THE
OLD-TIME
COWHAND

THE
OLD-TIME
COWHAND

RAMON F. ADAMS

Illustrated by Nick Eggenhofer

University of Nebraska Press
Lincoln and London

First Bison Book printing: 1989
Most recent printing indicated by the first digit below:
    2   3   4   5   6   7   8   9   10

Library of Congress Cataloging-in-Publication Data
Adams, Ramon F. (Ramon Frederick), 1889–1976.
The old-time cowhand / Ramon F. Adams: illustrated by Nick Eggenhoffer.
   p.   cm.
   "First Bison Book printing"—T.p. verso.
   Reprint. Originally published: New York: Macmillan, 1961.
   ISBN 0-8032-1025-6 (alk. paper). — ISBN 0-8032-5917-4 (pbk.: alk. paper)
   1. Cowboys—West (U.S.) 2. Ranch life—West (U.S.) 3. Frontier and
pioneer life—West (U.S.) 4. West (U.S.)—Social life and customs. I. Title.
F596.A33   1989   88-38636
978—dc 19   CIP

In memory of my beloved son, Elman

Foreword

It SEEMS like all books not branded as fiction call for a foreword. Maybe it kinda serves as a windbreak, so I'll trail with the herd, and build one. In case you're the kind that don't care to read 'em, I'm makin' this'n as short as the tail hold on a bear.

Book writin', I reckon, should be brushed and curried till it's plumb shiny and elegant. In writin' this'n, I could maybe slick up my grammar some, but because it's 'bout the old-time cowhand I want to write it in his own language jes' like he talked at the old chuck wagon. It seems more friendly, and it shore gives more flavor. Besides, it'll save me a lot of dandruff scratchin' and keep the editors from wearin' down a heap of blue pencils. If someone attempted to put the cowboy's speech into correct English, he'd only succeed in destroyin' its strength and flavor. The cowboy had no use for the feller who used words that nobody could savvy without an encyclopedia and two dictionaries.

You won't get no lesson in good grammar by readin' this book, but I hope it won't corrupt your education too much. The cowhand had an active mind, but because he lived in a well-nigh bookless country he had to derive his intellectual diversion mostly from applied logic rather than from readin'. He wasn't a man of many words, but the words he did use were full of meanin'. Most Westerners had a fondness for paintin' word pictures and sayin' a great deal in a mighty few words.

The cowman spoke a different lingo from any other breed on earth. It was all his own, and nobody else could fool 'round with it 'nough to deceive 'im. I've been interested in it for so many years it's got to be a kind of hobby with me. His language took on the character of the land, and, bein' both resourceful and courageous, he best expressed his thoughts with comparisons and exaggerations.

There's been a lot wrote 'bout the cowboy over the years, givin' certain phases of his life; but I'd like to cut the deck a little deeper and tell you all 'bout 'im, his rig and equipment, ever' phase of his work and his moments of relaxation. You'll notice I'm writin' most chapters in the past tense because this book's 'bout the old-time cowhand, but parts of some of the chapters, like the ones on his riggin', are in the present tense because some things are still as they was in the old days. Even cowhands born after the first fences and windmills would be considered old-timers now.

I want to thank the *Arizona Highways, The Cattleman, Southwest Review, Western Horseman, True West,* and *Western Story* for the chapters which appeared in those magazines at various times.

RAMON F. ADAMS

Dallas, Texas

Contents

x   Contents

Part Two

AT WORK

Part Three

AT PLAY

The Cowhand

The Old-Time Cowhand

THERE's an old sayin' that "a cowboy's a man with guts and a hoss," and that's 'bout as good a definition as anyone could give. If he didn't have guts he wouldn't last long; if he didn't have a hoss he couldn't be a cowboy. When one old cowhand described his breed, he said, "Cowboys is noisy fellers with bow legs and brass stomachs that rides hosses and hates any kind of work they can't do on one."

Some of us know 'im as a man who follows the cattle business as a profession. A generation ago the East knowed 'im as a bloodthirsty demon of disaster, reckless and rowdy, weighted down with 'nough artillery to make his hoss sway-backed, and ever ready to shoot. Today he's mostly knowed as the hero of Wild West stories, as the eternally hard-ridin' movie or TV actor; as the *git*-tar pickin' yodeler of the radio, or the loudly dressed rodeo follower. The West, who knowed 'im best, held 'im to be "jes' a plain, ever'day bowlegged human," carefree and courageous, fun-lovin' and loyal, uncomplainin' and doin' his best to live up to a tradition of which he was mighty proud. If he was from Texas, like all good Texans, he had the rep'tation of havin' been raised to vote the Democratic ticket, to love good whisky, and to hate Mexicans.

No class of men were ever so unfaithfully represented, and in consequence so misunderstood and unfairly judged by people generally, as the old-time cowboy has been. He suffered severely from the bad publicity of ill-informed writers who had no real conception of his life and work.

3

They pictured the rough, crude, brutal aspects of the cattle country; the reckless, happy-go-lucky visits to town, the careless use of the six-shooter, the drinkin', the fightin', practical jokes that were rough, the gamblin', and the profanity. All them things were subjects for the writer who painted, in the most lurid colors, slanderous accounts for eager Eastern readers.

So a variety of opinions regardin' the cowhand were developed. To the Eastern youngster he was tops in bravery, ferocity, cunnin', and Western skill. To the ignorant he was a badman, and the embodiment of whisky, blood, and murder. But still, in spite of all that's been wrote 'bout 'im, them who knowed 'im best and lived with 'im found 'im to be good-natured and a rollickin' whole-souled feller, quick to do a kindness, and as quick to resent an insult.

So thorough was that misrepresentation that part of the public, even today, will have no other way of lookin' at 'im. They see the wide hat but not the honest face beneath it. They remember the wild stunts he'd pulled in a moment of relaxation, but forget his lifetime of hard work and endurin' faithfulness. Few people of this generation realize that they was as brave as it was possible for a man to be. Bullies were almost unknowed among 'em. They kept their places 'round a herd under all circumstances; and if they had to fight they were always ready. No timid men were among 'em—the life didn't fit such men. They were he-men with fur on their briskets. Most of 'em had been raised to the cow business, and had been in the country so long they knowed all the lizards by their first names.

Romancers saw color but not the form in them wild men of a wild country. They saw traits but didn't see the character beneath 'em. Seekin' to tell of what they hadn't seen, they became inaccurate and unjust. Dallyin' with the pleasant sensations of excitin' themes, they distorted their handlin' of 'em.

It's utterly unfair to judge a whole class by what a few individuals do in the course of two or three days spent in town, instead of by the long months of weary, honest toil, common to all alike. One might as well judge all college boys by the one who turned out to be a drunkard or a thief. To properly appreciate his real qualities, the wild roughrider of the plains should've been seen in his own bailiwick. There he passed his days; there he did his lifework; there, when he met death, he faced it, as he'd faced all other perils, with quiet, uncomplainin' fortitude.

Fiction's made the cowboy the most romantic part of the West. He may have been a dashin' two-gun individual on paper, but he wasn't so on the range. No Westerner thought of 'im as bein' a type or character, or anything at all unusual. He certainly never thought of 'imself as bein' anything extraordinary or heroic. He'd likely been born to the cow business and had rode a runnin' iron for a hobbyhoss. He became a cowman from the bootheels up.

Most people enjoy readin' a good Western novel, yet they should realize that the true cowboy spent long, lonely months on the range workin' cattle, and wasn't forever skally-hootin' into town all spraddled out in fancy trappin's worth a couple of year's wages, and performin' marvelous shootin' stunts with a six-gun. His life was anything but the excitin' round of pleasure and thrills pictured in most stories and movies. He might crave action on the range, but when he hit town his cravin' was mostly for ham and eggs and other truck he couldn't get at the chuck wagon.

The real cowhand's typical day was anything but romantic. There was no romance in gettin' up at four o'clock in the mornin', eatin' dust behind a trail herd, swimmin' muddy and turbulent rivers, nor in doctorin' screw worms, pullin' stupid cows from bog holes, sweatin' in the heat of summer and freezin' in the cold of winter.

Prairie fires, swollen rivers, stampedes, storms, freezin' blizzards, man-killin' hosses, fightin' cattle, holes for hosses to step into and trees for 'em to run against, desperate men and savage Injuns to lie in wait for 'im, a rope that might betray 'im constantly in his hand—all them perils and more were a part of the cowboy's daily life. Small wonder he suffered the pains of rheumatism in his later years, brought on by too much rough ridin' and too much sleepin' under the stars in all kinds of weather, often with nothin' but a saddle blanket for cover.

In this day of scientific balanced diets and caloric study, his eatin' habits would make a dietitian shudder, but in spite of his monotonous fare of meat, biscuit, and beans, he was a fairly healthy cuss. Maybe it was the hard work and open air. He seemed to be all rawhide and whalebone. One of his chronic conditions was bad blood. This was due to his diet and the drinkin' of alkali water.

It was common for 'im to have runnin' sores on his hands. These could be from many causes, maybe a rope burn, the kick from a calf whose hoofs were sharp as glass, the prick of a mesquite thorn, the shoein' of a bronc, or from many other causes. Them sores healed mighty slow and sometimes got "proud flesh" in 'em. There was usually a can of powdered alum at the wagon or at headquarters to burn out them sores, or sometimes they were smeared with axle grease.

Then, too, there was a supply of pills and powders kept on hand for a man's innards, but the cowhand avoided 'em as long as he could, and it was only when he got down that he resorted to their advertised curative powers. Most of the time there were a few hands sufferin' from boils. These could be treated by a chaw of tobacco tied on with a strip of flour sack or his bandanna. But mighty often them boils were on that part of his anatomy that set on the saddle, makin' 'im want to do his ridin' on the bedrolls in the bed wagon. But rather than let the boss think he was throwin' off on the job, he'd keep tryin' to ride even if he did have to set his saddle off center. Sometimes he had carbuncles, and then he'd really have to take off to treat 'em with some sowbelly or dung poultice to try and draw 'em to a head. He'd be joshed a-plenty for havin' 'em, but the thing that hurt 'im the worst was the thought that someone might wonder if he was jes' soakin' on the boss.

It made 'im wish, too, that he'd taken his sulphur and molasses before he left town. But out on the range, though he could get the molasses, there wasn't no sulphur for fifty miles, unless you counted that in the matches he packed with his makin's.

But on the whole he never needed a doctor except for broken bones. When the poison in his system had worked out through them boils and carbuncles, he was rarin' to go again.

If, when he got to town, after long months out in the brush, on the lone prairie, or on the long, long trail, the cowboy cut his wolf loose and had a little fun, he could hardly be blamed. He was a robust animal, full of vinegar and pride. He generally came from venturesome ancestors, the makers of frontier homes, and he was likely honest and truthful and against outlawry and viciousness. Cowboys were hard and diligent workers, and men who work hard in the open generally lead straight lives.

The movies picture the cowboy as always goin' at a sweepin' gallop over the plains, his hair flyin' wildly and his hoss close to the earth, its eyes bulgin' with the joy of speed. These movie cowboys can run a hoss uphill, over rough trails, at great speed for unheard-of hours. Most of 'em are mounted on a turpentined charger which, when restrained, rears and tries to paw the moon. They're usually chasin' some villain, and though the whole posse is shootin' up a peck of shells they never hit nothin'.

Sometimes the real cowhand did ride hard on the roundup or when at other work which made it necessary, but when he set across the range on his day's work at the ranch, he didn't spur and gallop his hoss. He went in a steady, ceaseless, choppy little trot that would tire out a tenderfoot to follow all day. This short trot was a natural gait for the cow hoss, and he'd maintain it for a long time if not crowded too hard. The rider poked along completely relaxed to save both 'imself and his hoss.

The true cowboy's life, with its hardships, isolation, and dangers, developed all the sterner qualities to a high degree. To a lithe and sinewy body he joined courage, indifference to sufferin', and dogged industry when work had to be done. For them qualities it would be hard to find his equal. He was his own overseer. He needed no instruction or advice. No higher-type employee ever existed or one more dependable. Perhaps rude in some ways, he was the very soul of honor in all ways of his callin'.

The old-time cowhand lived in the saddle. He was strictly a ridin' man, and detested walkin', even for short distances. A self-respectin' cowhand would never be caught goin' far on foot. Even if he only had to go two or three hundred yards, he preferred to ketch and saddle a bronc rather than furnish that motive power 'imself. From the bunkhouse to the corral was quite a passear for 'im. Most of 'em had forked a hoss so long they straddled chairs instead of settin' like a human.

This was why he was mighty particular 'bout a straight ridin' job. When he was out of work and rode to a new range to get on some ranch's pay-roll, he was careful to inquire 'bout the outfit before hittin' 'em for a job. He didn't want to sign up with some little three-up outfit that didn't own 'nough beef to hold a barbecue. On such an outfit there'd be chores to do that was beneath his dignity, such as feedin', diggin' postholes, and cuttin' stove wood, and the only place a cowhand could cut wood and not hurt his pride was at a line camp where it was chop wood or no eat. Worst of all he was afraid of havin' to milk cows. He had no use for them hornless critters that wore bells and were punched with a stool. His profession might be considered that of a laborer by some folks, but he thought 'imself above most wage earners. He had that pride held by all men on hossback, and considered 'imself a specialist in his line—a cavalier, not a laborer.

When he hit a fenced ranch for a job, he hoped all the fencin' and cross fencin' had been done and there were no more postholes to dig. He didn't want to be caught on the blister end of no damned shovel. High-heeled boots weren't made for footwork, and he wouldn't be caught in a low-heeled shoe. But he didn't shirk any duty as long as it could be done from hossback. He worked without complaint long hours through flood and drought, heat and cold, dust and blizzard, never once thinkin' of his own discomfort if the cattle or the welfare of his boss demanded his attention.

Fightin' prairie fires, the dangers of stampedes, the loneliness of range ridin', the discomforts of standin' guard in the rain or sleet, none of them things seemed unusual if he could do it from the back of a hoss. On the other hand, he didn't even want to open a gate unless he could lean over and do it from the saddle. His profession was born of necessity, and with it was born a tradition that he followed jealously until he became the most colorful and picturesque hired man ever knowed. 'Bout the only footwork he considered honorable was ropin' in the corral, or doin' the brandin'.

They were sincere in their efforts to maintain the dignity and prestige of a callin' they'd perfected in their lifetime and for which, without mass thought or organized effort, they'd set certain standards.

Their profession in the United States was born in the years followin' the Civil War, reached its peak in the middle eighties, and waned before the nineties were finished. They had no formula for their work other than to get the job done; no workin' hours other than from sun to sun, and such hours permitted little or no time for menial chores or trainin' in any line other than that of handlin' cattle from hossback.

Certainly he'd never sink to herdin' sheep. This was a shore-'nough foot job, fit only for greasers, who didn't mind livin' alone with a couple of dogs, and didn't care how many funny stories were told about 'em. If there was anything the old-time cowman hated, it was sheep. He couldn't see how any man could favor mutton instead of beef. In his opinion there was nothin' dumber'n them woolies, except the man who herded 'em. It seemed a sheepherder always had a grouch and a Waterbury watch, and when he wasn't a-nursin' the one he was a-windin' the other. Some cow ranges was so against sheep that it wasn't safe to ride through it with a wool shirt on.

Neither did a cowhand propose to get 'imself "galded" followin' a mule's tail from behind a plow. Had the boss insisted, he'd have politely asked for his time, packed his bedroll on his pack hoss, and started toward the settin' sun. There were still Arizona, New Mexico, and the steer outfits of the Northwest where a man could be respectable. The cowhands were always goin' to quit and go to a new country, but the first little town they hit after bein' paid off was usually the end of the journey they talked 'bout, and they was back for the spring roundup to sweat out the likker till they smelled like humans again.

In them days a cowhand could always go back to the ranch after he was broke and eat till the spring roundup began. Since there was nothin' to do on the ranch except look after the saddle hosses (and there'd be paid men to do that), he had no cares or worries. He'd jes' play cards and ride broncs by a hot stove—which was the easy way to do it.

Another way the cowhand could live in the winter when he run out of a job was to ride the grub line. Any worthy cowboy might be forced to ride chuck line durin' this season, but the professional chuck liner was jes' a plain range bum, despised by all cowboys. He was the kind that took advantage of the country's hospitality and stayed as long as he dared wherever there wasn't any work for 'im to do and the meals were free and reg'lar. Some cowhands took this way to spend the winter for the sake of variety, and if such riders weren't too plentiful they were welcome. People who'd been shut in all winter was glad to see new faces, and them riders brought news from the outside.

A heap of sunshine put that squint in the old-timer's eyes, and a lot of prairie wind tanned his face. That ten-gallon hat and them fancy boots wasn't what made 'im look like a cowman. It was the elements, the corral dust, the hoss smell, and the cow-camp chuck that branded 'im. He could go away from the cow country and dress in fancy society togs, and another cowman would still know 'im to be a cowman.

A cowman had to get pretty old before he hung his saddle up, but when he did get long in tooth and couldn't travel like a colt no more, he liked to set 'round with old-timers and talk 'bout cows that wore horns. They liked to go back in history, too, and prove to the younger set that the life they was now livin' was soft as bear grease. He maybe set there a-shakin' his head like a hoss with a bee in his ear, tryin' to put the saddle on the younger punchers by tellin' yarns as long as a rustler's dream, and doin' his best to convince 'em that he'd once been so wild they had to tie his foot up to give 'im a haircut.

After the fences came, most of them old-timers were always bellyachin' with a yearnin' to go somewhere where they could spread a loop without gettin' it caught on a fence post. Most of the real old-time cowmen have now saddled a cloud and rode into the Great Beyond, and their like'll never be seen again.

The old-timer was an inveterate cigarette smoker. If there ever was a badge of a callin' it should be that little Bull Durham tag a-hangin' by its yeller string from the vest or shirt pocket.

When he hunkered down to take comfort in a frog squat, the first thing he did was jerk a leaf out of his prayer book and commence bundlin' up a new life of Bull Durham. When somethin' was eatin' on 'im and he was worried, he rolled a pill; when he was embarrassed, he rolled a pill; in fact, you'd find 'im buildin' a smoke whenever he found his hands free to do the job.

He didn't have much taste for a pipe. He left that tobacco furnace to the sheepherder, the nester, and the prospector. He couldn't see much fun in jes' a-settin' puffin' on an old pipe to fill the air with more smoke than a wet wood fire, especially when that pipe was strong 'nough to derail a freight train.

Most of the old-timers tried to be all-'round cowboys, and in order to do so he had to have some ability at readin' sign. Ever' track told 'im a story plainer'n if it'd been printed in a book. By his ability at readin' sign a good cowhand could save his ranch time, money, hossflesh, and sometimes save his own life. If out huntin' hosses, he could tell by the tracks if them hosses were grazin', goin' somewhere in a walk, or bein' drove in a hurry.

A cowboy ridin' down the trail might seem to be half asleep to an outsider, but his eyes didn't miss a thing. If he saw cattle spread out and grazin', he knowed ever'thing was hunkydory, but a bawlin' cow showin' nervousness was a sign her calf was dead or in trouble. If he came across an animal with thin flanks, a swollen jaw, and droopin' head, it was a sign she'd stopped a rattlesnake's fangs.

Readin' sign generally referred to trackin', but other things came under that headin' too. A cowman could see a rider from a great distance and tell whether that rider was a white man or an Injun. The white man'd be ridin' straight up and straight-legged; the Injun'd be swingin' a quirt and diggin' his heels into the hoss's belly at ever' jump. When the wagon boss, on roundup, caught his best circle hoss, the cowhand didn't need words to tell 'im that a big circle was goin' to be made. When the boss took the top hoss from a cowhand's string, he knowed that the boss was tellin' 'im, stronger'n words, that he wanted 'im to quit before he had to fire 'im.

On a clear day he didn't need a watch to tell 'im the time of day, and at night he could tell by the stars. He could tell a change in the weather by watchin' the action of the cattle. Somehow they always seemed to know. He could even tell what state a man came from by his riggin' and the clothes he wore. Words ain't needed to tell a range man a heap of things.

There was a true feelin' of friendship among old cowboys, even if they'd unsaddled for the last time. If a couple of 'em met and never saw each other before, they got to talkin' cow. Even if one of 'em had rustled a few mavericks they'd still have a warm feelin' for each other.

When so many of the ranches got to be small pasture outfits with their fencin' and footwork, a heap of the old-time cowhands quit and got a job in town as a bartender or a livery-stable chambermaid. Here he could still be with cowhands and hosses. He still claims that bob-wire and bib-overalls was what ruined the cow country. By the time modern ranchin', with its flivvers and helicopters, had caught up with 'im, he'd passed over the Great Divide, or was too old to care.

Book Learnin'

THE early cowman wasn't an educated hombre. He never had a chance to study the higher branches of information through book learnin'. Such things would've had 'im fightin' the bits all the time. Neither was dictionary talk to his likin', because he didn't read Webster. If you'd a-mentioned the name to 'im he'd probably asked what brand that hombre run. The cowman's grammar was rough and rugged like his hills, but his short cuts were practical and he didn't need words that showed up as big as a skinned hoss to make you understand his meanin'. This lack of education didn't cause any feeling of inferiority and he felt equal to any man.

There's a heap of truth in that old sayin', "Put a cowman afoot and he don't know a thing." Yet the sayin' itself's a compliment to his savvy of hosses and cattle. His sons rode in the dust of his trail, learnin' cattle, lovin' hosses, studyin' the rope, and shyin' at book learnin'. Some of them ranch kids jes' growed up with the rest of the yearlin's.

Their schoolin' started by watchin' their dads and the hands at work. In a few years they were practicin' with their little ropes on fence posts and chickens till they got big 'nough to tackle the smaller calves. When they got old 'nough they developed into hoss wranglers to make 'emselves useful. Here their real education started. Beginnin' as the butt of the rough jokes, and doin' the petty hard jobs of the cow camp, they progressed by stages that gave 'em fuller understandin' of the habits of cattle and hosses, of the range, of man and Nature till their ambition was stirred to make a hand and ride with the boys. By this time they was so big they was ashamed to start to school in case there was one in ridin' distance. Mostly they learned their alphabet from cow brands, and their three R's were Ridin', Ropin', and Roundups.

Some of the best wagon bosses of the old West couldn't read or write. Yet they wasn't so handicapped. They got their news from the outside by word of mouth. Reps brought it in on roundup, and in the winter grub-line riders scattered it from one end of the range to the other. Neither did them old wagon bosses have any letters to write or papers to sign. If their word wasn't good, neither was their bond. But the cow business was an open book to 'em, and they knowed ever' leaf in it.

Later, when scattered schools were established, and teachers imported from the East, the range-bred boy didn't have much respect for them wisdom-bringers because they were pilgrims. To 'im anybody that didn't savvy cows was a greener that couldn't teach a settin' hen to cluck. If a man teacher came out to teach school he had to be a fighter, for the cowboys framed it up with the bigger pupils to run 'im off so they'd have a lady teacher.

Often the pupil never got further'n the flyleaf of the primer before he quit. Others stuck with it till they got to "baker," the first two-syllable word in the old Blue Back speller. By this time they thought they was plumb educated. There used to be an old sayin' in Texas that "when a man learns to count to a hundred he's ready to teach school." Of course, this was kinda stretchin' the blanket a little, as most of 'em stayed in school till they outgrowed the benches and learned to read and write the simpler words, and that was all they had any need for. Anyway, they didn't give sheepskins in a cow country.

If you're so hobbled with a high education that you shudder ever' time a maverick tense hits back for the chaparral in the cowhand's talk, and refuse to listen, you'll be missin' a heap of colorful talk and pullin' leather from the first jump. Jes' because a cowhand don't use college grammar you mustn't get the idea he's plumb ignorant. Common cow sense sometimes assayed higher'n a heap of book learnin', and he savvied a cow till he knowed what she said to her calf. He had plenty of wrinkles on his horns, too, when it came to knowin' life, nature, honesty, and honor, which, after all, is worth more'n writin' half the alphabet after your name.

Hand the average old-time cowhand a pen and he was deaf and dumb, but he could talk so his conversation didn't make no boggy crossin' for 'nother cowman. He didn't have to fish 'round for no decorated language to make his meanin' clear. He was kinda shy of the educated feller who strayed over in the tall grass with his highfalutin' words. When he heard some educated feller usin' them four-legged words that run 'bout eight to the pound, or lingo so polished you could skate on it, the chances were he'd have to ask 'im to ride over that trail again, and chew it finer so he could get the meanin'.

Even when a cowboy'd learned to read he didn't get much chance to put it into practice. In the first place, he didn't have the material to practice with, except the air-tights and bakin'-soda cans. The printin' on them he memorized till it developed into a game, and most ever' puncher "knowed his cans." In the second place, while with the wagon, he worked all the daylight hours. By daybreak he was ketchin' his hoss and soon after supper he was unspoolin' his bedroll, with no time in between for readin'. In the third place, if he was at headquarters in the bunkhouse, or at a line camp, he was discouraged by smoky lamp chimneys and the shortage of coal oil, or "lump oil," as he sometimes called it.

The boys of the line camps never had much different printed matter, but in their spare time they read what they had, well and often. John

Hendrix, an old-timer friend of mine I'd always visit when in Fort Worth, Texas, before he died, used to tell a story of a cowhand who declared the best winter he ever put in was when he was sent out to an old abandoned nester shack to make a line camp. The shack was a one-room affair, papered with old newspapers and farm journals. Accordin' to his story, he read the north, south, east, and west walls durin' the winter and was jes' startin' in to read the ceilin' when they called 'im to headquarters.

Maybe some bull nurse who'd made the trip to Kansas City or some other cattle market with a shipment of steers would come back on the passenger train. Most always he'd make the news-butch richer by bringin' back some yeller-backed novels, or some other book the butch let 'im have at a high price after this cowboy'd promised he wouldn't tell no one where he got it, and wouldn't open it till he got home. When he did look into it he wondered about all the secrecy. It was a great event when he got back to the ranch with them thrillers, and they went the rounds over and over till they was worn plumb to a frazzle.

Then the boot and saddle makers began sendin' out catalogues, and the bunkhouse library was started. The merits and demerits of the different styles in saddles, boots, spurs, and other riggin' detailed in them catalogues was discussed by the boys till you'd a-thought they'd organized a debatin' society.

When the mail-order houses started sendin' out them old "shepherd's bibles," or three-pound catalogues, that got to be so common on the range, the cowhand had 'nough readin' matter to keep 'im interested for many moons. Many a cowhand got his education from them old wish books. By studyin' the pictures he knowed what practically ever'thing on earth was before he ever saw the real article. The women of the ranch did all their wishful window shoppin' from its pages too, if they could get it away from the cowhands before they wore it out. When it first came they'd burn the midnight oil thumbin' through this thick picture book, marvelin' at some of the things they seen there.

There's a story about one green cowhand who fell for a picture of a gal displayin' a pretty, fluffy dress in one of them catalogues. He sets right down and orders her for a wife if she ain't already took, and then he brags 'bout how it won't cost nothin' to have her delivered 'cause the company sends ever'thing *postpaid*.

When a new catalogue came in, the old one found its way out to a little house in the back like the one Chick Sale made famous. Which reminds me of a story of one old cowman who ordered some toilet paper from one of them mail-order houses. They wrote 'im back to look in his catalogue and give 'em the order number. He answered 'em right back that if he'd a-had a catalogue he wouldn't need the toilet paper.

Later, when mail routes were established, readin' matter got to be more plentiful, bringin' weekly, semiweekly, and monthly stock journals, papers, and magazines, so that the old bunkhouse library got to lookin' like a public readin' room. The modern cowhand's more educated. His old man sells off 'nough cows to send 'im through an agricultural college to learn scientific feedin' and breedin' now that bob-wire's changed the ways of raisin' cows.

Augurin' *

THERE'S an old sayin' in the West that "there ain't much paw and beller to a cowboy," and the rest of the world's got the impression he can't talk. A big part of the world's got no way of savvyin' the cowboy except through readin' 'bout 'im, and it's sad, but true, that most of their printed information's been wrote by town-gaited writers who've never been closer to a cow than a milk wagon. The few writers who did come West found the cowboy pretty close-mouthed because they didn't stay long 'nough to really get acquainted.

True, the wide spaces of the plains didn't breed chatterboxes, and bein' a lone wolf out on the range got 'im into the habit of usin' his eyes a lot and his mouth mighty little. There's a story on record where two punchers started on a ten-mile trip to town.

"When I get to town," says the first puncher, as he forked his hoss, "I'm a-goin' to get rid of this old kack and buy me a new one."

The second puncher didn't answer and there wasn't a word spoken as they rack that ten miles. When they reached town the first puncher continued where he'd left off with, "And she's a-goin' to be a damn good'n, full-stamped and ever'thing."

Of course, a cowhand didn't depend entirely on the sign language, and such silence wasn't always the case because he *can* talk, but he had a

---

* Augur is a word commonly used in the cattle country to mean (as a noun) "a big talker," and (as a verb) "to talk."

talent for sayin' a whole lot in a mighty few words, and he didn't use up all his kindlin' to get his fire started. He was of a breed that never let you know his business or what was on his mind till he got well acquainted. For all he knowed you might be reppin' for the law and lookin' for a friend of his that'd been careless with the statutes.

His code was to let you know as little as possible 'bout 'imself while he was findin' out all he could 'bout you through your talk. He early learned that the way to get information was through the ears and eyes, not the mouth.

When a tenderfoot came along, the cowman really put his jaw in a sling. Raised in two different worlds, they didn't speak the same language and had nothin' in common to talk 'bout. Because the puncher used his breath for breathin' instead of mixin' it with tongue oil, the shorthorn got the idea that the cowboy was snobbish or stuck-up or jes' plain dumb. And so rep'tations were made, but them wasn't the reasons the cowboy seemed to have busted his talk box. It was the greener's ignorance that made the range man hobble his lip and put a dally on his tongue, because the first time he said somethin' 'round a tenderfoot a herd of questions came foggin' his way. Some of them questions made 'im wonder if the person askin' 'em was full growed in body only, and ought'n to be playin' with a string of spools.

The cowboy wasn't much of a question maker 'imself. Too much personal curiosity wasn't good form, and met with a heap of discouragement. Besides, the early West found that it wasn't none too healthy, and the code's been handed down. He might be a-bustin' for information 'bout somethin', but he bided his time, kept his eyes open, and sooner or later he'd find out what he wanted to know. Or maybe, if he did ask a question, it'd be worded kinda indifferent like, and you'd never know he was seekin' information.

But don't let his silence 'round strangers fool you. Among his own kind he could really unplug his talk box, and when a bunch of them old flannel mouths got together they had more lip than a muley cow. However, a person too mouthy wasn't looked on with much favor. The cowman's philosophy was "the bigger the mouth, the better it looks when shut." A man that was slack in the jaw was called a "leaky mouth," and was said to have the "diarrhea of the jawbone."

After a lonesome ride, when a cowhand met 'nother hand on the trail or 'long a fence line, them two'd have plenty to talk 'bout. There was the weather, grass, and water conditions to discuss; calf crops to estimate, cattle prices to predict; and there was comin' events like rodeos and dances to exchange ideas on. Sooner or later the talk was hazed 'round to the merits of the different saddle and bootmakers, and they never got tired of talkin' hoss. Sometimes they'd augur 'bout the different lengths of rope, the best spur, or maybe the way they'd rod the spread if they was boss.

Soon after they met they'd be swingin' off their hosses and loosenin' the cinches to give the broncs' backs some air. They'd hunker down on their boot heels, twist a cigarette, and mighty soon be fishin' 'round for a

cowboy fountain pen, which was a broomweed stalk with plenty of loose dirt to draw in. Seems like a cowhand could talk better when he was a-scratchin' in the sand like a hen in a barnyard. There was always some brand to make a picture of, and some to be showed how they could be worked into another brand. Maybe some nester with a pretty daughter had squatted over in a certain valley and directions would be drawed how to get there. With a swipe of the hand he could have a clean slate and start 'nother lesson in cow geography. When they stepped across their hosses again, each one'd be loaded with the gossip of the range, and neither could say that his jaw hadn't been exercised a-plenty in puttin' in a big crop of words.

No, sir! In the West you didn't have to hire a hall for augurin'. The best of it was done in the shade of the chuck wagon, along the fence lines, and in the livery stables when in town. Of course, the real flowery kind was done in the saloons where likker started the flow of tongue oil, and here they could talk a pump into believin' it was a windmill.

In spite of the fact that the cowman had a rep'tation on the outside for bein' 'bout as talkative as a Piegan Injun, there were men on the early range with such talkin' talents they got big rep'tations as augurs. I don't know of any other part of the world that held reg'lar augurin' matches. There was nothin' like 'em. The rest of the world's got its debates where men augur 'bout a certain question pro and con, but one at a time. The Western augurin' match was jes' a case of two loose-tongued humans a-settin' cross-legged, knee to knee and face to face, talkin' as fast as they could to see which one could keep it up the longest without runnin' out of words and wind. There was jes' a constant flow of words that didn't make no sense a-tall, both of 'em talkin' at the same time and each one had so much to say it got in his way.

I'll never forget the time an old windbelly from the Pothook outfit sent a challenge to one of our boys with talkin' talents, sayin' he "wouldn't be talked down by no damned man." Our champion accepted the challenge and sent back word to this Pothook pelican that he'd "make 'im wish he'd never been born dumb and had to do his talkin' with his hands." Ever'thing was arranged and the time was set for right after payday so the boys'd have plenty of money to bet on their fav'rite. Them two augurs went into trainin' by tryin' to memorize the mail-order wish book, studyin' the printin' on all the cook's cans, and runnin' through what saddle catalogues they could find.

When the match came off, our champion, havin' some talent for poetry, started off with such giggle talk as, "The hoss he neigh, can you tell what he say? The cow she moo, the bull does too; the dog he bark, till the moon goes dark; the lion he roar, till his throat gits sore; the catamount squall, like a bronc in a stall; the rabbit he run, 'cause he's a-skeered of a gun; the kyote yip, like he's got the flutter-lip." He goes on like this till he runs plumb through the animal kingdom.

At the same time the Pothook man, not to be out-poetried, ranted such stuff as, "The lightnin' flash, the thunder crash; the rain she pour, and the wind she roar," till you thought you was in Noah's flood. Our man was as full of verbal lather as a soap peddler, but this here Pothook man had more wind than a bull in green corn time. Them two old jiggers jes' jabbered at each other like a couple of honkers on a new feed ground, their prattle soundin' like rain on a tin roof. At the start they talked fast and furious, but after an hour or so they slowed down to a trot to be savin' of both words and wind.

Either one of 'em could talk the hide off a cow, so they shouted this foolishness plumb through the night, the boys doin' their best to cheer their champion on to glory. It was daybreak when the Pothook man finally talked 'imself to sleep and our champion was leanin' over 'im at the finish still whisperin' the merits of his favorite brand of canned peaches in his ear, but he didn't have 'nough vocal power left to bend a smoke ring.

No, sir! You ain't seen a thing unless you've witnessed one of them old-time cow-camp augurin' matches. Ordinarily a cowhand don't unbutton his lip for giggle talk and foolishness, but an augurin' match was a parade of talent, and them old augurs went 'bout the business as solemn as a tenderfoot trapper skinnin' a skunk. Most of them old medicine tongues had 'nough wind to keep a windmill goin' and could augur a gopher into climbin' a tree, but don't get the idea that they panted like this all the time. Them matches were special occasions. When it was over they could sweat a little too, because they had work to do.

To prove again that the cowboy was not hogtied when it came to makin' chin music, one of his favorite sports was tellin' a circular story to a greenhorn. So far as I know, this kind of bedtime story originated in the West. Havin' a fertile imagination, he made up his story as he went, and after he got warmed up his tongue was plumb frolicsome.

Maybe he started out by tellin' 'bout ridin' over a certain trail and doin' certain things, but it wasn't long till he was ridin' in a circle and you heard the same things you'd heard before. Ramblin' on, he gave all the little details 'bout tracks, rocks, trees, and the like, callin' the names of the rivers, trails, and mountains. After a while he got to the point where he'd started from and began all over again.

Of course, by this time all the boys knowed they were listenin' to a circular story, and it was the tenderfoot now they were watchin', not the speaker. If the tenderfoot wasn't as chuckleheaded as a prairie dog he knowed by now that he'd listened to all this before, and he'd likely say, "You're ridin' over the same trail you started from," or somethin' to that effect. This was jes' what the teller had gone to all that long-winded trouble for. A sellout was what he was workin' for. Most any tale a cowboy told a tenderfoot had a sell at the bottom of it, and when the cork was taken under there was a heap of hilarity in camp.

But some of them circular stories didn't turn out so well. I remember a puncher who told one for the benefit of an old man from the East, and after this puncher'd talked till his tongue hung out like a calf rope, the old man said: "Would you mind talkin' a little louder? I'm hard of hearin' and haven't heard a word you've said."

In a case like this the cowhand tellin' the yarn felt 'bout as helpless as a dummy with his hands cut off, and wished he was so far away it'd take a week for a bloodhound to find 'im. Bein' beat at his own game made 'im feel like he might as well been talkin' Chinee to a pack mule. After such a backfire he lost all taste for circular stories, and went off talkin' to 'imself like a sheepherder.

Any story a cowhand told could leave a drummer's yarn kinda faded. When it came to tellin' tall tales he was a top hand. As a rule he was a plumb truthful critter unless he was tryin' to protect some friend. It's been said that "a good cowman has to lie to the sanitary man, the tax collector, and cattle buyers," but if he started out by sayin' he was "speakin' for the ranch," or givin' his "range word for it," you could count on it bein' plain gospel. But when he did lie he made you think Ananias was jes' an ambitious amateur. He could color up a story redder'n a Navajo blanket. The only man that could hold a light to 'im is the modern politician.

A man from the East could maybe lie in a small way, but when he came West he soon took lessons from the country where Nature seemed to lie some herself. Ever'thing in the West's got to be plenty big to be worth while, and this bigness of the country kinda broke down all small ideas. Writers of the East exaggerate the wildness and woolliness of the West so much the puncher was mighty glad to show the tenderfoot some real exaggeration.

Tellin' windies was a kinda natural product of the cow country, and it didn't take much persuadin' to start a puncher on one of them campaigns against truth. A lot of 'em got to be top hands at tellin' them tall tales, and a good peddler of loads was welcome at any cow camp. He was mighty entertainin' and it helped pass the time.

Any cowhand knowed when another was stringin' a whizzer, but, no matter how much he knowed the speaker's saddle was slippin', he always let his ears hang down and listened. In the first place he was bein' entertained, and it was one of the little courtesies of the cow camp not to interrupt a yarn; and in the second place he knowed that the teller was tryin' to uphold some sort of rep'tation as a yarn spinner.

Most cowhands could tell them yarns so serious-like they were as convincin' as a spade flush, and it was mighty hard for a greener to doubt their truthfulness. If he found a listener that wasn't alkalied, he piled it on plenty scary.

No cowman knowed all the windies that'd been unloaded 'round a cow camp, but most of 'em knowed 'nough to fill a mighty big book. Ever'-thing in the West had been lied about, from wind and weather, snakes and freak animals, to shootin' and runnin' and cattle and hosses.

Also there was always some man in ever' group that got callouses from pattin' his own back. Cowhands didn't mind listenin' to his tall tales, but when he started talkin' like a Texan and braggin' 'bout his prowess and accomplishments, he was soon left to chaw his cud alone; and if it got to be a habit with 'im it wasn't long till he'd bragged 'imself out of a place to lean against the bar.

Airin' the Lungs

WHILE we're on the subject of the cowboy's talk, we might as well say somethin' 'bout his cussin'. His blasphemy was from custom and habit, not from any wish to be wicked. It was a part of his slang, and he didn't hold it to be sacrilegious. It was more of a boyish desire to blow off steam, or a relief in the release of pent-up temper. In the words of Philip Rollins, "He holds that, while blasphemin' is bad for the soul, cussin' takes the strain off his liver."

The cowboy called cussin' "airin' the lungs." The average cowhand wasn't tryin' to bust any Commandments when he cussed. It was habit, and a natural part of his language, and he could shore cram plenty of grammar into it. When he uncinched this talent and turned 'er loose, he was a top hand at it, and had mighty few equals. Maybe such ripe language wasn't learned at his mother's knee, but it seemed to come natural from colthood up, and set on his tongue as easy as a hossfly ridin' a mule's ear. To hear 'im talk you'd think half his conversation was half-soled with cuss words, but without it his speech'd be a heap less effectual.

To appreciate Western cussin' you have to understand it. There's a lot of difference between profanity and blasphemy. In showin' his affection for you the cowhand might throw a language that'd blister the toughest hide. If he said 'em in a voice as frosty as a November night, he meant 'em for fightin' words. The tenderfoot, when he first hit the West, couldn't savvy why punchers called each other the foulest of names in the spirit of friendship and fun. Tryin' the same thing always got 'im into a jackpot with no openers because he didn't know how to put the proper tone into his cussin'. Neither did he know that a smile made a heap of difference in its meanin'.

Cussin' was the only effective language knowed to mules, and many a skinner's swearin' got so hot it would've burnt his throat if it hadn't been made of asbestos. But, in spite of the mule skinner's rep'tation as an expert, the cowboy could release some that any skinner'd be happy to get a copy of. He didn't depend on the commonplace, shopworn terms of the town plodder. He wanted a man's cussin' that could take the frost out of a zero mornin', and burn the grass to cinders for yards 'round.

Powerful cuss words demand courage and inventiveness, and the cow-hand had both them qualities. When he jerked off the bridle and turned loose you could smell the sulphur, and his cussin' would peel the hide off a Gila monster, or grow hair on a Mexican dog.

To observe the riot of imagination turned loose, you'd have to get one of them men mad 'nough to bust. He'd horn you with all the cuss words he could remember. It'd be unprintable, but you'd get a plumb new idea of what profanity meant. It's too bad we can't give you some examples of this full-growed language, but it don't look so good in print, bein' strictly a spoken tongue. But it was a part of his home-growed lingo, as thorny as the cactus through which he rode. The voice and manner of the speaker had a heap to do with its strength. Many a range man knowed how to swear in paragraphs with a reg'lar tune to it, and when a bunch of 'em turned loose it sounded like a mule skinners' convention.

In all fairness, however, it should be said that the cowboy didn't bust forth with his full power without cause. For this purpose he had a most astonishin' vocabulary. Sometimes his words were of no knowed language; he invented 'em for his own devices, but there was no misunderstandin' their meanin'. For use on such occasions he seemed to have plenty of English words that could be worked into cuss words, and if them wasn't 'nough he knowed some Spanish words that could be mixed in.

Ever' cowman had what was knowed as his private cuss words too. Them were a sort of individual creation of special phrases for which the public accorded 'im a kind of copyright. Maybe they wasn't even profane, but you soon learned the user turned 'em loose only when he was mad 'nough to kick his own dog, and their voicin' was a danger signal to all who knowed 'im.

When around decent women he tried his best to keep a lid on his can of cuss words, but force of habit didn't always let 'im be successful in this endeavor.

Back in the early cow country, men weren't ashamed of their cussin' talents. There weren't many women 'round to interfere, and it became a habit with 'em. Some got to be so good they had rep'tations as experts. For lack of entertainment others would make bets on certain fellers bein' able to outcuss certain others, and it wasn't long till a cussin' bee would be arranged. I reckon the early West was the only place in the world that had reg'lar cussin' contests.

There's a story of old Brimstone Wallace who had a big rep'tation as a cusser, and who the boys talked into a cussin' bee with a mule skinner from down Tombstone way. It was said that old Brimstone had come out of Texas ridin' a fast hoss jes' two jumps ahead of the sheriff. They say he'd cut his teeth on a cartridge and stood up to fight before he was weaned and that's what made 'im as bowlegged as a barrel hoop. He was so tough he had to sneak up on the dipper to get a drink of water, and he had the rep'tation of bein' able to whip his weight in wildcats. His old woman was the only human who could make 'im hump his tail at the shore end.

All she could talk was religion, and she preached to Brimstone all the time 'bout his sinful ways of cussin'. The worst part of it was, she was the leader of all the other calico in that section, and she had 'em all rulin' their menfolks with a half-breed bit. Life got to be plumb monotonous for the married men. They looked to Brimstone to help 'em out, but he declared 'imself hogtied when it come to augurin' with his old woman, and it was jes' as useless as barkin' at a knot.

'Bout the time all arrangements for that cussin' bee was made, the womenfolks got together, put on their war paint, and said it was high time the men stopped amusin' 'emselves by a-bustin' the Lord's Commandments. Old Sister Wallace was the bell mare of that remuda, and she made all arrangements for a sky pilot up in Tucson to come down and act as converter. At first there was trouble decidin' where to hold the meetin'. Ever' woman wanted it held on her ranch. Sister Wallace allowed she was entitled to first say since she was the originator of the whole idea. Sister Campbell came back that old Brimstone was so wicked he was in cahoots with the devil 'imself, and would have 'im and his pitchfork settin' right at the preacher's elbow, givin' trouble all the time, and she thought her place the best.

Then Sister Jones claimed Brother Campbell got his start in the cow business with a long rope and runnin' iron, and ain't got such a sanctimonious rep'tation 'imself. The menfolks were out at the corral passin' 'round hard likker while the women were at the house passin' 'round hard words, and that pore divine was as busy as a hen drinkin' a can of paint, tryin' to keep peace.

He finally settled the whole question by tellin' 'em it was his personal wish to have the boys build a pole arbor down by the river so it'd be handy for the baptizin'. Them old catamounts hated labor afoot worse'n pizen, but because their women said build it they went to work.

Ever'thing went along smooth, and it wasn't long till that sin-buster had old Campbell and a lot of other cow thieves weepin' at the mourner's bench and shoutin' hallelujah. Old Brimstone was there ever' night, settin' on the back seat, lookin' 'bout as uncomfortable as a camel in the Klondike. The boys figgered he'd floundered in the mire of sin so long he'd never find the straight and narrow, so they didn't worry 'bout losin' their champion cusser till he started movin' up a seat or two ever' night. Some of the boys persuaded 'im to stay outside with 'em where he could see and hear, but could keep his hat on and smoke. One of the boys even brought a bottle of redeye and got 'im to take a snort of that.

Old Sister Wallace got onto that game pronto, and ever' night after that she led Brimstone by the hackamore right up close to the front so she could watch 'im from where she was singin' in the choir. The preacher singled 'im out and preached right at 'im. With tears in his voice, he painted word pictures of the angels playin' their harps and of the terrors of the everlastin' fires of hell, and said a lot 'bout the wages of sin. It was as plain as paint who he was talkin' to, and old Brimstone felt as prominent as a boil on a pug nose. The preacher had the choir sing somethin' soft while he pleaded with Brimstone to cast out the devil and give 'imself up. Brimstone was blinkin' his eyes and all swellin' up like a frog in a churn, and pretty soon he was hittin' the trail to the mourners' bench, shoutin' so loud all the angels musta heard 'im. Then ever'body got to shoutin' and cryin' till it busted up the meetin', and the boys kissed their bets on the cussin' bee goodbye.

The next Sunday they held the baptizin', and when all them converts got into the river she looked like she was on a rise. Brimstone was standin' there belly-deep in water, nervous as a green bronc with his first saddlin'. Jes' as the preacher got to 'im, Brimstone reached into his pocket for a chaw of tobacco to quiet his nerves.

"God damn! My chawin's all wet," he shouted, and the boys on the bank let out a yell you could've heard in the next county.

"Don't let 'em git your wing-feathers wet, little angel," yelled one cowhand to Brimstone. The old sinner looked 'round so mad he could've bit a gap out of an ax, and opened his mouth to kick the lid off his can of cuss words; but jes' then he was ducked under, and before he could shut his mouth he was plumb water-logged. He come up a-spittin' and a-spewin', but considerably cooled off. Some folks claimed it was the nearest thing to a bath he'd had since the fall of the Alamo. Anyway, it shore washed off his war paint.

That baptizin' was followed by a drought, the worst in years. The water holes dried up, and what water in the river that wasn't sloshed out by the baptizin' jes' naturally vanished. It got so hot and dry you'd have to prime yourself to spit, and there wasn't 'nough grass left to chink 'tween the ribs of a sandfly. The boys were so busy tailin' up weak cattle they forgot all 'bout that cussin' bee. After watchin' his cows get as ganted as a gutted snowbird, till they looked like the runnin' gears of a katydid—what few there were left—Brimstone decided maybe religion wasn't such good medicine after all. His range was as bare as a farmer's feed lot, and the whole range wouldn't support a horned frog, but smelled like a packin' plant before the pure-food law. Folks forgot what water looked like outside of a pail or a trough.

He sent out word he was ready to do some real cussin' if they could find anybody who could make it interestin' for 'im. One of the boys rode down to Tombstone and made arrangements with the mule skinner who'd claimed to be some shakes as a cusser. The night of the contest Brimstone told his old woman he was ridin' out to tail up some more weak cows, and slipped off to town. He shore outdid 'imself that night. He'd been wantin' to cuss the weather, and been holdin' in his cuss words so long he was jes' a-bilin' over with 'em. He called forth all his private cuss words and a lot of new ones for this special occasion.

After he got started they could hardly cool 'im off 'nough to declare 'im champion. And believe it or not, that contest was hardly over when it started to rain, and there's folks there yet who declare the smoke from Brimstone's cussin' broke the drought.

Singin' to 'Em

THERE'S been a heap of paper talk lately 'bout cowboy songs. In fact, there's been a few books on the subject wrote by men educated to a feather edge. But all this writin's churnin' up a lot of dust that's hidin' the facts till they're as shy of the truth as a terrapin is of feathers. The radio's developed a heap of cowboy crooners in the past few years, and even if they don't know which end a cow quits the ground with first, they've done a lot to make cowboy songs pop'lar. But with all this bally-hoo, there's mighty few folks who've heard cowboy songs as they're really sung on the range. They only hear the editions that's distorted by some publisher to make 'em sell good. I'd like to tell you somethin' 'bout them songs as they're sung on the range.

Most outdoor men have kinda developed the custom of singin' at their work. It lightens the job and entertains 'em. Away back at the beginnin' of the cow business it didn't take the cowman long to savvy that the human voice gave cattle confidence, and kept 'em from junin' 'round. I reckon it started when the herder got to hummin' a tune to keep 'imself from gettin' as lonesome as a preacher on paynight. The practice got to be so common that night herdin' was spoken of as "singin' to 'em." Some claimed talkin' could've been jes' as effective because it was the human voice that kept a cow from bein' nervous. But talkin' out loud to yourself never got to be a pop'lar custom because no man wanted another to think he was so feather-headed he needed a wet nurse by talkin' to 'im-self by the hour.

Most old-time cowhands were good storytellers. As they rode 'long they'd make up a story in rhyme, then sing it to some tune they'd heard before. A lot of 'em were set to the religious tunes he remembered from the days when he had a mother ridin' herd on 'im. But the words he made up and set to them tunes wasn't learned at his mother's knee. They wouldn't make good parlor talk. He called them songs "hymns," but such hymns would shorely jar the clergy with shock they wouldn't get over soon.

Because all them words that wouldn't improve a Sunday-school book none have now been hazed into the cutbacks, mighty few folks outside the cow country have heard cowboy songs as they were really sung on the range.

The cowboy's songs are kinda like his yellin'—different from them of any other breed of men. His yells he learned from the bloodthirsty Comanches. They're sorta fiendish, savage-like, with a long-drawed-out, weird piercin' cry that shorely made your neck hair rise and set your pulse to racin' and your blood to tinglin'. His songs are different, too, havin' a kind of dismal heart throb like he's puttin' his mystery and misery into mournful melodies all his own. A heap of the charm of the cowboy's singin' and talkin' was in that peculiar inflection he gave his speech. It added a kind of native flavor to his language.

What most folks think of as cowboy songs are them they hear over the radio sung by some New Jersey cowboy. Judgin' by the singin' of them drugstore cowpokes, you'd think a real cowhand yodeled all the time, but you didn't hear none of that garglin' on the range. Seems like ever' feller that can yodel and claw a *git*-tar dudes 'imself up in hair and leather and gets 'imself a job bawlin' into a microphone, soundin' like a sick calf lost from his mammy till it gets as monotonous as a naggin' woman. He can shore punish the air with a noise like he's garglin' his throat with axle grease. Some of them tenderfoots that come out on the range seem disappointed when they don't find cowhands ridin' 'round with a *git*-tar strapped over their withers. What burns me up is to hear one of 'em singin' "Git 'long little doggie," like he's singin' 'bout a short-handled pup instead of the dough-guts of the range.

There wasn't many *git*-tar players on the range, and the instrument was too bunglesome to pack 'round. But there was a little instrument you'd find a heap of 'round a cow camp. That was the mouth organ that so many of 'em packed in their pockets. Maybe it'd be wheezy fom the tobacco crumbs in it, but when a cowhand could play one he poured his whole soul into it. You'd seldom find a cow camp or a bunkhouse that didn't have at least one good player in it. Maybe the city man didn't look on this little instrument as much, but a music-hungry cowhand far from radios and phonographs found it mighty entertainin'.

The cowhand never heard a lot of them songs the radio crooner sings. They've been composed by some educated professor who's never been closer to a cow than a T-bone steak. Some of the old cowboy songs have been changed till the old-timer wouldn't recognize 'em, and the original words have been forgot. One reason a cowhand don't like the radio and movin' picture singer's because he represents 'imself to be a cowhand when he ain't. I'll bet there ain't a one of 'em that could cut a lame cow from the shade of a tree. Maybe, too, he's a little jealous because this radio singer's got a better voice than he has. Some of the songs he sings are real pretty, but the trouble is, when a song makes a hit they sing all the nap off it till you get the trigger itch and want to shoot the singer where he looks biggest.

A heap of folks made the mistake of thinkin' a puncher sang his cows to sleep. He was only tryin' to keep awake, and wasn't tryin' to amuse nobody but 'imself. In the first place he didn't have no motherly love for them bovines. All he was tryin' to do was keep 'em from jumpin' the bedground and runnin' off a lot of tallow. In the second place them brutes didn't have no ear for music, which was a good thing because the average puncher's voice and the songs he sang wasn't soothin'. Mostly he was poorly equipped by nature for such endeavor. But when he opened his mouth to sing, some kind of noise came out. Mostly he had a voice like a burro with a bad cold, and the noise he called singin'd drive all the kyotes out of the country.

A lot of the songs he sang were mighty shy on melody and a heap strong on noise, but a man didn't have to be a born vocalist to sing when he was alone in the dark if he had a clear conscience and wasn't hidin' out. When we say strong on noise we're not speakin' of his singin' on night herd. If a feller did have a good singin' voice and started singin', you'd notice that the others would begin gatherin' 'round like a bunch of calves follerin' a cake wagon. Punchers were mighty fond of bein' entertained with good singin'. They heard so much of the other kind.

No matter how moody he got, he was mighty easy touched with one of them old range songs.

The trouble with most cowhands was, they'd lost their voices yellin' at contrary cows, sleepin' in the wet, or tryin' to explain to some judge how they'd come to have their brand on somebody else's cows. Usually he had an E-string voice that sounded like a rusty gate hinge, and when he opened his mouth to sing it sounded like the long-drawed squeak of a slow-runnin' windmill cryin' for oil. When one puncher I knowed started singin', I thought it was a scrub bull in a canebrake in cockleburr season. His singin' made me forget all my other troubles. You didn't notice trifles when a calamity like the sounds he let out hit you full in the face. Once when we was movin' camp, as one of the boys poured forth his soul in song the cook got off the chuck wagon to look for a dry axle.

If you ever want to compliment a singin' cowboy, jes' say, "I like that song," or, "That's a good song." Don't ever say, "You're a good singer." Even if he knows you're lyin' he's apt to get as full of conceit as a barber's cat.

A cowhand didn't know much 'bout rhyme and meter, but the rhythm had to match the motion of his hoss, and the words he used had to be familiar to the cattle country. If he heard some song with highfalutin words, it'd shore start 'im fightin' the bits. As he made up his song it never worried 'im if one line was a little too long or short, or some stanza had a couple of extry lines. When you hear a cowboy song that's correct in rhyme and rhythm, the chances are it's been worked over by some educated man.

Most cowhands could make the simpler words rhyme, but sometimes his rhymes didn't match so well. On his lonely rides he began to make up a story 'bout somethin' that happened durin' the day, or some incident he remembered from further back. Havin' made up a story with a jingle to it, he set it to some tune he remembered. While a lot of 'em could make up a rhyme, there wasn't many of 'em musician 'nough to compose a tune. He hardly ever knowed what tune he set his words to. It was jes' some old tune he knowed as a boy. The chances were it'd be an old religious tune so he could make it sound melancholy, but by the words he used you'd never think it was once a sacred tune. It seemed like most of 'em wanted to convince you that somethin' had shore swiped the silver linin' off his cloud. He liked to be knee-deep in pathos and picture 'imself as havin' more troubles than Job had boils.

In this way new songs were foaled. When a cowhand made up one he thought was all right, he sang it to his buddies. Then each one would criticize it, and all would make some changes so it'd be better. Maybe each one added some more verses, and pretty soon you forgot who started the whole thing. This was the reason the composer of a song was lost in the shuffle. When cowhands from different ranges met they swapped songs. They liked to learn new ones and teach others the ones they knowed.

Men goin' up the trail or from range to range scattered them songs as they rode, and the songs growed as they passed from mouth to mouth. Maybe verses were added, cut out, or changed to suit the singer as they made the rounds. That's why you see so many different versions of the same song in print. Take that famous song "The Old Chisholm Trail"—it growed till it was almost as long as the trail itself. You wasn't a real hand if you didn't add a verse or two. A lot of 'em was in pretty ripe language, and never got into print. They would've curled the paper. A cowhand was mighty free with his language. Most of 'em were unmarried and a long way from home, and they didn't care what kind of words they used in them songs.

That familiar *coma ti yi yippy yippy yea* you'd so often hear in the old trail songs wasn't put there to jes' fill in where the singer had forgot the words. It was his way of sayin' "Git to hell outta here you blankety-blanks." "The Old Chisholm Trail" starts out with

> "Oh, come along boys, an' listen to my tale,
>   I'll tell you my troubles on the Old Chisholm Trail."

Then ever' verse piled them troubles up thick. But the rhythm of that old song shore made them cows pick up their feet, and put new life in the tired riders as well.

Most of the cowboy's songs were doleful, slow, and melancholy. He wanted to let it soak in while he was enjoyin' his misery. He liked to sing 'bout the hard, dangerous life he lived and the troubles he had, but he wouldn't trade places with a banker if he had the chance. He lived in a big country and an empty one, but he liked it or he wouldn't be there. He liked to sing of tragic disaster because he saw so much of it all 'round 'im; he liked to sing of death because he was so full of life.

A heap of folks have the idea that a cowhand did most of his singin' when on night herd. If you was ridin' herd and passed your partner goin' in the opposite direction, most likely you'd jes' hear 'im hummin' some tune without words—jes' somethin' to keep the cattle quiet and help kill the time. Or, if he sang the words, it'd jes' be snatches of a verse now and then. Singin' a song from beginnin' to end was reserved for the campfire at the chuck wagon, the bunkhouse, or some social occasion. It was the music that had the quietin' effect on cattle, not the words. If they'd been able to understand the words, more'n likely they'd quit the bedground quicker'n you could spit and holler howdy.

Night-herdin' songs were always a croon. Loud singin' didn't quiet cattle. Any song could be sung for night herdin' if it had a lonesome-soundin' tune that could travel as slow as a walkin' hoss.

With the trail songs it was different. Even them were mostly sung soft-like except for a chorus breakin' out like a yell to urge the cattle on. Them yells invented by cowhands were a language best understood by cows. When you hear a verse of a cowboy song delivered on the radio with a lot of power, you can be shore it ain't bein' sung like a real cowhand'd sing it.

A real cowhand was always full of vinegar, and when he opened his mouth wide to yell at cattle to encourage more speed they knowed what he meant. Them yells were fitted to tunes and added to the chorus of some trail songs. Many was the time I've heard a cowhand let out a yell that'd drive a wolf to suicide.

Holdin' a herd on a dark and stormy night was a job for a man with fur on his brisket. If the weather was good and ever' hoof had a paunch-ful of grass and water, all was quiet. But if a storm blowed up and the weather got wholesale, the cattle were mighty apt to be so restless you'd have to ride a mile to spit. Maybe it was so dark you couldn't find your nose with both hands. That was when you had to do some real singin'—maybe till you was plumb tired of it. You might be cussin' the very steers you was ridin' herd on, but as long as you did it to a tune that had that soft accompaniment of squeakin' saddle leather and the tinkle of bridle chains, it was mighty soothin' to a spooky longhorn.

When on night herd, the cowhand's singin' was more or less mechanical because his eyes and mind were busy notin' ever' movement in the brush 'round 'im, on the lookout for anything that'd spook the cattle. One good eye was kept on his hoss's ears. If ever'thing was runnin' smooth his mount's ears'd be standin' up like he was enjoyin' that singin', but if he pointed 'em forward like he saw somethin' you could jes' bet your stack he wasn't lyin'.

In goin' on duty to relieve the guard, a new man approached the

herd singin' to let 'em know he was comin' so he wouldn't bulge up on
'em unawares. Charlie Russell used to say, "The confidence a steer's got
in the dark is mighty frail." Loom up on cattle without singin' and
they'd be off on a run that'd be noisier'n an empty wagon on a frozen
road. There was always some old stampeder or two layin' out on the
fringe lookin' for boogers.

When cowhands went to town, maybe three or four of 'em, after
nosin' their way to the bottom of a few glasses of joy juice, felt like
exercisin' their tonsils in song if the barkeep wasn't no music critic and
didn't have a bronc disposition. But you'd never see 'em standin' on a
street corner singin' like a bunch of college boys. Somebody'd be apt
to build a smoke under their hoofs and make 'em light a shuck without
waitin' to kiss the mayor goodbye.

A lot of cowboy singin' was done when no one was 'round. I think
his start in singin' was born of loneliness. While on some lonesome duty
singin' would help 'im while away the time. Most uncultured people
livin' far from communities naturally turned to song for amusement.

Usin' some old familiar tune, they'd make up parodies to bring back memories of their mothers, their sweethearts, or their boyhood home. The cowboy admired courage. It didn't matter if his hero was good or bad, if he had sand in his craw he was respected. That's why he made a hero of some outlaw like Sam Bass or Jesse James.

He liked men who loved danger or adventure. Usually his hero was red-blooded and square with his fellers. The cowhand condemned "the dirty little coward who shot Mr. Howard," and such traitors as Jim Murphy who squealed on Sam Bass. And you'd never hear 'im sing 'bout some cheap swindler like Soapy Smith.

Sometimes he picked up from some paper or magazine a poem wrote by some real poet like Badger Clark, Larry Chittenden, or Herbert Knibbs, and set it to a familiar tune and spread it over the range till it became a cowboy song.

Out in the cattle country went runaway sailors, and they took their songs along. The cowboy would take any old song and change the words to suit his callin'. There's that old sea chanty

> "O, bury me not in the deep, deep sea,
> Where the dark blue waves will roll over me."

He made this into one of the best knowed cowboy songs by changin' the words to

> "O, bury me not on the lone prairie-e,
> Where the wild coyotes will howl o'er me."

In spite of the fact that calico was as scarce as grass in a city street, the cowboy had his love songs. These, too, reflected the loneliness of his life. When he sang of his unfulfilled love he always tried to jerk a few tears. He had his religion too. He lived in God's great outdoors and studied the stars as he lay at night on the open prairie. On such an occasion the song "Cowboy's Dream" must've been thought up:

> "Last night, as I lay on the prairie
> An' looked at the stars in the sky,
> I wondered if ever a cowboy
> Would drift to the sweet by an' by."

The test of any song is its singability. Cowboy songs have that easy swingin' rhythm that appeals to us common folks. For years them songs have been handed down by word of mouth till a few educated men put 'em on paper. But now them printed editions have cut out all them words that could've raised hair on a currycomb, and the only thing we hear's songs all distorted to make 'em salable.

They tell me now that even them modern dude ranches hire some *gittar* strummin' crooner who looks like a mail-order catalogue on foot to sing to the visitin' dudettes. Maybe he's handsome as a new stake rope on a thirty-dollar pony—one of them kind that's so pretty you feel like tippin' your hat to when you meet 'im—and he can really sing good 'nough to give the romantic hearts of them gal tourists a flutter. But put 'im on herd duty and he'd find out there wasn't no romance in a cow's life and his pretty voice and fancy doodads wouldn't mean a thing.

The cowboy don't have to herd cattle no more and he's not so lonesome as he was in the old days, but singin's still a part of his life. As long as you can hear a cowhand singin' you know ever'thing's hunky-dory, even if the singer can't pack a tune in a corked jug, and his voice sounds like somebody's forgot to grease the wagon.

I never think of a singin' cowboy without rememberin' one down in the brush country of Texas. In one of the saloons he'd been lappin' up likker like a fired cowhand till he was becomin' limber-jointed, and ever' fresh drink seemed to raise his spirits to a higher cheerfulness. Ever' now and then he'd bust forth with a verse of "The Old Chisholm Trail."

Finally this high-heeled Caruso was refused more drinks—the bartender afterward said he wanted to get rid of that singin' before it soured the whisky. But this cowboy was enjoyin' life, and nothin' seemed to make 'im mad. The saloon was built high, with a wooden porch 'bout five feet from the ground and with wide steps that led to the street and hitch rack below. As he came through the swingin' doors to make his way across the street to 'nother bar where his welcome hadn't been wore out, he was liftin' his feet like a sandhill crane walkin' up a riverbed. Halfway across the porch he let go with his acid tenor to continue the song he'd started inside:

"With my knees in the saddle an' my seat in the sky-y-y,
I'll quit punchin' cows in the sweet by an' by-y-y-y."

Jes' then he missed the steps and landed five feet below, the jar rattlin' his bones like throwin' down an armload of wood, but he kept standin' straight up. With hardly a break in his song, he continued in correct rhyme and rhythm:

"An', by God, they shore built them steps damned high-h-h-h."

Cowboy Humor

THERE was an underlyin' humor in nearly ever' utterance of the cowboy. The country he lived in was vast and vivid; the life he lived was hard and lonely. This loneliness, his lack of education, and a certain restrained law-lessness all had their influence. His natural dislike for rule and restraint, his hatred for all authority, his extravagant and often grotesque humor, his exceptional capacity for word pictures—all these attest the spirit of the West, and from such qualities its language was nourished.

Though he led a hard and dangerous life, he could usually see the funny side, even if the joke was on 'im. Nobody relished the humor of bein' taken more'n the cowboy 'imself. His humor growed out of what he knowed and observed. It expressed itself in picturesque, full-flavored, fertile, and vigorous speech, in practical jokes and rough hossplay, and in the tall tales he spun 'round the campfire.

He was one of the great storytellers of our time. He observed closely ever'thing goin' on 'round 'im and had time to think. He developed this storytellin' into a high art, and few other men had more humor or re-vealed more clearly such colorful characters as the tellers themselves. The very life he led, his observations, his talent for word pictures, his closeness with Nature—all these made 'im witty.

While much of the cowboy's language needed some expurgatin' for parlor use, he didn't depend upon smutty stories for his taletellin', like so many of the stories the city man tells; nor did sex enter into the subjects he discussed or joked about. In the early days women were too scarce to be looked upon except with respect and admiration. There were only two kinds, good and bad, and the good were put on a pedestal while the bad were uncondemned.

Cowpunchin' was a hard old game, but most punchers could see the funny side of it, and part of their life's pleasure was tellin' some tall tale or some funny story to make another laugh. He'd act like a monkey on a stick if he could get a laugh. Even his ever'day speech was full of humor, and his capacity for humorous figgers of speech was unequaled.

Settin' round the wagon listenin' to some of that old bunkhouse jokin' was more entertainin' than a vaudeville show. His sense of humor often eased tensions and kept some of 'em from gettin' trigger happy.

Like in other walks of life, cowboys differed in their brand of humor. There were men others liked to work with because they were good at tellin' funny stories that pleased their sense of humor. This man usually had a talent for givin' his stories an original twist that made it his own. But most all cowboy stories were filled with cowtalk with which his listeners were familiar.

There was little that the cowhand took seriously. He was easygoin', indulgent, and held even his own misfortune with somethin' of detached amusement. Consciously or unconsciously, he still aimed to live so he could get up in the mornin', look the world in the face, and tell ever'body in it to go to hell—in a quiet and good-humored way. His language took on the character of the land. Bein' both fearless and resourceful, he could best express his thoughts with comparisons and exaggerations. He developed a vernacular in common with his occupation, and filled with reference to the familiar things of his life.

No group of men ever possessed a stronger, more vigorous sense of humor and made it a part of their lives. His loneliness gave 'im time to think and trained his powers of observation. He could see character in ever' clear-cut detail, and found humor in most of the incidents and situations of his life.

Ever'thing about the cowboy was the result of a young man's havin' to be watchful, proficient, and with a talent for self-reliance and self-protection in a big, empty country where much of the time he was alone and in danger. And this alertness, this necessity for close observation, this workin' with wild and unpredictable animals, this nearness to Nature made the cowboy exceptionally jocular.

In conversation his humor tended toward dry wit rather than gay humor. Most of his speech was of amusin' picturesqueness, and the humorous effect he wanted depended upon the poker face with which he attempted to affect seriousness. His capacity for humor was largely due to the fact that he was a young man, full of prank and play. His kind rarely considered the problems of life seriously. His humor wasn't merely an occasional flash of mood; it was a way of livin', a standard reaction to the problems of life. Even in his ordinary ever'day speech, his humor was evident.

'Round strangers he was brief of speech, and his conversation didn't generally flow freely unless he felt well acquainted and at ease with his listener. Ordinary words and phrases, freshened to novelty by his wit, showed his unpremeditated talent for brevity, as well as his never failin' aptness. There was little refinement in the life of a cowhand, or in his laughter. His was a laughter of men toughened to a hard life in the raw, yet it was a good medium for his own evaluation.

Most cowhands were full of humorous sarcasm toward another who had failed in an undertakin'. He never got sympathy. When a roper missed his throw at a steer for the third time, another cowhand rode up and asked, "Say, why don't you put a stamp on it and send it to 'im by mail?"

Another cowboy fixin' to mount a hoss notorious for his ability to throw riders high and often was asked, "You want me to throw you your overcoat up? It'll be cold up there."

Charlie Russell, the great cowboy artist, told a story of Bill Bullard ropin' two wolves, half dead from poison, and tryin' to bring 'em to camp on hossback, one on each end of his rope. His hoss went "hog wild" when he saw them two wolves so close, and he didn't slow down when he reached camp. Bill was welcomed with such sarcasm as, "What's your hurry, Bill, won't you stay to eat?" "Don't hurry, Bill, you got lots o' time," "If you're goin' to Medicine Hat, a little more to the left." Bill had maybe heard of killin' two birds with one stone, but he learned to never rope two anythings with one rope.

While much of the cowboy's sarcasm was in the nature of "kiddin'" or ridicule, he could also blister your hide with a sarcasm that had an entirely different meanin'. The old-time wagon boss was a diplomat and never publicly bawled out a hand, but when he took 'im aside and cut loose with his witherin' sarcasm it was plumb effective. John Hendrix once told of a wagon boss ketchin' a hand cruelly spurrin' his mount, and when the boss quietly told the hand, "It might be a good idea to borrow the cook's butcher knife if you *really* want to cut that hoss up fine," it had more effect than any command he could've given. And when he told 'nother rider, who was jerkin' his hoss's mouth till it was covered with blood, "If you want to split 'im why don't you use an ax?" that rider never let it happen again.

A green kid from the piny woods of East Texas arrived at a West Texas ranch and asked for a job, as he put it, cowboyin'! The boss put 'im on the payroll solely to give the reg'lar hands somethin' to poke fun at. But the kid was seriously ambitious to become a cowboy. At the first opportunity he roped and saddled a bronc that had been brought up and penned in the corral to await delivery to a buyer of rodeo hosses. Sabine—so named because he was from down on the Sabine River—tried to ride this gut-twister without anyone bein' the wiser. After he'd been throwed four or five times, the commotion attracted the attention of some of the boys in the bunkhouse. Several of 'em rushed to the corral jes' as he was draggin' 'imself up to make 'nother try.

Curly Mallison looked with interest at the ground the kid had plowed up in his many falls.

"What you doin', kid? Puttin' in a crop?" he asked dryly.

"The Ole Man won't like you cultivatin' a claim he's already got under fence," said another.

A third fun-lovin' cowboy squatted on his heels like he was doin' a job of surveyin', then solemnly declared, "You'll have to learn to plow your furrows straighter."

The cattle country had little use for the complainer. He didn't fit into their code. A small rancher in the Panhandle of Texas, classed as a "little feller" with jes' a cowpen herd, was complainin' bitterly one day 'bout the theft of some hides off his corral fence.

"You bellyache 'bout losin' a few hides off your fence," spoke up one of the larger ranchers in the crowd. "I've lost a bunch of hides too, but *mine* had cows wrapped up in 'em."

One cowboy picked up his hat that'd been shot off his head. Havin' no enemies, he supposed it'd been done by some rough joker. As he looked at the top of the crown shot away, he said: "That's a helluva joke. How'd he know how much of my head was in that hat?"

It's been recorded that Charlie Goodnight was once out on an Injun scout with General Baylor, a Texas Ranger. From their hidin' place in the brush they saw an Injun comin' toward 'em, and when he suddenly turned east Baylor begged Goodnight to let 'im do the shootin'. He raised his rifle and took careful aim, but when he fired, only a bunch of eagle feathers from the Injun's war bonnet flew into the air.

"Damn you," said Baylor, with typical Western humor, "if I can't kill you, I can pick you."

Rollie Burns told a story on 'imself when he got throwed tryin' to show off before some hoss buyers. He was young at the time, and tryin' to make an impression. After he'd picked 'imself up out of the dirt some feller walked out to see the "impression" he'd made, and added insult to injury by sayin', "If you'll square up the corners and timber 'er up, you kin hold this corral under the assessment law," and 'nother added, "If you'd try 'er ag'in and manage to hit the same place, you'd git water shore."

Philip Rollins told a story on Squinty Smith ridin' to a neighborin' ranch. When Squinty got to the bunkhouse, his hoss unloaded 'im through the door like he was deliverin' a sack of mail, then mighty sudden got homesick for his own feed trough and hightailed it for home. Squinty was welcomed with the three-word question, "Come to stay?"

The cowhand never lacked for a quick comeback. A young lady from the East became quite interested in a certain puncher. He was good lookin' and seemed better educated than the average cowhand.

"You haven't always been a cowboy, have you?" she asked.

"No'm," he came right back, "I was a baby once."

In the old days there was always some cedar breaker so full of vinegar he thought he couldn't have no fun without ridin' into a saloon on his hoss and shootin' out the lights. He didn't do this to be mean, but it was his idea of a joke, him havin' by nature, like all range men, the idea that all his jokes had to be rough to be worth while. Folks outside the cattle country took this spectacular play to be the earmark of the range, and it gave the whole West a rep'tation that's hard to blot the brand on.

They used to tell a story out in New Mexico 'bout the time three or four young punchers rode their hosses into a saloon when one of them overdressed Eastern drummers happened to be at the bar imbibin' his after-supper refreshments. Bein' considerably jostled by one of them hosses, he complained bitterly to the bartender 'bout all this goin's-on.

The barkeep, an old stove-up ex-cowpuncher, glared at 'im a minute and came back: "What the hell you doin' in here afoot anyhow?" Maybe this barkeep didn't appreciate all that livestock in the saloon, but he appreciated even less complaints comin' from an outsider.

On a New Mexico ranch one of the hands was a newcomer, havin' been there only 'bout a week. The old hands were a little suspicious of 'im because he kept his eyes on the horizon like he was expectin' a sheriff to bulge up on 'im. One of the old hands offered to bet the others that this new hand "came whippin' a mighty tired pony out of Texas," a common expression for "on the dodge."

The new man overheard the remark.

"No, fellers," he said, "I didn't have to leave Texas. The sheriff come to the state line and jes' *begged* me to come back."

Teddy Blue told of a cowhand who'd lost a lot of sleep on account of a troublesome herd on the trail. This hand let the world know his sentiments regardin' sleep by sayin', "I'm a-goin' to Greenland where the nights are six months long, and I ain't a-goin' to git up till *ten o'clock the next mornin'*."

There was 'nother yarn Teddy told 'bout the time they was out tryin' to gather some cattle after a hard winter and big die-up. The weather'd turned hot, the dead cattle stunk, and the only live ones they could find were a few ganted old steers. One old feller who'd owned a few of them dead cows stopped and, with the sweat pourin' from his face, looked up at the sun and, sober as a judge, says, "Where the hell was you last January?"

One cowhand had jes' come back from a certain ranch where he'd been reppin' for his brand. The boys wanted to know if they fed good at this wagon.

"Feed good?" says the returned rep. "Say, boys, they serve two suppers ever' night—one jes' before dark and the other plenty before daylight."

Which reminds me of a yarn Frank Hastings, manager of the Swensen SMS Ranch, told 'bout a cowhand from 'nother ranch spendin' the night at the Spur spread. This cowhand got to the Spur headquarters 'bout ten at night and was called out for breakfast at three o'clock the next mornin'. When he left he remarked, "A man can shore stay all night *quick* at this spread."

I sometimes wonder why the cowboy couldn't seem to resist usin' some figger of speech when a plain statement would serve his purpose. I've come to the conclusion that this is his natural attempt to give play to the humor with which he seems to be so filled that it has to find an outlet. I made a return visit to a ranch and missed one of the boys for whom I'd developed a likin'. When I inquired 'bout 'im, one of the other hands, instead of merely tellin' me he'd taken a job as deputy sheriff, said: "Oh, he's packin' a six-gun for the county and sportin' a tin badge on his brisket that shows up like a patent-medicine sign."

In tellin' of a Jewish merchant in town, one cowhand described 'im as bein' "one of them fellers that couldn't say 'hell' with his hands tied. Handcuff 'im, and he'd be tongue-tied."

Most cowboys took things as they came. They didn't stop to reason how or why. When a cowhand I know was asked, "How deep you reckon this snow is?" he answered: "What the hell difference does it make? You can't see nothin' but the top nohow."

Humor solved far more range problems than the six-gun ever did. Quite often the humor of some quick-witted cowhand relieved a tense situation that could easily have led to serious consequences. Elliott Barker, in his book *When the Dogs Barked Treed*, tells a story that illustrates this situation:

"Good humor," he wrote, "is almost traditional and its spontaneity is refreshing. Its effectiveness is often enhanced by, and largely dependent upon, the vernacular of the range. Cowboy wit often serves to break up what otherwise might develop into serious situations. It contributes to the moral of any cow outfit.

"One of the farm hands had a rather ill-mannered mongrel dog, which he thought a lot of and which followed him everywhere he went. The farmer and I were sitting on the edge of the porch one day when a cowboy rode up. He was a new hand on the ranch and didn't know either the farmer or his dog.

"The cowboy got off his horse and started toward us. The dog rushed out at him, barking and growling viciously. The cowboy was obviously afraid of the dog and backed off a little. The dog subsided somewhat when his master called him, but he didn't come back. Instead, with bristles up, and growling and snorting, the dog went up to the cowboy and sniffed at his chaps in a manner which raised some suspicion in the cowboy's mind as to the dog's intentions. The cowboy, acting on impulse, kicked the animal vigorously in the ribs, sending him howling back to the house.

"Instantly the dog's master came off the porch, fighting mad, and shouted, 'What the hell's the matter with you? Sport wouldn't bite you.'

" 'I wasn't scared of him biting me,' drawled the cowboy, 'but when he came up and smelled my chaps and then turned around and raised his hind foot, I shore thought he was a-goin' to kick me.'

"That broke the tension, everybody laughed, and the fighting mood vanished."

This kind of humor is heard from one end of the range to the other. Maybe it's not funny 'nough to make you laugh, but it'll shore keep you smilin' and in a good humor.

The Cowman's Religion

Most writers who write 'bout the early West would have us believe the cowman was mostly a drinkin', swearin', and shootin' individual. Consequently it's a rare occasion when one finds any reference to his religion. Somehow his profanity, poker playin', and drinkin' became a tradition as to his way of life. The preachers had nothin' to do with such activities and consequently became poor copy and were left out of the picture. But they were there. In fact, the missionaries preceded the cowman 'imself, even the trappers.

Though most cowhands wasn't pickin' any grapes in the Lord's vineyard, and the married rancher might grin his admission that most of his religion was in his wife's name, he did have his religion. Not the go-to-church, hidebound kind, but after his own way he knowed God had somethin' to do with Nature, and the cowhand was always close to Nature.

But because he wasn't a churchgoin', Bible-readin' man it was no sign he was irreligious and a godless person. The average cowhand had been raised in a Christian home and taught by a Christian mother. After he'd left home and gone out into the rough world, he sometimes forgot his early teachin', but he never seemed to lose his deep sense of religion. But religion to 'im wasn't somethin' to be fanatical 'bout, it was somethin' to use practically—to be lived instead of preached.

He felt that the Golden Rule was the basis of true, practical religion;

47

that true religion was in deed, not in words, in generosity, honesty, neighborliness, and hospitality. Followin' this code, the roundup wagon fed all who visited it. At the ranch ever' visitor was welcome to stay the night, even when there wasn't 'nough blankets to go 'round. Nowhere was found a more openhearted hospitality than on the range.

The average ranchman was honest, and when he came across an unbranded stray belongin' to a neighbor, even though they might not be on speakin' terms, he branded it with its proper brand and shoved it toward its home range. Bein' a lover of Nature, it was hard for 'im to disbelieve that some higher Bein' didn't have somethin' to do with the creation of things. He had a strong moral code and a definite philosophy that resulted from his closeness with Nature. Sincerity, loyalty, generosity, and simplicity were the four corners of this philosophy.

Many of 'em had their own code, which might be similar to that of Jesse Chisholm when he said: "I do not know anything about the Bible. I have no use for preachers. No man ever came to me hungry and went away unfed, or naked and departed unclad. All my life I have tried to live at peace with my fellow man and be a brother to him. The rest I leave with the Great Spirit who placed me here, and whom I trust to do all things well."

The cowman understood doin' good. He realized the insignificance of man as compared with the bigness of the universe and of Nature. He was sincere, and the thing he despised most was deceit. He had no use for the double-dyed hypocrite who was raised on prunes and proverbs and who sinned all week and then on Sunday tried to pull 'imself out of a hole by gettin' down on his prayer bones and taffyin' the Lord up.

Maybe the cowman felt that he'd been flounderin' in the mire of sin so long old St. Peter wouldn't recognize 'im as a candidate for wings, but at the final showdown he didn't want to be left out to starve on a bare range. He wanted to be up yonder where there was no end of harps and free music. He practiced sincerity rather than imitated it. The imitation article belonged to the accomplishments of polite society.

He had no thoughts on the creeds, isms, or cults that divided his civilized brother. Methodists, Baptists, Presbyterians, Lutherans, or Catholics might use the same church on alternatin' Sabbaths. He tried to keep cases on all them sky pilots, and get onto their curves.

But mostly his work took 'im away from religious activities. He was too busy with his daily tasks to consider churchgoin' as an important part of his life. Even when he did have the opportunity to go to town, he didn't want to spend this rare freedom listenin' to psalm singin' and exhortations on sin.

My friend J. Evetts Haley once told me a story 'bout two cowhands who went to town one Sunday to have some fun. They didn't know that there'd been a protracted religious meetin' goin' on for some time and that this had caused all the business houses to close on Sundays, not like it was in the old days. When they got there hopin' to have a few drinks and play some pool, they found all them places closed. Ridin' down the street they found that the little church was 'bout the only thing open, and hearin' the singin' they decided to go in as there was nothin' else to do. After listenin' to an hour-long sermon on how the Jews had crucified Christ and nailed Him to the cross, them cowhands rode back up the street to head back for the ranch again.

Halfway up the street they saw a store open, a clothin' store run by a little Jewish merchant. They dismounted and went in. The merchant looked up with a smile, rubbin' his hands together, and asked what he could do for 'em. He pictured a good sale from them two.

"I think we'd better take you outside and string you up," said one of the cowboys.

"Hang me?" gasped the surprised merchant. "For vat? I've done noddin' to you."

"No, but your folks crucified Christ," was the answer.

"But that was two thousand years ago," pleaded the merchant.

"Makes no difference," answered the first cowboy. "We've jes' heard 'bout it."

In the early days there were few reg'lar preachers who held down any specific church; the pop'lation was too sparse and scattered. Most of 'em were saddlebag preachers, or circuit riders, who rode from ranch to ranch and settlement to settlement. Sometimes the preacher was an educated man, trained in his callin', but often he was some former cowhand who'd got religion, and was devotin' his life to his convictions. This latter man was more understood by the ranchers because he spoke their language. His illustrations and figures of speech were drawed from the range. He might be as uneducated as his feller punchers, but he better understood their way of life. He wasn't squeamish 'bout enterin' a saloon. He preached in 'em, sought financial aid from their owners, ate their free lunches, and in doin' so gave the saloon man a different outlook on religion, often gettin' the money necessary to carry on his work.

As he went from ranch to ranch, from settlement to settlement, spread-

in' cheer and love and religion, the people began to look forward to his
visits. It seemed to the rancher's wife that they were always hungry.
Maybe it was because they never seemed to quite get filled up at home on
their small income. Whenever possible there was fried chicken, but the
children of the ranch knowed that when the preacher was there for dinner, all they got was the neck and that part last over the fence. So they
didn't look forward to a minister's visits.

It's been said that no man could herd the Texas longhorn and still be a
Christian, yet many were the times when the old trail drivers felt it im-
proper to bury a comrade along the trail without some kind of religious
word bein' spoken as they stood with bared heads and hopin' that this
unfortunate soul would be able to take off his spurs at the Pearly Gates.
No one knowed what struggles took place in the heart and mind of a
cowboy who rode away from the lonely grave of a fallen companion.

Some of the pioneer cowmen, especially if they had womenfolks, would
endure all kinds of hardships in order to get to church when one was not
too far away. Sometimes the preacher, in order to be a permanent addition to the settlement, also had to teach school durin' the week. Folks of
all denominations went to hear 'im preach, and considered his church their
own. Some of them frontier churches had log and plank seats, but the
people would sit still, no matter how uncomfortable, and listen to a sermon
an hour or two long. They didn't dare to relax and go to sleep on them
backless benches. Often the preacher's pay was only clothin' and food,
but he poured his whole soul into them messages he delivered.

The gatherin's that all ranch folks looked forward to was the protracted
meetin's held in the summer when the work was slack. These usually
lasted a week or more. The young ladies spent a heap of time gettin' their
glad rags ready so they could impress some saddle stiff they hoped would
be there.

All the young folks looked forward to them meetin's because they
could again see friends from distant ranges, and it broke the monotony
of ranch life. The older folks, too, were anxious to renew acquaintances
and make new ones. The women exchanged the latest gossip, and the
young girls told of their newest boy friend. Children, whose playmates
were few and far between, enjoyed the games they could play between
sermons, but they didn't escape the long-winded services. They were
brought in and made to set under the watchful eyes of their parents.

Them meetin's were planned in advance. A campsite near good water
and some timber was selected for the comfort of shade. Lumber was

hauled for seats, and these were placed on nail kegs or anything else that could be made to serve. The boards were placed smooth side up except when some prankish puncher put the splinter side up in hope of ketchin' a feller puncher unawares. The cowmen liked the open, and had little hankerin' for stained-glass windows, or bein' fenced in by a buildin'.

A brush arbor was built and some sort of makeshift pulpit put together for the preacher. On the day set, folks came from miles 'round, some in wagons, some in buggies, and most of the single men on hossback. Durin' the services the men sat on one side and the women on the other. The cowboys and young gals paid more attention to makin' eyes at each other than they did the preacher.

The preachin' was that old-time fire-and-brimstone kind that the preacher shouted in a voice you could hear a mile. When he got warmed up and began to sling his arms 'round like he was fightin' bees, it stirred their emotions, and most preachers seemed to rely on their appeal to the emotions to get conversions. When them old cowmen got their religious fervor all stirred up and got to singin', it was loud and lusty. Maybe they didn't have any singin' talent, but they had plenty of zeal, all of which made this singin' sound better from a distance where it'd be toned down.

But this singin' gave 'em a chance to express the emotion stirred up by the preachin', especially when some were goin' down the glory trail to have their sins washed away, while the preacher pleaded with the drags to come down and be saved. More'n one throwout went down the aisle steppin' as high as a blind dog in a wheat field, happy as a heifer with a new fence-post, and stacked his burden of sin on the altar. Some of them old coots had maybe outrun a hangin' bee in Texas because he got up earlier and had a faster hoss than the sheriff, but he was now shoutin' hallelujah louder'n anybody. By now the women, who were especially good shouters, were sheddin' a few tears and pleadin' with their sinnin' menfolks to change their way of life.

All durin' them meetin's the people camped 'round the brush arbor. Some families camped close together, and cooked and ate as one family. The women slept in the covered wagons, the family men nearby in the open, the cowboys in their bedrolls scattered over the prairie, while the children might sleep in the straw at the altar, placed there for the mourners.

There were usually several meetin's held durin' the day and night, most of 'em preachin's, but some of 'em "experience" meetin's. Most of the night services were prolonged by testimonials of personal religious experiences. Before the meetin' broke up the preacher would be hoarse from his exhortations and the people jes' as hoarse from their happy shoutin'. The whole thing was a picnic for the kids. Plenty of food was brought by the families to feed all the single cowboys, and there was plenty of grain for the hosses.

When the meetin' broke up and ever'body had packed to leave, there was much handshakin' among the men, and kissin' and tears among the women. The preacher was happy because he'd made so many see the light, and the people were happy because of the spiritual uplift they'd received.

The Cowman's Code of Ethics

BACK in the days when the cowman and his herds made a new frontier there wasn't much law on the range. Lack of written law made it necessary for 'im to frame some of his own, so he developed a rule of behavior that became a kind of code of the West. Them homespun laws, bein' merely a gentleman's agreement to certain rules of conduct for survival, were never wrote into the statutes, but became respected ever'where on the range nevertheless.

When legislated law did come to the frontier, it failed to fit the needs and conditions on this fringe of civilization. Men didn't respect these laws because they couldn't obey 'em, and survive. Thus the West got a rep'tation for bein' lawless, though the blame for this condition should've been placed on the white-collared lawmakers, and not the so-called law-breakers. Though the cowman might break ever' law of the territory, state, or Federal government, he took pride in upholdin' his own un-written code. His failure to abide by it didn't bring formal punishment, but the man who broke it became, more or less a social outcast.

One of the first rules of the code was courage. Men who followed this life wouldn't tolerate a coward, for one coward endangered the whole group. Through the hundreds of ways of makin' the life of a coward unbearable, he was soon eliminated. If a man had a spark of courage to start with, the life he lived on the range soon developed it to a high degree. He had to have bones in his spinal column and know how to die standin' up. His life was full of dangers such as mad cows, bad hosses rode over a country full of dog holes at breakneck speed, crossin' swollen rivers, quicksands, and many other things, not countin' the troubles the early cowman had with Injuns. If his craw wasn't full of sand and fightin' tallow, he wouldn't make the grade.

Cheerfulness was also a part of his code. The bigness of the country, the mighty struggles with a virile Nature wouldn't let 'im listen to the whimpers of a mere human. Privations and hardships were endured without complaint. No one knowed a man was tired; sickness or injury was his own secret unless it couldn't be hid any longer. You'd never know but that he was as happy as a lost soul with hell in a flood, and he was usually grinnin' like a jackass eatin' cactus.

The cowman laughed in the face of danger, laughed at hardships when laughin' was hard. Tragedy and its possibilities were all 'round 'im, and his cheerfulness was an attempt to offset this. As a man of action he had little time to mourn fatalities.

From the nature of his work, no cowboy could be a quitter; therefore he rarely complained, because he associated complaints with quittin'. He took a pride in his work, always tryin' to do better than the other feller. No matter how good they were, there was no room for excuses on the range. Grumblers simply didn't flourish in a cow camp.

One of the cowman's outstandin' codes was loyalty. He was one class of worker who didn't have to be watched to see that he did his work well. The nature of his work demanded that he be trusted. He took a pride in bein' faithful to his "brand" and in performin' his job well. He needed no overseer, or advice. He worked long hours and packed no timepiece. He belonged to no union, and no whistle was blowed orderin' 'im to knock off work. He worked from before dawn to after dark, and even later if need be. His loyalty to the boss came first, and he'd ride night herd on the cattle as faithfully on a rainy night, or in a stingin' sleet, as he would on starry, moonlight nights.

Personal comfort and safety were forgotten in lookin' after the welfare of the herd under his charge, and he'd lay down his life, if necessary, for the privilege of defendin' his outfit. Once a cowhand had throwed his bedroll into the wagon and turned his private hoss into the remuda of an outfit, he'd pledged his allegiance and loyalty.

He lived up to a law that held the obligation of friendship deeper than all others. Yet, accordin' to the unwritten law, he stood ready to offer friendly service to strangers, or even an enemy, when necessity called for it. The rule required that whoever caught a signal of distress was to render quick assistance. It sometimes happened that a cowboy laid down his own life to save an enemy that he might live up to this code.

No man had a greater sense of fair play than the cowman. He despised treachery. The very principle of his code demanded square dealin' with his feller man. That common expression, "He'll do to ride the river with," was 'bout the highest compliment that could be paid 'im. It originated back in the old days when brave men had to swim herds across swollen, treacherous rivers. The act required level-headed courage; and, as time passed, this phrase acquired the meanin' that the one spoken of was loyal, dependable, trustworthy, and had plenty of sand.

Gene Rhodes spoke the sentiment of the whole range when he said:

"To rise up from a man's table and war upon that man while the taste of his bread is still sweet in your mouth—such dealings would have been unspeakable infamy. . . . You must not smile and shoot. You must not shoot an unarmed man, and you must not shoot an unwarned man. Here is a nice distinction, but a clear one; you might not ambush an enemy; but, when you fled and your enemy followed, you might then waylay and surprise without question to your honor, for they were presumed to be on their guard and sufficiently warned. The rattlesnake's code, to warn before he strikes, no better; a queer, lopsided, topsy-turvy, jumbled and senseless code—but a code for all that. And it's worthy to note that no better standard has ever been kept with such faith as this barbarous code of the fighting man."

There was no prouder soul on earth than the cowboy. He was proud of his occupation, and held it to be a dignified callin'. The man on hossback has always held 'imself above the man on foot. You might see many men and boys from other walks of life try to palm 'emselves off as cowboys, but you'll never see a cowboy tryin' to hide his occupation. For this reason he avoids wearin' a spur on a single foot because it smacks of the sheepherder, and he shuns bib-overalls because it's the farmer's riggin'. In ever'thing he did he was as full of pride as a bull is of wind in corn time.

He'd do a tremendous amount of work in the line of duty, but his proud spirit wouldn't let 'im kowtow to anyone. No commands were given 'im; the merest hint was an order. To throw off on the boss was an unpardonable sin. In the saddle at frosty sunup, he rode through all kinds of weather, rain, snow, or heat, till the job was done, no matter how late the hour. But in spite of his loyalty, his proud spirit wouldn't let 'im do work that couldn't be done from the back of a hoss. Like the old sayin', he was "too proud to cut hay, but not wild 'nough to eat it."

Because of this great pride in his callin', the punishment that hurt the deepest was to be "set down" in the presence of his feller riders. This meant bein' ordered to surrender his "company hoss," and, if he didn't own a private mount, to hit the trail afoot. Very often the sting of this disgrace was so deep it ended in gun smoke.

The true old-time cowhand had a heart in his brisket as big as a saddle blanket. Nothin' he owned was too good to share with a feller worker if that puncher needed it. The night was never too dark or the trail too long or rough that it kept 'im from ridin' to the aid of a friend. He was generous with his money. Any stranger could make 'im shell out his *dinero* with a hard-luck story. Even if he was powerful narrow at the equator 'imself, he'd share with any other hungry man. Hearin' of some puncher bein' sick or broke and needin' medicine, the whole range would empty its pockets. He was generous with his life and would take all manner of risks to save the property of his outfit, even to goin' to war for it.

Far out on the range, a long way from where he could buy more, his supply of "makin's" might run low, but he never refused another a smoke unless he wanted to offer a direct and intentional insult.

Some folks wonder at the cowman's code of honesty. In his dealin's with another, his word was his bond, and the unwritten law put a premium on honesty and fair dealin'. Accordin' to romance, 'bout half the men in the cattle country were cow thieves. It was true that many cowboys, honest in ever' other way, didn't spend much time lookin' for the mother when they found a slick-ear, but all other property was perfectly safe 'round 'im. As a rule he was as honest as a woman's lookin' glass.

Property in the West consisted mostly of hosses and cattle. There was no such thing as petty thievery. As Charlie Russell once said, "I've known many old-timers who would hold up a stage or steal a slick-ear, but they was no camp robbers." Locks on doors were unknown till the nesters came, and in the old trail days bags of silver and gold lay 'round camp unnoticed with never a thought of theft. There was hoss and cattle stealin' to be shore, and the code of the West made a strange distinction between the two. To set a man afoot by stealin' his hoss carried a penalty of death, for deprivin' a man of his hoss could mean life itself on the plains. Public opinion regarded the cow as jes' property, and its theft was a case for the courts.

The cowman also had a code regardin' his hosses. No matter how hungry he got 'imself, he took care of his hoss before lookin' after his own comfort. When climbin' mountains on hossback, he picked the easiest way; when ridin' 'long a hard-surfaced road he rode at the side where it was soft.

When nearin' 'nother person on a trail, etiquette required that a man approach within speakin' distance and pass a word before changin' his course unless, for a very good reason, he was justified in such a change. The West held that ever' person had the right to find out the intent of all other persons 'bout 'im. Unwarranted violation of this was usually interpreted as a confession of guilt, or as a deliberate and flagrant insult.

When two men met, spoke, and passed on, it was a violation of the West's code for either to look back over his shoulder. Such an act was interpreted as an expression of distrust, as though one feared a shot in the back. If he stopped to talk 'long the trail, he dismounted and loosened the cinches to give his hoss's back some air. When greetin' a stranger on the trail, one was careful not to lift his hand if the stranger rode a skittish hoss. Some critters would bolt if a man lifted a hand near 'em. He merely nodded and said, "Howdy." If the stranger lit to cool his saddle, the other didn't stay mounted while carryin' on a conversation. The polite thing to do was dismount and talk with 'im face to face. This showed one wasn't lookin' for any advantage over the other.

If he met a rider on a grade, he gave 'im the inside. Thus he could always dismount without steppin' down in front of, behind, or against the other's hoss. This rule didn't hold good if the dust drift blowed his way. In that case, he rode downwind.

No buster hired to break hosses abused 'em. No outfit wanted spoiled hosses. If the buster was throwed, and not crippled in the fall, he was certain to crawl back on the animal. It never did a hoss any good to let 'im think he'd won the argument. A good hand never gave a hoss too much work; nor did he jump his hoss into a run if he had a long way to travel.

A cowboy saddled and unsaddled his own hoss, and an offer to help was unwelcome unless he was hurt bad. Only in a serious situation would he lend his hoss to another. He knowed a hoss was easy spoiled or crippled by the wrong person ridin' 'im. One of the worst possible breaches of range etiquette was for a man to ride another's "company" hoss without first askin' permission, even from his best friend, for no two hands train a hoss alike, and one spoils it for the other. To mount without leave another's private, or individual, hoss, his own personal property—well, slappin' a man's face could hardly be more insultin'.

When on roundup or on the trail, a good cowhand got up when he was first called. When he went to wash the sleep from his eyes, if there wasn't a pool or stream handy, he didn't use up all the water in the barrel. He knowed that good drinkin' water couldn't be found ever'where, and it was considerable trouble for the cook to fill that barrel. Also, he knowed he'd get a cussin' from the cook if he left the spigot on the barrel half open, and wasted water. If he left dirty water in the wash pan, he couldn't take offense at the cussin' he got from the hand that followed 'im.

Furthermore, he found out what relief he was on, who he was to call for the next watch, and where they'd be bedded down so he wouldn't be wakin' up ever'body in camp to find the right man. Nothin' made a cowhand so fightin' mad as bein' waked up from his needed sleep when he wasn't wanted. It was good to double with some rider on the same relief as 'imself and to make down his bed where it wouldn't be in nobody else's way. It was a good idea to sleep with your pants on, and to always put your boots under cover when sleepin' outdoors. You might wake up next mornin' to find 'em froze stiff or full of rain water. They could be used for a pillow if you'd put 'em down first, then your chaps and your jacket over 'em.

It was a good rule never to dismount within a hundred yards of a bedded herd. The shake of the saddle often given by a hoss freed from his burden was 'nough to cause a stampede. Also, no good cowhand would ride a hoss into the middle of a herd if that hoss was a bucker. 'Nother good rule was to never strike a hoss when you're mad. A man had to control 'imself before he could control his hoss.

Early in cattle raisin', the code of the range required ever' cowman to brand not only his own calves, but all others he rounded up. All honest cowmen branded them offspring with the brand of the mother, so no matter how far a man's cattle might stray he was shore to gain the natural increase.

It was not a statute law, but a range law jes' as strong, that two outfits coverin' the same territory should roundup at the same time. If one outfit covered it, then a second came 'long through the herd makin' their cuts, it not only made much extry work but was hard on the cattle.

In workin' cattle, if a man let an animal break from the herd and get by 'im, it was his job alone to bring it back, and he resented anyone givin' help.

A strict range law was "no whisky with the wagon." Nothin' would get a man fired quicker'n drinkin' while workin' cattle. The only man who could get away with this was the cook, and he didn't do any cattle work.

A standin' rule in the old trail days was to wake a man by speech and not by touch. The hardships and dangers of the drive frayed his nerves, and he was apt to come alive with a gun in his hand. No firin' of guns 'round a cow camp unless emergency demanded it was another unwritten law.

The cowboy might be rude and unlettered, and treat his companions with a rough-and-ready familiarity, but he accorded his neighbor the right to live the life and go the gait that seemed most pleasin' to 'imself. One didn't intrude on the rights of others in the cattle country, and he looked to it mighty pronto that nobody intruded on his. Ever' Westerner had such a dislike of intrudin' into other folk's affairs that he volunteered to the officers of the law hardly any assistance, except in such matters as pertained to his own cattle and hosses. They weren't close-mouthed because they approved crime. They jes' had a dread for hornin' in. They held in contempt anyone guilty of feedin' off his own range. One of the prime rules of a cowman's life was to keep his mouth shut and attend to his own business.

It was a violation of code to ask a man what his name was back in the States, even if you knowed his past was full of black spots, and he'd dropped his right name when he'd headed in the direction advised by Mr. Greeley. A heap of men drawed a new name from the pack when they came West. It was quite 'nough to know a man by his local and accepted name. He was valued for what he was, not for what his name was, nor what that of his father might've been. A man's past belonged to 'im alone, and should remain a closed book if he wanted it so. If a cowman felt any curiosity toward 'nother's past, there was no evidence of it. Too much personal curiosity wasn't good form, and met with many discouragements; besides, it wasn't healthy. The West cared nothin' 'bout a man's past, and willingly accepted any name he cared to volunteer if he was livin' up to the code. Many men've lived for years knowed only by a nickname.

As the cowman said, "Mindin' one's own business is the best life insurance." Nobody asked questions of a stranger. If he was jes' driftin' through the country seein' things, that was his business. If he had reasons for travelin' which he didn't dare tell, his silence was respected. Also, askin' a cowman how many cattle he owned jes' wasn't done. This'd be as bad as askin' a businessman how much money he had in the bank.

It was never good form to exhibit curiosity. A puncher, passin' a stranger or enterin' the latter's camp, wouldn't lower 'imself by seemin' to note the stranger's apparel or equipment. Custom also demanded that whoever approached a person from the rear should let his presence be knowed by a "hello" before gettin' within gun range. A like signal should also be used when approachin' a camp, and, if possible, the approach should be made from the direction most easily observable to the camp's occupants. As an incident of greetin' between strangers, it was good form for each to bow to the extent of temporarily removin' his hat, or at least to raise the right hand to his hatbrim. This took away the supposedly dangerous hand from the vicinity of the gun at his belt.

One of the strictest codes of the West was to respect women. No other class of men looked upon women with greater reverence. An abundance or oversupply of anything lessens its value and position. So it was with women of the range; there were so few of 'em. No matter who she was, or her station in life, the cowman held her with respect.

Range etiquette forbade a strange male guest to show an interest in the women of the household, or an appreciation of their hospitality except by eatin' heartily. The cook, if it happened to be the lady of the house, was jes' "the lady who cooks." Except for a duck of the head, she wasn't greeted when an unknowed man arrived.

A woman might live alone, miles from anyone, but she had no fear of any true cowman. She was as safe as in a church, and she knowed it. If any man, at any time, under any circumstances, mistreated a woman, he was culled from society. Men refused to speak to 'im, doors were shut against 'im, and he was an outcast. In spite of the movies, if one insulted a woman he was probably killed sooner or later, even if somebody had to get drunk to do it. All this kidnapin' of women you see in the movies never happened in real life.

So you see that even though the cowman failed to always observe man-made laws, he had a code of his own of great beauty, and one to which he strictly adhered.

Bosses and Reps

To HEAD the list of bosses came the owners, of course. These came under three different species. One was the owner who lived in some distant state, or territory, and under this head were the foreign owners who lived in Scotland or England. The absentee owner who lived in America usually made a trip or two each year to the ranch to check with their foreman or manager to whom they had assigned the runnin' of the outfit. The cowhands had various names for them absentee owners, such as Presidente, from the Spanish, meanin' a local government official; Big Augur, Big Sugar, Old Man, and when on his inspection tours if he didn't ride a hoss well, but preferred ridin' 'round in a buggy, he was called the "Buggy Boss."

While them owners were away from the ranch their property was in the keepin' of their cowhands, who were under the direction of their foreman. Them men had usually come up from the ranks, and knowed the cattle business. The success of the ranch depended on their knowledge, faithfulness, and prompt attention to ever' duty and their ability to handle men.

Regardin' the foreign owners, there's much to be said both for and against 'em. Rich Englishmen became very interested in the American cattle industry in the early eighties. Many Scots also bought ranches in the Northwest. While the Scots were businesslike and serious in the investment of their money, the English looked upon it as an interestin' adventure, and more of a lark. They came from wealthy families and didn't know the value of a dollar. Many of 'em had come to America seekin' minin' interests or on huntin' trips, and on bein' told that the cattle business was a quick way to get rich they either formed companies or bought individually some of the largest ranches in Wyoming, Montana, and other cattle states.

Many of them foreign investors belonged to the nobility and were used to luxury. They did ever'thing on a grand scale, such as buildin' expensive headquarters, importin' cooks and servants from London, even bringin' the furniture from Europe. American wines and whisky weren't good 'nough for 'em, so they imported this too. They throwed great parties and had frequent huntin' and fishin' trips. Most of them foreign outfits chose Wyoming as the place to try their hand at ranchin'. Some of 'em spent money lavishly in buildin' up their spreads; but after the winter of '86 and '87, with the terrific losses, the constant lowerin' of cattle prices, and the beginnin' of the influx of nesters, they soon gave up the sponge.

Most of them companies hired some native and experienced cowman to run the outfit, but took little interest in anythin' 'emselves except huntin' big game and havin' a good time. Their mode of livin', wantin' someone to wait on 'em at ever' turn, their speech, their softness—all them things disgusted the cowboys on their payroll. Of course, all this investment of foreign money, said to be forty or fifty million dollars, had tremendous influence on the cattle boom of the early eighties, and all this, too, caused the buildin' of railroads and many other improvements. Their influence on the whole stock-raisin' industry was felt in two ways.

On the good side were their interest and introduction of stock of better grade, such as Herefords; their help in formin' stock growers' associations, animal bureaus, and other organizations. But many of their ideas were impractical, and their influence for evil maybe offset the good. Their wasteful and extravagant spendin' of money made the hard-workin', poorly paid cowhand rebel in his own way. There couldn't be much loyalty to some such boss or corporation, the head of which never even came to America, much less to the ranch.

It wasn't long till a calf belongin' to some owner in London didn't seem quite so much a piece of private property as that of the adjoinin' ranch owned by a local man. Cowhands were very loyal to a native owner who they felt was one of 'em, but not some foreigner who had more money than judgment. Therefore cattle stealin' became common in that section till it developed into one of the great range wars. It was hard to convict a thief, because even the juries were against foreign ownership. So no matter how convincin' the evidence, the thief usually went scot free to steal more calves.

Them English knowed little 'bout the business, and overstocked their ranges, employed too many high-salaried officials, and paid too little attention to their losses. The Scots were more conservative, better businessmen, and thus were a credit to cattle raisers ever'where. Such men as John Clay, Murdo MacKenzie, and others left their good and lastin' impression, as well as a vast influence on the cattle industry.

'Nother type owner was the one who lived in town because maybe his wife wasn't happy on a ranch, with its hardships, and life away from other women and the things they liked, or maybe because it was easier to send the kids to school. However, he was a cowman, and made frequent visits to the ranch, and was much closer to things than the absentee owner who never came to the ranch more'n once or twice a year. Though he turned the actual runnin' of the outfit over to a foreman, he was at the ranch often 'nough to see that his orders were carried out.

The third type owner was the one who stayed at the ranch all the time and devoted his whole attention to its success. If his was big 'nough to justify it, he usually also hired a foreman to take some of the work off his shoulders. Thus he could devote more of his energies to the business end of things, or to the buildin' up of his blood lines and such.

The foreman of a good ranch didn't have no easy job, and it was one of great responsibility. He was knowed by such titles as "top screw," "high salty," "head taster," "cock-a-doodle-doo," and, accordin' to his immediate duties, was the "range boss," "wagon boss," or "trail boss." As a range boss he mostly worked with company-owned outfits, and his duties were to secure and protect the company's range, run its business, keep its men and wagons at work, and see that the cattle were bred up. He saw that fences and buildin's were kept in repair, that the water supply was in runnin' order, and did ever'thing he could to better the interests of his company.

First of all he had to be a good cowman, and that meant he had to understand cattle, their natures, and their diseases, and to know how to remedy them diseases. He had to know his range thoroughly, ever' water hole and other piece of water, its bogholes, a river's quicksands, and its fordin' places. He had to understand men, know their limitations, and command both their respect and obedience. He should have 'nough experience to make wise decisions, and good judgment because he had access to his employer's purse and could make or break 'im. He had charge of the buyin' of supplies on both roundup and trail drives, as well as for the home supplies, the purchase of blooded bulls, and such. He had to be a man of courage, one who wouldn't ask any man to do somethin' he wouldn't do 'imself.

Before a roundup the cattlemen of a district met and chose some experienced cowman to be the general superintendent of the approachin' district roundup. The man chosen to act as boss of the roundup was called the "roundup captain" or "wagon boss." He stood out above the rank and file. One who knowed the cattle country could ride up to an outfit at the chuck wagon, or the brandin' pen, for the first time, and go straight to the boss, though he was hard at work and dressed like all the others of the outfit. His appearance and attitude denoted leadership. He was usually quiet, reserved, and had to have better'n average intelligence to understand the nature of the average cowhand.

He was chosen because of his knowledge of cattle and men, his honesty, ability for leadership and for fair play. He had to arrange each man's work and place, day and night, without appearin' to give orders, and all this called for a lot of tact and understandin'. On the roundup he saw that the drive for cattle was thorough, that there was no unnecessary abuse or heatin' of the cattle, hosses, or men, and above all that there wasn't any dissension between the various owners of the cattle or their hands.

He was absolute boss and his word was law, no matter if he didn't own a hoof. The owners of the cattle were as much under his orders as any common puncher or hoss wrangler. He had to know all the brands of the country and had to be a diplomat to keep peace between warrin' factions. He had to know men and select the right man for the right job, as well as the proper roundup grounds. Certain men knowed certain ranges better'n others; accordingly he sent them men out to scour this range for cattle. He selected from among the cowboys he knowed to have good judgment as many lieutenants as he needed. These he put in charge of small units to run the cattle out of the brakes, arroyos, and other parts of the range. One cowhand described the roundup boss as "the feller that never seems to need sleep and it makes 'im mad to see someone that does."

On the ranch the ability of the wagon boss was gauged by the condition of the hosses in the fall after the roundup. Many a good wagon boss has decided to accept or reject the offer of the job of roddin' a spread on the number and kind of hosses owned by the ranch and their condition. A good foreman would make his men understand that he'd get out and do the things he asked them to do. He was generally agreeable, but firm in his demands. Because a hard-boiled foreman was never liked and couldn't get real service from his men, the foreman had to be well liked to hold his job long.

A good trail boss had to know men and cattle too. He had to be resourceful, aggressive, and quick in emergencies. He belonged to a class of men who made history bossin' the herds up the long trail north from Texas, and the world'll never see his like again. He had to be a man of character, a leader, and one of quick and just decisions. He selected his men with care because he knowed what lay ahead and that he needed men who could be depended upon in ever' emergency, men who'd obey orders without question; men who had faith in his judgment and experience.

He had to be honest because he was trusted with the owner's cattle, sometimes amountin' to a fortune. He had to be diplomatic in handlin' quarrelsome nesters 'long the trail, or the hostile Injuns while crossin' through their country. Above all, he had to know cattle and how to handle 'em, their nature and their faults. On the trail, he usually rode ahead in the mornin' to look up waterin' places, grass, and possibilities of flood water or quicksand, or sign of hostile Injuns, one of the great menaces of the trail driver. He usually had more hosses in his individual string than the reg'lar hands because he had to ride long distances lookin' for water and river crossin's. It was said that a good trail boss fed his hands out of the herd, lost a few en route, yet got to his destination with more cattle than he had when the owner counted 'em out as they left the home range.

He not only had to use good judgment in crossin' flooded rivers, selectin' the right bedground for his cattle, selectin' the proper riders for certain night guards and all other such duties, but he had to keep a trained eye on the hosses of his saddle band for sore backs, and the shoulders of his chuck-wagon teams. His good judgment allowed the cattle to graze their way northward and arrive at their destination in better flesh than they started with. All in all he was a most important cog in the success of the drive.

THE REP

A cowboy selected to represent his brand at outside ranches durin' a roundup was called the "rep." His task developed from the efforts of ranch owners to recover their stray cattle. It became a reg'lar part of the open-range system to have one man of each ranch work with the roundup to look out for and carry 'long cattle of his employer's brand till he could return 'em to their home range, brandin' their calves at the roundup. He assisted in the work of the roundup, but his first duty was to look after the cattle of his brand, or brands, for sometimes he represented more'n one of the smaller ranches.

As a rule, the top hand of an outfit was given this enviable job, and he was considered a notch higher'n the common puncher and got a little more pay. He had to be a reg'lar ridin' encyclopedia of brands and ear-marks, and his eyes were so well trained he could discover cattle belongin' to his outfit in a vast millin' herd through a dust fog that an ordinary man couldn't even see through. His was a responsible job, too, but he liked the work because he could travel 'round, mingle with old friends, and make new ones in other outfits.

He got the pick of the best hosses because the owner wanted 'im well mounted so he'd make a hand and his hosses would be representative of the kind they had at home. He needed a string of good-lookin', well sea-soned hosses that were steady and would follow 'long with the strays when he went to pull for home. Among his band also was a dependable pack hoss, for he had to pack his bedroll on this animal and he had to have one he could trust for the safety of his "thirty years' gatherin'" of worldly possessions. Also among his hosses were a top cuttin' hoss, a good rope hoss, and a dependable night hoss.

He usually started early 'nough to let his hosses travel at a walk in order to save 'em for the hard work ahead at the roundup. He knowed he'd have to have them hosses in good shape if he showed up as a good hand, for a lot depended on the hosses. Some reps packed a brand book, but most of 'em knowed most of the brands offhand for many miles 'round.

The big outfits were always buyin' up cattle carryin' all kinds of brands, and turnin' 'em loose on the range, where they often scattered over a wide area. A rep with his string of hosses was sometimes away from the home ranch durin' the entire summer, lookin' after the scattered and widely flung interests of his employer.

When he arrived at the roundup he turned his string into the cavvy, and he was knowed by the brand of his hosses. If he wasn't already knowed, no one asked his name. He jes' reported to the wagon boss and pitched into the work. He did his work in an orderly manner and didn't need to be told what to do or how to do it. He worked under this new boss, though maybe he'd never seen 'im before, jes' like he'd always worked under his boss at the home ranch.

It didn't take 'im long to get ready. All he had to do was cut out eight or ten hosses, pack a change of clothes, some makin's, and maybe a six-gun in his war bag, tie it on a gentle hoss, and be off. He didn't need money because there was nothin' to buy and nowhere to buy it, and gamblin' wasn't allowed.

One of the courtesies extended the rep was that he didn't have to do

any day herdin' because he was there to see all the cattle bein' rounded up so he could pick out them he represented. Maybe the other riders didn't know his brands, and anyway had no interest in 'em. Neither did he have to stand night guard unless it was absolutely necessary. Them are the things that were high on his wish for the job. He was also knowed as the "outside man," or "stray man."

When he'd reached the outside limit of the drift from his company's range, he cut from the day herd, or sometimes held in a separate cut knowed as the "rep's cut," the cattle of his brand or brands, took his mount from the remuda, packed his hoss with his bedroll, and dragged it for home, drivin' his gather before 'im. Durin' the work he could handle his own hosses as he pleased, but the wagon boss told 'im when he could cut his cattle, jes' givin' 'im so much time to do it. If he couldn't be a good feller and cut 'em in the allotted time, he'd better get his hosses and beat it for the home ranch, call for his time, and fog it out of the country. As a rep and cowhand he'd be laughed off the range.

10

Slickin' Up

TODAY'S Western romance writers always have their hero fresh and handsome and duded up like a ridin' advertisement for a leather shop. But the real cowhand didn't look like no fresh daisy. Follow 'im for a day and you'd know he wasn't attendin' no ladies finishin' school. His hours were long and hot, his work hard and dusty. With his hide soakin' up dust, the smoke of brandin' fires, the stench of burnin' hair and the blood of calves' ears, he was liable to get considerable whiffy on the lee side.

The cowboy didn't have no shower and one of them val-*lays* to lay out fresh linen after a session at the brandin' pen, but he wasn't water shy. Dirt wasn't his idea of comfort, and he kept as clean as conditions allowed. Ever' time he found a water hole he took a cold plunge without soap or towels and let his underriggin' dry while washin' out the old canyon, which, in cowboy language, means takin' a bath.

Back in the early days, if a puncher fooled 'round much with Injuns he was apt to inherit a cavvy of graybacks 'cause most redskins pastured a herd of this crawlin' stock. As soon as a hand found 'imself supportin' any of them seam squirrels, he'd picket his clothes on an anthill and give them cave dwellers a chance to fatten. If no anthill was handy he'd go to the creek, wash his clothes, and then, layin' 'em on a big rock, he'd take a smaller one and pound the seams to slaughter some of the biggest and fattest ones that didn't drown.

If some puncher was lazy and didn't mind givin' them varmints free bed and board, the boss read the Scriptures to 'im pronto. Then, if he didn't do somethin' to wash his sins away, he was ordered to pull his picket pin and drift to other ranges.

When one of the boys failed to show up for supper on a Montana ranch, the boss asked 'bout 'im.

"He's out in the bunkhouse readin' his shirt by lamplight," answered one rider between mouthfuls.

Ever'one then knowed that the absentee was tryin' to rid his clothes of seam squirrels.

'Nother rider in Montana returned to the ranch from a week's visit to an Injun camp where he'd acquired a collection of them insects. Not wantin' to let 'em get established in the bunkhouse, the other hands made 'im undress and throw his clothes out into the yard where they had a pot of water boilin'. After he quit throwin' clothes through the door, the fire tender yelled to know if there were any more.

"I can't go no deeper without a skinnin' knife," replied the other, "I'm naked as a worm."

I remember an amusin' argument about which was the most annoyin', fleas or lice. To clinch his argument in favor of lice, one of the debaters finished by sayin': "I'd rather have graybacks than fleas anytime, 'cause them pants rats graze and bed down, but a flea ain't never satisfied. After he locates paydirt on one claim he jumps to stake 'nother, and he's a damned nimble prospector."

In the old trail days when a hand had been on the trail for three or four months, his clothes would get plenty stiff with grease and river mud. The first thing he did when he hit town at the end of the trail was to rattle his hocks for a barbershop where he could take a civilized soakin' in hot water with big woolly towels and sweet-smellin' soap.

Splashin' there in the suds, he'd enjoy life like a kid pullin' a pup's ears. After he came out of that dippin' vat he bought ever'thing the barber had. When he left that place, clean and brown as if he'd been scrubbed with saddle soap, his own folks wouldn't have knowed 'im either by sight or smell. Then, after outfittin' 'imself with new wearin' gear, he proceeded to try and ketch up on the fun he'd missed.

Out on the range haircuts didn't bother 'im much. He jes' let 'er grow till he got to town. In case his hair started down his back and clogged up his ears before he got in, he got some puncher who was handy with the shears to gather his wool crop. In the old days an Injun haircut was the only one he was shy of. This called for a certain amount of hide, and no puncher wanted to see his hair hangin' from an Injun's belt. Havin' his hairpins undone that way was a shock to his idea of barber work. Seems like 'bout the only ambition an Injun had was to raise hell and hair. He shore wouldn't take no blue ribbons at barberin', accordin' to the white man's standards.

To protect his face from the sun and wind, the puncher let his whiskers grow, unless he was ridin' over to see some nester filly, or goin' to a stomp. On them occasions, he dug out the outfit's dull razor, stropped it on a latigo strap, and tried to make lather with laundry soap and gyp water. But makin' lather with them two ingredients was like huntin' a hoss thief in Heaven, and divorcin' them bristles was 'bout as refreshin' as bein' burned at stake. When he finished, it looked like he'd grubbed 'em out instead of cuttin' 'em off. He was dewlapped and wattled till he looked like he'd crawled through a bob-wire fence, had an argument with a catamount in a briar patch, and come out second best.

On roundup he didn't pack much more'n 'nough extry clothes to dust a fiddle, but them he tried to keep clean. Ever' time the work slowed up he'd boil out his underriggin' and socks. If he couldn't find time to boil 'em he jes' rinsed 'em out and hung 'em on a mesquite to dry.

Let a woman visit a roundup wagon and you'd soon see them cow nurses sneakin' away to feel 'round between their soogans for cleaner pants and shirts. They wouldn't come back till they'd been to the creek, if there was one handy. Shinin' faces and wet, slicked-down hair gave 'em away like a shirtful of fleas.

A cowhand was mighty careful of his feet, and never passed up a chance to soak 'em in some shaded water hole while he let his hoss blow. His foot rags might not be much more'n a chinstrap to keep 'em from climbin' up his legs, but he tried to keep 'em clean. Tight boots and cotton socks made feet sweat, and sweatin' meant scalds.

On gettin' up in the mornin', the first thing a cowhand reached for was his hat. After that came his pants and boots; then he reached for his sack of Bull Durham. A few drags on a cigarette and he hoofed it over to the washbasin to snort in it a couple of times to get the sleep out of his eyes. That done, he pawed over a towel which, judgin' from its complexion, had been plenty pop'lar. If he was more particul'r than some, he used the broken-toothed comb that was tied to the wagon bed, tryin' to get out the tangles that broke out a few more teeth.

On most ever' ranch there was a fashion leader, one of them dudes that spent his wages on his back. After payday, by the time he got through addin' fancy doodads to his wardrobe, he could count his coin without takin' it from his pocket. When he got all spraddled out in his low-necked clothes, and went swallow-forkin' to town in his full war paint, you could jes' bet that fancy trimmin' wasn't the least in his thoughts.

He might be as handsome as an ace-full on kings, but it mighty often happened he was more ornamental than useful. In rough range work he was inclined to favor his duds for fear he'd scar up some garment that cost 'im a month's pay. You rarely saw a cowhand ridin' in a fancy rig that was much good.

Lookin' glasses on the range were mighty scarce, and so them fellers admired 'emselves by shadow ridin', feastin' on the picture their shadows made on a sunshiny day. They was knowed as sunshine riders or shadow riders, and clouds had no silver linin' for this breed.

The California buckaroo was a top hand at puttin' on the dog, and

went in for a lot of fancy riggin'. When the sun blazed on his silver
conchas and fancy trimmin's, you could see 'im for miles. The Texas
puncher wasn't so much for pretty. The chances were he was dodgin'
some sheriff and avoided sun-reflectin' gadgets like he would a swamp.
But he had his vanity too. His weakness was five-pointed stars stitched
in his boots, chaps, and saddle. For a Texan not to be totin' stars on his
duds was considered most as bad as votin' the Republican ticket.

The average hand felt dressed up in a pair of old worn Levis, but you'd
never ketch 'im wearin' a pair of bib-overalls like a laborer wears, any
more'n he'd be wearin' the clumsy, heavy cowhide boots of a sodbuster,
nor a spur on a single foot like a sheepherder. Fancy riggin' was in the
drag of his thoughts.

If you really wanted to see some fancy cow duds you'd find 'em on
some stall-fed tenderfoot who'd come West huntin' some of that romance he'd read in books. Chances are, he'd been raised on the Brooklyn
Bridge and had never been closer to a cow than a can of Eagle Brand,
but when he sallied forth from the outfitters he looked like a dime novel
on a spree. The first one of them shorthorns I ever saw I thought he was
a mail-order catalogue on foot. Put 'im with a bunch of cowmen and he'd
a-showed up like a tin roof in a fog.

Some of them greeners at a dude ranch dress up in heavy, hairy chaps
which made 'em walk like a man in a new suit of wooden underwear.
Cowboy riggin' jes' didn't seem to fit so good on a man that'd growed
up with a collar 'round his neck. I remember one who came ridin' to town
wearin' so much hair and leather it was sweatin' 'im down like a tallow
candle. You'd a-thought the weather was cold 'nough to make a polar
bear hunt cover, but it was July and hotter'n hell with the blower on.

After buyin' a big hat and a pair of ridin' boots, he got one of them
silk shirts that made you want smoked glasses to ease the strain on your
eyes. There was nothin' gaudy 'bout the shirts of the old-timer. He
usually wore dark shirts, because they didn't glare in the sun, nor show
dirt so easy. It's the modern rodeo rider that advertises the colors of the
rainbow and makes the tenderfoot think they're the style. The range man
usually wore dark flannel or black sateen, loose and open at the neck,
and he wouldn't be a cowhand if the shirttail wasn't hangin' out most of
the time. At night, when the day'd been hot and the calves big, them
dark shirts maybe showed a white salty rim across the back, but they
kept 'im from coolin' off too quick. Unlike the movie hero and the con-

test riders, a workin' cowhand's whole dress was more likely to be on the shoddy side than full of pipin' and embroidery till he looked like the map of Mexico.

The cowhand of the range never wore a coat unless it was cold, and not often then if he had any ropin' to do. He needed freedom of motion in ever'thing he did. Maybe he hadn't owned a coat for years, but he always had a vest. Usually it was ripped up the back by cactus and cat-claw and was hangin' to his neck by the neckband. He didn't wear this garment for the warmth it gave, but for the storage room it furnished to pack matches, a short pencil, a little tally book where he kept a record of the salary due 'im, or other notes; a plug of tobacco, or his sack of makin's. That little Bull Durham tag hangin' outside was a sign of the callin'—like the city cop's badge. He wore this vest loose and open to let the air to his body, and not bind 'im. At night, after a hot day's work, he maybe buttoned it to keep his body from coolin' off too soon. Mostly they're jes' ordinary vests, but sometimes you'd find a rider who was considerably dudish and went in for Injun beads or wore a woolen one that looked like some painter had upset the color pot on it.

The brush hand wouldn't be hampered with a coat either, but he did wear a jacket, one that was close fittin' and without a tail. They were made of heavy duckin' that'd turn thorns, and were sometimes rein-forced at the elbows with leather. Most of his ridin' was done with his elbows throwed over his face to protect it from the whippin' brush.

On the colder ranges the cowhand wore an overcoat in winter. Them garments were usually of knee length, made of heavy canvas, light brown in color, and fleece or flannel lined. To make 'em more windproof some covered 'em with a coat of paint, and daubin' with a paint brush always invited the drawin' of the brand the owner of the coat worked for.

His pants were mostly of hard, close-woven material that could stand rough usage. Call 'em trousers and he wouldn't know what you was talkin' 'bout. To 'im they were never anything but pants. The old-timer wore 'em stuffed inside his high-topped boots; the modern cowhand wears 'em outside his short boots, with usually one side of each leg crawlin' up over the top like it ain't on speakin' terms with the boot heel.

The style now is the denim Levi, an overall without a bib. He buys 'em long and turns 'em up at the bottom for a turn or two, till they're jes' above his spurs. Them turnups make a handy place to pack hoss-shoe nails and such.

No matter whether they were pants or Levis, they'd be hangin' from his hips without any other support. Galluses were never seen on the range because they bound the shoulders and interfered with work, and belts were apt to cause hernia when ridin' a pitchin' hoss.

The cowman took a heap of pride in his gloves. The cowtown merchant might be able to sell 'im shoddy clothes at high prices, but he knowed better'n to show 'im anything but the best in gloves. If he tried to sell 'im sheepskin or anything but genuwine buckskin, he'd be called some names that wasn't in the Sunday-school book, besides gettin' some free advertisement that wouldn't be to his advantage.

A cowhand wanted gloves of good quality that wouldn't stiffen when they got wet. Stiff gloves interfered with ropin' and didn't make it easier to get the right hold mountin' a plungin' hoss. Most of the early Western gloves were made with gauntlets that were covered with fancy patterns of silk designs; for a time patterns in Injun beads were also pop'lar. Most of 'em had long, heavy fringe on the little-finger side, but that was soon discarded. The fringe would often get tangled in the turns of a dally man, and his hand would be badly injured. The wrist gloves soon became the style, yet some cowhands wore stiff leather detachable cuffs, too, to protect their wrists and keep their shirt sleeves from botherin' 'em. No cowboy ever rolled his sleeves up. That was a shore sign of the tenderfoot.

Many old-time cowhands were so vain they'd wear gloves all the time they wasn't sleepin'. They weren't sissies, but were advertisin' the fact that they were too good at ridin' and ropin' to stoop to manual labor. Good gloves were a big help in ropin' to keep from gettin' rope burns, and some men wouldn't rope without 'em. On the other hand, some cowmen scorned their use and didn't have much use for a gloved puncher. They claimed it was cheaper to grow skin than to buy it. Their hands were usually tougher'n the calluses on a barfly's elbows.

11

Cowboy Riggin': Chaps and War Bonnets

BECAUSE the cowboy's riggin' was so different from that worn in any other callin', a lot of folks figger it was worn for show. Such a notion's as shy of the truth as a goat is of feathers. Town-gaited writers call this riggin' picturesque, and maybe it is for them that wasn't raised in the cattle country, but ever'thing the cowboy wore was designed for a necessary use and not for ornament.

Maybe he decorated his riggin' with some silver conchas and fancy hoss jewelry that wasn't essential, but you couldn't hold it against 'im for wantin' a little style, and an outfit to be proud of, 'specially when he made his livin' in it. A city cop, too, decorates 'imself with more leather and iron than a nigh-wheeler of a jerk-line string, but all this trimmin's not necessary to uphold the law; he jes' wants a little style.

There's nothin' a cowhand could wear that'd be as useless as a city man's stiff collar and necktie, which he called a "collar and hames." Duded up in such an outfit he'd be hurrahed plumb off the range unless he took it good-natured, and admitted, like one puncher did, that he was wearin' 'em to "keep his feet warm." Somebody'd be shore to ask 'im if he didn't have to mount a cracker box to spit out if he had one of them high collars on. Put a necktie, or "choke strap," as he called 'em, on any old-timer and he'd a-thought he was tied to a post. To a cowhand the most useless clothes in the world would be the city man's dress suit with no front in the vest and jes' a little windbreak down the back with tails that flapped like a damned scissortail bird. He called 'em Herefords because of the white front.

A heap of men in other callin's would like to palm 'emselves off as cow-hands, but they didn't have no more success at it than a hare-lipped hombre tryin' to whistle. You'd never see a cowhand tryin' to hide his occu-pation, and you'd have to be some persuader to make 'im shed his cow riggin' for any of that gearin' of the shorthorn. He didn't feel at home in civilized harness, and even when he was afoot and dressed in his visitin' clothes there was no disguisin' a cowman.

CHAPS

I reckon the most conspicuous part of the cowboy's riggin' was his chaps, or leggin's, as they were mostly called. The shorthorn looked upon 'em as the most affected part of the costume of a vain man, but it was a product of conditions that was adapted to the service it had to render. Handed down by the Mexicans, chaps were jes' two wide and full-length trouser legs made of heavy leather and connected by a narrow string called the "chap string." This held the legs of the chaps together in front at the waist. It wasn't so strong that it wouldn't break when the wearer got hung up in the ridin' gear.

Viewed from the front a cowhand afoot wearin' chaps looked like some prehistoric animal waddlin' 'long on its hind legs; viewed from the rear it was kinda disgraceful to see his seat cut out thataway. Which reminds me of a story John Hendrix told me 'bout the jackpot a pair of chaps got one old wagon cook into. Havin' gotten his noon meal well under way, this cook goes to a nearby creek to take a bath 'cause the sun was hot and his trip across the flats that mornin' had been plenty dusty.

While he was frolickin' 'round in the water like a kid in rompers, a couple of old dry cows came nosin' 'round. Them salt-hungry brutes proceeded to make a meal of the cook's clothes he'd left hangin' on a mesquite. After a while he looks toward the bank and sees what's goin' on and he fogs out of that water like a turpentined cat. But he's too late. What's left of his pants and underriggin' wouldn't pad a crutch. All he could salvage was his shirt, and by the time he grabbed it the tail was missin'.

Back at camp he gophers through the wagon for some clothes, but all he could find was a pair of chaps one of the boys'd left behind. All this time he's mad 'nough to eat the devil with his horns on. Goin' back to his fires to put on his sourdoughs, he's still sore as a scalded pup. When he stoops over his skillets, the rear view looks like a full moon risin' over the hills.

He's still sullen as a soreheaded dog when he looks up and sees the boss's wife bringin' a buggyful of town ladies to have dinner at the chuck wagon. Now he's really got a skunk by the tail.

He knowed he could never tend his fires and get that meal ready without turnin' his back to them women. The only thing he could think to do was act as crazy as popcorn on a hot stove. He shook his gouch hook at 'em, laughed like a hyena over a dead lion, and cut such didos that them women thought he'd gone plumb loco.

The boss's wife didn't waste no time gettin' that surrey turned 'round, and they was soon foggin' over the flats, leavin' so much dust it didn't settle all day. The old cook saved 'imself some embarrassin' moments, but he had some tall explainin' to do later to the boss.

Chaps were not only a protection against thorns, brush, and cactus, but they protected a rider's legs when he was throwed, or when a hoss fell on 'im, pushed 'im against a fence or another animal. The word "chaps" is an American abbreviation of the Spanish *chaparejos*, meanin' "leather breeches," or "overalls." This Spanish word was too much of a mouthful for the American cowboy, so he bit shallow and called 'em "chaps," pronouncin' it "shaps."

There're several styles in chaps, all developed from the *armitas*, a sort of loose-ridin' apron. This word's from the Spanish *amar*, meanin' to arm, to plate with anything that adds strength. Them were well cut aprons, usually made of home-tanned or Injun buckskin and tied 'round the waist and knees with thongs. They protected the legs and clothes and were cooler in summer than chaps. Their use practically passed with old-time range customs, although they're still used to some extent in southern California.

The first chaps in Texas to be developed from the snug-fittin' *chaperras* of the Mexican vaquero were the "shotgun chaps." These were pulled over the boots, and usually carried a leather fringe down the sides. The way the outside seams were sewed together they looked like the twin barrels of a shotgun, with a choke at the muzzle. In the more northern ranges they used "hair pants" a lot. Them were chaps made from skins, such as goat, bear, deer, and other animals with the hair left on and worn hair side out. They were a protection against cold, but in snow, sleet, or rain storms they proved mighty uncomfortable, for they got wet, soggy, and heavy, sometimes smellin' stronger'n a wolf's den. They wasn't so pop'lar on the range as in the movies.

Closed leg   Angora

Chinks

The most pop'lar chaps were the heavy, bullhide bat wings. They have wide flappin' legs that're fastened with snaps. Ever' cowhand lived with a pair of spurs on his heels, and he liked bat wings because he didn't have to take off them spurs to put on his leggin's like he did the shotgun style.

The Texas brush hand never wore chaps with hair, flappin' wings, or ornaments on 'em. The less surface he gave the brush to grab, the better. Cowhands of all other sections shed their chaps when they dismounted for ground work, but the brush hand kept his on because he never knowed when he was goin' to have to tear a hole in the brush. He got so used to 'em that he felt jes' as naked without 'em as he would without his pants. The Texan called chaps "leggin's." He rarely used the word "chaps." Chaps often went by the slang names of "open-shop pants," or "twelve-hour leggin's." A type of wing chap was developed in Wyoming called the "Cheyenne leg," or "Cheyenne cut," that became pop'lar. The wing was narrower and straight, the underpart of the leg bein' cut back to the knee, with no snaps below that point.

Rodeo chaps were another style, strong 'nough to protect a rider's legs against chute fences and Brahma hoofs and horns, but most of 'em were slicked up with a lot of fancy inlay and monogram doodads to satisfy the owner's ideas of showmanship. Parade chaps were of still another breed, made for show only. Shake a thorny bush at one of 'em and they'd fall apart. The plain cowhand with his shabby chaps was the one who could be depended upon to do an honest day's work. He had no time for fancy duds.

Unless a cowhand was mighty vain, or was tryin' to conquer the heart of some filly not range bred, when he rode to town he left his chaps hangin' on a nail in the bunkhouse. If he did wear 'em he took 'em off when he arrived, and either hung 'em over his saddle horn or throwed 'em in the corner of some saloon where he was knowed. They were mighty uncomfortable things to walk in. You'd never think it, though, to watch some of them dudes and actors walkin' 'round in their "dude chaps." These were specially made fancy chaps that a cowhand would be ashamed to be seen in.

Some rider who didn't have much confidence in his ridin' ability, or was afraid of bein' grassed and havin' to walk back to camp, might wet his chaps on the inside of each leg. This helped 'im with his leg grip and made it harder for the hoss to dump 'im, but the real rider had a name all his own for this breed, so he tried not to be caught at it.

Chaps could be used as an instrument of torture and punishment too.

If some kangaroo court found you guilty of breakin' a law of the range, you'd be bent over a wagon tongue and the chaps applied where they'd do the most good. If the man wieldin' 'em didn't like you and had been filin' his teeth for you, he could make 'em take the hide off.

WAR BONNETS

A lot of folks make shore that a man's a cowboy when they see 'im wearin' a ten-gallon hat. A big hat's the ear-mark of the cattle country all right, and is the first thing a tenderfoot buys when he comes West. He's plumb ignorant of quality, but is mighty particular 'bout the brim width. When the first rain ketches 'im he discovers he's bought a cheap woolsey that leaks like a sieve and flops in his eyes till he thinks he's wearin' a blind bridle.

It's true nothin' made a man look more like a cowboy than a cowboy hat, *if* he knowed how to wear it. The cattle country could tell a cow-hand as far as it saw 'im by the way he wore this old war bonnet. The greener has got to stay on the range a long time before he learned to wear this hat at jes' the right jack-deuce angle over his off eye.

Different sections of the cattle country had different styles in hats, but whatever the style, it was the puncher's pet object of his outfit. The Southwest used a wider brim for sunshade, and the Northwest used a higher crown and narrower brim because of the wind blowin' stronger there. A bone-seasoned man of the range could almost tell what state a man was from by the size and shape of his hat, and the way he creased it. Riders of the plains and desert country used a wider brim and higher crown than the hands of the mountainous country, while the brush hand'd wear one that a tenderfoot never would class as a cowboy hat. Wide brims didn't help in the brush.

A cowhand might crease the crown of his hat either accordin' to his own taste or the custom of the section he was ridin' in. Some left the crown flat on top, some creased it on all four sides, while others liked jes' a crease in front. In a hot country the four-creased peaked crown kept the head cooler, while in a rainy section a front crease made a better watershed.

A lot of folks can't savvy why a cowhand paid so much money for a conk cover when there was nobody to see 'im in his splendor except a few of his own kind and a lot of cows. It wasn't vanity that made 'im invest so much wealth in a hat. By nature he was a proud cuss and he took a heap of pride in the quality of all his riggin', but he put a lot of dependence in this hat, too. He knowed the fine quality in it would stand the rough use it got. Maybe he'd throw it on the floor and hang up his spurs on a nail, but it was because he knowed it could be tromped on without hurtin' it, while trompin' on a spur didn't do either the tromper nor the spur any good.

N. ELLENHOFER

The cowboy was mighty particular 'bout his hoss and his gun because he never knowed when his life depended on 'em. Likewise, his life sometimes depended on his hat, and the limber brim of a cheap hat might flop in his eyes at jes' the wrong time without givin' 'im a chance to ask old St. Peter for a passport.

Ever'thing the cowboy wore had a lot of uses besides coverin' his nakedness, and a good hat has got more different uses than any of 'em. When you're ridin' the plains in the summer with the sun tryin' to soak all the tallow out of your spinal column, that old wide brim made it like ridin' in the shade of a cottonwood, and the high crown furnished a heap of space to keep the head cool. With it shadin' the eyes you could see long distances without gettin' sun blind when a lot depended on your vision. If the sun was at your back you could tilt that old John B. to cover the back of your neck for protection. The wide brim made a good shelter, too, when you was tryin' to snatch a little daylight sleep. In rainy weather it made a fine umbrella, keepin' the rain from runnin' in your eyes or down your neck.

The crown made a handy water bucket. Many a grateful hoss has stuck his soft muzzle into a hat crown filled with water when he was unable to get to water 'imself. Sometimes a cowhand had to ride out into a pond, or tank, to where the water was cool and clear to get a drink 'imself. Here he couldn't lay on his belly and stick his own muzzle in like he could on the bank of a runnin' stream, but he always had his drinkin' cup 'long. He jes' scooped up a brimful, and when you was thirsty there was no drinkin' cup on earth that'd beat it.

He might use it for a water bucket to put out a fire when he broke camp, and more'n one hat has been used to beat out a grass fire before it got too much start. Fires were started with it too, by usin' it as a bellows to encourage a sickly blaze. Old-timers who had to burn bull-chips wore out many a hat tryin' to persuade that prairie coal to burn.

In the winter the brim pulled down and tied over the ears has saved many an ear from bein' gotched by frostbite. At the line camp it could be stuffed into the window to take the place of a busted pane when it was cold and the snow was blowin' in. The old trail driver used it to wave signals that saved long rides, and the cow thief used it to "wave 'round" some approachin' puncher, givin' this intruder the signal that he wasn't wanted, and if he expected to stay healthy he'd better make a wide detour.

There was an old sayin' that "humans dress up but a cowboy dresses down." His hat was the last thing he took off when he crawled into his soogans, and the first thing he put on when he crawled out the next mornin' to the cook's call of "Crawl out snakes."

But there were a lot of times in his day's work when a cowhand jerked off his hat to use as a mighty handy implement. There were times when its sudden wave saved lots of hard work, a long ride, a nasty fall, or even sudden death. Maybe he was pennin' a bunch of snaky critters when the wave of a big hat would turn a stampedin' bronc from dangerous ground by fannin' his head when a pull on the reins wouldn't mean a thing. It was mighty useful, too, in splittin' a bunch of hosses in two when you're afoot in a hoss corral. The little city hat'd be useless and look kinda comical for such work.

You've seen balancin' acts where the performer used a pole. A big hat in the hands of a top rider could be used to the same advantage. A sudden loss of his hat and a rider lost a lot of his balancin' power. It maybe sounds silly to say that a rider's hat made any difference in his ridin', but many a rider makin' a good ride by balance, if he suddenly lost his hat, found 'imself tryin' to eat gravel with the chickens. When some puncher got throwed he might try to alibi that he lost his hat and got off to look for it, but he expected nobody to believe 'im.

Maybe a cowhand was afoot brandin' calves when some old mama cow who'd heard her youngster's beller came a-runnin' in a horn-tossin' mood to help 'im out. Monkeyin' with one of them old mama cows when you're afoot and she was on the prod was more disastrous than kickin' a loaded polecat. A big hat came in mighty handy to throw into the old gal's face when she got too close. She wasn't used to seein' a cowboy come apart in pieces like that, and if it didn't change her course it'd shore make her hesitate long 'nough to let 'im get to a hoss or a fence. Without that hat he'd shore have to keep step with a rabbit to keep her from scratchin' the grease off his pants at ever' jump, 'cause that wasn't love light in her eyes. As Jim Houston once said, "a cow with a fresh-branded calf might be a mother, but she shore ain't no lady."

The color of a hat was a matter of personal choice, but to stand the gaff it had to be of good quality. The more expensive the hat the lighter the weight and the more durable it was. The best grade, four or five X Beaver, came high, but they'd last a lifetime. The quality of the felt made the brim stay put whichever way it was turned. The cheaper hats were sometimes soaked in water, then shaped to suit the wearer. The front part of the brim on both sides was usually trained to curve, comin' more or less to a point in front. It provided a grip for easy handlin' and seemed to give the hat character.

Most riders decorated their hats with a band, both as an ornament and for the purpose of adjustin' the fit to the head. What they used was mostly a matter of personal taste. Some liked a leather band studded with silver conchas, some used a string of Injun beads, while others were satisfied with a band of rattlesnake skin or woven hosshair. Whatever he used, it'd likely be the storeroom to keep his matches dry and handy.

Some riders equipped their lids with bonnet strings by fastenin' a buck-skin thong from either side of the brim at the edge next to the crown and runnin' the ends through a bead or string. By pullin' these up under his chin he had a hat that'd stay on durin' a fast ride or in windy weather.

There was one case on record, though, where a good hat worked to a disadvantage. Jack Potter, an old-time cowhand friend of mine, now passed away, once told me a yarn 'bout a puncher who took a heap of pride in a good hat. This rider came to Clayton, New Mexico, with a herd, and after the cattle were delivered he collected his wages of sixteen dollars. After buyin' a pair of socks and some makin's, he spent the other fifteen dollars for a Stetson.

At that time there was an outlaw gang summerin' nearby in Road Canyon. The other boys had a little wad of money between 'em, and as they rode back to the ranch they stopped before they got to Road Canyon and held a powwow to decide where to hide their wealth in case them holdups were still on the job. The old boy who'd jes' bought the new Stetson suggested that they hide it in the linin' of his new hat. They hadn't rode far till they were asked to stick up their paws by two or three men that were holdin' some mighty able persuaders. One of 'em started searchin' for the money, and he went clear down the line, friskin' ever' man from forelock to dew-claws without findin' anything but small change.

The boys were feelin' pretty good 'bout the wisdom of their choice of a hidin' place for their money when this man doin' the searchin' reached the feller with the new hat who was hangin' back with the drags. Gettin' mad at not findin' any bigger money, and seein' this brand-new Stetson, this holdup made a Pecos swap right there. This left one hat-proud puncher minus a hat that he'd hardly got warm and the rest of the herd between a rock and a hard place, meanin' bankrupt.

Some punchers wouldn't let any other man wear a wider brim than them. If they found one with a hat an inch wider'n theirs they'd order a wider one, even if it cost a month's pay. I hope I never live to see the day when you can't find a wide brim in the cattle country. It's a kind of symbol of the cowman, a mark of his callin'. He's still big 'nough to wear 'em, and the country's still big 'nough to furnish the room.

Cowboy Riggin': Boots and Spurs

LIKE the good hat he wore, the cowboy was mighty proud of his boots, and they were generally the most expensive part of his riggin'. When he had the money to match his pride, you'd see 'im wearin' boots so fine you could nearly see the wrinkles in his socks. If he couldn't put his feet into a decent pair of boots, he shore wasn't goin' to put 'em into an entire cow.

In the earlier days he wore "mule-ear" boots, which were a high-topped boot with pull-on straps, and are still used in the brush country. Rarely would his boots be less'n seventeen inches. This length prevented brush and gravel from gettin' into the leg. Later, the style changed to "peewees," a short and dressier boot with less weight. However, this low-topped boot has only retained its pop'larity with the dude and city man because the workin' cowhand preferred one with more height, due to the fact that them low-topped boots were always full of somethin' besides his feet. When the foot was in the stirrup and the heel was pressed down, the top of the low boot was pulled down below the bottom of the pants in the rear, creatin' a funnel to receive all the rocks, dust, and twigs the hoss's hind feet kicked up. The higher boot left no space of this kind to act as a "ketch all." Besides, they could be worn inside or outside the pants. Then, too, higher tops were a protection to the rider's legs from the stirrup leathers, bumps and scratches, brush and rocks and such.

But no matter what style he wore they were high-heeled, thin-soled and of good leather. The tops were made of lightweight high-grade leather, and all that stitchin' you see on 'em wasn't jes' for fancy decoratin'. Up to a certain point this fancy stitchin' had a practical value. It helped stiffen the leather so the tops wouldn't break down and become sloppy; kept 'em from wrinklin' too much at the ankles where they contacted the stirrups; and preserved the tops and kept 'em from comin' to pieces after they got old. Some used stitchin' on the toe which made the foot look smaller, and the cowboy always wanted to make you believe he had small feet. This stitchin' on the toe also kept the leather over the linin' of the boot to the outside leather, makin' it more comfortable to the wearer. Leanin' against a stirrup without ankle protection gave 'bout as much comfort as a bob-wire fence gave shade.

His boots were custom made, that is, handmade and made to order. He had no use for hand-me-down, shop-made footgear, and no respect for a cowhand that'd wear 'em, but held to the opinion that they was made for furrow-flattened feet and not intended for stirrup work. In orderin' a new pair of boots, he'd spread out an order blank on the bunkhouse floor and trace a picture of his socked feet on the paper. When he got his measurements on paper and the directions as to the style of heel, toe, and so on, he waited till somebody rode to town to mail it—which maybe wasn't for a month. He usually ordered his boots 'bout six months before he needed 'em, to allow for delays. He didn't wait till his old ones were wore plumb out, for he held that a man was gettin' pretty low that'd wear boots so frazzled he couldn't strike a match on 'em without burnin' his feet.

For looks, Nature kinda stacked the deck against the seasoned cowman. Wind and sun put wrinkles on his face; dust and brandin' fires ruined his complexion. Rough food and hard work gave 'im strength, but didn't allow tallow to grow on his bones. Raised in the saddle, by the time he'd cut his tobacco teeth he was so bowlegged a yearlin' could run between his legs without bendin' a hair. It wasn't till we looked at his feet that we found he'd any claim on daintiness. The range-bred button (boy) never had a chance to go barefooted and let his feet spread. He was a descendant of ridin' ancestors and inherited small feet. His dad put made-to-order boots on 'im by the time he was fryin' size. When he growed up he still had small feet because he'd never exercised 'em 'nough to let 'em grow.

Most punchers were as sensitive as a woman 'bout their feet. I remember one puncher we used to kid a lot because he admired his feet so much. Someone would joke 'im 'bout "most of his weight bein' on the spur end."

"I only wear a six and a half," he'd come back, plenty riled.

"Yeah, six cowhides and a half-keg of nails," said one of the boys, mighty sarcastic.

By the time we got 'im so ringy his horns drooped, we'd walk off and leave 'im grittin' his teeth like he could eat the sights off a six-gun. Of course, we were only jokin' 'im, 'cause, like most range-bred men, his feet were small and looked like they'd been poured into his boots and allowed to harden.

When a cowhand worked in the rain and muddy corrals, he paid for his vanity in tight-fittin' boots. Wet boots contracted and were hard to pull on and off. He skinned his heels, tugged and cussed without success. He greased the insides with laundry soap, dusted some flour in, and tried again and maybe didn't succeed till he worked up a sweat. All this time he was cussin' boots in general and tight-fittin' boots in particular, but he never cussed the bootmaker because he knowed he'd never have paid a nickel for 'em if they hadn't fit close. No matter how loose he wanted his other garments, he wanted his boots to fit tight.

When a puncher once got a fit that suited 'im, he never changed bootmakers. Them old bootmakers took a heap of pride in their work, and their business was handed down from father to son. Likewise, they made boots for father and son cowmen for generations. A man who knowed the cattle country could tell, almost at a glance, who made 'em.

There was a heap of folks who wondered 'bout the high heel the cowboy wore on his boots, but that high heel was the most important part of it. It kept his foot from slippin' through the stirrup and hangin'; it let 'im dig in when he was ropin' on foot and gave 'im a shore footin' in all other work on the ground, and there was a lot of times when he shore couldn't afford to slip when he was handlin' a hoss with flyin' hoofs. He never knowed when he'd need the shore, quick footin' them high heels gave 'im.

Examine the heel on a cowboy boot and you'd find it more'n jes' high. It was narrow, set under the foot and sloped under from behind. This was mostly for his comfort and safety. Settin' the heel under the foot let 'im put his foot safely in the stirrup and have his weight on the arch and rest against the stirrup with the boot heel. On a long ride this was a heap less tirin' than havin' the weight on the toes or ball of the foot.

A narrow heel with a decided underslope was made to prevent bein' hung up in case the rider was throwed and brought a stirrup up over the seat of the saddle with his foot. When a man got throwed and went over the saddle with his back toward the ground, his toe pointed up with the stirrup from the opposite side holdin' his toe, and his heel held against the saddle by his own weight, he was apt to be hung up. A high heel without the underslope would hold a man firm, but the undersloped heel gave 'im a better chance of comin' loose. This kind of heel also gave the spur a better chance of pullin' off if it got caught. There was nothin' that made chills run up and down a cowboy's spine more'n hearin' 'bout a man gettin' hung up, or thinkin' of it happenin' to 'imself.

Maybe high heels wasn't made for walkin', but a cowboy took mighty little exercise on foot. When he walked in town he liked to hear the *poppity-pop* of them high heels on the board sidewalk. Then again, if he wanted to be in style, he didn't wear any other footgear but ridin' boots to a dance. They didn't make a bad dancin' pump, and high heels could pop out a might pretty rhythm on the floor. The high heel was a kind of tradition, a mark of distinction, and the sign that the wearer was a ridin' man; and a ridin' man, as I've said before, always held 'imself above the man on foot.

A cowhand wanted the toes of his boots more or less pointed to make it easier to pick up the near stirrup on a wheelin' or buckin' hoss, and also to find that right-hand stirrup after he hit the saddle. He wanted a thin sole so he had the feel of the stirrup. He wanted the vamp soft and tight, and the top wide and loose to allow the air to circulate and prevent sweatin'.

For rodeos, conventions, and town visits he maybe had an extry pair made more fancy and of calfskin, but he didn't use 'em on the range. The goin' was too tough and they wouldn't last long. You'd never ketch a range man wearin' a pair of "stogies," what he called cheap hand-me-down boots, nor low-cut shoes. He'd jes' as soon ride barefooted. Price was no object. Quality was the main consideration. They might squeak like they was made of goose quills, but he wasn't worryin' as long as they fit close and cost 'im plenty.

SPURS

In spite of the fact that some folks thought a cowhand wore spurs for show, they were not on his heels for ornament. Them hooks, or galves, as he called 'em, were mighty necessary in his work. He used 'em more'n he did the reins. In takin' short cuts to head a bunch of cattle, they was necessary to urge the hoss over rough places he maybe didn't want to cross. They were necessary, too, in signalin' a hoss for turnin', or a quick start or stop.

A pair of them big spurs looked mighty wicked to a shorthorn, and if he'd had 'em on 'imself he'd most likely have stumbled over 'em at ever' step.. But a cowhand was raised with 'em on his heels; they were jes' as much a part of 'im as his feet. He wore 'em all the time whether on hoss or afoot. 'Bout the only time he took 'em off was when he went to a shindig, or a-visitin' in someone's home. Many a pair of spurs have stayed on a pair of boots till them boots were worn plumb out. He used 'em at night for a bootjack to help pull off them boots. In some sections a cowhand kinda lost his social standin' when he was caught without his spurs, but in most of the West range etiquette ruled that a man take off his spurs when he entered another's home. They wasn't made to rip up rugs and scar furniture. There was an old sayin' that "gentlemen wear spurs in a saloon, but never in a friend's house." But the cowboy didn't do much visitin'.

A real cowhand didn't use spurs for punishment, but jes' as a reminder. He loved hosses and didn't want to be cruel to 'em, even when he was tryin' to ride some jughead that was doin' his damndest to kick 'im into a funeral procession. The man that used spurs for cuttin' machines didn't last long on the range. Things would soon get so unpleasant for 'im that he'd be glad to drift to other ranges. If he was kept on because the outfit was short-handed, he'd likely be given such a rough string to ride he'd be kept so busy tryin' to hang on he wouldn't have time to put spur marks on their hide. When the boss saw them panther tracks on that hoss's hide, it didn't take 'im long to tell that rider to pull his picket pin and drift.

Spurs were merely to signal quick action, as in cuttin' and ropin'. The fact is that on long trail drives they were seldom worn. Lengthenin' their stirrup leathers so as to take the cramp out of their legs, and in them long, tedious eighteen-hour days trudgin' 'long they were allowed to shift positions in the saddle, which was guarded against in roundup work as much as possible because it had a tendency to create sore backs on the hosses.

If the real hand had to be cruel because he wore spurs, he'd never put 'em on. Of course, them grapplin' irons could be a wicked tool, but the cowboy knowed how to use 'em. Sometimes a mere motion of the leg was all that was necessary. At the most a mere touch was as far as he went. He never sank 'em in like a lot of folks think. It was the feller that'd never rode much that did the damage.

The first thing a cowhand did when he bought a new pair of spurs was to file the sharp points off the rowels till they were blunt. He knowed sharp rowels wasn't of much use to 'im when he wanted to do good work, because they kept the hoss fightin' and nervous, shrinkin' from their touch. He usually bought a big spur, not because it looked scary, but because it was less cruel. He knowed that the bigger the rowel and the more points it had, the less damage it did. It was the little spur with the few points that sank in. 'Bout all the damage he wanted to do was maybe ruffle the hair a little. Even the old Mexican Chihuahua gut hooks weren't so cruel on his heels as they looked because he knowed how to handle them can openers.

Spurs have changed some since the parade and rodeo have become a national institution, but not so much as some other parts of a cowboy's outfit. Work spurs were usually plain, light ones, with or without chap guards, and usually with small, dull rowels, and medium-light heel bands.

Parade spurs were big and showy with silver inlays, great big rowels, and wide heel bands to create flash. Dude riders should never be allowed to wear spurs, for a gig in the wrong place at the right time'd shore put 'im reachin' for the saddle horn, and chances are he'd find his arm too short.

It made no difference what part of the country a bronc man might hail from, his spurs'd be made followin' one of three patterns: the long shank, the straight, or drop shank. Each style of shank might carry any one of a dozen types and sizes of rowel. The length of the shank and its style depended on the rider's size and build, and the type and size of the hoss common to the particular section in which he might work.

The Southern man who was used to handlin' and ridin' small hosses would, particularly if long-legged, be apt to use long-shanked spurs. The early California vaquero, and the Oregon, Nevada, and Montana buckaroo who followed, favored a short, drop shank spur since they, on an average, rode a larger hoss than the Texan. The shorter the man's legs or the larger the hoss, the closer the spur rode to the hoss's barrel, so that only a short spur shank was needed.

Like ever'thing else he wore, the cowboy took a heap of pride in his spurs. Unless he was plumb down and out he wouldn't be caught wearin' a cheap, inferior pair, which he called "tin bellies." He had a lot of slang names for his spurs, like he had for ever'thing else, such as "persuaders," "steel," "can openers," "diggers," "gads," "grapplin' irons," "gut hooks," and "hell rousers." Various-shaped rowels had their names too. There was the one with a few long, sharp points he called a "buzzsaw"; one havin' few, but long points was a "cartwheel"; one shaped like the petals of a daisy was a "flower rowel"; one with five or six points was a "star rowel"; and a "sunset" or "sunburst" was one with many points set close together.

The shank of a spur was that part to which the rowel was fastened, and the "gooseneck" was a long shank shaped like a goose's neck, the rowel fittin' into its mouth, while the "gal-leg" was a shank shaped like a girl's leg.

The spur leather was a broad, crescent-shaped shield of leather fittin' over the instep to hold the spur on the foot. A spur whose rowels dragged the ground when the wearer was afoot was knowed as a "California drag rowel." It was the Spanish California type, straight heel band, with a small button on the end to loop the spur leather on, and the heel chains passin' under the instep to hold it in position on the boot.

The jingle of a spur was mighty sweet music to any cowhand. Some of 'em loved this music so well they added little jingle-bobs, or danglers, to the rowel axle. These were little inch-long, pear-shaped pendants loosely hangin' from the end of the spur rowel and whose sole function was to make music. This music kept 'im from gettin' lonesome, and as long as he heard that jingle at his heels he knowed ever'thing was hunky-dory. The shank of many spurs turned downward, allowin' the rowel, when the wearer was afoot, to roll noisily 'long the ground. When in town afoot maybe a cowhand made more noise than one of them old knights that had his clothes tailored by a blacksmith, but he was livin' amongst a breed that didn't object to that music in public, and they knowed, too, that he wasn't tryin' to slip up on 'em.

Cowboy Riggin':

Slickers, the Wipes, and Bedrolls

THERE was one garment that rarely got any attention by writers of Westerns. Maybe it was because the modern cowboy didn't use it much. With fences and no trail work, he don't need it like the old-timer did. I'm speakin' of that old yeller slicker, or "fish," as the old-timer called it. In the old days a picture of a mounted cowboy wouldn't look quite natural without that old yeller slicker tied behind the cantle of his saddle.

He might pack it there till he wore it plumb out and never need it, but jes' let 'im leave it in camp for half a day, and he'd shore get soaked to the hide. When he had to leave his saddled hoss outside in the rain, his slicker could be used to cover his saddle and a good part of his hoss. On the range in wet weather when he had to leave his saddle on the ground, he put his slicker under and over it to keep it dry.

Sometimes, if he was ridin' a bronc that he was afraid he'd have trouble settin', and his saddle was a slick-fork, he'd tie this old slicker behind the horn and use it as a saddle roll to kinda help wedge 'imself in.

The slicker has played an important part in helpin' to train a bronc, and they was good for sackin' out a green colt. Some riders, when they were ridin' a spooky hoss that they were interested in trainin', tied the slicker behind the cantle so it'd nearly touch the ground on the left side. Of course the hoss tried to kick it to ribbons, but he soon got used to it and quit tryin' to stampede. This was called "slicker breakin'," and by this trainin' the hoss got so he didn't spook at other boogers jes' as harmless. A slicker-broke hoss was always safer'n one not so trained.

When rain drove the hands into their slickers and set the hosses to humpin' backs and turnin' tails, saddlin' wasn't no kindergarten game. Rain made hosses spooky, and a cold, wet hoss was dangerous. Cowhands movin' 'round in the hoss corral like so many yeller ghosts gave them broncs a fine excuse to tear things up. They didn't like the cracklin' noise them old slickers made, and the riders didn't look natural in such long, loose garments.

It handicapped the rider, too. Maybe he was already hindered by mud-clogged boots and a slippery footin'. Wet, slippery stirrups and muddy boots didn't make hairpinnin' a snuffy hoss any less dangerous, and when this bronc felt that cold slicker touchin' his flank, he didn't lose no time in breakin' in two. Sometimes, when it was slick, that hoss needed more legs than a centipede to keep his footin', but the rider usually hung on and rode 'im through.

Durin' that ride he'd cuss this old slicker for causin' such a ruckus, but when the rain was over he'd skin out of it, fold it carefully behind the cantle, and be thankful he was as dry as a covered bridge.

It was no good to keep out the cold, and wasn't made for warmth. A rider I know got caught out in one of our sudden Texas northers without a coat. He comes back to the ranch wearin' his slicker as an emergency coverin', but by the time he put his hoss up and reached the house, he was blue as a whetstone. He was plenty loud in condemnin' slickers as overcoats.

"If," he says, "I'd had *two* of the damned things on I'd a-froze plumb to death."

Slickers have been knowed to take the joy out of life in other ways. Once there was a cowboy ridin' drag on a trail herd, and he was cussin' a lazy old steer that'd been givin' 'im trouble all day. By all the signs it wouldn't be long till a gully-washer'd be on 'em, and they were tryin' to reach open country before they bedded down the herd for the night. This cowhand unrolled his slicker to put it on when he was hit by the happy thought that maybe a prod with it might speed up this old drag steer.

It did. When he whacked that old sore-foot on the rump with it, a button caught in the matted hair of his tail. The slicker was jerked from his hand, and that old wrinkle-horn went tearin' through the herd stampedin' ever' hoof in it. That yeller flag rattlin' behind urged 'im to faraway places with a speed that made the rest of the herd look like they were backin' up as he passed. All hands spent the night gatherin' scattered cattle and cussin' that slicker and the man who used it for a bullwhip.

Then there was 'nother feller who duded up and started on a long ride to town to enjoy a Fourth of July celebration that he'd been lookin' forward to for a month. Comin' to the river, he found it big swimmin'. Not wantin' to get his low-necked clothes wet, he stopped, stripped, and rolled 'em carefully in his waterproof slicker.

Now he could cross the river and dress on the other side and ride on as dry as a cork leg. But his hoss had different ideas. When this bronc looked 'round and seen somethin' that was a-wearin' nothin' but his hat and hair tryin' to crawl his back, he made a nine in his tail and lit a shuck. This cowboy was so shocked he couldn't even cuss till he realized that both his wardrobe and his transportation had disappeared over the same hill, leavin' a cloud of dust that told the world he was in a hurry. Wherever he was goin' it was a cinch he wouldn't be late.

It wasn't long till this hossless cowboy's feet felt like he was walkin' on a herd of porcupines and the sun was fryin' the tallow out of his naked spinal column, but that Fourth of July celebration was ancient history before he found a sheep wagon to raid and got back to the ranch with his feet and nakedness wrapped up in sheep pelts, lookin' like a woolly, overripe tomato on the hoof, and smellin' of mutton.

Yep, that old fish was a grand old garment to keep you dry if you wore it on your shoulders where it was intended, but it wasn't no play toy.

THE WIPES

One of the smallest things in a cowboy's riggin' was his neckerchief, or "wipes," as he called it. It had more uses than most anything he wore, and it wasn't used as an ornamental necktie like a heap of folks thought.

It couldn't be too big, and the color was mostly red, blue, or black. White wasn't pop'lar because it showed dirt and reflected light. Rodeo riders went in for bright colors, but the range man wanted to dodge attention either of people or of animals, and these shore advertised the things he was tryin' to hide.

Folded diagonally, like the first garment he ever wore, he tied the two farthest corners in a square knot and hung it on the safest peg he knowed— his neck. In this way he was never without it in case he needed it, and he most generally did. Mostly he wore it draped loose over his chest with the knot at the back. If the sun was at his back he reversed it for the protection of his neck against the sun. Ridin' in the drag of a herd, he pulled it over his nose and mouth so he could breathe without suffocatin' from the dust they kicked up. Likewise, it was a protection against cold wind and stingin' sleet. Pulled up under his eyes it was a guard against snow blindness.

If he was ridin' in a stiff wind, and didn't have bonnet strings on his hat, he'd tie it on with his bandanna; sometimes, when it was cold, he used it for an earmuff, or when the weather was hot he'd wear it wet under his hat to keep his head cool. Caught in a country where there was no runnin' water when he was thirsty, he spread it over a muddy waterhole to use as a strainer to drink through.

When he washed his face at the water hole, or creek, in the mornin', he packed his towel with 'im, tied 'round his neck. In the brandin' pen when the sweat was runnin' down in his eyes this old mop was hangin' handy. It made a rag for holdin' the handle of a hot brandin' iron, too.

He maybe used it as a blindfold when saddlin' a snaky bronc. Some riders didn't like a leather blind. He could use it as a piggin' string, too, when he run across a calf critter that'd been overlooked in the brandin'. He sometimes used it to hobble his hoss to keep from bein' set afoot when makin' camp at night. One end tied to the lower jaw of a gentle hoss made a kind of Injun bridle that'd do in a pinch. It's been used as a sling for broken arms, a tourniquet, and a bandage for wounds. Men have been handcuffed with 'em, too, and a few have been hung with 'em when there was no rope handy. It was also the favorite mask for the holdup man. And more'n one cowhand has been buried out on the plains with one of 'em spread over his face to keep the dirt from touchin' it.

THE BEDROLL

All this chatter 'bout cowboy riggin' wouldn't be complete without a mention of his bedroll, or hot-roll, the warehouse where he kept his worldly goods.

This shakedown, or velvet couch, as he sometimes called it, consisted of a waterproof tarpaulin or "tarp," 'bout seven by eighteen feet, made of Number Eight duckin', weighin' eighteen ounces to the square yard, and thoroughly waterproofed. It was made with a series of flaps and was equipped with rings and snaps so he could pull the flap over 'im and snap it. Inside there was a couple of heavy quilts, or soogans, folded double, and a blanket or two to take the place of a mattress. Them soogans were heavy comforts or quilts made of patches of pants, coats, and overcoats. When made from scraps of faded overalls and jumpers they were called "Mormon blankets." A soogan usually weighed 'bout four pounds—"a pound for each corner," the cowboy said. They claim that what run so many sheepherders crazy was tryin' to find the long end of a soogan. If ever so often you didn't hang 'em out in the sun, or wash 'em in the creek to get that Rover smell out of 'em, they'd maybe crawl off some night.

There was one cowhand whose life was made miserable because his best gal embroidered some sachet bags on his soogans. Ever' time the other boys got near his bed they'd hold their noses, and somebody'd make some such remark as, "There's a sachet kitten loose 'round here." The cowboy often called a skunk a "sachet kitten."

Soogans were better'n a mattress because they could be taken out for a shakin' and airin'. Some riders used a thin, feather-filled comfort they called a "henskin." A feather pillow was called a "goose-hair." Mattresses were barred at the wagon because they made the bedroll bulky and took up too much room when loaded. As it was, most punchers had gathered so much plunder in their driftin' 'round the country it took an extry hoss to pack the load when they wasn't with the wagon. 'Bout the only mattress the cowhand knowed was the one at the cheap frontier hotel, stuffed with "prairie feathers," and knowed as "Missouri featherbeds," or "mule's breakfast." But he did get to enjoy clean sheets, which he called "clean straw," when he hit town.

With his bed went his "war sack," his "thirty years' gatherin' " as he often called it, because in it was his savin's of a lifetime. Next to his hoss and saddle, his bedroll was the cowboy's most valued possession. It served as his safety deposit box, and it wasn't what you'd call healthy for a man to be caught prowlin' through another's bedroll. His bedroll and his string of hosses were touchy spots, and jes' half 'nough cowboy sense told a feller to leave 'em both alone.

His bed was his home, and no matter where he went his bed went with 'im. If he was workin' from headquarters, it was spread on the bunkhouse floor or his bunk; if he was out with the wagon it was rolled and loaded to go 'long; when he went to town for a spell this old lay was taken and dumped in the corner of his hotel room, for it was his trunk; and when he was driftin' over the range it was loaded on his pack hoss, and mounted on his "individual" saddle hoss, he was free as a bird. He never cared, when night came, whether he hit a ranch or not, for he had his bed and shelter with 'im, a home free from taxes and overhead.

It was the boys that wasn't on speakin' terms with the law that had to travel light. They missed this old hot-roll more'n anything else, but when a sheriff was campin' on your trail you didn't have time to drag a pack hoss 'long. Them brutes might wonder at the hurry you're in, but the only cooperation they gave was to pull back on the halter like they was in cahoots with the law. There wasn't much comfort in a "Tucson bed," which was usin' your back for a mattress and your belly for a coverin', but when you're jes' two jumps ahead of a sheriff you couldn't be choosy. Lots of 'em had to do a "star pitch" and do a little "sage hennin'," that is, sleep in the open without coverin'.

A certain ranch in Wyoming had a rep'tation of workin' its hands early and late. The owner rode into Laramie to hire 'nother hand or two for the spring work. A Texas cowhand who'd jes' drifted into the country hit 'im for a job, and was hired.

"I'll be ready," he says, "jes' as soon as I can buy a bedroll."

A native cowhand who'd worked on this ranch followed 'im outside.

"Hell, you don't need no bedroll on that spread," he says. "Jes' buy yourself a lantern."

When a cowhand unspooled his bed at night, he picked high ground that'd drain in case of rain, but avoided hillsides where his bed'd be apt to work downhill. Before spreadin' it out he stomped the ground to rout out any varmints that might try to split the blankets with 'im, as he didn't have no hankerin' for them crawlin' bedfellers. In the daytime he'd maybe crawl under the wagon for a little snooze if the work was slack and the cook wasn't so mean he'd pour dishwater under there to prevent such luxuries, but at night he wanted to be in the open. A sudden wakin' under a wagon might cause 'im to crack his skull on the runnin' gear, and the scars of others' scalps had taught 'im not to bed down under wagons at night.

If it rained, he was as dry and cozy in his bedroll as a toad under a cabbage leaf. Water couldn't get through his tarp, and with the flaps pulled up he kept his bed as dry as if he was under a good roof. On rainy nights his hat, rope, boots, and spurs went to bed with 'im. Wet boots were hard to pull on, and a stiff rope didn't make it easy to ketch his mornin' hoss. Wet beds meant tired, stiff cowhands with dispositions as techy as a teased snake. But the range man with a well equipped bedroll who couldn't keep it dry ought to get a job as chambermaid for a livery stable—he didn't belong on the range.

The cowboy's bed was warm in winter. The tarp kept out snow, sleet, and wind, and even if it was covered with snow and ice the extry weight made it warmer inside. In the mornin' when he woke up to find the weather freezin' outside, he dressed à la Pullman berth, without quittin' his warm blankets. In cold weather a lot of thoughtful cowhands took their bridles to bed with 'em so they'd have a bit that wouldn't frost their hoss's tongue the next mornin'.

When he crawled in between his soogans at night, he was layin' amongst ever'thing he owned, except maybe his saddle hoss and saddle. Under his head for a pillow was his war sack, which held all the useless ditties and do-funnies that he'd gathered in his years of followin' the wagon. There he kept his makin's and supply of cigarette papers, an extry spur, some whang leather, an extry cinch or bit, and maybe a carefully wrapped picture of a gal, or some tattered letters that'd brought 'im news from the outside. Among this plunder there'd likely be a box of cartridges, a greasy deck of cards, and a bill-of-sale for his private hoss.

Under this pillow was his six-gun, which didn't make it any softer. If that spur dug into his ear, he turned the pillow over, but huntin' a soft spot was like tryin' to find hair on a frog. Between his soogans were his extry shirts, socks, and underriggin'. Maybe there, too, you'd find some pretty fancy shirts and an extry suit that he wore when he went gallin'. In this storeroom they'd not only be kept clean but pressed as well.

Scattered near the foot you'd find his pet rope, some latigo straps, a pair of hobbles, his clothes that needed washin', and all the rest of his personal plunder. Lookin' into a cowboy's bed was like visitin' a clothin' store, a hardware store, and a saddle shop all in one.

Sometimes he cut the bed, or split the blankets, with a feller puncher, either to keep warm in cold weather, or to save space when the wagon was heavy loaded and the outfit didn't use a hoodlum, or bed wagon.

There were few things a cowhand liked more'n stretchin' out full length after a long day's ride, even if he wasn't tired. He crawled into his soogans early because the nights were short, but before he dropped off to sleep he'd likely lay there gazin' up at the big stars that looked close 'nough to reach up and touch. Scattered over the ground 'bout 'im were other sleepin' punchers lookin' like so many huge cocoons spread over the prairie.

Off in the distance maybe he heard a coyote howl, or an owl hoot. Out toward the herd a cow critter bellered, or maybe a hoss nickered out where the tinklin' of a bell told 'im the remuda was grazin'. Maybe he heard a rider or two come in and others ride out at the change of guard. The jingle of their spurs and all them other soft noises made a music that soon soothed 'im to sleep.

He was usually waked up before daylight by music that was always sweet to his ears, a music comin' from the wagon where the cook was grindin' the mornin' coffee. He knowed that he still had half an hour to doze and dream and that when he was routed out by the cook's yell there'd be plenty of good strong coffee to start the day on.

The first thing he did after he crawled out was to spool his bed and strap it together. Packin' it over to the wagon, he dumped it where it'd be handy for loadin' when camp was ready to move. Then, makin' his way to the washbasin, he snorted in it a couple of times and was ready for breakfast, the smell of which had whetted his already keen appetite. Fillin' his cup and plate at the steamin' pots, he hunted a place where he could squat cross-legged on the ground and fill out his equator, or maybe he used his old hot-roll for a combination sofa and dinin' table. When loaded, his bed had to be tied down good or some cowhand would be shy a bed that night, because that bed wagon traveled over some mighty rough places durin' the day.

For a cowhand to leave his bed unrolled and not packed for loadin' when camp was to be moved was a serious breach of range etiquette. The cook was shore to make the air cloudy with cuss words. If this careless puncher committed the offense more'n once, the cook was mighty apt to drive off and leave it behind.

One old cook had a shore cure for such carelessness. 'Bout the third time a certain puncher rode off with his bed unrolled, this king of the pots tied it to the rear axle of his wagon and dragged it behind at high speed. By the time he reached the next campsite it was worn plumb to a frazzle, and as useless as a .22 cartridge in a twelve-gauge shotgun.

When this puncher rode into camp at noon and saw his puny lookin' bedroll still tied there, he turned green 'round the gills. He started diggin' through the remains for a gun he couldn't find. Cookie, when he saw what he was after, didn't waste no time in gopherin' for his own hogleg that was cached under the wagon seat, and if that puncher'd found his gun that camp'd probably looked like beef day at an Injun agency.

His bedroll not bein' worth rollin' up, he rescued what little plunder he had left and, without a word, stuffed it in his war sack. He saddled his private hoss and rode off madder'n a rained-on rooster, backtrackin' the wagon like he was searchin' for that gun and expected to come back and use it. I reckon he failed to find it because he never came back, but I'll bet he never left 'nother bed unrolled.

Hoss Jewelry: Saddles

THE cowboy's saddle was his workbench and throne. His love for it is a tradition of the range. It was his most highly prized possession, and in the old days often cost more'n the hoss he slapped it on. The company might sell the hosses he rode up the trail behind a herd of steers, but he kept his saddle and brought it back in a gunny sack. The expression "He's sold his saddle" meant he was utterly broke or in disgrace. Even in death his saddle was associated with 'im, and "He's sacked his saddle" meant he'd gone over the Long Trail. When he was too old to ride, it was said he'd "hung up his saddle," or "hung his saddle on the fence."

Our first saddle came from Mexico, but the American cowboy made a heap of changes and improvements to suit his needs. Without the Western saddle no man could have rode the buckin' hosses of the range and there'd been no cowboys and no ranches.

Over the years there developed many different styles in saddles, as to tree, cantle, horn, or riggin', but once a rider got one that suited and fit 'im, he wouldn't part with it of his own accord. One correctly made with stout tree and prime leather would last a long time unless it was the victim of some accident. If a hoss throwed a rider and got away, this cowhand was shore to yell, "Ketch my saddle!" The hoss belonged to the company, but the saddle was his own private property.

Startin' with the old Mexican saddle, the cowboy has always given his rig nicknames. *Fuste* is a Spanish word meanin' "wood," or "saddle tree."

The American cowboy sometimes called the Mexican saddle by this name. The Mexican used less leather than the American, so the American looked on the Mexican saddle as bein' made principally of wood. The *fuste* had a flat horn, a low cantle, and was noted for its ability to make a hoss's back sore. The broad-horned Mexican saddle was called a "dinner plate" because its horn was big 'nough to play a game of seven-up on. A "skeleton rig" was an early saddle consistin' of nothin' but a tree, the riggin' for the cinch, and the straps reachin' to the wide, oxbow stirrups. It had no skirts or fenders.

Still 'nother early-day saddle was the "Mother Hubbard," the first improvement on the Mexican saddle. It consisted of little more'n a tree and stirrup leathers, but had a housin' like a mochila, an almost square piece of leather with a hole for the horn and a slit for the cantle, the whole bein' detachable. Later this was made a permanent part of the saddle, and designed to give more comfort to both hoss and rider. Durin' the evolution of the American saddle the cowboy gave it such nicknames as "wood," "leather," "geldin' smacker," "Visa" (short for Visalia), and many others. The style of the horn, the placement of the cinch, and its riggin' gave it other names which we'll tell you 'bout as we go 'long.

In the early eighties a new saddle came out and was called the "apple horn." It took this name because of the small horn whose top was round like an apple as compared with the flat ones it replaced.

Since we've given you some nicknames the cowman called his own saddle, we might as well tell you what he called them little Eastern saddles that he held in such contempt. Such saddles as the Easterner rode on some city bridle path were called "chicken saddles," "henskins," "kidney pads," or "kidney plasters," "pancakes," "pimples," "postage stamps," or "pumpkin seed" saddles. A saddle without a horn was called a "muley." While the cowboy had a pretty big vocabulary of forceful adjectives at his command, he never seemed able to find any strong 'nough to express his disgust for them little pad-saddles and short-hitched stirrups of the Eastern rider.

The "tree" is the foundation of the saddle. It's the wooden frame that the leather covers. As the saddle went through its evolutions, different makers designed different shapes of trees, and each took its name after the model or maker. The "tree" has three parts, the "fork," or front to which the horn is fastened; the "cantle," or back rest; and the two side bars connectin' the fork and cantle. All parts are fastened together with glue and heavy wood screws, but as few screws were used as possible because they might rust or become loose with rough usage. The whole tree was covered with green rawhide laced on while wet. As it dried it shrunk, holdin' the whole frame together strong and tight. No good saddle could be built on a poor tree.

A saddle often took its name from the shape of its tree, such as the California rig, Visalia, White River, and others, or from the name of its maker, such as the Taylor, Nelson, Ladesma, Porter, Hamley, and Ellenburg. The "bronc saddle" took this name because of its specially built tree which made it easier to ride a bad hoss. It was made with wide, undercut fork, with built-in swells and deep-dished cantle. There were no copyrights on the saddles of early days, and many of them have been copied, especially if they proved to be good ones. The Ellenburg proved to be one of the best trees and had been copied by many other makers, with various modifications. The "Association" or "contest" saddle adopted by the Rodeo Association in 1920, and now compulsory at all large contests, is but a modified Ellenburg. We'll tell you more about this saddle in a later chapter.

The "fork" is the front part of the tree which supports the horn. This name dates back to early days when Texas cowmen built their own crude saddles by shapin' the fork of a tree to fit over the withers of the hoss. Because no bulge was possible in them days, all saddles were "straight forks." After "swell forks" were invented, the straight fork became knowed as a "slick fork." The swell fork had projections built on each side of the fork below the horn. The rider could hook his knees under them projections when ridin' a buckin' hoss, and they helped keep 'im in the saddle. Some called these "bronc saddles," and if the projections were too pronounced they became knowed as "freaks."

The curved portion of the underside of the saddle fork is called the "gullet." The larger the swell of the fork, and the higher the horn, the longer the gullet. The swells originated from the "buckin' roll," or "saddle roll," a roll of blankets tied across the saddle, jes' behind the fork, to help wedge the rider in the saddle, and make it harder for the hoss to unseat 'im. Sometimes it's a leather pad, stuffed with hair, three or four inches high, and tied down on each side of the fork jes' behind the horn. Swells are now built in. A saddle with large swells and deep-dished cantle is called a "form-fitter." Only the professional bronc rider gives them swell saddles much thought.

The "cantle" is the raised back rest of the saddle. It might vary in width, height, and slope, accordin' to the owner's choice, or the custom of the section in which he worked. Riders in a flat country, and good ropers, prefer a low cantle. A low cantle makes it easier to mount and dismount. The contest rider liked a low, full-slope cantle. Riders in mountainous sections liked a high-slope cantle. This cantle might be round, oval, or flanged. The outside of the cantle's called the "cantle drop."

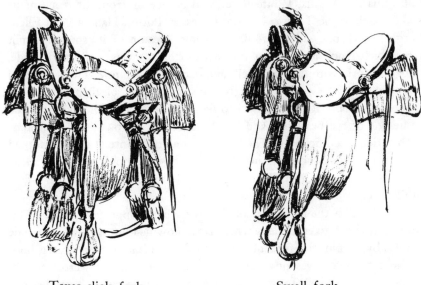

Texas slick fork   Swell fork

Some cowhands had a way of ridin' loose and hittin' the cantle as the hoss traveled. This was called "cantle-boardin'," but it wasn't the sign of a good rider.

Some of the old Mexican saddles had a slopin' cantle with a hand slot in the center, sometimes two. Frank Meanea, a saddle maker of Cheyenne, Wyoming, to create somethin' different from the current saddles of his day, made a saddle with a leather flange extendin' over, to the rear, of the cantle board, and this was called a "Cheyenne roll." This saddle was brought out 'bout 1870 and became very pop'lar through the seventies and eighties, especially east of the Rockies.

The hand slot of the Mexican was doubtless the forerunner of the Cheyenne roll. It gave the rider a hand hold in case of an emergency. The modern rider, however, don't take time to hunt a hole in his cantle. If he grabs anything it's the horn. It's easier to find.

Now we come to the seat of the saddle, that part said to be the easiest to find but the hardest to keep. The two side bars of the tree runnin' from fork to cantle form the seat. A strip of galvanized iron, called a "strainer," is placed over the middle of the saddletree, when it's bein' built, to cover the open space between the sideboards. This metal further strengthened the frame, and prevented the seat from sinkin' or breakin' down. Upon this was laid a piece of soft, thick leather fashioned to the form of the rider.

The length of the seat's the distance from the center of the fork at a point 'bout an inch below the base of the horn to the center inside edge of the cantle. The proper length of the seat for each individual depends to some extent upon the height and weight of the rider, and whether he likes a fairly tight-fittin' saddle or one with plenty of room. A great deal of his comfort depends on the fit of this seat. The seat's often called the "dish," and accordin' to its depth is spoken of as bein' "shallow-dished" or "deep-dished." Its coverin' of leather also has some influence on its style. The "full seat" is when the seat's entirely covered with leather; the "half-rigged" saddle's one with a triangle of leather tacked on for a seat, while the "three-quarter seat's" one whose seat coverin' extends only to the rear edge of the stirrup grooves.

The horn's that part of the saddle above the fork. Its technical name, "pommel," is never used by a cowman. First let us tell you some of the slang names it's called in different sections. It's knowed by such names as "apple," "biscuit," "handle," "Lizzie," "nubbin'," and "pig." Good riders try to avoid grabbin' the horn, but when he does he's said to be "huntin' leather," "pullin' leather," "reachin' for the apple," "shakin' hands with grandma," "soundin' the horn," "squeezin' the biscuit," "squeezin' Lizzie," and many others. Various saddles have different slopes of horn, accordin' to the style the rider likes. Horn heads can have a different pitch too. A roper uses a different shaped horn than a rider might want for ordinary use.

The horn's one of the most important parts of the saddle. Without it no ropin' could be done. They're also an important factor in mountin', and they've been knowed to keep a man from bein' crushed when a hoss has throwed 'imself backward, ketchin' the rider before he could get out of the saddle. In ropin', all riders either tie their ropes fast 'round the horn, or take a turn, or dally, 'round it. Many dally men wrapped their horns with an extry coverin' of leather. In doin' this, the horn has to be wrapped the opposite direction from which he takes his dallies. Thus when a roped animal pulled on the rope the wrappin'd tighten instead of gettin' loose. Because most ropers make their turns to the left, the wrappin's done toward the right.

The wooden tree of the saddle's covered with leather, and these leathers have various names. Some of the first saddles were covered with what was called a *corus*. This was a coverin' for the tree, at first made of two pieces of leather stitched together through the middle with a hole cut for the fork and a slit for the cantle. It was worked and shaped to fit the tree, and, after the riggin' was in place, was slipped down over the saddle and buckled or laced in front of the horn. The early-day "Mother Hubbard" saddles were made on this style, and though they gave both hoss and rider more comfort than the original Mexican saddles they were crude affairs, and it wasn't long till they were improved upon.

Many of the saddle's leathers are called "jockeys." The "front jockey" is the leather on top of the skirt of the saddle, fittin' close 'round the horn. The "back" and "rear jockeys" are the top of the skirt of the saddle, bein' the uppermost broad leathers joinin' behind the cantle. The "side jockey" is the leather extension of the saddle's seat, while the "seat jockey" is the flat plate overlyin' the stirrup leathers when the latter issue from the seat of the saddle. This is also called the "sudadero," a Spanish word meanin' "a handkerchief for wipin' the sweat," or "sweat pad." This term's sometimes incorrectly applied to the "rosadero."

The little semilunar tailpiece of the saddle's called the "anquera," from the Spanish meanin' the round coverin' for the hindquarters of a hoss. Americans use this term as meanin' the broad leather sewn to the base of the cantle when there's no "rear jockey," and extendin' beyond the cantle. A "full-rigged" saddle's one whose tree's entirely covered with leather. When a saddle's covered with fancy stamped designs it's called a "full-stamped" saddle. Them hand-stamped saddles aren't merely to satisfy a rider's ego. The rough indentations cause a friction between the leather and the rider's smooth trouser legs, allowin' 'im to set tight in the saddle without the tiresome crampin' of his legs that would result from ridin' a fractious hoss with a smooth saddle.

"Basto," a Spanish word, means a pad. Americans use it as a technical term for the skirt of the saddle. A "California skirt" is short and rounded, while the "Texas skirt" is a long, square skirt as used on Texas saddles. Other little leathers on the saddle are the "whang strings," or "saddle strings," little rawhide strings to hold the saddle leathers together. The ends are tied and left hangin', which allows packages or slickers to be tied on, as well as servin' as decorations. A "six-string" saddle's one usin' six strings to hold the various leathers in place. Bronc saddles are usually six-string saddles. The work saddles are usually eight-string ones. A "buck strap" is a narrow strap riveted to the leather housin' of the saddle jes' below and on the off side of the base of the horn. Top riders have nothin' but contempt for this hand hold, and it's barred at contests. The "horn string" is a leather string fastened to the horn for securin' the rope.

A saddle's riggin' is the middle leathers attached to the tree and connectin' with and supportin' the cinch by latigo through the "riggin' ring." This riggin' ring's an iron ring attached to the saddle for fastenin' the cinch, and it's also called a "tree ring" or "saddle ring." The style of the saddle takes its name from the position of its riggin' and cinch. It may be a "single-rig," or one-cinch, saddle, or a "double rig," or two-cinch, saddle. A lot depends on a saddle's riggin' as to how it'll hold its position on the hoss. The farther forward the cinch is set, the better the saddle'll stay. A double-rigged saddle usually has a narrower front cinch than the single-rig.

A saddle with one cinch, placed near the center, is called a "center-fire," "single-rig," "single-barreled," "single-rigged," or "California rig." When the one cinch is placed far to the front, it's knowed as a "rim-fire," "rimmy," or "Spanish rig." A two-cinched saddle's knowed as a "double-barreled," "double-fire," or "double-rigged" saddle. A one-cinch saddle with the cinch halfway between the "center-fire" and the "rim-fire" is a "three-quarter rig." One with the cinch between the "rim-fire" and the "three-quarter" is a "seven-eights," and one between the "three-quarter" and the "center-fire" is a "five-eights" rig. Neither of the latter rigs is commonly used, but the "three-quarter" is a pop'lar rig. California uses the "center-fire," but a one-cinch saddle's no good in a mountainous country or for ropin'. Texans use the two-cinch saddle and tie fast when ropin'.

Cinch is from the Spanish *cinchas*, meanin' girth. It's a broad, short band of coarsely woven hosshair, canvas, or cordage. On each end's a metal ring called the "cinch ring." On each side of the saddle are "saddle rings," and through them rings the saddle's fastened on the hoss's back by the "latigo," a long leather strap. Its name's from the Spanish meanin' "end of ever' strap which must be passed through a buckle." It's passed successively through the cinch ring and the riggin' ring, and tied like a four-in-hand necktie. The "flank riggin' " is a flank strap from the rear of the saddle, goin' far back on the flank of the hoss. Used in rodeos to make the hoss buck, it's also called a "scratcher cinch."

Texans call the cinch "girth," pronouncin' it "girt." The front cinch's called "front cinch," or "front girth," while the rear cinch's either "rear cinch," "rear girth," "hind cinch," or "flank girth." A "billet" is a wide leather strap looped through the tree on the off side of the saddle. Holes are punched in it to accommodate the tongue of the cinch buckle. A "nigger catcher" is a small slotted leather flap on one or both sides of the saddle, usually at the base of the fork or cantle, in a two-cinched saddle. It holds the long, free end of the latigo through the slit when cinched up. A latigo which buckles is called a "trunk strap," and the name's used as ridicule. A cinch buckle carryin' two wraps of the latigo and hookin' into the cinch ring's a "tackberry buckle."

Stirrups are the foot supports of the saddle, usually made of wood, sometimes bound in iron, brass, or rawhide, but often all iron or brass. Most earlier stirrups were made of wide, tough wood, bent into shape and bolted together at the top, and strong 'nough so they wouldn't be crushed by a fallin' hoss. Stirrups are at the end of the broad leathers that hang from the bar of the saddletree, called "stirrup leathers." The vertical, wide leather shield sewed at the back of the stirrup leather's called the "rosadero." The heavy leather shields sewed on the outside of the stirrup leathers are "fenders," and these protect the rider's legs. A Spanish term sometimes used in California and on the southern border, in speakin' of the stirrup leather, is "acion."

The old wide wooden stirrups of the early range were called "dog-house stirrups," "ox-bows," or "ox-yokes." With the evolution of the saddle came narrower stirrups which made it easier to mount and dismount. All of 'em were made stout 'nough to resist crushin' if the hoss fell on 'em. The Visalia style was a fav'rite, and was wide 'nough to let a man put his weight on the ball of his foot. It had flarin' sides and a flat bottom. The bronc stirrup has a narrow bottom, as most riders like to have their feet well in the stirrups, but can easily kick their feet free.

When stirrups are connected with a strap or rope passed under the hoss's belly, they're called "hobbled stirrups." These furnish an anchorage when ridin' a buckin' hoss, but are held in contempt by real riders, and barred at rodeos. Though they practically tie a rider in the saddle, they're extremely dangerous, for if a hoss falls the rider's got no chance to free 'imself quickly. In the cow country a man who rides with hobbled stirrups is considered plumb loco, and he shore ain't a top hand.

The word "tapadero" is from the Spanish *tapaderas*, which comes from the verb *tapar*, meanin' "to close or cover." It's a wedge-shaped piece of leather which covers the stirrup in front and at the sides, but is open in the rear. Its literal meanin's "toe fender." The word's usually shortened to "taps." Made of heavy cowhide, and occasionally reinforced by a wooden frame, they're used mostly in the brush country to protect the rider's feet. They also prevent the rider's foot from passin' through the stirrup, avoid scuffin' of the brush, and the bite of a mean hoss. Their style takes the name of their shape, such as "bulldogs," short ones; "monkey nose," short upturned front; or "eagle-bill," longer hooked front. Stirrups without tapaderos are called "open stirrups," or "tapless" ones.

Some saddles don't fit the hoss they're on, and cause sores, "set fasts," or "kack biscuits," as they're sometimes called, and the hoss is "baked," "beefsteaked," or is said to be "nigger branded." More riders have lost their jobs over back-eatin' saddles that had teeth in 'em than over any other one thing. Some of them early-day saddles could eat out of a wire corral in one night. Riders of double-rigged saddles claim the center-fire saddle's "meat and hide hungry" because it's hard to keep in place on the hoss's back.

When a hoss shows up with an empty saddle on his back there's a lot of concern, for an empty saddle has great significance in the cattle country. There is much anxiety concernin' the rider, because an empty saddle signifies he is either dead, hurt, or left afoot, perhaps far from home, which in itself might also mean tragedy.

Well, I've told you most ever'thing 'bout the saddle, but it couldn't be used without a saddle blanket, the paddin' that goes next to the hoss's back beneath the saddle. That is a necessary piece of equipment to keep the hoss's back in good condition. Yet no matter how good a blanket you use, if the saddle's an old worn-out kack that's been warped out of shape, it doesn't protect the hoss from a sore back. A good deal depended on how the cowhand rode, too, in keepin' down sore backs. If he was always shiftin' his weight from one foot to the other with his weight on one stirrup ridin' on one side it was mighty apt to have a tellin' effect on the hoss.

The Navajo blanket became a favorite because its wool absorbs sweat, protects the hoss's back, is durable and made in many different attractive colors and designs. Any blanket should also be kept free of wrinkles, bunches of shed hair which has a way of knottin' up under the blanket, and all other foreign matter.

One good blanket was all they needed. Too much paddin' under the saddle made a hoss sweat, and an overheated back got tender. After the saddle was throwed on, and before it was cinched up, a couple of fingers were inserted under the blanket where it came over the withers to work up a little slack, for it was important to avoid any unevenness while a hoss was bein' rode. If a "set-fast" did develop it was a real menace to the usefulness of the hoss.

Hoss Jewelry:

Bridles, Bits, and Hackamores

ORDINARILY we think of the bridle as the headgear of a hoss, composed of head-stall, or bridle-head, crown-piece, brow-band, throat-latch, and, on each side, a cheek-piece. While the purpose of them various leathers is to hold the bit in the hoss's mouth, they're not, strictly speakin', the complete bridle unless the bit and reins are included.

The head-stall, the foundation of the bridle, is that part of the bridle encompassin' the head. There're two main types of head-stalls, but many styles, the two most common bein' the "one ear," or "split ear," open-face style, and the reg'lar style with a nose and brow-band and throat-latch. Bridle-heads are made either of hand-carved leather or braided rawhide, and sometimes decorated with conchas, but the workin' cowboy preferred a plain head-stall with nothin' to interfere with his ropin'.

Of the various parts of the bridle, each has its name and function. The brow-band's the front part of the bridle which assists in holdin' the bridle in place; the crown-piece's the top part passin' over the hoss's head behind the ears, and is really a continuation of the cheek-pieces; the cheek-pieces are the side parts, and the throat-latch is the leather strap fastenin' the bridle under the throat for security. Some bridles have a nose-band, chin, or curb strap for better controllin' the hoss. In some parts of

the range bridles are never used, but hosses are broken with a hackamore.
If, after the hoss is well seasoned, a bridle's used it's introduced gradually
and at first in conjunction with the hackamore.

The "ear bridle," or "ear-head," is a head-stall made in two pieces, with
a loop for the right ear, one buckle on the left cheek, no nose-band,
throat-latch, or brow-band. The bit ties in with buckskin thongs. This
form of bridle's used only on well broke hosses. It usually has the loop
made for the right ear only, but can be made with loops for both. The
loop's adjustable to slide to fit the hoss's ear. If the hoss has the habit of
rubbin' the bridle off, a reg'lar head-stall's used, or if the rider still prefers
the ear bridle, a throat-latch is attached. This bridle can be made from one
piece of leather with a buckle at the left side, or a buckle can be placed
on both sides, so the head-stall can be adjusted to a uniform length for
various size hosses.

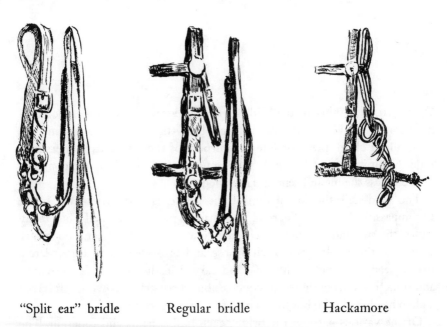

"Split ear" bridle   Regular bridle   Hackamore

The original name for the "curb," or "chin strap," was the Spanish word
barboquejo. It's a piece of adjustable leather under the hoss's chin. Sometime a chain curb's used if the hoss is hard-mouthed. This is a short piece
of chain instead of leather, but it can be covered with leather. Sometimes
bits come with curb straps attached, and these are all right for one who

can't adjust or handle a chain curb, but they soon become loose and have no leverage. They often become dry and stiff, and gall and cut the hoss with their sharp edges. This can be eliminated by soakin' in a good grade of oil frequently. It will then get soft and pliable and stay that way. Once it loses its leverage, it's useless in controllin' a hoss.

'Bout the only bridle a cowhand was shy of was a "biddy bridle," what he called a bridle with blinders as sometimes used by a nester who couldn't afford a ridin' bridle, but used the same one on hossback that he used on his plow hoss.

BITS

The first bits of the range were inherited from Mexico, made on the Spanish and earlier Moorish types. The early artisans tried to outdo each other in fashionin' intricate designs, givin' no consideration to cruelty toward the hoss. American common sense modified them bits and held to the theory that the function of the bit was to suggest physical sufferin' rather than cause it. Bits are not so important as the nature and disposition of the rider and the lightness of his hand. Severe bits are never necessary, and when they seem necessary it's an indication that the hoss has been spoiled and abused by such bits. A good hossman controls his hoss with a light hand, and the hoss is never conscious of the possible punishment of the bit in his mouth.

The bit's the metal bar that fits into the hoss's mouth. There're many kinds and styles of bits, some of 'em extremely cruel when misused. Yet it was a rare case when a cowhand used a bit for cruelty. His idea of a bit was that it was merely to hang in the hoss's mouth for a psychological effect. When turnin' to the right, for example, he didn't pull the right rein; he merely moved his bridle hand a couple of inches to the right, bringin' the left rein against the hoss's neck. It was merely a signal. A well trained hoss turned 'imself; he didn't have to be pulled 'round. There're three basic types of bits—the bar, snaffle, and the curb, and the various designs fall under one of them three types or combination of 'em.

The bar bit's a straight or slightly curved round bar for a mouthpiece, and, like most bits, has a ring at each end, called either the "bit ring," or the "bridle ring," to which the reins are fastened. Where the bar's straight it's called a "straight bit." Bar bits are not common on cow hosses, but more suitable on drivin' teams. This type bit rests on the hoss's tongue, which is not particularly sensitive, and with his tongue he can hold the pull away from the tenderer gums. Cowboys don't favor these bits because they're not severe 'nough to make the hoss obey in quick stops and quick turnin' in cuttin' and ropin' cattle. Besides, this bit encourages a "puller," a hoss wantin' to go in spite of no such desire of the rider.

The "snaffle bit" is similar to the bar bit except it's made in two pieces and connected with two interlockin' eyes at the middle. Some call it a "broken bit," or "limber bit"; the "chain bit," made of a short piece of chain, could come under this classification. The center hinge acts as a pincher when pressure's applied and can cause a heap of pain if not used right. Some ranchers use this bit on young hosses, but fit it with a jaw strap between the bridle rings to keep the bit in position. When there's no pull on the reins its position's so that it jes' touches the corners of the mouth. Like the bar bit it's not widely used on the range.

The "curb bit" is one with an upward curb, or port, in the center of the mouthpiece, and is sometimes called a "grazin' bit." It's one of the most widely used bits in the cattle country. Workin' on a leverage, it's more severe than the bar or snaffle, but can be used humanely by a good rider. The port, or raise, in the mouthpiece should be low, never high to bruise the roof of the mouth. The bit should fit snugly into the corners of the mouth, not high 'nough to wrinkle the mouth, nor low 'nough to leave a space. If there's slack the corners of the mouth'll be pinched ever'time the reins are used. The lower the bit, the more severe on the hoss. On the curb, the curb strap should be snug against the chin groove, and not work up on the lower jaw.

The "half-breed bit" is one that has a narrow, wicket-shaped hump in the middle of the mouth bar, within which a "roller," or vertical wheel with a broad and corrugated rim, is fixed. The half-breed, and all bits with extry high ports, are not for beginners and should never be used by 'em. The "roller" in such a bit's called a "cricket" because it makes a chirpin' noise, givin' the hoss somethin' with which to amuse 'imself with his tongue and creatin' a music the cowboy loves to hear. Sometimes them rollers are of copper, called "tasters." They've got a taste that's pleasin' to the hoss, helpin' 'im to accept the bit in his mouth. A hoss that fights his bit's called a "sour mouth." The copper roller makes 'im more contented.

The "spade bit" is one with a piece shaped like a broad screwdriver on the mouth bar, three or four inches in length, and bent backward at the top. The most sensitive spot in a hoss's mouth is its roof, and when the spade bit touches this spot the hoss is aware of its possibilities. A good rider never forgets it's a spade that can do damage, and handles his reins light. Because of this flat piece of steel which curves upward, it's sometimes called a "stomach pump." To most spades has been added a roller, and to some two wires closely strung with short metal tubes, extendin' on either side of the spade to the cheek-pieces. These can be of copper for tasters too. To ensure the spade restin' on the roof of the mouth, the reins have little knots on 'em to determine the pressure applied on the bit.

A "ring bit" is one with a metal circle slipped over the lower jaw of the hoss and a whole set of hardware in his mouth. This cruel Spanish bit's sometimes called a "Chileno," and ain't looked on with favor by American cowmen. It's extremely severe unless handled carefully, and is capable of breakin' a hoss's jaw. A cold-jawed hoss is always one that's been abused 'round the mouth, perhaps pulled up hard with a ring bit until the nerves have been killed. The most cruel bit ever put into a hoss's mouth is this bit, and it's practically disappeared except in Mexico. A similar brutal hitch of rope in the mouth and 'round the lower jaw's called a "war bridle." When the rider adds to his bit any contrivance to make it cruel, it's called a "tool chest," and such a man's soon cold-shouldered off the range.

THE REINS

Reins are the two leather, rawhide, or hosshair lines runnin' from the bit ring to the rider's hand, and are used to guide and control the hoss. There're two types of reins, but many styles. One type's the flat leather, usually buckled onto the bit. The other's braided rawhide with "romal," and is attached to the bit by "bit chains," or "bridle chains." These are short pieces of chain fastened to the bit ring on one end and the reins on the other end. Some riders like chains because the reins don't get wet when the hoss drinks, and they also keep the hoss from chewin' the reins. A good rider handles his reins light, especially with spade or curb bits with a long shank. Even stoppin' a hoss should produce little strain on the reins.

"Open reins" are them not tied together, each independent of the other, usually 'bout seven feet in length. Most cowhands prefer open reins because if the hoss falls or the rider's throwed, the reins'll fall to the ground and the hoss'll step on 'em, givin' the rider a chance to ketch 'im. Tied reins'll often hang on the hoss's neck, and away he goes. Dismountin' in a hurry, you simply drop open reins instead of stoppin' to strip 'em over the hoss's head. Most hosses are trained to stop when the reins are dropped. Steppin' on a rein pulls on the bit severely, and this hurts the hoss's mouth. Some hosses are so well trained that they're thus "tied to the ground," and won't move till the rider picks up the reins to remount.

"Tied," "closed," or "California reins," as they're sometimes called, are tied together at the ends or the entire rein's made in one piece. Often they're made of braided rawhide and worked into a romal at the home end. When tied reins are left over the saddle horn, they keep the hoss from gettin' his head down to graze, but don't prevent 'im from walkin' off. If they're stripped over the head and dropped to the ground, the hoss's liable to get tangled and fall or otherwise hurt 'imself. Tied reins ain't pop'lar with most cowmen, especially in the plains country. California's where they're used most, bein' handed down by the early Spanish settlers. Open reins are also easier tied to a hitch rack.

The "romal" is a flexible whip made on the bridle reins when they're fastened together. The Spanish *el ramal* means literally "a branch road," "a division," or "ramification." Thus, attached as it is by the loop to the bridle reins, the romal becomes but a ramification of the rein, a handy addition that can be used as a quirt and dropped from the hand without fear of it gettin' lost. The romal's removed when ropin' and placed 'round the roper's waist, which was the reason most old-timers ordered romals to their waist measure. A light romal's no good if used as a quirt in windy weather for the lash'd be hittin' the user in the face. A long romal's no good either, for it might cause the hoss to stumble and fall over it.

The "quirt" is a flexible woven-leather whip made with a short stock 'bout a foot long and carryin' a lash of three or four heavy, loose thongs. Its stock's usually filled with lead to strike down a rearin' hoss which threatens to fall backward. A loop extendin' from the head provides an attachment to either the rider's wrist or the saddle horn. For ordinary ridin' the cowboy seldom packs a quirt, and never on his wrist when ropin'. Usually he's satisfied to use the long end of his reins as a whip. The word "quirt" is derived from the Mexican *cuarta*, meanin' whip; this in turn's from the Spanish *cuerda*, meanin' cord. One can get more out of a tired hoss with a quirt than with spurs. It wakes 'im up, don't cut the skin, but is effective for quick moves.

THE HACKAMORE

The hackamore's part of the equipment of the cowboy in some sections, as they never use bridle and bit. The word's corrupted from the Spanish *jaquima*, meanin' a halter. The American cowboy pronounces his Spanish by ear. When he first heard the word *jaquima*, he pronounced it hackamer, as it sounded. Gradually it became hackamore, as it's found in the dictionary today. Some look on the hackamore as merely a halter with reins instead of a lead rope, but it's more'n that, and hossmen west of the Rockies consider it necessary in breakin' and trainin' hosses. It takes more time to break by hackamore than it does by bit, but they claim it makes better cow hosses. Makin' a hackamore's an art, each part requirin' certain materials and specifications.

The hackamore consists of a head-piece somethin' like a bridle with a bosal in the place of a bit, and a brow-band 'bout three inches wide that can be slid down the cheeks to cover the hoss's eyes, but it's got no throatlatch, except when the fiador's used. For best results a hackamore must be firm, not flexible. A limber one's useless. Its stiffness is built to balance with the nose button and heel knot. The balance that's essential in a good hackamore depends a great deal on the way the nose button and heel knot's made. The correct position to place the hackamore's 'bout an inch above where the cartilage joins the bone. Like the bit, it can punish a hoss too, but it don't punish through a tender mouth.

The cheek-pieces are that part of the hackamore that fit 'round the sides of the hoss's nose and run up 'longside the face close under the eye prominence and tie at the poll. Some have buckles at the left side for easy adjustment. They shouldn't be so stiff that there's no spring, neither should they be flimsy. When too stiff they're hard to shape to the animal's nose and'll fit too tight, and thus hurt the hoss from the corners of his mouth to the edges of his jawbone. Flimsy cheeks won't pinch, but neither will they keep the nose button and heel knot in place for proper action. The fewer strands used in makin' a hackamore, the coarser the finish, and a rough finish'll chafe the hoss's jaw.

The word "bosal" is from the Spanish *bozal*, meanin' a muzzle. It's usually a plaited rawhide nose-band placed jes' above the mouth, used in place of a bit. Its top rests at the crest of the nasal bones and plays an important part in controllin' the hoss. When placed too high it's practically useless. Its shank should be jes' long 'nough to let the heel knot swing free of the jawbone when the mecate's relaxed, yet short 'nough to contact the bone, lettin' the shanks hug the facial nerves 'long the sides when the rein's pulled up. Properly adjusted, it has practically the same effect as a bit, except that in cold weather there's no danger of freezin' the hoss's mouth with a cold bit. It's also effective on hosses with a cold jaw or spoiled mouth.

At the top of the bosal there's an increase in diameter, extendin' from two to three inches each way from the center. This is called the nose button. It should be made with a gradual taper from the center down evenly on both sides. This taper's got to be centered to an exact length. The nose button averages 'bout seven inches in length and should be made so it'll balance in proportion to the diameter of the hackamore body. A little below the nose button there's a slidin' button on either side which holds the cheek-pieces in place high up on the bosal shanks. The nose is a tender spot, and the purpose of the nose button's not to abuse this spot till it becomes calloused, but to keep it tender to better control the hoss.

The "heel knot" is that enlarged plaited knot at the end of the shank of the bosal comin' jes' under the chin. A pull on the reins slaps the heel knot back into the jaw, and such action will get the jaw pretty sore. If a sore jaw gets too much abuse it'll become calloused and insensitive; then more pressure or sharp instruments will have to be added for it to be effective—somethin' to be avoided if possible. The heel knot's the balance wheel of the bosal. If it's too tight the bosal won't rest securely on the nose and will move up and down when the hoss walks, thus causin' unnecessary irritation. All the strands of both ends of the bosal should be used in securely tyin' the heel knot.

In breakin' hosses with a hackamore, some riders use a *tapaojos*. This Spanish word's from *tapar*, to cover, plus *ojos*, eyes. It's a blind or eye cover for animals, and is made from a strip of leather 'bout three inches wide. It's fastened to the head-stall of the hackamore and is long 'nough to extend across the brow of the animal. It slides up and down the cheek-pieces, and is thus used either as a blind or a brow-band. When used as a blind to saddle or mount a green bronc, it can be raised after the rider mounts by his reachin' over the hoss's head and slidin' it up. Its use dates back to the time hosses were first brought to America. All hackamore men don't use 'em, but when breakin' out a green bronc they're handy implements.

The word "fiador" is from the Spanish verb *fiar*, meanin' to answer for, to go surety for. It's a looped cord passin' over the poll then down under the throat where, after a series of fancy ties, it ends at the heel knot. Some Americans have corrupted it into "theodore." It's made of braided hoss-hair, or cotton cord. It takes seventeen feet of hair rope one-fourth inch in diameter to make a fiador. Hair's best because braided cotton cord's too stiff when new and takes away from the action of the hackamore. It also hinders the action of the heel knot by takin' away the flexibility of the bosal shanks. Like any other breakin' equipment, the fiador'll lose its effectiveness if not adjusted with the bosal to the hoss's head, and set well behind the ears for a straight pull over the gullet.

Most hackamore men only use the fiador in advance trainin', due to its takin' away the action of the heel knot. The main advantage of the fiador's its grip on the head of the hoss, and many times means keepin' the hoss and rider together because it's a safety device. A hackamore without it'll pull off over the ears if much force is exerted from the front. When the fiador's made of coarse tail hair it's apt to be prickly, and this is likely to be very irritatin' to a tender-skinned hoss. Finely twisted mane hair's softer and more flexible, thus makin' better fiadors. The humane hossman takes this into consideration when makin' or selectin' this piece of equipment. The irritation of prickin' hair takes the hoss's mind off his trainin'.

The "mecate" is a hair rope used as reins with the hackamore. Corrupted from the Spanish, it's usually called "McCarty," and is made 'bout twenty-two feet in length. This allows eight feet for reins, two for wraps, and twelve feet for lead rope. The wraps're taken 'round the shanks of the bosal jes' above the heel knot. The best mecate to use at first's a tail-hair one because, bein' rough, it gives the hoss some feelin' on his neck and helps in his trainin'. Later it can be changed to the smoother mane-hair rope. When made they should be twisted even and tight so they won't hang lifeless in the hand. They're usually 'bout one inch in diameter and made in six or eight strands. When usin' the mecate for reins, the reins should be pulled down and toward the rider's knee, not up or yanked.

Ropes

THE rope's a simple thing, but it's the most important tool of the cowboy. Without it there'd have been no cattle business. In the early days it was the only way to ketch and hold hosses and cattle; the only way to throw an animal for brandin' and doctorin'. Even now, with fences, corrals, and chutes, it's still a necessary implement. Ever' workin' cowhand's got a rope coiled below his saddle horn, and it ain't there for pretty. No matter what job was to be done, he'd look it over to see if it could be done with a rope and saddle hoss. Ropin's an art, the most difficult of all cowboy attainments, and an expert started learnin' while he was fryin' size, and kept practicin' till he'd sacked his saddle.

The word "lariat" is a contraction of the Spanish *la reata*, which literally means a "tie back." The term was originally used for a rope in picketin' hosses. Some Eastern folks like to say "lariat" and "lasso" because it sounds Western, but the cowhand called his rope jes' plain "rope." "Reata," or "riata" is 'nother Spanish word meanin' "rope," and is sometimes used, but usually it refers to a braided rawhide rope. Lariat may be used as a verb, as to fasten, or ketch with a lariat, but reata's never used as a verb, only as a noun. Some sections of the cattle country never used the word "lariat." California, for instance, don't like the word, but prefers "reata," or "lass rope."

The term "lasso" usually meant a hide rope, generally a long one with a runnin' noose. Mexicans introduced this name to the cattle range, although the word's not of Spanish origin, but comes from the Portuguese *laco*, which has a meanin' equivalent to "snare." Early in cattle-raisin' history cowboys began callin' a rope jes' plain rope. Out on the Pacific Coast, where they still use a lot of rawhide, they still say "lasso," but not in other sections except in fiction. In the Southwest where they mostly use a thirty-five-foot-length manila for ordinary ropin', a rope's a rope—without any fancy label. And when they swing a loop and ketch a critter, they "rope" it. They don't "lasso" or "lariat" it in spite of movie talk.

'Bout the earliest rope was the "skin" rope, sometimes called a "skin string." Made of plaited strips of rawhide, they were used first in Spain and Mexico. Buffalo hide was used in the early days. They're not so common now, as the braidin's becomin' a lost art. It held a good loop and handled well when throwed, since it was small for its weight. It was tough, though not as strong as some other materials, and was slower runnin' through the honda. It was strictly a dry-climate rope, and no good in wet weather. It was also a better rope for dallyin' than for tyin' fast.

Ropes are made of several different materials, and I'll try to tell you a little 'bout each of 'em. The "maguey" is a four-strand rope, of a scant three-eighths inch in diameter, made from the fiber of the century plant. American cowboys call it the "McGay." It's extry hard, holds a wide loop, and can be throwed fast. This is the fav'rite rope of the trick roper for fancy ketches, as the size of the loop's easy controlled. In wet weather they get so stiff you couldn't throw one of 'em into a well. These ropes are better for dallyin', as they break easy when tied hard and fast. For light work such as heelin' calves or ketchin' hosses in a corral, they can't be beat.

The "manila" is now the most common rope used in the ranch coun-try, as it can be bought cheap in any length and size at any supply store. It's made of manila fiber, constructed on three strands, and laid extry hard for strength and smoothness. Some ropers waterproof them ropes by mixin' beef tallow or Vaseline with melted paraffin, but cowboys of the dry country don't go to all this trouble because they figger the rope'll be wore out before it rains anyway. These ropes come in several diam-eters. The smaller ones are excellent for light ropin', and the heavier ones good for steer bustin' and other heavy work.

A good rope that's becomin' pop'lar's the one made of twisted linen thread. Like most fiber ropes, they're made of three strands. A good coatin' of wax worked in waterproofs 'em and makes 'em last longer. Unless well waxed they have a tendency to become soft and raggy, all of which creates some disadvantages in ropin'. They handle a heap like a rawhide rope, bein' stronger and faster if kept in good condition. These ropes are more expensive than some others, and as the cowhand likes to furnish his own rope some of 'em stick to the serviceable but cheaper manila or maguey.

Cotton ropes are used some in the range country, but are not common as ketch ropes. While they're smooth to handle, hold a good loop, and seldom kink, they're springy, stretch, and are both hard to set on an animal and hard to tie to the saddle horn. They're not as strong as other ropes and are better for fancy trick rope spinnin' than for anything else. A short cotton rope makes the best piggin' string for tyin' down, as it's easy to handle, soft, and don't skin the animal's legs. But a good roper never chooses the cotton rope for his heavy range work.

The hair rope's made of hosshair, either the tail or mane hair, or mixed. The tail hair makes a stiffer rope. Them ropes are never used as reatas because they kink easy and are too light to throw. They're therefore made short and used for hackamore reins, tie or lead ropes. Because a hair rope for this purpose has long been traditional, there's a tendency to call all hair ropes "mecates." In trainin' colts most trainers at first prefer the tail-hair rope because the stiffer hair ends against the colt's neck make him aware of its pressure. When woven of alternatin' black and white hairs, it's called a "pepper and salt" rope.

The "honda" is a knotted or spliced eyelet at the business end of a rope for makin' a loop. *Hondo* is Spanish, meanin' eye, and originally meant a receptable in a sling for holdin' a stone to be throwed. It's made of a small loop tied in the end of the rope itself, the rope here bein' protected with a piece of slick leather sewed 'bout the upper end of the loop so the rope won't burn through. This honda's best for the rope to "set" on an animal after the ketch. Some use a metal honda. The rope slides through this better, but it don't pull the loop taut 'nough to keep a strugglin' animal from freein' itself. Used for a head ketch on hosses, it can knock his eye out.

The home end of the rope can be tied in various ways to keep it from ravelin'. Sometimes a little noose is tied or spliced to make a "horn loop" when the rope ties hard and fast. A good roper's careful of his rope, as his ropin' ability often holds his job. He even takes it to bed with 'im to protect it from the weather. When not in use it's found in a neat coil tied by the horn string to his saddle. The first thing he learns is to properly coil his rope. It has to be coiled neat and even if it's to play out when throwed without gettin' tangled or fouled.

Ropes are made in different lengths, dependin' on the section used in and the work to be done. They also have diameters of various sizes, rangin' from a scant three-eighths inch up to a half-inch. Ropes for light work are three-eighths inch and for heavier work seven-sixteenths inch. In a country where the roper dallies, like California, they use longer ropes, sometimes bein' as much as sixty feet. The tie-fast man of Texas uses a rope of thirty or thirty-five feet, and contest ropers like an even shorter one, for it speeds up their work and shortens the distance to the animal to make his ties. Calf ropers, too, like a short rope of 'bout twenty-two feet.

Until a rope's limbered up it'll neither throw good nor coil well. New maguey and manila ropes're especially stiff. To take out the kinks and limber it up the cowboy fastens a chain to one end, attaches the chain and the rope to a couple of trees or fence posts. With a bar in a link of the chain he twists till the rope becomes tight. He leaves it stretched like this a couple of days. Or, he might fasten one end to a tree, the other end to his saddle horn, mount a good gentle hoss, pull the rope tight, and hold it a while. Sometimes he draws it over a flame to singe the whiskers off. After it's properly stretched and softened, a rope comes to life in the hands of a smooth roper.

Like ever'thing else in the cowboy's life, he's got a lot of slang names for his ropes. A rawhide rope's called a "skin line," "catgut," "skin string," or "gut line." His grass rope's called such names as "line," "clothesline," "string," "twine," "hemp," "manila," "fling line," "lass rope," "whale line," "coil," or "Tom Horn." He often called his lariat a "ketch rope," to distinguish it from other ropes. When a rope slipped through a roper's hand till it burned the flesh it was a "hot rope." When he throwed a loop intent on a ketch it was a "hungry loop," but if he missed he "wasted a loop."

The cowboy uses a rope for ever'thing. The short piece of cotton rope used for hogtyin' he calls a "hoggin' rope," or "piggin' string." At the wagon on roundup a rope's used to make a corral to ketch his hoss, and this is called a "cable." A rope used to fasten packs on a packsaddle is called a "lash rope," or "sling rope." A "lead rope" is a short rope used to lead a hoss, and is also used as a "tie rope." A "choke rope" is used by some Wild West show riders. When the hoss lowers his head to buck, the rope slips down near his jaws, allowin' the rider to steady 'imself as well as choke the hoss down. Also, there was the "picket," or "stake rope."

A rope had a lot of uses in the cattle country. Its first duty in the mornin' was to rope out the mounts to be rode that day. Out on round-ups where there wasn't any corral, ropes became the "cable" when used to encircle the remuda while riders roped out their mounts. A rope snubbed a fractious bronc to a saddle horn or a snubbin' post so he could be saddled or mounted. It pulled mired cattle from bogholes. When the chuck wagon hit quicksand or a bog in crossin' a river, the boys tied on and pulled by their saddle horns. As a cow whip an experienced hand could make a rope crack like a blacksnake, slip hair, and tear hide. He could kill a rattlesnake as far as his rope'd reach.

Many a load of wood was snailed into camp by rope and saddle horn. A rope furnished cowboy entertainment by ropin' wildcats, mountain lions, wolves, and bears. He used his rope to tie his bed, secure his packs, stake his hoss, and to fight grass fires by pullin' a drag. In a snow-storm a rope'd be his guide from his bunkhouse door to the stable or woodpile. And a rope was sometimes used to mete out justice in the ab-sence of judge and jury. The result was a spectacular warnin' to other hoss thieves and cattle rustlers.

Hobbles and Stake Ropes

TODAY hobbles come in handy only on rare occasions, but they were the part of a necessary equipment of the old-time cowhand. There's a lot of difference between ranch and range work. The modern cowhand on a ranch rides within a limited area of leased or owned land. The old-timer on the range before fences rode after cattle no matter how far they went. The old-timer didn't need hobbles when workin' at the home ranch because then his hoss, if not placed in a corral, was turned loose to be rounded up when needed. But when out on the range or travelin' through the country, he needed hobbles to fetter his hoss while campin' so he'd have a hoss to ride the next mornin' and still give the animal 'nough freedom to graze. When not in use, he packed his hobbles on the saddle, or looped 'bout the hoss's neck where they'd be handy when needed. When workin' with the roundup he'd toss 'em into the wagon.

There were many styles in hobbles. Some were homemade, others manufactured. The plains Injuns used a one-piece twisted rawhide pattern, and then there were the various carefully braided and ornamentally knotted or buttoned Spanish-California models and the more modern strap-buckle-and-ring, called a "figger eight." Some, made on a figger-eight base, were both hobbles and quirt combined. Yet the cheapest to make and the easiest on a hoss was nothin' more'n a ripped-up and folded gunnysack.

Many men used the government-style hobble, a leather cuff buckled 'round each foreleg above the pastern joint, the two cuffs bein' connected by a short length of chain which worked on a swivel. These gave a certain amount of freedom in grazin', but some hosses were smart and soon learned to travel by walkin' with the hind feet while makin' short jumps forward with the front. Such a hoss could travel several miles in a night, thus discountin' the value of hobbles to a certain extent. One way to break a hoss of this habit was to tie a rope on his hobble and the other end to his tail.

'Nother way to keep a hoss from travelin' at speed was to "sideline" 'im. This was placin' hobbles on the front and hind feet on the same side, the two bein' connected with a rope. The smart aleck who had learned to travel with a hoppity-skip with hobbles on both front feet would now be considerably handicapped and wouldn't be able to go far. Some men used the "cross-hobble" on such hosses. This meant hobblin' one front foot to a hind one on the opposite side. If the hoss was of a nervous type, this method was dangerous because it throwed 'im into a panic. If this happened, he'd fight the hobbles, throw 'imself, and be injured. The thoughtful cowhand would rather go back to camp "by hand" than have a good saddle hoss injured or spoiled.

The old-timer made his own hobbles from fresh beef hide or buckskin. These were simply wide bands of hide tied into cuffs at the ends with a center length twisted into a sort of rope as a substitute for the modern chain. A buttonhole and wooden button, or sometimes a crossstick, were used for the final knot. Most cowmen augured for the hobbles as against the stake rope because a staked hoss would graze in a circle and if left any length of time would have the circle grazed down till it'd be as bare as a farmer's feed lot, while a hobbled hoss could always find new grass. 'Nother argument was that a hoss trained for hobbles didn't fight and cut 'imself up when he got his feet into brush or wire. Also cowmen claimed that a staked hoss was forever gettin' rope-burned or crippled; on the other hand, many augured in favor of the stake rope. It was mostly a matter of opinion or experience.

In good tall grass a short hobble for the front feet would give the hoss plenty to eat, but if the grass was scanty a long side-line hobble was sometimes used. If it rained, though, and the hoss was side-lined with rawhide, he could walk right out of them hobbles because rawhide stretches when wet.

Some cowhands refused to pack heavy hobbles 'round. When they needed a pair they simply used a piece of half, five-eighths, or three-quarters inch sisal rope, and unstranded it 'bout five feet. For proper length most of 'em measured 'round their waist once and allowed two feet over. They took a single strand, doubled it, and tied the ends together like a seamstress ties her thread. Throwin' the knot end 'round the hoss's leg, he brought the knot and loop end back, twisted one 'bout the other four or five times, left 'nough to go 'round the near leg and fastened on the outside. The knot was slipped through the loop from the inside out, then laid over the lower strand, passed up between the strands and the animal's leg, comin' out between the two strands of the loop end.

Some cowhands used a chain hobble because they were easy to put on. This was the fastenin' of a short chain, 'bout two feet long, to the hoss's foreleg, the other end bein' left loose. This method of hobblin' wasn't commonly used, because the loose end struck the hoss's legs if he started to run, and besides causin' pain, often tripped and injured 'im. As long as he grazed slowly and merely dragged the chain, he could travel a distance in the night. This was 'nother point in their disfavor. When the hoss attempted to run or go somewhere in a fast walk, the chain was slung 'bout, bangin' his legs, and he stopped from pain. Frequently the skin was broken, and flies blowed the wound. Its disadvantages greatly outnumbered its merits.

"Clogs" were a crude but effective hobble. They were made by takin' forked sticks 'bout an inch and one-half or two inches in diameter and 'bout two feet long, and lashin' 'em with rawhide thongs. These were used only in the brush country. The brush was the brush hand's worst enemy, but he also made it serve many useful purposes. Such unsightly hobbles'd shock the plains cowhand, but the brush hand had never been as dudish as the plains cowboy. He went in for service instead of looks, both in dress and equipment. He knowed the brush soon tore up his clothes and scarred his leather. So, when he wanted to hobble his hoss, he didn't have any false pride, but used his handiest material, the brush he worked in.

One of the simplest hobbles to make, the cheapest and most practical, was the "sack hobble." It was made by pullin' the stitchin' in a reg'lar gunnysack, openin' it, then foldin' cross-cornered to make a triangle. Startin' at the center, it was rolled up and a four-inch lengthwise slit was cut 'bout the middle. Divided evenly, the hobble was twisted 'round itself three times to give space. One end of the sack was put 'round one leg and the two ends twisted together; then the other end was tied together securely with a couple of square knots. This kind of hobble was easy to make, and as strong as one ever needed. It wouldn't skin up or burn a hoss's legs as much as ropes and straps no matter how much jumpin' 'round the hoss did.

The "Scotch hobble" don't belong to the other hobble family. It was made different and served a different purpose. It was made with a large soft rope and looped 'round the hoss's neck where it joined the shoulders and was arranged so that a bowline knot lay back of one shoulder. The long end of the rope was then placed 'round a hind leg jes' below the ankle joint, the end run back into the neck loop and tied, jes' short 'nough so the foot, when the animal was standin', would be three or four inches off the ground. To keep the hoss from kickin' out of the rope, it was necessary to take an extry turn 'bout the ankle, or twist the rope back on itself. A half-hitch on the ankle would stay on, but as the cowhand says, "You'll play hell gittin' it off." This hobble was used to keep a hoss still while sackin' 'im out, gettin' 'im used to throwin' the saddle on, and other breakin' maneuvers. It's called a "Crow hobble" in the Northwest.

The stake rope was one of the oldest ways to fasten a hoss and keep 'im from runnin' away. Many cowhands preferred it to hobbles as bein' safer and givin' less punishment and more freedom. A hoss can't relax and roll if hobbled, and when allowed to graze he might learn to travel with 'em in a short time. If staked out, he could roll and feed nearby without anyone worryin' 'bout his takin' off across the country. Teachin' a hoss to be staked out was very simple if done correctly. For the first few lessons, it was better to play safe by tyin' the rope 'round the neck with a bowline knot, runnin' the end through the halter ring and fastenin' it to the anchor. It was a good practice to set the halter high up on his nose.

Stakin' was good trainin' for the hoss, and he'd soon learn not to be afraid of a trailin' rope, and he'd learn how to avoid gettin' 'imself tangled up. A few rope burns helped to teach 'im. The Southwest called it a "stake rope," while in the Northwest it was called a "picket rope." The latter section "picketed" his hoss; the former "staked out." A twenty-five or thirty-foot rope was used, as this gave the hoss 'nough freedom to graze and didn't pull 'im up too short if he started to run.

A special rope was used for stakin'. The cowboy wouldn't use his lariat for this if he could help it. Some used a halter, but usually the rope was tied 'round the hoss's neck. To do this an extry knot had to be made in the slip noose to prevent chokin'. This caused kinks and spoiled a lariat for ropin'. Besides, when a rope was dragged through the dew it became unfit for other use. When on the trail or roundup, the cowboy staked his night hoss handy. If the weather was good and no emergency was expected, he staked 'im without the saddle so the hoss could get more rest, but if expectin' sudden trouble the saddle was left on ready for quick action.

There were several ways to stake a hoss. Some used a halter, some tied the rope 'round the neck, and some 'round the forefoot, but the last wasn't common. Some tied the rope to a heavy rock or fallen log. This was called "loggin'," and since a log'll move it allowed the hoss more freedom and eliminated the danger of entanglements from more rigid stakin'. Tyin' to a bush was avoided, as sudden fright might cause the hoss to pull it up by the roots and take to the tules. Some liked to use a fallen tree limb with the branches still on it, as it made a noise when dragged and was harder for the hoss to pull any distance.

The most common way to stake a hoss was by usin' a stake or picket pin. This could be made of iron or wood, and driven into the ground.

When stakin' night hosses was the practice, picket pins were packed as part of the chuck-wagon equipment. Near the Canadian border they were called a "putto," from the French *poteau,* meanin' post. Short stake pins held surprisingly well because the pull on 'em was lateral. The picket pin has become a part of the cowboy's language, and when he left the country he was said "to pull his picket pin," and the expression "pulled his stakes" is now commonly understood ever'where. When a woman has a man bound by love ties, she's said to have 'im "picketed." In the Northwest it was "picket pin" and "picket rope"; in the Southwest it was "stake pin" and "stake rope."

If caught in a timberless country without a picket pin, and a cowhand had to camp overnight without hobbles, he dug a deep hole with his pocket knife. He tied a big knot in the end of the rope, stuck it in the hole and packed the dirt 'round it. His hoss would be there in the mornin' unless it rained to loosen the dirt. Sometimes he used a prairie-dog hole the same way. If his hoss was untrustworthy, he'd dig a trench in the shape of an *L,* and bury 'bout two feet of the rope's end in it. This was stronger'n the straight hole. It was surprisin' how well such a simple method would hold, but a gentle saddle hoss didn't pull much when he felt the rope taut.

The Remuda

THE Spanish word *remuda* is from the verb *remudar*, meanin' "to exchange"; *remuda de caballos* means "relay of hosses." The cowman uses the word to mean the extry hosses of each cowboy herded together and not at the time under saddle. The word's pronounced "remootha" in the Southwest, but most Texas cowmen merely speak of "the hosses." The remuda's to the Southwest what the "cavvy" is to the Northwest, though the Northwestern cowhand usually calls them hosses the "saddle band." "Cavvy" is a shortened corruption of the Spanish *caballado*, meanin' a "band of hosses." It, too, refers to the broken hosses maintained by a ranch.

Cut a cowhand a good string of hosses, and he'd take most any trouble that came. But cut 'im a bunch of plugs, and he shore wouldn't be workin' for that outfit long.

The number of hosses allotted to each man for his individual string, or mount, varied accordin' to the kind of country worked, the size of the ranch, and the work to be done. In the mountain country a greater number were required than on the plains. Generally seven to ten head might be considered an average mount. These consisted of mornin' hosses, afternoon hosses, among any of which would be a good rope hoss, a cuttin' hoss, a night hoss, and in trail days each man liked to have a good river hoss. Also, ever' man was allowed all the broncs he wanted to ride. Therefore, each man generally had several half-broke hosses in his mount. They were used on short rides and gradually broken, for in actual cow work a bronc was worthless. If the boss thought a hoss had the makin's of a good cow hoss, he tried to assign 'im to a rider he knowed would train 'im right. He knowed a man had to have more sense than the hoss if he was able to teach the animal cow sense. In his second year's work a green hoss was referred to as "last year's bronc."

A hoss usually went into the remuda when he was four years old. By the time he was six he was fairly well trained for cow work, but didn't reach his full period of usefulness till he was 'bout ten years old. Each year the remuda was culled of hosses too old for the best work. A good faithful hoss was pensioned for a life of ease and grass; the ordinary hoss was sold for farm work. Durin' roundup the life of the cow hoss was a hard one, but with each year he became better trained till he was too old for active duty. Their life in off season was one of ease. All they had to do was graze and run free.

In assignin' the hosses the same men rode the same hosses each year. There was no fixed rule as to that, but the boss felt that the men liked it better that way, did better work, and it was easier on the hosses. He sized the hands up accordin' to their ability and what he might use 'em for durin' the summer. Some ranches jes' held a choosin' match for the hosses. The choice rotated accordin' to seniority with the firm, and each puncher chose his string from the remuda of the ranch. His choice was final, and even the boss respected it. Of course, the foreman had first pick of the remuda in choosin' the hosses he wanted for his mount. Old hands had the next choice, and then the new hands in the order hired were given the pick of what was left. Each man's string of hosses was the same as his own while he was ridin' for the outfit. He had the say over 'em, and takin' a hoss out of his string would be the same as askin' 'im to quit. Cowboys who have worked at one ranch for years have been knowed to quit because some higher-up had come out to the ranch and decided they wanted to ride one of his pet hosses.

Each man realized that the hoss was his motive power and that his work was handicapped unless them hosses were in top condition. Because each man became acquainted with the characteristics and dispositions of the various hosses a string was never split. If a rider quit, or got fired, the hosses in his string weren't used till he came back, or another rider took his place. A rider takin' a new job had a string of hosses pointed out to 'im by the boss. He received no information 'bout 'em. Information was often taken as an offense, as it implied a lack of confidence in his ability. Any cowhand that interfered with 'nother man's hoss was askin' for trouble.

The rule of most remudas was that all hosses be geldings. These made the best cow hosses, as stallions fought and disturbed a peaceful remuda, and mares were bunch quitters, failures as saddle hosses, and a constantly disturbin' element. Some outfits used a bell mare in the remuda so that if the band spooked and left in a hurry, the men on night herd, or the wrangler in camp, would be warned. There was somethin' 'bout a belled mare that seemed to fascinate a bunch of geldings. While a bell helped the wrangler, most cowhands objected to it because it sounded too many false alarms and kept 'em awake at night. Anyway, most remuda-broke hosses settled down after a short run.

Outside the bell mare the old-time cowman never run mares with the remudas. Mares were like their human sisters. They were always wantin' to go places, and as Charlie Russell says, "There's always some gentleman cayuse willin' to see that she gets there." Mares were for raisin' other hosses and not for the remuda, as the other hosses were always fightin' over 'em. Nowadays the modern rancher rides a mare occasionally to see if they possess cow qualities. If they didn't have good cow sense and the makin's of a cow hoss, he didn't have to breed 'em.

Though a cowhand didn't own his own mount, it became his most prized possession. They loved the hosses in their string, and treated 'em well. They'd fight for their hosses as quick as for a friend. To take a hoss from his string'd make 'im quit an outfit quicker'n you could spit and holler howdy. The hardest experience the old-time trail hand had to bear was to ride his string up the trail and have the boss sell 'em with the cattle at the end of the trail.

When the work was over in the fall, the hosses were turned out to run the range for the winter to rest and heal their scars. They could forget for a while the wrangler on their tails ever' mornin', forget the rope corrals, and the hard workdays of roundups. Jes' before they were turned loose, the boss gave 'em a goin' over to check their ages, condition, feet, and how they'd stood the year's work. If he found one slowed up by age, with bad knees and feet from the jarrin' stops that go with cow work, he was either condemned or put on a pension. Cowhands didn't like to ride a hoss that was apt to stumble or fall when workin' because of old age and stiff joints.

Them hosses were replaced with younger ones that were broke to ride but had a lot to learn before makin' good cow hosses. If in a year or so of trainin' they still didn't show evidence of ability to learn, they were soon gotten rid of. But most range hosses ketch on kinda quick and by the third year were pretty good cow hosses.

Most cowmen wanted hosses of solid colors, browns, bays, sorrels, and duns, but no paints. The latter found little more favor in the average remuda than did a mare. Paints were the favorite hosses of the Western story writers, but they didn't meet with any favor in the cattle country. It was a rare thing to find one that developed into a cuttin' hoss, or a hoss fitted for any quick close work. They were mostly for show, and got to be pop'lar with town folks. A cowboy didn't mind havin' one in his string to use for a Sunday, or "gallin' " hoss, but when it came to workin' a herd, he'd rather have a solid color hoss with some breedin'. Like the old sayin': "All a paint's fit for is to ride 'im down the road."

When the hosses were turned out on the range in the fall, there was sometimes a few kept up to be used as winter hosses, and grain fed, so there'd be somethin' to ride when needed. Out on the winter range the remuda growed long coats of hair and looked in better shape than they really were. When driven up in the spring they were maybe weak and had to be fed hay before they could be rode for more'n a few hours. Their long hair caused 'em some worry and overheatin', but a few good sweatin's took care of that. The boys worked out a few cockleburrs from the hoss's mane and tail each time he was rode till these were all gone, and he was soon ready for the spring work again.

Some springs the hosses didn't come in so frisky or lookin' so good; this was after the winters they'd been through a siege of distemper. It was seldom fatal, but it left 'em lean, long-haired, watery of eye and nose, coughin', and too weak to work. It almost always resulted in a runnin' sore between and under the lower jaw; when this busted the hoss began to show improvement immediately. When there was an epidemic of this, the spring work had to be postponed. Both the cowboys and the owners dreaded a distemper epidemic.

When the hosses were drove up in the spring, the wagon boss was there to look 'em over. They constituted the tools of his trade, and he knowed his work could be no better than his hosses. He knowed, too, that in the fall his ability as a wagon boss would be judged by the condition of the hosses. Sometimes he made up his mind whether to take or reject a job of runnin' an outfit on the kind of hosses it owned.

Ever' hoss in the remuda had his name and ever' hoss was well knowed by ever' man in the outfit if he'd been on the payroll long. Ordinarily them names came from some peculiar markin', his disposition, or some occurrence in the hoss's life. Some of them names were printable, others not. With ever' hoss there was a history as individual as the hoss 'imself, and, though a cowhand might forget many incidents of life on the range, the names of his hosses and much of the history connected with 'em lived in his memory. A good cowboy could identify and rope out any hoss in the remuda by name as long as it was light 'nough to see 'im.

Cowhands workin' on roundup changed hosses ever' few hours because the work was hard on hosses and a change also helped rest the rider. "Changin' mounts" was mostly routine as he changed his circle hoss for his cuttin' hoss or rope hoss accordin' to the duty he was goin' to perform. Later, if goin' on night herd, he changed to his night hoss. There was always a few broncs in his string, and he worked 'em in rotation to give his other hosses a rest. He used them hosses on circle, and when he put his saddle on one of 'em, the changin' was a thrill producer. On cool mornin's a hoss always had a hump in his back, and when a crew mounted the first hosses in the mornin' you'd see buckin' all over the place. On one roundup so many were bein' bucked off that one cowhand remarked, "They was fallin' off like wormy apples in a high wind." Very often riders were afraid to tackle their broncs in the early mornin', but waited till the nooday change when their courage rose with the warmth of the sun. After things settled down they rode back to help hold the herd, while the cutters, on gentle cuttin' hosses, began their work.

Ropin' hosses from a remuda was a science, and had to be learned from experience. The job had to be done with extreme caution, for the average cowhoss was skittish and feared the swing of a rope, particularly when used by a man on foot. If a man ever attempted to swing a rope 'round his head like they do in rodeos, the chances were that some snortin' hoss would break through and stampede the whole bunch.

The roper had to do some figgerin' he hadn't learned at no blackboard. He had to figger the direction of the wind, its rate of speed, and how far astray the rope'd be carried while sailin' through the air, and the distance between 'im and the hoss. He also had to know how high in the air the loop would have to be tossed in rainbow fashion for it to lose momentum and fall over the hoss's head. He also had to calculate the movement of the hoss and determine which position the hoss's head would be in by the time the loop was sailin' through the air. With all them calculations in mind, the throw was made with one quick movement of the right arm.

When changin' mounts on roundup, three or four cowhands, each holdin' the end of a rope in their hands, formed a circle 'round the hosses. The tenderfoot couldn't understand why the hosses didn't run against the rope and jerk it from their hands. It was simply a matter of schoolin' that from the very first taught the hosses to respect a rope. A colt usually made its first acquaintance with the rope when branded. Later, when the bronc buster started teachin' a bronc good manners, he learned more 'bout the rope and avoided runnin' against one.

If a young hoss failed to respect a rope, and ran over it, he was apt to be stagin' his own downfall. The boss would have one of the best ropers on a good hoss, and when the bronc broke away from the remuda the cowman'd rope 'im by the forefeet, which meant a nasty fall for the hoss. It sometimes meant a broken neck, but that was preferred to havin' a hoss get the habit of runnin' away from the remuda when the men were changin' mounts.

The boss usually picked one or two of the top ropers to do the ropin' for all. Each man told 'im the hoss he wanted; then, knowin' each hoss by name, the roper proceeded to locate 'im in that circlin' bunch of hosses. Too many ropers excited the hosses, and ropes were apt to get tangled. Most hosses were rope wise and seemed to sense they were wanted. They hunted the middle of the bunch and stuck their heads between their front legs, givin' the roper no target. It was a job for a man with patience, but once a hoss was caught he came out meek 'nough.

It was a joy to watch a top roper send an accurate loop past a dozen tossin' heads, and over as many backs, to land over the neck of an animal in the middle of the band. It was also interestin', if the roper missed, to see how that wanted hoss would now dodge, twist, and turn to escape a second throw. He now knowed for shore he was wanted, and so did his companions, who realizing they were not wanted, pushed 'emselves between the roper and his intended victim, and did ever'thing they could to protect their companion.

Some hosses were inclined to pitch when saddled no matter how many years they'd been in service, especially in the spring when the grass got green, or on cold mornin's. Sometimes they were saddled and allowed to "soak" for a spell to forget their friskiness, but if a rider mounted without untrackin' his hoss there'd be some buckin' without that ten-second limit provided for rodeo contestants. Some riders would walk their mount 'round a bit when they saw a hump in his back. They didn't mind swallerin' their pride and walkin' a hoss 'round to make 'im change his mind, even if the boys were yellin' at 'im, "You're gonna walk that hoss plumb down pretty soon."

From the dawn of ranchin' the cowman has been dependent on the hoss for his work and transportation. He might brag 'bout his saddle, his boots, or his spurs, but it was his hoss that always came in for his big praise. His hoss became his pal, his constant companion with whom he talked as though with a human to break the lonely hours on the silent trails. Small wonder that the pride of ever' puncher was his hoss and that much romancin' was engaged in by 'im as he set 'round the campfire and told stories of the skill, ability, and almost human understandin' of his hoss.

The cowman usually called his hoss a hoss, or cow hoss, and this was the universal name for 'im, not "cow pony." A good cow hoss had to possess strength and intelligence, both well trained. He had a natural instinct for sensin' direction and detectin' danger, both day and night. He was game and would drop dead in the performance of his work if need be. He was well adapted to his place, tough and inured to the hardships of his life. His lightness of foot and quickness of motion fitted 'im for the work better'n any other type hoss.

Of necessity he was shore-footed and always had an eye for the trail. He had to have good feet, good limbs, heart and lungs, so he could have endurance, or bottom, and above all he had to have good sense. A good hoss had one eye for the cow ahead and one for the ground. He inherited that gift. If he fell, he was lost; such were eliminated. Nothin' on the range caused so many serious accidents as fallin' hosses; and of nothin' else was a cowhand more afraid, except bein' dragged.

There was as much difference in cow hosses as there was in cowboys. One hoss might look pretty much like 'nother to a stranger, but to a puncher ever' hoss had its own individuality. Real top hosses were as scarce in a cow outfit as top hands, but it was seldom a top hand was found without a top hoss. The work which showed up a top cow hoss was cuttin' and ropin'.

A hoss highly trained for cuttin' out cattle was called a cuttin' hoss, and he was the top-rankin' and most talked-of hoss in cow work. This coveted title came only after years of trainin' and experience, and the rider who could boast of such a hoss in his string was the envy of his comrades and the pride of the whole outfit.

When a good cuttin' hoss began his work, he was made to understand which animal was to be cut. He worked quietly till the animal was urged to the edge of the herd. Naturally the cow tried to stay with her companions, and here was where the cuttin' hoss proved his worth. A good cutter was both mentally and physically alert, possessed speed and action, and knowed how to use 'em. He must spin and turn faster'n the cow; and it took an expert rider to stay on, for he had to anticipate the hoss's turnin's to keep from gettin' spilled. All the work had to be done in such a manner as to excite the herd as little as possible. When the edge of the herd was reached, the animal had to be rushed to send it away from the herd, and the hoss and rider'd go no further'n necessary in order to save time and extry steps.

Durin' the open-range days most cuttin' hosses had several years of actual ranch work to their credit before they earned the distinction of bein' a top cuttin' hoss. Once a hoss gained that rep'tation, he didn't do much reg'lar ranch work but was saved for the important work of cuttin' cattle out of a herd.

A good rider on a good cuttin' hoss was able to go into a herd and cut out the wanted animal without chousin' the herd, because this would cause the cattle to lose flesh and that meant the rancher would lose money. One of the main essentials of a good cuttin' hoss was that he could work on a loose rein, it bein' used only when pulled up or stopped. Most good cutters needed no cuein' at all, but if his rider did give any help it was done with words, leg action, or a slight movement of the reins.

A cuttin' hoss which had a talent for stoppin' short in his tracks when gallopin' in one direction, changin' his direction, and instantly boundin' off on a new course was called a "peg hoss." He was highly valued by the cowman because he could turn on a button and never scratch it when a quick turn meant ever'thing.

'Nother high-type hoss in cattle work was the rope hoss. A man could learn to ride and do ordinary cow work in a short time, but to become good at ropin' required years of practice; yet no matter how expert a roper might become, he'd have small success without a good rope hoss. Mind, rope, saddle cinch, nothin' could be allowed a second's slack, or accidents would happen.

When we speak of rope hosses we don't mean the rodeo rope hoss, or any hoss that simply pounds after a calf, stops at the ketch, and backs up. Them hosses, like their riders, are professional, and highly trained for that purpose. They're not what you'd call all-'round ranch rope hosses.

To look at a ranch rope hoss he'd look a little droopy and unexcitable. He led a monotonous life heelin' calves in a corral all day, or draggin' 'em to a brandin' fire; or ketchin' and holdin' down heavier stuff for doctorin' or markin'. He went 'bout his business serenely like it was all in a day's work.

Many think that to ketch was all there was to ropin'. In ketchin' the critter the work'd jes' begun. Ropin' required the most skill and was the hardest and most dangerous of all cow work. When the roped animal was tied onto, slack had to be instantly taken and kept up. The cow at the other end of the rope wasn't asleep. A top ropin' hoss knowed when the rider took his rope down and what he wished. He'd go like a bullet to the left of the cow, but never past her. There he'd stay till the rider cast his loop; then he'd do his stuff, and he knowed when the throw missed. The slightest pressure on the rein caused the well trained hoss to set back, hind feet well under 'im, forefeet braced well out in front to receive the shock. The slightest pressure on the side of the neck with the reins caused 'im to whirl instantly to face the ketch.

A good rope hoss never allowed a cow to get a side run on 'im, nor did he allow an inch of slack to let the rope wind 'im up. Experience had taught 'im the consequences of such blunders. The instant the roped animal fell, the hoss'd pull against the rope, draggin' the dead weight 'long the ground. At a roundup where a large crew was workin', the top ropers and top ropin' hosses stood out above the rest. Some hosses were afraid of a rope, and so never made a good ropin' hosses.

In ever' remuda there were certain hosses knowed as night hosses, no matter what cowhand might inherit 'im for his mount. A good night hoss was invaluable. One of his chief requirements was good night eyes. The old-time cowhand selected his night hoss with a heap of care, for more depended on 'im than any hoss in his string. He had to be gentle, dependable, shore-footed, have keen eyesight and a sense of direction. Them tests usually came durin' a stampede at night in the rain, thunder, and lightnin', which called for all a hoss could give. In such runs the rider usually gave the hoss his head and depended upon his many senses to see 'im through.

He mustn't be high-strung, but must be gentle, unexcitable, and intelligent. He was never used except for night work, and durin' stampedes much depended on 'im. He held his rider's life in his ability to see, run, dodge, and keep his footin'. His ability to detect an animal in the dark was plumb uncanny. He'd see an animal strayin' from the herd and turn it back without bein' guided, and he could find his way back to the wagon on the darkest night. Many night guards have been rode by dozin' cowboys who, noddin' through the two-hour guard, set in the saddle on a hoss that needed no touch of the bridle rein, but jes' jogged the circle 'round the herd with faithful regularity, and put back ever' cow that made any move to escape from it.

A seasoned night hoss was likely to know within a few minutes when it was time for the rider to quit the herd. If he knowed, he tried to convey his knowledge by pullin' on the bits and shakin' his head. Some of 'em could be depended upon as certainly as readin' the stars. On the early day drives, if a cowhand had a good night hoss in his string, he valued 'im far above any other hoss he rode, because this was the hoss his life depended on at night. He not only packed the cowboy on his back, but had to do his seein' and hearin' in most cases. He had to know what to do in the dark no matter how stormy it got. Often when a herd would start to stampede a good night hoss was in front of 'em quicker'n St. Peter could slam the door in the face of a hoss thief, and he knowed how to handle 'imself in a stampede. When an old-time cowhand thought of what could have happened if it hadn't been for a shore-footed night hoss, it filled his old heart with love for that animal. He never forgot the name of any night hoss he'd rode durin' the many years he rode the range. He might not be the best lookin' hoss in his string, but he'd be the most dependable.

Unless an outfit was short-handed and the herd they was handlin' was jumpy and nervous from a run or two, each man unsaddled his night hoss before stakin' 'im out so that he'd get all the rest possible. But when the cattle were scary and the weather threatenin', the hoss was left saddled to save time in case of a run. A man's night hoss might be so well thought of that he'd name 'im after his best gal.

In the old trail days one of the most essential hosses was the river hoss, or swimmin' hoss. The steady, not easily spooked, night hoss was a necessity jes' as important as the cuttin' hoss, but the river hoss that loved to swim and knowed what to do in deep swift water was second to none; that alone put 'im in a class by 'imself. Not all hosses were good swimmers, and durin' them days when there were many rivers to cross, much depended on a good swimming hoss.

Them hosses had a special fitness for river work, for crossin' and re-crossin', for leadin' or drivin' a herd through the water, for anything that was to be done when water was high or deep or dangerous. They seemed to know where the water was swimmin' depth and where the bottom was firm and safe. Besides bein' strong, a good river hoss had to be gentle and never get excited when he got into a close place.

If a man had a good river hoss in his string, he'd stop and change to 'im before attemptin' to cross. He knowed that many a young cowboy had been buried near the banks of some river because he didn't have such a hoss in his string.

Most ever' ranch had a good, well built sensible hoss that was quiet and gentle 'round the place. He was dependable, and you could walk up to 'im in a pasture and put a bridle on 'im after you discovered the night hoss had escaped the corral, leavin' the outfit afoot for hosses. He could be used by the woman of the ranch if she wanted to go with her husband to some distant part of the ranch when he went to a line camp or a neighbor's, and had no fear of his runnin' away or pitchin'. He could be trusted to pack a dead bear over a trail that'd make a mountain goat nervous. Such a hoss was often used in an emergency. When the kids came 'long and they outgrowed their daddy's arms, them old steady hosses was the first ones they got their ridin' practice on.

"Talkin' hoss" was a subject that never growed old with a cowhand. If one could listen to the conversation of a bunch of punchers at work, he'd find two-thirds of it 'bout hosses. Bad hosses came in for a lot of talk, but the old reliable hosses came in for the fondest memories. They bragged on the merits of some hoss in their string and deplored the shortcomin's of 'nother. They'd sometimes do some tradin' and swappin', but there was always some hoss that money couldn't buy.

A hoss's intelligence and gentleness were developed in proportion to the extent of his contact with man. In the old days, when hosses were caught, saddled, and rode to be turned loose again without other handlin', it was natural that them qualities didn't show. It was due to their treatment, and not their disposition, that they got a bad name.

The Western hoss had an individuality and a self-reliance not often found in hosses raised in confinement. It wasn't necessary to guide 'em 'round treacherous holes when lopin' across prairie-dog towns, nor to look out for stones and such 'long the road. When he was led to a strange waterin' place he was mighty careful to satisfy 'imself that the bank wasn't boggy, and before he'd trust his weight in the mud he'd test it with one foot and then the other.

Really, to know hosses, how to care for 'em, keep 'em in good shape, and, at the same time, get the most work out of 'em was a heap more necessary to the cowboy than merely bein' able to scratch hell out of anything that wore hair.

The Wrangler

THE hoss wrangler never has stood very high in a cow camp. Even
though he was an important cog in cow work he's never gotten credit for
bein' more'n a chambermaid to the cook. One reason was, he was usually
a kid wantin' to be a cowboy, and wranglin' was the first step in his education. Ranch-raised kids knowed hosses before they did cows because
they was throwed more closely with 'em. Bein' too young and light for
heavy work, his first job was nursin' the hoss band. He had nothin' to do
with cattle.

However, the wrangler wasn't always a kid. Sometimes he was some
feller too old and stove up from rough ridin' to hold any other job, and
from his past loyal service he was kept on the payroll and put to wranglin'. But usually wranglin' was done by some kid breakin' into the cow
business, and he was selected for his good judgment and his likin' for
hosses. Bosses and owners watched his development carefully.

He was always the butt of the cowhand's rough hossplay and jokes.
This was part of his education, and it kept 'im from gettin' as full of
conceit as a barber's cat. The boss usually shoved the sorriest hoss on
'im. If he happened to draw one that looked good, the chances were it'd
be wind-broke, or have somethin' else the matter with it. His initiation
into the cow business was liable to be a pretty bitter pill, but if he had
the guts to take it he'd wind up by bein' a good cowhand.

While the cowhand looked down on 'im, forgettin' that this was probably how he got his own start, the boss didn't overlook his importance. A wrangler could make or break a remuda; he could keep the hosses in good condition, or set the outfit plumb afoot. One of the first lessons he learned was that a cow outfit was no better'n its hosses.

First of all, he had to love and understand hosses. He studied the hosses under his charge till he knowed each one like a mother cow knows her calf. As he hazed 'em from camp to camp on roundup, he got a mental picture of each hoss's characteristics and habits. By doin' this he was able to control 'em by his own brains, and not the speed of the hoss he rode.

Durin' spring roundups a lot of stray men joined the outfit and turned their string of hosses into the remuda. Now the wrangler had more strange hosses to study, addin' to his cares and worries, sometimes givin' 'im more trouble than a rat-tailed hoss tied short in flytime till he got acquainted with them new arrivals. Some bunch quitter might try to high-tail it for his home range, keepin' the wrangler ridin' the hocks off his hoss to break 'im of this habit. When he drove the hosses into camp with a complete remuda, he got no praise, but let a hoss be missin' and he'd shore ketch hell from the boss.

The wagon boss not only counted the remuda ever' day to check up on the wrangler, but he was careful to watch each rider to see how he handled his hosses. He knowed that the work of the outfit depended on the condition of the saddle band. Each cowboy was responsible for the condition of his own string; while the boss never interfered with that string, if he saw some cowhand's hoss developin' set fasts from some back-eatin' saddle, or noticed too many spur marks, unless he was exceptionally short-handed he ordered this puncher to saddle his private mount, and drift.

Many people thought wranglin' was a job for a lazy man; all that he had to do was ride 'round a bunch of grazin' hosses. But his job wasn't as easy as jes' settin' in the shade eatin' a can of peaches. He had plenty to do. If the hosses got restless and spooky, he was kept as busy as a little dog in high oats. And durin' his spare time he was rustlin' wood and water for the cook, helpin' wash and dry the dishes, or grindin' coffee. He didn't do much tree choppin', but he'd gather loose limbs, put his loop 'round the pile, and snake it to the wagon.

When the cook called 'im in the mornin' he took his time crawlin' out, stretchin' and scratchin' till he was shore the coffee was 'bout ready. If it wasn't quite ready he lit a cigarette from a coal of the cook's fire, and kept stallin' till he saw the bubblin' coffee runnin' down the sides of the pot. He wanted that first cup before goin' out to drive the hosses in.

When camp was moved, he helped pack the camp plunder and load the wagon. This roustabout job wasn't held to be very elevatin', and that was why the wrangler wasn't considered to amount to much. If he was good kitchen help, the cook usually took up for 'im, and saw that the hands didn't get too rough on 'im. He made it easier for 'im to get a little extry food, too, or snatch a little sleep.

If he had the makin's of a good wrangler, the boss took a personal interest in 'im. Any kid that took his job seriously and learned his business thoroughly was apt to receive some favors. A good wrangler studied the disposition of each hoss and kept an eye on them likely to give trouble. He'd head his hosses out in the same direction when leavin' camp, and would drive 'em to open country away from timber, even if he had to go farther. Hosses saw shadows in timber, and got pretty spooky. Flies and insects were in timber, too, and if it was "cat" country cougars were apt to be hangin' 'round.

A good wrangler tried to teach his hosses remuda manners, such as standin' in a rope corral, even when ropes were whistlin' through the air. A single rope held by three or four men to form a corral would hold the hosses, for the first thing a range hoss learned was respect for the rope. He didn't forget the burns he'd received when roped and throwed for the first time. If some hoss hadn't yet learned his lesson, and broke out, the boss nodded to a smooth roper, who picked up this break-away's forefeet and gave 'im a heavy tumble. It might break his neck, but the boss figgered he'd rather have 'im dead than spoilin' the other hosses.

Because too many ropers excited the hosses, one or two top ropers snared the ones the hands called for. There wasn't any rope twirlin' over the head, but each roper tossed some big flat loop like the hooley-ann. The wrangler set nearby on his hoss, waitin' for the rope cable to be dropped so he could haze his hosses back out to grass. He learned to love all his hosses, and didn't want help for fear someone would get rough with 'em. When movin' from camp to camp he preferred to drive 'em 'imself. Extry help was liable to crowd 'em too much.

Most outfits used but one wrangler, and he was responsible for the hosses at all times. In the early days some of the bigger outfits, however, used two men for the hoss band, a day wrangler and a nighthawk. The day wrangler had charge of the saddle band from sunrise to sunset; the nighthawk stayed with it durin' the night to keep it from strayin' or mixin' with the other remudas of the big open-range roundups. He was the feller that was said to have "swapped his bed for a lantern." He drove the hoodlum wagon, or bed wagon, when camp was moved durin' the day, but he could lay back on the bedrolls and snatch a little sleep while his team followed the chuck wagon ahead.

If the nighthawk had learned his business, he loose herded his hosses, and didn't hold 'em close and ride 'round 'em all night. This wore out his mount and gave the remuda no chance to feed or rest. Hosses held better in a rough country. On the flats they were apt to drift. However, if he was in a rough country he didn't let 'em scatter too much, or some wise old bunch quitter might graze innocently 'round a hill and then flag it for home. Some of them wise hosses, when they left the band, didn't leave 'nough tracks to trip an ant, and in a country of canyons and hills he was as hard to find as a fly in a currant pie. A remuda that stayed together was much less trouble than one which was always splittin' up and strayin' apart.

On a still, dark night with no stars or moon showin', it wasn't easy to find the hosses, especially if the grass was short and the hosses had to graze over a lot of ground to get their bellies full. If it was too dark to see any trail or sign, the wrangler would stick one finger in his mouth to wet it, then hold it up. The side that was cold would show 'im the direction from which the slight breeze was comin'—that was the direction to take in search of the hosses, for in warm weather they always grazed against the breeze.

If the feed was good a hoss'd fill up in a couple of hours. Then he'd lie down and sleep a while. If the ground was rough he'd sleep standin' up, and he'd never lie down with his feet uphill. However, hosses didn't all sleep at the same time, and there was always some who seemed to do their grazin' at a long trot.

Hosses didn't give much trouble before midnight. They spent this time browsin' 'round and cat nappin'. When they woke up from a snooze they were easy spooked. After four o'clock they rested and slept again till herded to camp.

When a hoss started strayin' from the bunch, the wrangler rode 'round 'im and hazed 'im back. His hoss could see better at night than he could, and usually did the job if he was properly trained. The saddle band was kept clear of camp at all times so the work of the roundup wouldn't be interfered with. The wrangler brought 'em in to camp at reg'lar intervals so the riders could have fresh mounts. Usually this was at mornin', noon, and night, but if the weather was hot and the work hard he might bring 'em in oftener, for while no hoss is overworked, no hoss is overlooked.

He rounded 'em up in the mornin' so the riders could rope out their circle and cuttin' hosses. Then at noon he brought 'em in so they could change for the afternoon work when they came in for dinner. Many of 'em needed their ropin' hosses by this time. Jes' before sundown he brought 'em in again to let the riders rope out and stake their night hosses. After that he drove 'em out to water and good grass for the night, and, if there was a nighthawk, he would take over.

As he loped 'round 'em to bunch 'em and bring 'em in, he took an inventory by name, color, or disposition to see if any were missin'. If it happened one wasn't in the bunch, he tried to think up an alibi, but no matter how good the excuse it didn't set well with the boss. The remuda was seldom crowded into a run when driven in. He tried to round 'em up and get 'em to camp with as little chousin' as possible. Certain hosses always took the lead; some of the younger ones followed, nippin' and kickin' at their companions, but the old steady, less frisky wise ones were always found in the drag.

Maybe some night the sky was soggy with rain when the day wrangler brought in the band, and the nighthawk went sloshin' through the mud to rope his hoss. Before he could get a rope on this drippin' hoss he'd taken a roll in the mud. Then he had to bog 'round for a mesquite branch and scrape the mud from his back before he could saddle. By the time this was done his own feet were caked with gumbo till they were the size of loadin' chutes.

Slippin' into his fish, he finally mounted and drove the band back out to the prospect of spendin' eight hours in a wet saddle, pelted by a cold rain without a chance to roll a smoke. As he set his hoss, watchin' the band, or ridin' 'round 'em to let 'em know he was on the job, he was hopin' nothin' would happen to spook 'em into a run, and longin' for daylight when he could drive 'em into camp again. Sometimes the night was so black the bats all stayed home. On such nights he had to keep his ears open, and ride by instinct.

When fresh hosses were caught next mornin' he hazed the rest back out to grass. If he was the only wrangler, he let 'em quiet down again before he went back to camp to eat a bite and augur with the cook. If camp was to be moved, the wrangler helped pack and load the wagon while the cook was washin' the dishes and pourin' his dishwater over the coals. He drove the hosses on the trail to the next camp. Maybe he had a mouth organ to entertain 'imself with as he rode, with one knee crooked over the saddle horn, or perhaps he jes' rode 'long dreamin' of the day when he'd be a full-fledged cowhand.

Cow Critters

MAYBE the most interestin' thing I can tell you 'bout the cattle of the plains are the various names by which they are knowed to the Westerner. The cowman originated many technical distinctions in speakin' of cattle. No matter what the sex, it was a "calf" when it was "born," "dropped," or "come 'long." If a male, and reserved for breedin' purposes, it became in turn a "yearlin' bull," a "two-year-old bull," a "three-year-old bull," a "four-year-old bull." If not so reserved, it was castrated and became a "steer yearlin'" for a year and then a "steer" till he was full growed, when he became a "beef." On the other hand, a female after her first year became a "heifer," then a "two-year-old cow," and so on successively till she also went into the "beef" grade. A spayed heifer was called an "open heifer." Any steer or cow over four years old was called a "beef." When the cowman used this word as a verb, it meant to kill an animal for food. Cattle below three years of age were said to be of "short age." Young cattle 'bout two years old and beginnin' to fatten were called "pony beeves," while grown cattle were referred to as "grown stuff."

Yet in spite of all them distinctions, the cowboy, when speakin' of cattle, more often used the word "cow," and by this he meant ever'thing from a sucklin' calf to a ten-year-old bull. Animals of exclusive feminine gender were called "she stuff," or if an individual was pointed out, the sex was designated as "that three-year-old heifer," or "that line-backed steer." "Critter" was 'nother word he used to designate cow as a general term; and 'nother common reference to general range stock, which might include yearlin's, bulls, steers, weaners, cows with calves, and dry cows, was "stuff." Followin' his distinction still further we find that he was apt to call a cattle ranch a "cow ranch," but seldom spoke of the range as a "cow range."

The ranchman spoke of cows as "head," as "I have three thousand head on this range." Speakin' of cattle grouped together, he referred to 'em as a "bunch," while he called a group of hosses a "band." In usin' the word "stock" or "livestock," he used the word "bunch," as a bunch of livestock," and in this case "band" was incorrect.

A cow carryin' an unborn calf was called a "heavy cow," and calves born durin' the season were referred to as the "calf crop." A calf which lacked a little of bein' a year old was called a "short yearlin'," and one eighteen months old or older was called a "long yearlin'." A calf raised on skimmed milk was referred to as a "pail fed," "skimmy," or a "churn dash calf." Calves old 'nough to wean were called "weaners."

Some ranchers used a system of "blabbin'" their calves when they found some lusty calf was still nursin' an emaciated cow after he should have been weaned. This "blabbin'" was done by fastenin' to the nose of the calf a thin board, six by eight inches in size, at the center of one of the long edges. He could graze, but was shorely weaned. Them boards were called "blab-boards," or "blab-board weaners." A "spike weaner" was also used, and this was a circle of wire spikes fitted 'round the calf's nose and used with a halter, the spike band bein' like the bosal of a hackamore. Durin' brandin' season when cows were seekin' out their calves in the confusion, this gettin' together was called "mother'n up."

A scrubby calf that hadn't wintered well and was anemic from the scant food of the cold months was called a "doggie," also spelled "doby," or "dogy." Although the word was commonly used in the West and understood by all cattlemen, there has, in recent years, been some controversy over its origin. One version is that, durin' trail days, when it was discovered that the northern range was good cattle country, especially for fattenin' beef, there arose a demand for young animals. It became the custom to call these "dogies," especially yearlin' steers, to distinguish 'em from steers that were fat 'nough for market. 'Nother version is that the term originated in the eighties after a very severe winter had killed off a great many mother cows and left a number of orphan calves. Grass and water was too heavy a ration for them little orphans, and their bellies very much resembled a batch of sourdough carried in a sack. Havin' no mother whose brand could establish ownership, and carryin' no brand themselves by which they might be identified, them orphans were put into the marverick class. The first to claim 'em was recognized as the owner, no matter where they were found. One day on roundup a certain cowman who was tryin' to build up a herd drove a bunch in from the river bottoms.

"Boys, there's five of them dough-guts in that drive and I claim ever' damn one of 'em!" he yelled excitedly.

Durin' that roundup all orphans became knowed as "dough-guts," and later the term was shortened to "dogie" and has been used ever since throughout cattleland to refer to a pot-gutted orphan calf. This term has recently become pop'lar through Western songs, yet too great a percentage of singers call it "doggie" as if they're singin' 'bout a pup. The Mexcian name for dogies and scrubby calves was "sanchos," and sometimes used by the American cowboy.

Sometimes stockmen purchased calves in the corn belt, or from farmers, and shipped 'em to their ranches to restock their range. These were called "bucket dogies." An orphan calf was also called a "leppie," "poddy," or a "buttermilk." A poor, runty, and weak calf was called an "acorn calf," or "deacon." Usually he was "fat in the middle and pore at both ends" so he was called a "windy," or "wind belly," and was said to be "grass bellied," "kettle bellied," or "potbellied." Poor calves were said to be "jes' a ball of hair," "ganted," "slab-sided," or said to have "bed-slat ribs."

From the beginnin' of the cattle industry in America, the cowboy exercised his talents in givin' the animals in his charge nicknames and slang titles.

The old "longhorn" of the brush country of Texas were called "brush splitters," and "cactus boomers." Them of the coast country of Texas were "coasters," or "sea lions" that "come right out of the Gulf" of Mexico. A "scalawag" was a worthless "cutback," generally wild and old, while a "mossy horn" was a Texas longhorn steer six years or more old, whose horns had become wrinkled and scaly. He was also called a "mossback," or "wrinkle-horn." Because of the many twists and turns of the horns of the old longhorns they were sometimes called "twist-horns," or "spraddle-horns," and because of their long horns and speed they were often referred to as "horned jackrabbits." A breed of cattle with short horns such as the Herefords are knowed as "shorthorns."

Outlaw cattle of the brush country were called "landinos," from the

Spanish word meanin' "crafty" or "sagacious." A common reference to all wild cattle was "wild stuff." To get them cattle to the "shippin' pens" or "shippin' points," it was often necessary to resort to "neckin'." This word, on the range, had an altogether different meanin' from what the young city feller knows it to be. On the range an unruly cow, or one inclined to prefer the faraway places, was often "necked" or tied to a more gentle animal, the animal used for this purpose bein' called a "gentler." This was especially resorted to in the days of the longhorn. After the two animals had worn 'emselves out tryin' to go in different directions at the same time, the wilder one was 'nough subdued to move 'long in company with its fellers. A good neck animal was valued highly by its owner. "Kneein'" was also sometimes resorted to. This was the splittin' of the hide on a wild steer 'bout an inch and a half between the knee and the ankle on one foreleg, and cuttin' a small leader, or tendon. When the steer was turned loose, he found that he could walk, but his runnin' days were over. This operation was also called "doctorin'."

A "maverick" was an unbranded animal of unknown ownership. The story of the origin of this word has often been told, but often incorrectly, so I'll repeat the true version here. It was derived from Samuel A. Maverick, a Texas lawyer, who took over a bunch of cattle for a debt before the Civil War and placed 'em in charge of a Negro on the San Antonio River 'bout fifty miles south of San Antonio. The Negro, knowin' nothin' of cattle and havin' taken to the bottle, failed to brand the increase, and let 'em roam wild over the country. In 1855 Maverick sold his entire outfit, brand, range, and all the rest to Toutant de Beauregard, a neighbor ranchman. It was a kind of blanket deal, and accordin' to the terms Beauregard, in addition to the number of cattle present and actually transferred in the trade, was to have all the others, branded and unbranded, that he could find on Maverick's range. Beauregard, bein' a careful man, then, it is said, started a systematic search, a roundup that covered not only Maverick's range, but several counties, and wherever his men found an unbranded cow-beast they claimed it as a "Maverick," put Beauregard's brand on it, and drove it in.

It was under these circumstances that the term "maverick" became applied to unbranded cattle. The term spread over the entire cattle country, and found such common usage that it's found its way into our dictionary. "Orejano," from the Spanish *oreja,* ear, literally meanin' an eared animal, or "long-ears," as meanin' not earmarked, was also used in the sense of maverick, but used mostly in California, Oregon, and Nevada. An unbranded animal, especially a calf, was also called a "hairy dick."

"Bueno" is a Spanish word meanin' "good," but durin' the open-range days in the Southwest it was also used as a cattle term, and meant that the animal called thus was "good" in that it had not been claimed by anyone at the roundup, and that its brand couldn't be found in the brand book. Such animals were "good" pickups because they were supposed to get by brand inspectors at shippin' points and market centers.

A case of theft at Springer, New Mexico, in 1895 against three men who had shipped a trainload of such cattle to Cheyenne, Wyoming, proved the pop'lar use of this term. At this time New Mexico was a Territory, and the judges of the courts were men from the East. Defendant witnesses swore that the defendants, accordin' to their knowledge, had bought so many head of "buenos" from a certain party. The judge, bein' unfamiliar with the word, called for expert testimony on the meanin' of the term and learned that an animal of unknown ownership was commonly called a "bueno." Some of the noted brands of the West were so well knowed that their animals could stray a thousand miles from home and their identity could be determined by the brand, and consequently this animal could not be a "bueno." The term was applied only to animals bearin' brands that were unknown in that section.

Cows without horns were called "muleys," "bullheads," or "can't hook cattle." Bein' handicapped in defendin' herself from other cattle, she bedded down at night on the outside edge of the herd, away from the horned stuff. Comin' thus under the cowboy's personal observation as he circled the herd, she was either cussed or called somethin' endearin' by 'im. The cowhand didn't like to drive muley cattle because they jammed together, suffered from the heat, and lost more weight than horned cattle. Then, too, they caused 'im to use the greatest patience. 'Nother name given 'em was "pelon," from the Spanish meanin' "bald." "Dehorn," used as a verb, meant to remove the horns from cattle. Cows that had been dehorned were also said to be "snubbed."

An animal with droopin' horns was called a "droop horn," and the word "mocho" was also sometimes used. This was from the Spanish *demochar*, meanin' "to decapitate, to cut off, to be cropped or dishonored." An animal which had lost part of its ears or tail was also a "mocho." When ticks had undermined the supportin' cartilages of an animal's ear, causin' it to droop, this animal was spoken of as a "gotch-ear."

Cattle which have been drove out of canyons onto the plains durin' a roundup were called "windies." Them cattle were usually contrary and hard to drive, and by the time they'd been gotten out of the canyon, they, the hosses, and the cowboys were 'bout exhausted—hence the name. Wild stock that ranged high in the cedar brakes were called "cedar brakers"; them of the mountain country were "mountain boomers," and a scrawny steer of the timbered country was called a "blackjack steer." The word "Cimarron" is Spanish, meanin' "wild, unruly." The Mexican used it in referrin' to an animal that ran alone and had little to do with his own kind. Literally it signified one who had fled from civilization and become a fugitive. It was therefore also used in speakin' of a human who was "on the dodge."

Cattle that were shipped or drove to the corn belt for fattenin' before marketin' were spoken of as "feeders," or "poverty cattle." Weak stock that hadn't wintered well were referred to as "hospital cattle"; a weak cow was also a "rawhide," and a "Nellie"; a scrawny, poorly developed animal was a "rusty," "rough steer," "scrag," "cull," "shell," "scrub," or "cutback." A "downer" was a cow that after a drought or a hard winter, was too weak from undernourishment to stand. Ever' time she attempted to move faster'n a walk she'd fall and have to be "tailed up." Such animals were said to be "on the lift." The term "down steer" was used in speakin' of an animal off its feet in a stock car. When the cattle began to fatten and put on flesh they were said to "put on tallow," or were called "warmed-up stock." Long-legged thin cattle were said to be "leggy."

Speakin' of cattle bein' "locoed" meant the result of feedin' on the toxic loco week. An animal addicted to it would run about frantic and crazy, as though intoxicated." Such animals were said to be "weedy," or to have the "grass staggers," while animals sick from eatin' sage were said to be "saged." An animal with screw worms was spoken of as a "case of worms," while one sufferin' with the "lump jaw" (actinomycosis) was said to have the "big jaw." It was believed by old-time cowmen that "splittin' the tail" would prevent "black leg," a disease common among cattle. "Hollow horn" was a run-down condition in cattle pop'larly ascribed to hollowness of their horns. As a cure a small hole was bored in the horn. From this practice the old sayin' "he ought to be bored for the hollow-horn" originated, meanin' that the one spoken of was a person who seemed to be feeble-minded.

A sexually imperfect female calf born as a twin with a male, and as a rule sterile, was called a "free martin." Cattle not thoroughbreds were called "cold-blooded stock," while thoroughbreds were "hot bloods," or "pures." To "warm the blood" was to place purebred bulls with inferior cows for breedin' up the stock. This was also called "gradin' up." "Line breedin'" was the breedin' of cattle of the same strain, usually to secure descent from a particular family, especially the female line.

Bulls come in for their nicknames too. The old-time cowboy would use any word to avoid callin' a spade a spade in the presence of ladies. In earlier times "bull" was a word unsuited for parlor use, but today we're not so modest, and we hear "throwin' the bull" on ever' hand. The cowboy, in the presence of the opposite sex, would often refer to a bull as an "animal." He also used the Spanish word *toro*. When he spoke of an animal "bullin'" on 'im, he meant that it balked or refused to move. An old bull whose horns were clipped and broken from many fights was called a "stubhorn." He often spent his time rubbin' them horns on rocks and trees, attemptin' to sharpen 'em for the next battle.

An animal which jumped over or crawled through fences was knowed as a "breachy" or "fence crawler." Sometimes such animals were "canned," that is, had a can tied to their necks to prevent fence breakin'.

To hold a herd of cattle on a new range till they felt at home was called "locatin'" 'em. To keep 'em scattered somewhat and yet herd 'em was called "loose herdin'." To hold 'em in a compact mass was "close herdin'." Cattle were inclined to remain in a territory with which they were acquainted. That became their "home range." Yet there were always some that moved farther and farther out, seekin' grass and water. These became "strays," the term bein' restricted to cattle, however, as hosses, under like circumstances, were spoken of as "stray hosses," not merely "strays."

Cattle would drift day and night in a blizzard till it was over. You couldn't stop 'em; you had to go with 'em or wait till the storm was over, and follow. Such marchin' in wholesale numbers was called a "drift," or "winter drift," and if the storm was prolonged it usually resulted in one of the tragedies of the range. The cowboy made a technical distinction in reference to the number of them animals. The single animal or a small bunch were referred to as "strays"; but when a large number were "bunched up" or "banded up," and marched away from their home range, as long as they stayed together the group was said to be a "drift." Drifts usually occurred in winter in an effort to escape the severe cold winds, but it could also occur in summer as the result of lack of water or grass because of a drought, or as an after-math of a stampede. Drifts usually happened only with cattle, for hosses had 'nough sense to avoid 'em, and to find shelter for 'emselves.

The wholesale death of cattle as a result of blizzards, and sometimes droughts, over a wide range of territory was called a "die-up." Followin' such an event there was usually a harvest of "fallen hides," and the ranchers needed skinnin' knives instead of brandin' irons. Cattle were said to be "potted" when "blizzard choked," that is, caught in a corner or a draw, or against a "drift fence" durin' a storm. Cattle which died from them winter storms were referred to as the "winter kill." When cattle in winter stopped and humped their backs up they were said to "bow up." This term was also used by the cowboy in the sense of a human showin' fight, as one cowhand was heard to say, "He arches his back like a mule in a hailstorm." Cattle drove to the northern ranges and held for two winters to mature 'em into prime beef were said to be "double wintered."

Cattle brought onto a range from a distance were called "immigrants." Them new to the country were referred to as "pilgrims." This word was first applied to the imported hot-blooded cattle, but later was more commonly used as reference to a human tenderfoot. Hereford cattle were often called "white faces," or "open-face cattle," and the old-time cowman gave the name of "hothouse stock" to them newly introduced cattle. Because Holstein cattle weren't a beef breed, they were rarely seen on a ranch, though one might be found now and then for the milk supply. The cowboy called this breed of cattle "magpies." A "cattaloe" was a hybrid offspring of buffalo and cattle. "Dry stock" denoted, regardless of age or sex, such bovines as were givin' no milk. A "wet herd" was a herd of cattle made up entirely of cows, while "wet stuff" referred to cows givin' milk. The cowboy's humorous name for a cow givin' milk was a "milk pitcher." Cows givin' no milk were knowed as "strippers." The terminology of the range, in speakin' of "dry stock" and "wet stock," was confusin' to the tenderfoot. The most common reference to "wet stock" was with the meanin' that such animals had been smuggled across the Rio Grande after bein' stolen from their rightful owners. The term soon became used and applied to all stolen animals. "Mixed herd" meant a herd of mixed sexes, while a "straight steer herd" was one composed entirely of steers, and when the cowman spoke of "mixed cattle," he meant cattle of various grades, ages, and sexes.

In the spring when penned cattle were turned out to grass, this was spoken of as "turn-out time," or "put to grass." "Shootin' 'em out" was gettin' cattle out of a corral onto the range. When a cow came out of a corral in a crouchin' run she was said to "come out a-stoopin'." To stir cattle up and get 'em heated and excited was to "mustard the cattle," and the act was called "ginnin' 'em 'round," or "chousin' 'em." After a roundup the pushin' of stray cattle of outside brands toward their home range was called "throwin' over."

A cow rose from the ground rear end first. By the time her hind-quarters were in a standin' position, her knees were on the ground in a prayin' attitude. It was when she was in this position that the name "prayin' cow" was suggested to the cowboy. They were said to be "on their heads" when grazin'. "On the hoof" was a reference to live cattle and was also used in referrin' to cattle travelin' by trail under their own power as against goin' by rail. Shippin' cattle by train was called a "stock run." A general classification given grass-fed cattle was "grassers."

When a cowboy spoke of "dustin'" a cow, he meant that he throwed dust into her eyes. The cow, unlike a bull or steer, kept her eyes open and her mind on her business when chargin', and a cow "on the prod" or "on the peck" was feared by the cowhand more than any of his other charges.

The Injun's name for beef was "wohaw," and many of the old frontiersmen adopted it from their association with the Injun on the trails. The first cattle the Injuns saw under the white man's control were the ox teams of the early freighters. Listenin' with wonder at the strange words of the bullwhackers as they shouted "Whoa," "Haw," and "Gee," they thought them words the names of the animals, and began callin' cattle "wohaws." Rarely did a trail herd pass through the Injun country on its march north that it wasn't stopped to receive demand for "wohaw."

"Tailin'" was the throwin' of an animal by the tail in lieu of a rope. Any animal could when travelin' fast, be sent heels over head by the simple process of overtakin' the brute, seizin' its tail, and givin' the latter a pull to one side. This throwed the animal off balance, and over it'd crash onto its head and shoulders. Though the slightest yank was frequently capable of producin' results, many men assured success through a turn of the tail 'bout the saddle horn, supplemented sometimes, in the case of cattle, by a downward heave of the rider's leg upon the strainin' tail. Such tactics were resorted to frequently with the unmanageable longhorns, and a thorough "tailin'" usually knocked the breath out of a steer, and so dazed 'im that he'd behave for the rest of the day. It required both a quick and swift hoss and a darin' rider. When cattle became more valuable, ranch owners frowned upon this practice and it was discontinued, at least when the boss was 'round. When the cowboy used the word "tailin's," he meant stragglers.

"Bull tailin'" was a game once pop'lar with the Mexican cowboys of Texas. From a pen of wild bulls one would be released, and with much yellin' a cowhand'd take after 'im. Seizin' the bull by the tail, he rushed his hoss forward and a little to one side, throwin' the bull off balance, and "bustin'" 'im with terrific force. Rammin' one horn of a downed steer into the ground to hold 'im down was called "peggin'".

Colors of cattle came in for their special names. An animal covered with splotches or spots of different colors was called a "brindle" or "brockle." A "lineback" was an animal with a stripe of different color from the rest of its body runnin' down its back, while a "lobo stripe" was the white, yeller, or brown stripe runnin' down the back, from neck to tail, a characteristic of many Spanish cattle. A "mealynose" was a cow or steer of the longhorn type, with lines and dots of a color lighter'n the rest of its body 'round the eyes, face, and nose. Such an animal was said to be "mealynosed." "Sabinas" was a Spanish word used to describe cattle of red and white peppered and splotched colorin'. The northern cowboy called all the red Mexican cattle which went up the trail "Sonora reds," while they called all cattle drove up from Mexico "yaks," because they came from the Yaqui Injun country, or gave 'em the name of "Mexican buckskins." Near the southern border, cattle of the early longhorn breed whose coloration was black with a lineback, with white speckles frequently appearin' on the sides and belly, were called "zorrillas." This word was from the Spanish, meanin' "polecat." "Yeller bellies" were cattle of Mexican breed splotched on flank and belly with yellerish color. An animal with distinct coloration, or other marks easily distinguished and remembered by the owner and his riders, was sometimes used as a "marker." Such an animal has frequently been the downfall of the rustler.

Countin' each grazin' bunch of cattle where it was found on the range and driftin' it back so that it didn't mix with the uncounted cattle was called a "range count." The countin' of cattle in a pasture without throwin' 'em together for the purpose was called a "pasture count." The counters rode through the pasture countin' each bunch of grazin' cattle, and drifted it back so that it didn't get mixed with the uncounted cattle ahead. This method of countin' was usually done at the request, and in the presence, of a representative of the bank that held the papers against the herd. Them notes and mortgages were spoken of as "cattle paper."

A "book count" was the sellin' of cattle by the books, commonly resorted to in the early days, sometimes much to the profit of the seller. This led to the famous sayin' in the Northwest of the "books won't freeze." This became a common byword durin' the boom days when Eastern and foreign capital were so eager to buy cattle interests. The origin of this sayin' was credited to a saloonkeeper by the name of Luke Murrin. His saloon was a meetin' place for influential Wyoming cattlemen, and one year durin' a severe blizzard, when his herd-owner customers were wearin' long faces, he said, "Cheer up boys, whatever happens, the books won't freeze." In this carefree sentence he summed up the essence of the prevailin' custom of buyin' by book count, and created a sayin' which has survived through the years. "Range delivery" meant that the buyer, after examinin' the seller's ranch records and considerin' his rep'tation for truthfulness, paid for what the seller claimed to own, then rode out and tried to find it.

When a cowhand said that a man had "good cow sense," he meant to pay 'im a high compliment. No matter by what name cattle were called, there was no denyin' that they not only saved Texas from financial ruin, but went far toward redeemin' from a wilderness vast territories of the Northwest.

21

Swingin' a Wide Loop

THE first use of the word "rustler" was as a synonym for "hustler," becomin' an established term for any person who was active, pushin', and bustlin' in any enterprise. Again it was used as the title for the hoss wrangler, and when the order was given to go out and "rustle the hosses," it meant for 'im to go out and herd 'em in. Eventually herdin' the hosses was spoken of as "hoss rustlin'," and the wrangler was called the "hoss rustler." Later, the word became almost exclusively applied to a cow thief, startin' from the days of the maverick when cowhands were paid by their employers to "get out and rustle a few mavericks." In the beginnin' this practice of ropin' and brandin' any calf not at the time followin' its mother was not considered stealin', but legitimate thriftiness. Calves of this kind were considered anybody's cattle.

Them same cowboys soon became interested in puttin' their own brands on motherless calves to get a start in the cattle business. They figgered they could "steal a start" the same as their boss, but as soon as the cowboy began takin' a few for 'imself the ranch owners looked upon this practice as stealin'. Yet many ranchers, who wouldn't condone theft in any form, sent out their cowhands to do a little maverickin' at so much per head.

When the cowboy saw how easy it was to build up a herd for his boss, he began wonderin' why it wouldn't be jes' as legitimate and a lot more profitable to 'imself to maverick on his own hook. The trouble with 'im was that he was in too big a hurry to become a big cattleman, and started "runnin' a maverick factory" by killin' the mother to get the calf.

In the early days of Texas, cattle were so plentiful and wandered over such a wide territory that maverickin' was more or less legitimate cow huntin', and an honest game. Some men jes' naturally hate to see anything go unbranded whether it was theirs or not, and bein' the critter didn't look jes' right to 'em without a brand, they were most apt to plant one on, and sometimes the brand didn't always fit.

An old sayin' of the early range was that all a man needed to start a brand of his own was "a rope, a runnin' iron, and the nerve to use it." The struggle for existence on a fierce frontier developed nerve; ropes and runnin' irons were cheap, and cow thieves developed till rustlin' became quite an industry. The rustler was given such titles as "brand burner," "brand blotter," "brand blotcher," "brand artist," "long rope," or "rope-and-ring man," and he was said to "have a sticky rope" "pack a long rope," "throw a big loop," "swing a wide loop," or was "handy with the runnin' iron." One accused of stealin' was said to be "careless with his brandin' iron," "His calves don't suck the right cows," "His cows have twins," "His cows have a calf ever' wash day," "He don't keep his twine on his tree," "He keeps his brandin' iron smooth," "He rides with an extry cinch ring," or "He's too handy with the rope."

Stealin' unbranded cattle was the easiest, less dangerous, and therefore the most pop'lar. Brand changin' was easy botched, and often left telltale results that might cause the brander to be invited to be the guest of honor at a string party, and mighty few men wanted to ride under a cottonwood tree to look up at the leaves. It took a heap of skill to change a brand successfully, and the average cowhand wasn't expert 'nough to fool a real cowman very long.

Because the cattlemen themselves knowed ever' trick of the cow thief, the rustler had to be smart 'nough to outwit 'em. He knowed that his very neck depended on his cunnin'. His constant danger sharpened his wits, and by reason of 'im bein' the aggressor he did a heap of thinkin' 'bout the cattleman, much more'n the cattleman did 'bout 'im. He was an adventurous soul to start with, and the excitement of the game was what he liked most. He was usually honest in most other ways, and in the early days tried to take calves from them who wouldn't be hurt too much by the loss.

The practice of "burnin'" cattle, that is, of alterin' brands so that the old part and the new would form a perfect and quite different brand, was raised to an art by some experts. He had to be mighty skillful to deceive not only the average stockman but also the shrewdest and most expert cowman among 'em. The rustler's greatest nemesis was the stock detective, a man with nerve and a thorough knowledge of cows, hired by the cattle associations to trap and run down them thieves.

Once a man got the taste of the easy money of rustlin', it was as hard for 'im to quit as it was for a loser in a poker game. He had to be mighty wary to survive. He never knowed when he might pick up a "marker" that would be his downfall. Them "markers" were animals of distinct coloration or other marks easily distinguished and remembered by the owner and his riders. Caught with one of them with his worked-over brand was 'nough to turn a cottonwood tree into a court. His captors considered his neck too damned short and used a rope to stretch it.

He did most of his stealin' from the big ranches, and most of the settlers were in sympathy with 'im, especially if his thefts were against Eastern or foreign owners. One cause for rustlin' bein' profitable in the early days was the remoteness of the law. And it was hard to get a nester jury to convict 'im, for most of them jurors were not past takin' a few mavericks 'emselves. When the big owners took matters into their own hands, it developed into wars such as the Johnson County War, of Wyoming. The difficulty of convictin' rustlers in court was why so many necktie parties took place before the rustler had a chance to see a lawyer.

Most rustlers started out in a small way. He was usually some feller who became tired of workin' for thirty dollars per month while seein' his boss growin' rich. He first perhaps squatted on a little land and bought a few head of cattle for an excuse of bein' there. In ridin' over the range he saw no harm in puttin' his brand on a "slick" or two because he knowed other men who'd gotten their start that way and were now looked upon as solid citizens. Havin' gotten away with the first few thefts, his appetite was then whetted for ownin' a herd large 'nough to make 'im independent. This was where he made his big mistake, for it was a rare case when one was satisfied with the gradual buildin' up of a herd. And once he was placed under suspicion he was watched, and sooner or later the smartest of 'em slipped up.

The rise and development of the range stock-raisin' industry opened the gates of opportunity to many enterprisin' Western men of loose ideas 'bout the rights of property. The conditions that have run with the business from its beginnin' have been very favorable for the operations of them who regarded as a dead letter that part of the Tenth Commandment that tells us we shall not covet our neighbor's ox. In years gone by, the number of men regularly engaged in this stealin' of range cattle was so large that their operations was raised almost to the rank of an established industry.

Winter was open season on the rustler, for then he was the busiest. Dodgin' range riders, he rode through the grazin' cattle, pickin' up big calves that had been missed durin' the summer and fall brandin'. There were many ways of stealin' cattle. On circle durin' roundup, he could push some unbranded and likely lookin' cattle back from the drive to be picked up later to run his brand on. If he got into the business in a serious way, and wasn't satisfied with jes' brandin' unbranded cattle, he'd pick and register a brand that one or two of his neighbor's brands could be worked into.

One method of stealin' was the use of the "slow brand." It was against the law to mutilate any brand, and the law required the registration of ever' brand in the county of its origin. A man who blotted a brand and put 'nother in its place might be afraid to put his new brand on record. He simply run it, trustin' to get the cattle out of the county at first chance. Such a brand was called a "slow brand." Unrecorded brands were also called "maverick brands." A thief could easily hold an animal on the range with one of them unrecorded brands till he was able to drive it off. In case suspicion was aroused, there was no records to connect 'im with the theft.

Takin' an unbranded calf, ear-markin' it with the mother's ear-mark, and turnin' it loose unbranded was called "sleeperin'." The ear-mark was used as a quick means of identification. Thus durin' roundup, when ranch hands saw such an animal, they'd naturally take it for granted that it'd been branded when it was ear-marked, and leave it to roam. If the calf passed the notice of them ranch hands, the thief returned when the calf was weaned, and slapped his own brand on it. Then he changed the ear-mark to go with his brand, and the new ear-mark would be one which destroyed other ear-marks, such as the "sharp," or the "grub."

Some rustlers, if not hurried, "pick" their brand. This was done by pickin' tufts of hair in the lines desired with the aid of a jackknife. It was seldom used except to get an animal out of the country, as it was only temporary. The "hair brand" was easier and more common. This was made by holdin' the hot iron against the animal jes' long 'nough to burn the hair and not the hide. The rustler usually ran the owner's brand, and by the time the hair growed out again, effacin' the sign of the brand, he had the calf out of the country and could then put his own brand on it.

The rustler knowed cows and their motherly instinct and took this into consideration. Mother cows and their calves, on becomin' separated, backtrack for miles to reach the spot where each had last seen the other. Because of this instinct, he was forced to wean the calves he stole before he applied his brand. In doin' so, he used many different methods. He might "sand" the calves, that is, put sand in their eyes so they couldn't see to follow the mother. The calf was then drove off to a distance, and by the time he reached his destination he was weaned.

'Nother method employed by the rustler was to "hotfoot" the mother, that is, burn her between the toes with a hot iron, makin' her feet too sore to walk, thus makin' it hard to follow her calf.

Sometimes he cut the muscles that supported the calf's eyelids so they'd droop closed. Thus unable to see, it would be separated from its mother, and would bawl his head off for a few days. Bein' unable to return to its milk supply, it'd grope 'round for food and soon become weaned. The muscles healed in time, but the lids always drooped slightly, and them calves were referred to as "droop-eyes." Most rustlers avoided this method because a droop-eyed animal created suspicion.

Occasionally some rustler followed the brutal practice of splittin' the calf's tongue so it couldn't nurse. When the calf was weaned, them "tongue-splitters" put their own brand on it.

Mighty often the man followin' this dangerous industry made genuwine orphans of the calves by butcherin' the mother. Pinnin' crape on the kid this way was 'bout the quickest if he was in a hurry. He could drive the mother into the brush, shoot her down, cut out her brand, and drive the calf away.

Some ranchers, in tryin' to trap a smart rustler, would pick out some choice unbranded animal and place a small brand on the animal's belly. This was called a "decoy brand." Then this otherwise unbranded animal would be turned out on the range with the hope that it'd tempt some cow thief. Also, they might slit the leg skin of a yearlin' and insert a dime or a quarter, which would be proof 'nough if this animal was found wearin' 'nother's brand. But them ruses were rarely successful because it took mightly little to arouse the suspicions of the rustler, for he was usually as smart as the rancher. All ranchers used their utmost talents to create brands that couldn't be altered. But none of 'em ever succeeded, because there never was a brand that couldn't be changed in some way by a clever rustler.

Corrals of some friendly small rancher, or them of the larger ranches placed at a distance from headquarters and seldom used except in roundup season, were often used by the rustler for a temporary holdin' of stolen cattle till they could be pushed out of the country. These were called "roadhouses."

A good rustler could change the old brand into a new and entirely different one by addin' lines, numerals, curves, and symbols with a piece of hot telegraph wire, a cinch ring, or a runnin' iron. Or, again, he might use a wet-blanket process whereby a scrap of wet woolen blanket was laid over the old brand and a hot iron applied to it, through the blanket. This changin' of brands was called "workin' over brands," but a botched job was mighty mortifyin' to any rustler.

A runnin' iron was made in the form of a straight poker curved at the end and used much like the free style of writin' on a blackboard with chalk. In the seventies Texas passed a law forbiddin' its use. This was a blow aimed at the brand blotter, whose innocent single iron didn't tell no tales if he was caught ridin' across the range with it tied to his saddle. The law made an object of suspicion the man found with a single runnin' iron, and he was sometimes obliged to explain to a mighty urgent jury.

The rustler then found that he could use a cinch ring by heatin' it and holdin' it between two pliable sticks such as green twigs from trees. Also, it was easy to hide in his saddle linin' or some other convenient place. Later, and best of all, he discovered that telegraph wire or balin' wire could be used to make a better brand. It could be curved into any shape he wished to use and could be quickly folded and hidden in a small place. It could make a brand that easily melted into the old scars of the cow's present brand. The smart rustler discovered that, no matter how cleverly done, to place his brand over the old brand left a telltale mark. The scar would peel off and show that it had been tampered with. The clever rustler bent his wire so that the new mark it made would simply be an addition to the old lines without coverin' the old lines of the brand. Some brands were so cleverly done that the only way to prove that it'd been tampered with was to skin the animal and read the inside of the hide.

If the rustler, while at his fire workin' over a brand on an animal, was approached by a rider in the distance, he waved 'im 'round. In cowboy language this meant that he waved a hat or other object in a semicircle from left to right, and in the sign language of the plains it meant that the one approachin' was not wanted and had better stay away if he didn't want to stop hot lead. The sight of a lone man, with a downed animal and a fire meant only one thing, and it was dangerous to investigate too closely, for the rustler usually packed a Winchester, while the rider, if he packed any iron at all, usually had a sidearm.

Occasionally women became implicated with rustlers. Them women were called "Cattle Kates," this name bein' taken from "Cattle Kate Maxwell," whose real name was Ella Watson. She was hanged with Jim Averill for cattle stealin' in Wyoming in 1889 at the beginnin' of the Rustlers' War. Though history didn't prove her to be a thief, her name has gone down as such, and she was certainly associated with one.

In the early days of the unfenced range, when the big ranches were run by Eastern and foreign capital and absentee owners and the country was full of mavericks, it was easy to steal yourself into the cattle business. With the crowdin' of the range and the organization of stock associations with their stock inspectors, it got to be harder and harder. But there's always someone who thinks he can get away with it, and cattle are still bein' stolen, jes' like banks are still bein' robbed in spite of the fact that the James boys have been dead for many years.

The modern cow thief operates with a truck. Their spy will locate a herd to be raided, study the country and the pasture of the cattle. At night a truck like a movin' van is drove near the fence and the long end gate let down. The fence is cut and the selected cattle rounded up. 'Bout a half-dozen of the choicest steers are cut out and hazed toward the cut in the fence. Then they're drove as quietly as possible into the truck. The truck is drove without lights till they're well away and only turned on when they're clear of the section.

Most modern rustlers are jest' meat thieves. They steal a steer or two, butcher 'em, and sell the meat to some town butcher shop which asks no questions. Them thieves are careful to destroy the hide by buryin' it in some out-of-the-way place. He usually safeguards 'imself further by cuttin' the brand out of the hide and the ears off to destroy the ear-marks. A hide so cut is said to be one with a "stovepipe hole" because it resembles a tent with a stovepipe hole cut in it. He does ever'thing he can to hinder the identification of a hide by its rightful owner in case it's found. When a man kills an animal that belongs to someone else, either for food or for sale, he's said to "slow elk it," and such animals are called a "slow elk" or "big antelope."

Ridin' the High Lines

Some folks think that because a man wears a pair of boots and a big hat he's bound to be a cowboy. This kind of thinkin's one of the things that gives the cowboy such a wild name. In the early days there was a lot of men runnin' the range that wasn't cowboys. The West was also a grazin' ground for gunmen and desperadoes because they liked the freedom of a new country. Study the lives of any of the old Western desperadoes and you'll find mighty few of 'em actual cowboys, though the cowboy has had to suffer for 'em.

Many of 'em didn't even belong to the West, but were foaled in the slums of Eastern cities, came from penitentiaries, or from the armies of the Civil War, and had flocked west because there was a longer distance between sheriffs. Most of 'em came to dodge a strangulation jig in some other section of the country.

Them fellers hived up in town, not the range. The range was too lonesome for their breed. To read some magazine stories on the West, or to see the movies and TV, you'd think the thieves and killers was so thick they had a bill of sale for the whole damned country. The good citizens didn't like this breed, and most of 'em died young. A mighty few of 'em got a chance to quit this life in bed, with a preacher hoverin' over 'em and a doctor takin' their pulse count. When they was put to bed it was with a pick and shovel, usually with a pill in their stomach they couldn't digest, and there wasn't nobody there to let 'em down easy with their hats off. There wasn't many tears shed at a Boot Hill buryin'.

Most of them old gunmen lived a life that'd make some of them scary yeller-backed novels look like a primer. Their past was plumb full of black spots. They spent their time tryin' to show how wild and wicked the West growed her men, and you'd never find 'em settin' on their gun hand. That hog-leg hangin' at their side wasn't no watch charm, and they didn't pack all that hardware for bluff or ballast.

A man who wore his guns low didn't do much talkin' with his mouth. He was mighty short on conversation. He knowed that high talk led to gettin' leaded. He mostly talked in quiet tones because his nerves were always under control. They had to be. His finger might have the trigger itch, and maybe he had no more conscience than a cow in a stampede, but he was wise as a pack rat all the same. He liked a shade start, and wasn't too good to get you from a sneak if he thought he could get away with it, but the West's code of fair play put hobbles on most of his coyote work. The West still has men who've got a sensitive disposition and who're impulsive with a gun, but the old-time hell-on-wheels is a thing of the past. He either wiggled his finger once too often, or else the better citizens took all the slack out of his rope.

When a gunman saw the leadin' citizens of some town takin' down their ropes, he got a sudden hankerin' to sniff Gulf breeze, and rolled his tail south, or he headed in the direction advised by Mister Greeley. When he hit the breeze for a healthier climate, he didn't stop for no kissin', and maybe kept some sheriff ridin' the hocks off his hoss. When he seemed settled in some town for a few days, he kept his eyes on the horizon like he was expectin' some sheriff to bulge up on 'im. Maybe the town ahead didn't look like no health resort as long as a certain sheriff spread his blankets there, and he'd keep his hat well down over his eyes till he found out if they had the same sheriff they had a few years back.

Sometimes he packed a pair of them bring-'em-close glasses, and when he saw a posse on his trail he started fixin' for high ridin'. Or when he was ridin' the trail and looked over his shoulder to see a sheriff-lookin' man followin' 'im, it shore had a stimulatin' effect on his rate of travel. Sometimes the sheriff got close 'nough for 'em to swap lead, and then there'd be 'nother hoss race. Together they stirred up more dust in five minutes than Noah's flood could've settled, and they didn't pay no more heed to distance and fatigue than a steer does to cobwebs.

The old-time range man wouldn't have felt completely dressed without a gun hangin' at his side. He'd packed one so long he felt plumb naked without it and would've caught cold. But, contrary to pop'lar opinion, he didn't pack that iron for the purpose of killin' men. There were wolves and snakes to be killed, and crippled stock or mad cows to be shot when a gun meant a matter of life or death. There were times, too, when it was needed for givin' signals of distress when help meant a lot. The one time he hated to use it was for a mercy shot when his hoss fell and broke a leg. The early-day cowhand needed it in the days of Injun raids, and later when rustlers got bold. He might wear it all his life and never need it, but when he did he needed it bad, and it was kinda embarrassin' to be caught short.

Later the more modern cowhand found little use for guns. His trigger finger would've gone to sleep for lack of exercise. Even the old-timer seldom had to be lookin' over his shoulder at anybody on the trail, or have any fears of sheriffs and warrants.

But life, accordin' to the pulp-magazine cowboy, was jes' one long battle. He'd shore have to draw down good wages to burn up all that powder with cartridges at the price for which they sold. Had all their killin's actually taken place in such a thinly settled range, the survivors would've been as scarce as hiccoughs at a prayer meetin'.

I hate to take all the so-called romance away from the cowboy, but the cowman never packed two guns like they do on TV and in the movies and pulps. In real life he packed only one, and that was all there was any need for. He didn't need all that ballast to keep 'im in the saddle. The old-time professional gunman sometimes packed 'nough hardware to give 'im kidney sores, but the man who packed the most guns was considered the biggest coward in camp. It was a rare case where two guns had any advantage over one, and the man who could really use *one* was scarce. Also, when among strangers, he had to be mighty careful with the motion of both hands. He was kinda handicapped in doin' the little things other men could do. 'Bout the only advantage of two guns was the threat of an ace in the hole, or as a show of force when a lone man stacked against a crowd. A gunman "lookin' for someone" might bog 'imself down with all this weight, but the cowhand had ridin' and ropin' to do, and he rode light unless there was war in the air and he was drawin' fightin' wages.

In real life the average cowhand would run his bootheels over, side-steppin' trouble, but when he did fall from grace and stampede to the wild bunch it wasn't long till he was jes' two jumps ahead of a sheriff. And once he started ridin' the high lines, he couldn't quit no more'n a loser in a poker game. He was sometimes forced to ride over trails that'd make a mountain goat nervous and in a country so rough an ordinary man couldn't find his saddle seat with a forked stick.

Many a long-rider got mighty tired of usin' his back for a mattress and his belly for a coverin' before he could find an open trail out of the country. He spent so much time bellyin' through the brush he was as weary as a fresh-branded calf. All this layin' among the willows and waterin' at night wasn't from choice, but if he didn't know you for a friend you couldn't get close 'nough to 'im to borrow a chaw. Most men didn't like history too near home, but a man of this breed was usually kept on the end of a runnin' iron till he couldn't settle long 'nough to call any place home.

Back to them pulp writers. They'd have us believe the cowboy spent one day in the saddle and twenty-nine in the saloons, shootin' up the back bars and fillin' up the town's Boot Hill. Thus the Eastern reader got the idea that he was a man quick to shoot, one who held life cheap while paintin' the town red. He was a man who stole cattle from his employer, bulldozed inoffensive people, was a bold, bad man, and a holy terror at all times.

But cowboys weren't such lawless bein's as they've so often been painted. They were hardy, fearless, and reckless products of the condition by which they were surrounded, but not vicious as a class. Their life was one of hardship, isolation, and self-denial, yet through it all, loyalty to the interests of their employer was steadfast; and whatever might be the privations of their occupation they met and endured 'em uncomplainingly.

Many of these stories 'bout the West have their gunman packin' a nickle-plated gun with a fancy ivory stock, but he shunned a bright gun in real life like he would a swamp, because the sun shinin' on it would give 'im away like a shirtful of fleas, and make 'im as prominent as a new saloon in a church district. He usually packed a .44 or .45 single-action Colt with a blue steel barrel and a plain cedar stock.

Neither did the cowman, in real life, whittle away his gun makin' commemorative notches of his victims, in spite of the way romance wants it. A few professional badmen might carve some scallops for the sake of brag, but with ever' notch they shortened their own lives, for sooner or later some other flannelmouth would have 'im fingerin' music out of a harp for the rep'tation it'd bring 'em.

Maybe some story has the hero "firin' six shots so rapidly that the report blended into one continuous roar." How them romancers can imagine! In the first place, men of the West never packed but five beans in the wheel. The hammer was always down on an empty chamber. He did this for safety to ensure against accidental discharge of the gun while in the holster, because of the hair-trigger adjustment of the gun. Gunmen have too much respect for guns to take unnecessary chances, and a man who packed six cartridges in the cylinder of his gun, as one said, "Jes' didn't know dung from wild honey." If he couldn't do the job in five shots, it was time to get the hell out of there. As for the "continuous roar," common sense shows us that the old single-action couldn't humanly be cocked fast 'nough for such rapid shootin'.

Of course, fannin' a gun could fire bullets pretty fast, but this trick was seldom used in real life. Fannin' was done by holdin' the gun in one hand in the usual way and strikin' the hammer back repeatedly with the heel of the other hand, thus bringin' the hammer to a full cock. If the trigger was removed, held down, or tied down, the hammer wouldn't stay cocked, but as the hand continued with a rapid circular motion to strike the hammer again, it fell and fired the shot. Maybe fannin' makes good readin', and a heap of gun fanners have shot their way through the pages of romance, but when a man's life was at stake he didn't depend on the inaccuracy of such shootin'. The stunt's interestin' in theory, but of doubtful practical value. When a large-caliber gun was fired, the recoil after each shot caused it to buck up into the air. Though it's possible to work an unloaded gun fast in this way, in actual shootin' the gun won't stay still to be slapped, at least not long 'nough for accuracy.

Maybe, too, you read in some story how a man used the butt of his six-gun for a club in a saloon brawl. It shore makes me wonder why he wastes all this time and motion reversin' his gun to club a feller when he could comb that same hombre's hair with the barrel, and still be ready to shoot in case his skull was ivory. The West never used the butt for a club because the barrel was more potent, quicker, and a lot safer. This is what he called "buffaloin'."

Again, no old-timer gettin' the bulge, or drop, on a man and wantin' to disarm 'im would for an instant think of askin' his captive to do what modern tale writers require 'im to do, to "hand over your gun, butt first." The old-timer knowed that "butt first" meant a finger in the trigger guard, and that a quick snap of the wrist would spin or flip the gun with the muzzle pointin' forward and a bullet borin' into 'im. Chances are that before he could reach for the gun he'd be wingin' his way to St. Peter to take harp lessons. The old-timer jes' ordered his enemy to simply drop his gun, together with his belt, and back away from the spot where they fell.

A fav'rite theme of romancers is speed on the draw. It's true some gunmen who lived by the gun practiced in makin' their draw faster, and used all manner of methods to make this trick easier, such as special holsters, filed sights, and such, but mighty few cowboys lost any sleep over such matters because he didn't figger on gettin' into fast gun work. In the first place he wasn't gunnin' for nobody, and nobody was gunnin' for 'im. He could always skin a gun fast 'nough to do what shootin' he did on the range.

Mighty few real cowhands like gunplay. They rarely practiced fast draws and the fancy tricks of the gun fighter. If they did, it was jes' for the fun of it and to get used to the feel of a gun. With the professional gunman it was different. He had good reason for practicin'. To the tale writer, not the historian, is due the commonly believed windies as to the uncanny speed and deadly accuracy of all cowboy shootin'.

The real gun fighter had nothin' but contempt for the gun fanner, and the fanner had small chance to live against the man who took his time and pulled the trigger once. Unless a man was mighty quick with a gun, he'd better stay out of fast company. It was a fatal weakness to reach and fumble. Such a case of "slow" was a quick way to take his place with the angels. Like the old axiom, "Fingerin' that gun you're totin' ain't motion, it's suicide."

In real life the average cowhand was only an ordinarily good shot. Others, with talent and practice, became good at it. Even then they wasn't like the cowboy in fiction who always hit the enemy "right between the eyes." It's uncanny how the fiction cowboy can shoot the gun out of the villain's hand and never take aim. Now, a gun barrel makes a mighty small target. Jes' try hittin' a hangin' rope sometime and see how easy it is to miss. It's true that if you're at close range you can hit a man in the middle where he looks biggest without takin' aim, but if you're at some distance you'd better aim if you want to live long 'nough to pull another trigger.

Maybe a real gunman's scars was a reg'lar war map, and if all the lead he'd had mined out was in 'im at the same time he couldn't walk uphill, but at the showdown he was as cool as a skunk in the moonlight. It was the coward with a gun that he was skeered of. He knowed that the feller he had to watch was the one whose finger trembled on the trigger.

Only a fool spent his time makin' the town smoky, for there was always someone willin' to scratch an itchin' trigger finger. A heap of the cowhand's troubles happened in some saloon after he'd filled up on fightin' whisky, and when there was any shootin' somebody was apt to buck out in smoke with sawdust in his beard. Sometimes friends took sides and there'd be a reg'lar feud, and at the end the town's undertaker'd be ridin' high on the wave of prosperity.

And speakin' of Western stories, it's kinda refreshin' to run across one that ain't filled with blood and barroom battles. Most of 'em make you think the cowboy's biography would have to be tallied on asbestos paper, and writers seem to forget that there's plenty of action and romance in the West without fillin' their stories with booze, bullets, and badmen.

If the average cowhand did use a gun in a fight, and he was at close range, he preferred to use it to buffalo his enemy. Partin' his hair with a six-gun barrel might leave 'im with a knot on his head that'd sweat a rat to run 'round, but he'd eventually wake up and you wouldn't have to be ridin' the coulees and waterin' at night. Ridin' the owl-hoot trail didn't appeal to 'im. Like the old sayin', " 'Nother man's life don't make no soft pillow at night," he knowed that the folks who have to ride at a high lope miss all the fun 'long the trail.

More men in the West have been killed bluffin' with their guns than was ever killed because they didn't have one on. The West's code shore made it tough on a man who shot an unarmed man, and its sense of fair play demanded an even break. A man who packed a gun jes' for show or because it was customary, but who couldn't use it, was shore adoptin' a careless way of committin' suicide. Some folks think it takes nerve to be a gun fighter, but nerve is jes' a case of which end of a six-gun you happen to be lookin' at. The winner in a gun fight was the man who took his time, and shunned tricks and grandstand play like he would poison; and the one who kept the bridle on his own temper always shot the truest.

Flannelmouths

In the early days some of them old-time long-haired, man-eaters would wild up for the benefit of a tenderfoot audience, and orate plenty savage of their bold, bad deeds. They'd brag 'bout bein' the worst he-demon of the plains and doin' their damnedest to fertilize the West's rep'tation for bein' wild and woolly.

Some of them brags have found their way into song and story and become a part of the lore of the West. Even the later-day cowhand, when he gets a few drinks under his belt, sometimes declares, "I'm a wolf and it's my night to howl," but there's a twinkle in his eyes which convinces you he ain't so bad as he sounds.

It's needless to give more'n a few examples of them brags because they all wear the same road brand, even if they've been gathered from different ranges.

"I'm the daddy of all the badmen that ever come from Buzzard Hole. I wuz nursed on whisky, cut my teeth on a circular saw, and rattlesnakes wuz my playmates. Us reptiles bite each other to see who's the most piz'nous, and I always win."

"I'm a death-dealin' demon from Dead Man's Gulch. The further up you go, the tougher they get, and I hole up a mile past the last camp. I wuz cradled on cholla spines. Grizzlies and catamounts wuz my early playmates, and I'm so hard I kick fire outa flint with my bare toes. I have to put tarantulas and vinegaroons in my whisky to give it flavor, and mix it with strychnine and wolf pizen to give it bite. When I come to town, all the other killers hide under their mammy's aprons. Hide out little ones, it's my night to drink gore."

Or: "I wuz born in an eruptin' volcano and suckled by a lion. I got nine rows of jaw teeth made of iron with holes punched in for more. I'm wild and woolly and full of fleas. Never been curried below the knees. I'm a tornado of destruction, a killer that nourished on blood and it's my night to devour."

But such a character don't skeer nobody with bones in his spinal column. Usually he's as yeller as mustard but without the bite, and you could take a bunch of corncobs and lightnin' bugs and make 'im run till his tongue hung out like a calf rope.

I never hear of one of them old flannelmouths that I don't think of the story Butch Ikard once told of Rattlesnake Jake.

"This reptile," said Butch, "spent his time makin' life miserable for tourists and doin' his damnedest to make ever'body think he was wild and woolly. Seems like he was growin' in his mean ways, and the progressive citizens of Mule Shoe figgered he was makin' them said tourists give their growin' city a wide berth. They figgered he was hurtin' business, and in their civic pride they took 'im out and let 'im play cat's cradle with his neck.

"In the first place Mule Shoe inherited Rattlesnake from Burnt Fork when the citizens of that metropolis chaparoned 'im down the trail to the west and give 'im a rousin' farewell with powder smoke and utter disregard for his unappreciated talents. When he first came a-siftin' into Mule Shoe, he's a-wearin' a load of hay on his skull, and packin' 'nough artillery to make his hoss swaybacked, and he looks mean 'nough to have a reserved seat in hell. He orates to us Mule Shoers as how he's the big daddy of all the badmen that ever come from Buzzard Hole, and he shore looked 'er. He declares that he was nursed on whisky and cut his teeth on a circle saw, and that rattlesnakes was his playmates. He was one of them reg'lar storybook badmen that you read 'bout but seldom see.

"Us boys soon sized 'im up and didn't pay no attention to 'im. We soon learned that he had a yeller streak down his back so wide it lapped plumb 'round his brisket bone, and we figgered he ain't even fit to shoot at when you want to unload and clean your gun. He'd git drunk and ride up the street a-shootin', but even the marshal figgered he was harmless as a chambermaid, and that soon somebody'd git tired of his pesterin' and

would send 'im to hell on a shutter with his hide so full of holes it wouldn't hold hay.

"His fav'rite meat was tenderfoots, and he did his best to show them shorthorns how wild and wicked the woolly West growed her men. To them he looked meaner'n a centipede with the chilblains, and when he bellered 'Scat,' they shore hunted their holes.

"One day a young feller come to town lookin' for health. His lungs wasn't stronger'n a hummin'bird's, and he's so puny he couldn't pull my hat off. He'd have to stand twice to make a shadder, and when Rattlesnake seen 'im his mouth jes' dribbled water. He started to campin' on that kid's trail, dealin' 'im misery till he's as worn and weary as a bull cat walkin' in mud.

"I cornered this kid one day and says to 'im: 'Buddy, how come you let Rattlesnake run over you like this? Don't you know a hard-boiled **egg**'s always yeller inside? He's as yeller as a dandelion. Buck up. **Git** your back up and show 'im you ain't built of butter. I wouldn't let no man swipe the silver linin' off *my* cloud.'

"He looks at me with them big eyes a minnit and perked up kinda hopeful, but he soon shook his head, and I knowed my advice didn't have no more effect than pourin' water on a drowned rat.

"One day an old prospector rode into town for supplies. He'd been gopherin' in the hills 'round there for years. There ain't no tellin' how old this old sourdough is. He's as wrinkled as a burnt boot, and the oldest citizens said he'd looked like that for as long as they could remember. He came in a-ridin' an old crowbait hardtail and wearin' a spur on one boot like a sheepherder.

"He heard 'bout the lunger and Rattlesnake first thing, and, huntin' up the kid, he offered to take 'im out in the hills where the air was purer and the rattlesnakes crawled on their bellies and warned you with their alarm clocks 'fore they struck. It wasn't no time till them two was gittin' 'long like two pups in a basket, and when they rode out of town Rattlesnake gritted his teeth like he could eat the sights off a six-gun. He swelled up like a carbuncle and swore vengeance ag'in this corrigated old party for robbin' 'im of his play-pretty.

"Time hung heavy on his hands after that till finally he got desperate for his fav'rite amusement and he picked on a snoozer [sheepherder] who'd come to town for supplies. But you never can tell which way a dillpickle's goin' to squirt, and this snoozer put a head on Rattlesnake big 'nough for 'im to eat hay with the hosses, and told 'im to hunt up somethin' he could use for a backbone. This slowed 'im down for a spell, but didn't cure 'im. Curin' *him* was like tryin' to scratch your ear with your elbow.

"Next he jumped a chili [Mexican], but this oiler stuck a knife in his flank, then tried to walk 'round 'im till old Rattlesnake thought there was a general holiday in hell. Figgerin' his luck was runnin' kinda muddy ag'in anything but shorthorns, he finally confined his amusement to this latter species as they occasionally dropped into town. He never quit talkin' 'bout what he was a-goin' to do to the old sourdough that stole his pet though, and if he done ever'thing he said he was a-goin' to do, that old prospector would soon be hoppin' over hot coals in hell.

"In a couple of months old Wrinkles brought the lunger back to town to see the sawbones. Seems like he wasn't gettin' no better, and the old man was worried. Of course, they soon hear 'bout Rattlesnake's talk, and and it wasn't good news to the old prospector 'cause he was a peaceable man and had always kept his boot heels run over side-steppin' trouble. He wasn't no coward, but he was old and didn't want no trouble now that he was in the shank of life.

"He took the kid down to the doc's office and told 'im that he'd go order dinner while he waited so they could save time and get out of town earlier. So, leavin' the kid, he made it back to the Chink's swaller-and-git-out trough. The sawbones, who'd had more experience with hosses than he'd had with humans, looked the kid over and shook his head. He spluttered 'round a while tryin' to figger how to break the news, and fin'lly he told the kid that he ain't got but 'bout a month to live at most.

"At first the kid trembled a little at this news, which I admit ain't pleasant for no man to hear, but he soon bucked up, his jaws kinda clickin' together with a snap, and payin' the pill roller, he follered his old friend to the Chink's. He stopped at a gun shop on the way and bought a flame-thrower, a .44 Colt. I reckon it was the first gun he'd ever handled, and he got the clerk to load it and show 'im how it worked. He tried to cock it, but was too weak; a kitten was plumb robust beside 'im. He got the clerk to cock it and asked 'im to leave it that way 'cause he'd seen a snake down the street and he wanted to try and kill 'im 'fore he bit some friend of his.

"When Rattlesnake seen the old man go into the Chink's to give his tapeworm nourishment, he went over as salty as Lot's wife, 'cause he seen the old man wasn't packin' an ounce of iron. He started low-ratin' old Wrinkles and usin' language ag'in 'im that a man wouldn't take from no one but his wife, and lowed it was 'bout time to carve 'nother scallop on his gun. The old man knowed he didn't have as much chance as a wax cat in hell, but he got up archin' his back like a cat at the sight of a dog. Of course, Rattlesnake was jes' fourflushin' 'cause he knowed mighty well what the boy'd do to 'im for shootin' an unarmed man. He hadn't figgered on the lunger, though, and didn't know that invalid had made up his mind that if Death already had 'im branded for the Eternal Range he might as well buck out in glory. This coffin fodder came in at a side door, seen Rattlesnake's gun out, and heard his threats, and he didn't wait for nothin' else. He jes' swooped down like forty hen hawks on a settin' quail, raised his gun with both hands, and with both forefingers he pulled the trigger.

"That old hogleg let out an awful beller, and the bullet smashed a bottle of ketchup on the table in front of Rattlesnake, splatterin' 'im with its contents. When Rattlesnake looks down and sees his shirtfront covered with red, he thinks it's gore, and with a howl that'd drive a wolf to suicide he starts makin' far-apart tracks for the sawbones to have the lead mined out. Old Wrinkles heaved such a sigh you could feel the draft. Rattlesnake was laughed plumb out of the country. He headed for the settin' sun, but I later heard that the next town he landed in didn't like the color of his eyes, and they took 'im out and hung 'im so high he could look down on the moon."

Most of them old flannelmouths tried to make you believe they were so tough they'd growed horns and were haired over, and most of 'em were 'bout as sociable as an ulcerated tooth. They were as cold-blooded as a rattler with a chill, and tried to make you believe they'd been reared in a country so tough the hoot owls all sang bass. But as a rule at the showdown their guts turned to fiddlestrings.

There were times in the early West when the rope was resorted to as a final justice, but no man livin' there made it more'n an occasional subject of conversation, nor would he admit that he had anything to do with one. Them were mighty stern and solemn matters, and not subjected to jests nor pop'lar mention.

When some posse got in a hangin' mood and went lookin' for a guest at a string party, they were mighty shore to have the goods on the one they hung up to dry. Most cowmen were too proud of their Adam's apple to want to be exalted, but now and then there were them who couldn't resist pickin' up a rope that somehow had a hoss fastened to the other end of it when they got home. When a man admired other folk's hoss flesh too much, he was doin' his best to ride under a cottonwood limb and do a strangulation jig. When he was used to trim a tree in this manner, he was said to have "throat trouble," a "case of hemp fever," or "they made a cottonwood blossom out of 'im." More'n one hoss thief has climbed the Golden Stairs on a rope.

On the Prod

As a rule the cowman kept a dally on his temper. He knowed that hot words mighty often led to cold slabs if there was any guns involved. In the early days ever' man packed a gun, but he wasn't so quick to use it as some romancers try to make us believe. You'd find the cowhand mighty quiet with his words in a crisis. He was no coward, but he wasn't so bloodthirsty he'd take a life for the defense of a little pride. He'd shoot quick 'nough for self-protection, but he'd take a lot of ridin' before he'd start a powder-burnin' contest. He had no hankerin' to ride the high lines. When he did go after his gun he did it with a serious purpose. Ever' sense he owned was keyed to shootin' as fast and as accurate as possible to make the first shot the last of the fight. But the real cowhand didn't like to dabble in gore. When he did get his bristles up, however, there was nobody settin' on his shirttail, and there was usually a battle that'd make an ordinary fight look like a prayer meetin'. When two men, toughened by hard outdoor life, and used to takin' chances, got into combat, there was shore to be a hide hung up.

When a cowhand went to town it was usually to replenish his wardrobe, or jes' for a good time. It always did rile a workin' cowhand when he saw them town porch perchers all ragged out in fancy doodads and a shiny gun. Many of 'em had the pronto bug, and spent their time practicin' a fast draw and dry shootin'. There was usually a gun fighter or two in their midst too, but they didn't scare the cowman. In fact, there was only two things the old-time cowpuncher was afraid of—a decent woman and bein' left afoot.

Most ever' town had a bully who was all horns and rattles with too much spread. Some of 'em seemed to always be pawin' 'round for turmoil, but at the showdown they proved to be all gurgle and no guts, and had mighty cold, feet for such a hot country. Mighty often he'd make a mistake and rile some feller that didn't have no use for his breed anyway, and he'd wind up by losin' 'nough skin to half sole an elephant, and his own folks wouldn't have knowed 'im from a fresh hide.

Sometimes two long-time enemies hit town at the same time. Each had been packin' a grudge against the other as long as an Injun could remember. One wouldn't speak to the other if he met 'im in hell packin' a lump of ice on his head, and the other didn't have no more use for the first one than he did a temperance lecturer. But both had craws jambed plumb full of sand and fightin' tallow, and they'd fight till hell froze over and then skate with you on the ice.

It wasn't long till each had heard the other was in town and lookin' for 'im. The whole town seemed to sense that peculiar tenseness of such a moment—a moment of crisis, of taut nerves, of impendin' disaster. There was that odd quiet that precedes certain gunplay. From the windows and doors along the street would peer the faces of interested onlookers. There might be a careful lack of all expression, but you knowed they were interested. It was never well to openly express approval of a shootin'. The shooter had friends, and little breaches of etiquette were always remembered. An ironclad rule of the old West was that ever' quarrel was a private one. No outsider had any right to interfere.

Because there were times in life when a man had to fight or lose his self-respect, when these enemies did meet they both immediately went into the gunman's crouch, leanin' slightly forward with knees a little bent, hand near his gun butt, fingers spread and bent like bird claws, alert, ever' muscle tense—that familiar gesture, catlike and perilous. While each waited for the other to make the first move, native caution made the bystanders scud out of the way of future activities.

For a second there might be an intense silence, heavy, strained, and sickenin'. Then suddenly guns crashed and spat their slantin' tongues of flame. It might be a case of slow with one, and he'd be settin' on a damp cloud learnin' harp music, or both shooters might be takin' off their spurs at the Pearly Gates at the same time.

Mighty few cowhands wanted to actually kill anybody. A man didn't care 'bout havin' to ride the willows and belly through the brush. If some bully dug up the tomahawk and went on the warpath, this cowboy'd usually comb this bully's hair where it was thinnest, with the barrel of his six-gun, and knock 'im cold 'nough to skate on.

Looks like some folks were as full of venom as a rattlesnake in August and were forever pawin' 'round for turmoil. But there was always somebody ready to pounce on 'em like a road runner on a June bug, and it wasn't long till he'd lost 'nough hide to make a saddle cover and 'nough blood to paint a house. By the time he woke up he'd been stripped of that bric-a-brac he packed at his waist, and the man who'd cleaned his plow promised 'im that the next time they met he'd squirt 'nough lead into 'im to make it a payin' job to melt 'im down.

When the cow towns passed laws that made the cowhands check in their artillery while in town, they had to do their fightin' with their fists. The early cowman felt that such combats were beneath his dignity. He called 'em "dogfights." As one said, "If the Lord had intended me to fight like a dog, He'd a-give me longer teeth and claws."

But when he did get his bristles up and pull his hat to a fightin' angle, he did a good job of it because he was hard and strong. When he got in a sod-pawin' mood it wasn't past 'im to do a little scratchin' and eye gougin' too. One cowhand, describin' a fight on the ranch when he was passin' the bunkhouse, said, "It sounded like they was shoein' a bronc inside," and when he went inside he found that one of 'em was walkin' up and down on the other's backbone like he was climbin' a ladder.

I never think of a gun fight I don't think of a tale Bugeye Lawson told on a roundup of the old Swingin' L.

The circle riders had combed the rough country for any outlaw cattle. The cattle 'emselves seemed to be unusually contrary and on the prod, and more'n one bullfight had been witnessed before the cattle had been drove to the *parada* grounds. One of them fights was the most comical any of us had ever seen.

In the drive we'd brought in a relic of the longhorn days. He was a little long-legged, long-horned, slab-sided bull that looked like a calf in size compared with the heavy-bodied stock we had on the range, and them outlandish long horns made a person rub his eyes to realize he wasn't "seein' things." No one knowed where he'd come from, and we all grinned when we saw 'im acceptin' the challenge of 'nother bull that'd make two of 'im. We paused in our work to watch, shore that it wouldn't take long for the larger bull to save us the trouble of runnin' the scrub off the range. Many of the boys offered heavy odds on the big bull, shore that they'd find no takers. No one stopped to consider the aggressiveness and stamina of that wild, longhorn breed—that is, no one but Bugeye Lawson. He covered ever' bet.

There was much pawin', bellowin', and throwin' of dust, but ever' time the larger one charged, he found the scrub too agile for 'im. The latter quickly side-stepped, and in doin' so got in some wicked work with them swordlike horns. Time and again the larger one charged, only to get the worst of it each time, and with each new charge he became more bewildered. He'd never fought such an adversary before. The fight didn't last long, for the pure-bred suddenly realized that he had more cud than he could chew. He whirled quickly, and, humpin' his tail at the shore end, he rattled his hocks away from there; not quick 'nough, however, to avoid a thrust of the other's long horn in his rump to urge 'im to greater speed. The last we saw of 'im was when he disappeared over the hill, makin' us poorer and Bugeye richer as he went.

Naturally, after supper, when the day's work was over, there was a heap of laughter over the comical appearance of that fight, and, too, there were some regrets because the victor had to be butchered. He'd won much admiration, even though it did prove costly to us. But the wagon boss declared the owners were raisin' beef, not soup bone and horn, and that they were breedin' up, not down.

"There's jes' one thing I'd like to know for my money," says one of the boys. "Bugeye, how come you snaps up all our bets in such a confident manner? You acts like you was shore of the outcome."

"Well," answered Bugeye, "them two critters fightin' reminded me a heap of a fight I seen 'tween two men a long time ago. There was as much difference in the size of them men as there was in them bulls, and it jes' came to me in a flash to take them bets on account of seein' this other fight.

"To begin with, you can't tell nuthin' 'bout a man from his build. Now I've seen fellers so beefy you'd think they'd pack a wallop like the kick of a mule, but maybe at the same time they couldn't lick their upper lip 'cause they didn't have no nerve. Likewise, ordinarily you figger that one of them tall skinny hombres that don't pack no meat on his bones can't fight, but don't git fooled. Of course, in a fistfight it usually requires a more even match in beef, but in a gun fight like the one I'm tellin' 'bout I believe the skinny feller has the edge.

"I was jes' a button at the time, a-workin' for the TJ spread in the Cherokee Strip as hoss jingler. This long-legged anteater I'm speakin' 'bout come from down in the Skillet, and went to ridin' for the outfit. He's so long he had to shorten his stirrups to save his boot soles, and the boys called his hosses walkin' sticks 'cause his feet nearly dragged the ground. He was so thin I'll bet he could've taken a bath in a shotgun barrel, and if he'd a-shut one eye he'd a-looked like a needle—in fact, that's what the boys named 'im.

"He was the funniest-lookin' sight on a hoss I ever seen, but he shore loved them animals. Most all good cow prods love their hosses, but this feller jes' dotes on 'em and talked to 'em and petted 'em like they was his sweethearts. He didn't spend much time makin' up to the boys, but could usually be found, when he didn't have nothin' else to do, out huggin' some hoss 'round the neck with them long arms of his.

"When the boss cut his string, he wasn't stingy with the raw broncs, and figgered he'd have some fun watchin' that moon scraper tryin' to ride 'em. But he got fooled. When Needle'd tie hisself on with them long legs in a half-hitch, there wasn't a hoss that could warp his backbone 'nough to untie that knot. It was jes' like buckin' off a porous plaster, him stickin' there tighter'n a tick makin' a gotch ear. It wasn't long till he had all them broncs eatin' out of his hand and follerin' 'im 'round like a pet coon. He plumb ruined their appetites for grass by feedin' 'em sour-doughs, and they near run the cook crazy hangin' 'round camp nosin' among the cookin' pots—reg'lar pie biters they were.

"It jes' seems natural to think them skinny fellers don't have no sand and'll take anything. Needle seemed to be that way, too, and he soon became the butt of all the jokes and pranks in camp. He was a game rider, though. I guess it was 'cause he loved hosses so. But with men he seemed to be different. He took ever'thing pretty good-natured, and the boys soon figgered he was as yeller as a dandelion.

"There was 'nother feller workin' with us as a stray man for the Open A outfit that was jes' the opposite in ever' way. His name was Bat, and he was big 'nough to hunt bears with a switch. He tried to make you think he was the toughest longhorn that ever shook his antlers in the Injun country. He looked like he could knock you so far it'd take a week for a bloodhound to find you. He'd worked a good many years down in Mexico, and had took up the greaser's ways of bein' mean to a hoss. He used a stomach-pump bit, and wore a big pair of Chihuahua can openers that he used overtime. Nearly ever' hoss in his string wore marks where he'd beefsteaked 'em, and 'bout half of 'em'd been baked or jiggered.

"The boss can't say much, 'cause the Open A was payin' his wages, but he shore thought a-plenty, and wished this hombre was workin' for the TJ. When Needle looked at them hosses' backs and seen how savage Bat treated his mounts, he got so mad he lost his head. He jumped Bat 'bout gimletin' them hosses. We didn't think he had the nerve, 'cause Bat was as big as an eight-mule baggage wagon compared to 'im, and he was so tough he had to sneak up on a dipper to git a drink of water; but Needle jes' went crazy, and didn't stop to consider consequences.

" 'Haul in yore neck 'fore I tromp yore britches, you long drink of water,' snarls Bat, gettin' his bristles up when Needle jumped 'im 'bout them hosses' backs.

" 'Hop to it you hoss killer,' says Needle, nearly in tears he was so mad. 'There ain't nobody settin' on yore shirttail.'

"Bat made a play to hit Needle, but when he looks 'round and seen the other boys edgin' in, he backs down. Needle'd made a friend out of ever' T J puncher right there, but you could see 'im and Bat loved each other like a cow does heel flies. The boss said if he'd had a stepladder, he'd a-patted Needle on the back.

"Looked like after that Bat hammered his hosses 'round mor'n ever, and he allus looked over and sneered at Needle, who was watchin' 'im, white and sick lookin'. There wasn't 'nother break 'tween 'em, though, till the last day of the roundup when Bat roped his top whittler to saddle 'im for the afternoon work. He'd fought his mounts so much they was all scairt of his shadder. This hoss fell out of bed [pulled back on the halter] till Bat shore got in a fightin' mood. When he finally dragged his hoss out of the rope corral, he tied 'im up short to a wheel of the hoodlum wagon and went 'round huntin' somethin', and he was madder'n a drunk squaw. Pretty soon he finds a big club, and when Needle seen what he was goin' to do he went to the other side of the wagon, climbed a wheel, got his bedroll, and dragged out a hog-leg, and by the time Bat had hit that bawlin' hoss the first lick Needle combed that puncher's hair with the barrel of a six-gun quicker'n hell could scorch a feather.

"Before Bat could git up, the boss was right there on top of the play.

" 'Bat,' he says, 'git yore string and yore cut and rattle yore hocks for the Open A 'fore I let Needle fog you till you're as full of lead as Joplin. Tell Old Man Henderson to keep his hoss fighters off my range or I'll hang up his hide. Now git!' The longer the boss talked, the madder he got.

"Bat give the boss a look that'd make icicles look feverish, and turnin' to Needle, he says, 'Next time I see you, you'd better be heeled.'

"Needle still stood by the wagon, watchin' 'im go, like a man in a daze. He musta gone crazy for a minnit. The boss climbed a wheel and put his arm 'round Needle's shoulders.

" 'Son,' he says, 'I'm right proud of you, but you want to watch out for that skunk. He's got snake blood, and he'd eat off the same plate with a rattler. I'd go 'round 'im like he was a swamp if I was you.'

" 'Bout a year later Needle quit the TJ and got hisself a job in town as deputy. His badge danged nigh covered his whole chest, and looked as big as a soup plate. Meantime, Bat had started a little spread of his own, but he got kinda careless with his runnin' iron, and folks got to noticin' his calves didn't suck the right cows. But they didn't say much till he got greedy and organized a gang and began pinnin' crape on the kids [killin' the mothers to steal the calves].

"Most of Needle's work was collectin' taxes and servin' civil papers, so when the sheriff handed 'im a warrant to serve on Bat it kinda took his breath away. Some said the sheriff didn't have the nerve hisself, and was gittin' Needle all killed up. Needle was a hog for duty. He was representin' the law now, so he kinda forgot his personal feelin's and started campin' on Bat's trail. Bat sent 'im word that his whole gang is gunnin' for 'im, but Needle was as chuckleheaded as a prairie dog, and all hell couldn't keep 'im from servin' that warrant, 'cause now it was his duty.

"Tales were packed back and forth, and you know how rilin' water makes it muddy. It wasn't long till Bat and his gang comes rackin' to town with blood in their eyes. It so happened that Needle had gone over to Lobo Springs to serve some papers at the time. When Bat heard this, he 'lowed he'd camp right there till Needle come back. The whole town got interested, and the big gamblers laid heavy odds on Bat, jes' like you boys did on the big bull today. Needle's friends wasn't shore of his nerve. He'd never been in such a tight place before. Deep down in their gizzards they didn't think he had any sand in his craw. They shook their heads and wondered what show a little feller like 'im had ag'in a big tough like Bat, and besides, there was his whole gang behind 'im. They augured that Needle didn't stand as much show as a hen at a mass meetin' of coyotes. Some few admitted that a Colt was a good equalizer, and size didn't count if the gang'd stay out of it.

"The town settled down to wait, but as the hours dragged by it got on men's nerves. Gradually the street got empty. Men even moved their hosses to the back alleys. Doors were closed, and upstairs windows were filled with faces waitin' for the showdown. It was like them box-seat things at one of them op'ry plays. Needle was due back any time now. One of his friends 'lowed he couldn't stand it no longer, and that Needle was at least due a warnin', so he sneaked out the back way, forked his hoss, and slipped down the trail to put Needle wise to the play. When Needle still didn't show up, the town figgered that this friend's news had sent 'im high-tailin' over the back trail.

"At last Needle comes ridin' in. He left his hoss at the end of the street, and after lookin' to make shore his gun was workin', he made his way up the wooden sidewalks. He'd been told what to expect, but that empty street would've told 'im anyway. He come slow and cautious, half crouched, and a-walkin' on the balls of his feet. He knowed the town was a-watchin' 'im from them closed windows, and he reckoned they figgered he was yeller 'cause he'd taken backwater on one or two occasions before. But them occasions had been personal matters. Now he was representin' the law. If only the sheriff was in town he'd have some backin' ag'in a whole gang. He wondered if the sheriff'd left 'im holdin' the sack on purpose.

"He figgered he wouldn't last as long as a keg of cider at a barn raisin', but he kept a-comin'. He got slower and slower, but he kept a-comin'. Now and then he'd take a look back over his shoulder and dodge behind the corner of some buildin', but he kept a-comin'. He could feel the eyes in them windows borin' into 'im, and he didn't know if they was friendly eyes or not. He was pale, and lookin' like a motherless calf out there alone. That musta been one hell of a feelin' to be huntin' an enemy that's layin' for you, with you out in the open and not knowin' where that enemy is hid nor from which angle you'd git that hot lead you're expectin' ever' minnit.

"Jes' as he got opposite the Silver Spur Saloon, Bat stepped out with a gun in his hand.

" 'You lookin' for me, Needle?' he asks in a voice that sounds like an iron tire on frozen snow.

" 'Yeah, I got a warrant—' But Needle didn't git any further 'fore Bat started the fireworks.

"Now here is where my previous remarks 'bout a skinny feller havin' the edge in a gun fight is proved. Needle turns sideways, and don't give Bat much to shoot at. It was like tryin' to hit a rope hangin' from a limb. Needle sways 'bout, makin' a still harder target, and ever' time he squeezed his trigger he let sunshine through Bat like he was a pane of glass. Needle was as good a shot as he was a rider. By the time Bat was down his gang starts pilin' out of the Silver Spur like red ants out of a burnin' log, and a-smokin' as they came.

"Bullets got as thick as hossflies in May, but Needle jes' stood there puttin' windows in their skulls and givin' each of 'em a pitchfork for the Eternal Beyond. When that corpse-and-cartridge occasion was over, they had to pick them rustlers up with a blotter. Right then the undertaker was the most prosperous man in town, and Needle could of been elected sheriff in a walkover.

"After it was all over, Needle walked down to the office, throwed his badge on the sheriff's desk, and wrote out his resignation. He was satisfied now that he'd put Bat where he couldn't be mean to no more hosses, and he proceeded to go out and git so drunk he couldn't hit the ground with his hat in three throws, while his friends was lamentin' that they didn't have the nerve to put their money on *his* nerve."

At Work

Ridin' the Range:
Ridin' Line and Ridin' Fence

WHEN a cowhand rode across the range, whether he was on the prowl or goin' someplace, force of habit made 'im keep his eyes skinned for anything goin' on 'round 'im. No matter if he was goin' to town and wanted to get there in a hurry, if he saw anything unusual goin' on he'd ride out of his way to look after his boss's interests.

His trainin' taught 'im to see great distances and to interpret signs of ever'thing goin' on 'bout 'im. From force of habit his eyes searched ever' flat and ridge within his vision. If he heard some cow bawlin' in a coulee, he'd ride over to investigate, and maybe he found her calf had died. He'd rope her, tie her down, and milk her out to keep her bag from spoilin'. He might run across an animal with a swollen jaw and low-swung head and know it'd been bit by a rattler. A twitchin' hide and peculiar odor told 'im of a case of screw worms he'd have to doctor with his limited equipment.

Screw worms always gave the rancher a heap of trouble, especially in the Southwest durin' the warm months. If an animal with any kind of wound was exposed to blowflies, the screw worms started workin' the same day the wound was blowed. The heat of the animal's body soon hatched the eggs, each a maggot 'bout three-fourths of an inch long, with each forming its own cell in the flesh of the victim and eating its way till it reached some vital spot.

If the animal didn't get attention in a day or two, great damage was done. A cowhand could tell a wormy animal as far as he could see it. It held its head sideways like it had a tick in its ear, and shook its head a heap. Freshly branded and castrated calves had to be watched to see that the blowflies didn't get to 'em. Later-day cowboys swabbed the wounds with dope, and also packed a bottle of screw-worm medicine on their saddles to have when wanted.

The dope most cowmen used contained carbolic acid, persylic ointment, and axle grease. The acid killed the worms, the ointment healed and the axle grease was to keep the acid from blisterin'. Some used chloroform and cresyllic ointment.

The cowhand might ride out of his way to inspect a water hole, or a boghole he knowed to be in the vicinity. As he rode he watched for tracks of animals, varmints, or other riders. He read the story of them tracks as he would a book. He could tell by the tracks if a hoss was shod or barefooted, if he was walkin' or runnin'; if he was bein' driven, rode, or was jes' wanderin' of his own accord. He could tell by the twigs and bushes and the bent grass approximately how long ago an animal had made the track. What he called "sign" were tracks and other evidence of their passin' left by animals or men. The act of interpretin' them markin's in followin' a trail was called "readin' sign." To "cut for sign" was to examine the ground for tracks or droppin's, and when them signs were clearly visible it was called a "plain trail." When the sign was old and indistinct it was a "blind trail" or "cold trail." To go back over a trail was to "back trail," and the vernacular for followin' a trail so clearly marked that it couldn't be lost was called "slidin' the groove." The cowman often used his trail vernacular in ordinary conversation, and when he spoke of someone deceivin' 'nother he was said to be "cloudin' the trail." When he was followin' someone he was said to be "campin' on his trail." When his immediate duty was to ride the range to follow animals that had strayed too far, and turn 'em back, or pull cattle from bogholes, turn 'em away from loco patches, or do anything else in the interest of his employer, he was said to be "ridin' sign."

A "tracker" was one expert in trackin' and readin' sign, and some of 'em were so good that it was said of 'em that they "could follow a wood tick on solid rock in the dark of the moon," or, "He had a nose so keen he could track a bear in runnin' water," or "He could track bees in a blizzard." Because the cowboy always used exaggerations in his descriptions, if he was speakin' of one with no trackin' ability he'd likely use such expressions as, "He couldn't find a belled calf in a corral," "He couldn't find a baseball in a tomato can," "He couldn't follow a load of loose hay across a forty-acre field of fresh snow," or "He couldn't track an elephant in three feet of fresh snow."

In the early days before fences, cow outfits employed line riders and maintained line camps 'long the borders of their range in which were quartered one or more cowboys whose duty it was to keep the cattle of their brand throwed back on their own range, and to prevent 'em from driftin' in winter. If cattle began to drift in masses, it was then impossible for a small number of men to hold 'em. Then the only thing to do was to let 'em go and have a crew from headquarters go after 'em.

Them camps were ordinarily small, one- or two-room shacks, or maybe a dugout, all scantily furnished with only such equipment as would not tempt prowlin' visitors and which could be left unprotected in the summer, when camp was deserted, without much loss. They were called "hoodens," "sign camps," or often referred to as "Jones's place," and when such a camp was in an untidy condition, which was usually the case, it was often called a "boar's nest." This name was used because its occupant was more interested in his duties as a cowhand than in his rep'tation as a housekeeper.

The kitchen held a small wood-burnin' stove. Maybe one leg was gone, and this corner was propped up with a stack of flat rocks so common in some parts of the range. His cookin' utensils consisted of a black coffeepot, an iron skillet of the same color, a few pots and pans, a water bucket or two, and a dishpan that doubled for his bread pan. On one wall was a wooden box, nailed within easy reach, in which he kept his eatin' tools, tin plates, cups, knives, forks, and spoons. Here he also kept an empty beer bottle with which he rolled his biscuit dough. On 'nother shelf he kept his dried beans, salt, soda, bakin' powder, syrup, coffee, flour, lard, and his small supply of canned goods. On the wall, suspended from a nail, was a slab of sowbelly coated with a thick crust of white salt. Also on the wall was a coffee grinder with which he tried to keep two or three days' supply ready for use. There was too much waste in killin' a beef for one or two men, and unless a kindhearted boss sent out a supply of beef when killed for the home ranch, they had to eat Kansas City fish, and like it.

There was a cheap pine table covered with red and white checkered oilcloth, a few straight-backed chairs, either with cane or cowhide bottoms, and all likely held together with balin' wire. If company dropped in, the host could usually rake up a nail keg or a wooden can-goods box for extry seats. His bed was usually one of them cheap iron affairs, from which most of the white paint had been chipped. Though it had a thin mattress and blankets, he usually used it to spread his hot-roll on. Of course, if company stayed overnight he spread his hot-roll on the floor and gave his visitor the bed, splittin' what blankets he could spare.

He got up in the mornin' by a dollar alarm clock, and he found no cheerful light of a campfire, nor the savory odors of fryin' meat and boilin' coffee. He got up in the bone-chillin' darkness of the early mornin', slipped on his shirt, pants, and boots, and made his way to the cookstove. Liftin' the lids, he scraped 'round in the cold gray ashes of the night before, put in his kindlin' and wood and lighted a fire. He waited to wash his face till the pot of water on the back of the stove had time to warm up some. He threw out the old coffee grounds, put in some new, poured some water in the pot, and put it on the fire. If the coffee supply was gettin' low, he maybe used the old grounds over, or, if he figgered the coffee'd be too weak, he'd make it with half old and half new grounds. While the cold white grease in the fryin' pan was meltin', he sliced off some more of the sowbelly. While this popped and sizzled he sprinkled some water over the half-dozen sourdoughs left from the night before, and slapped 'em in the oven. He promised 'imself he'd make some fresh ones that night.

Before eatin' his own breakfast he'd go out and grain his hosses, or give 'em some hay if the grass was still green. Then, after eatin' his own lonely breakfast and decidin' he'd wash the dishes when he got back that night, he caught and saddled the hoss chosen for the day and which by now was through with his grain. If it was a frosty mornin' and his hoss felt frisky, he'd likely have to iron the humps out before he got 'im straightened out.

Men selected to winter in them camps were usually single men with few or no home ties, and didn't mind the life of a buck nun. When more'n one man was in camp there was a rule among 'em that the first man to ride in should build the fire and prepare the meal. If one of 'em happened to be an extry good cook and housekeeper, the other always managed to be second in to camp, even if he had to scout 'long the ridges above camp till some smoke could be seen comin' from the chimney of the shack before he gave his hoss its head and let 'im come in the quickest and nearest way.

The cookin' duties consisted mostly of the ability to fry sowbelly, cook beans so they wouldn't rattle in the plate, make passable sourdoughs, with an occasional cobbler of dried fruit, and strong coffee. Usually the coffee was made by the standard recipe of a handful of coffee to a cup of water, for they liked it strong 'nough to kick up in the middle and carry double. They liked for the man doin' the cookin' to be clean, and would assist 'im in washin' the dishes and swampin' out the place. Some men didn't mind cookin', and preferred doin' that rather than take chances on someone whose cookin' qualifications they didn't know; but to most of 'em cookin' was a tiresome job and they'd resort to anything to avoid doin' it.

Each man patrolled a prescribed boundary to look after the interests of his employer. His was a lonely two-meal-a-day job, and he worked long hours. When two men were placed in camp, although they spent the day ridin' in opposite directions the job wasn't quite so lonely because they could keep each other company at night. Usually the uppermost thought in his mind was the day he could return to headquarters and hear a real cook yell, "Come an' get it!"

Line riders were sometimes called outriders, though, strictly speakin', outriders were commissioned to ride anywhere, while line riders had a certain territory to patrol. However, their many and varied duties were much the same. Each pushed strays of his brand onto the range and drove off of it them which didn't belong. If cattle were overgrazin' certain sections, they were hazed to new and better grass. The condition of the grass and water were always watched, as well as the physical condition of the cattle. Each rider had to be somewhat of a veterinarian and doctor cattle for lumpjaw or screw worms, and pick porcupine quills from the nose of some inquisitive cow.

Among some of the duties of the line rider was the drivin' of cattle away from patches of loco weed, or akaline water holes. If the wolves were bad he spent some time settin' traps, or puttin' out poisoned bait, though some ranches kept a professional wolfer hired for that purpose. If he saw a bitch wolf slinkin' 'long some ridge, he might follow her to a den where her pups were hid, and dig 'em out. If he ran across an animal mired in a boghole, he had to rope it and pull it to dry ground. Here and there he might find an overgrowed calf still nursin' a mother too thin for her own good. He had to drive 'em some distance apart, rope the calf, and put a blab board on its nose to wean it so the mother could gain her strength and survive the winter.

The worse the weather, the more ridin' he had to do. Some sudden norther might cause the cattle to drift, and they had to be pushed back into the brakes, or broken country, where they'd have some protection from the icy blasts. Holes had to be chopped in frozen waterin' places and weak stock helped in many ways. Durin' them emergencies he worked ever' daylight hour with cold feet and hands, and maybe frostbitten ears, only to return at night to a cold and cheerless shack.

After thawin' 'imself by cookin' a hot meal, he'd hit his blankets with the unpleasant thoughts of 'nother day's such work on the morrow, but with the satisfaction of a day's duties well done. Maybe it was a good thing he didn't stop to think how hard he had to work for $30 a month.

RIDIN' FENCE

The change from open range to fences produced the fence rider. This was also a job for a man who could stand loneliness and his own cookin'. He was stationed at a line camp and rode an ever deepenin' trail 'longside the fence for ten or fifteen miles, watchin' for breaks in the fence that needed repair to keep his outfit's cattle in and other ranches' cattle out. He usually rode till noon or a little after, then turned back so he could reach camp in time to grain his hosses before dark. If he met a rider from the next camp, they both swung off their hosses to twist a cigarette, give the hoss's backs some air, and exchange the range gossip.

The fence rider got up early in the mornin' so he could do his chores and get started on his patrol by good daylight. After buildin' his breakfast fire he went out to feed his hosses. He packed no lunch, but might take 'long a can of tomatoes for both food and drink. He ate a heavy breakfast and promised 'imself to wash the dishes when he got back.

His equipment consisted of a pair of fence pliers which combine wire cutters and hammer. Tied to the horn of his saddle was an old boot top, sewed at the bottom and filled with staples and a small coil of stay wire. Some fence riders packed a narrow hatchet which could be used to drive staples and cut new stays when needed. The open-range cowboy would shore have balked at packin' such an outfit 'round. He'd have done anything that could've been accomplished with a rope from horseback, but gettin' down on foot and hammerin' staples into a post would've been a blow to his pride.

The fence rider usually patrolled a four- or five-strand fence with cedar posts placed at thirty-foot intervals. Some fence builders "dodged" ever' other post, that is, placed alternate posts on opposite sides of the wire to give additional strength. This was called a "dodge fence." Posts at corners were usually larger and were braced with "dead men." These were made by twistin' several strands of barbed wire into a cable and fastenin' it to the top of the post, the other end bein' fastened 'round a large rock which was buried deep into the ground. These braced the fence with steady strength, and prevented too much strain bein' placed on the corner posts.

After the posts were set the wires were usually put on with a "fence stretcher," a tool for pullin' the fence wires tightly from post to post. A roll of wire might also be attached to a wagon which stretched the wire by its progression. Important gates near headquarters were usually made of lumber and placed on hinges, but often other gates were makeshift affairs called "Texas gates," made of barbed wire fastened to a pole. This long pole, which served as a latch, was called a "belly buster," and if you've ever tried to open or close one of them gates and had the pole slip from your hands, you'd know it was well named.

Lots of things could happen to make fence ridin' necessary. Lightnin' could strike and destroy panels of fence; bulls fightin' on opposite sides of the fence could snap tightly strung wires, or push staples out and let the wires sag; heavy rains could wash up "dead men" and let a mile of fence go slack, or wash out water gaps where erosion would deepen a hole large 'nough for cattle to crawl under if wire, weights, and brush weren't added to fill the gap. Gates might be left open, or some rider crossin' a pasture might remove staples to lower the wires and forget to replace 'em. Sometimes the staples in a top post on a sharp hill would have too much strain and would snap out, lettin' the wire to the ground. As the fence rider followed the fence he watched closely for any damage caused by destructive nature or the carelessness of man. Ever' so often he left the fence to ride up a hill to survey conditions of the cattle.

There wasn't many things his eye didn't ketch. If there was a wolf track among them made by the coyotes, he'd notice it. He checked the tracks 'round the gates to see what animals had gone through since his last trip by.

26

Ridin' the Range:
Ridin' Bog, Ridin' the Mills,
and Ridin' the Brush

HEEL-FLY time was bog-ridin' time. This was the dreaded season in the cattle country. From the middle of February to the middle of April in the more southern states, and at later dates as you went north, them insects were at their worst. To escape the torture of the heelfly, cattle ran to bogholes where they could stand for protection. They soon became so bogged they couldn't free themselves. The men chosen to patrol the boggy sections and pull cattle to dry ground were called "bog riders," or "pothole riders." In sections where bogholes were unusually bad, the rancher either built fences 'round 'em or established a reg'lar bog camp nearby where the bog riders camped durin' the fly months. Many Western rivers were also treacherous with quicksands, and when thirsty cattle entered 'em and worked out into the stream they became bogged. So the bog rider not only had to watch the knowed bog holes, but also had to ride the rivers.

In the open-range days when a rancher started lookin' for a location, the first thing he sought was a stream of livin' water, and the establishin' of his camp on this gave 'im the water rights. As long as them water rights existed he could control all the range adjacent to and surroundin' it, even if he didn't own a foot of ground. There wasn't many of 'em who didn't claim both sides of the stream as far up and down as they dared. Grass without water was useless.

The only time the old-time cowhand really worried 'bout cattle gettin' thirsty was on a dry drive when trailin', or when there'd been a severe drought on the range. There wasn't much he could do 'bout it except watch the cattle suffer and be glad he wasn't the boss. He didn't worry much 'bout his own thirst. If water was plentiful he could lay on his belly and stick his muzzle in a runnin' stream, or he could ride out into a pond, shoo the skimmers away, and brush back the top waters with his hat and dip up 'nough water to quench his thirst. He didn't always look toward the other end of the water for fear he'd see the carcass of some old cow who'd give up the ghost.

If it was an unusually dry year he could find a quicksand bed in what had been a stream, and work it till some moisture came to the top. Chances are he'd have to chew it before he could swaller it, and he'd need sandpaper to get what he didn't swaller out of his mouth, but it was wet. Some of them Western streams were so full of alkali that it was said they'd give a killdee the diarrhea to fly over 'em. The cowhand used to say that this gyp water was so mean it'd run uphill and you couldn't keep it in a jug.

Life in a bog camp was monotonous and lonely, far from the activities of headquarters. There was nothin' romantic 'bout pullin' cows from the mud, and there was too much footwork in it to suit a cowhand.

The boghole rider rode a stout hoss, packed a strong rope, and frequently a short-handled shovel. The main qualifications of a bog hoss was that he be strong, winter fed, and selected for good bottom. Bog riders rode in pairs, for the work was too strenuous for one man. Placin' his rope 'round the animal's horns, he wrapped the other end 'round the horn of his saddle. After cinchin' up his saddle as tight as the latigo straps could be drawed, he mounted and started his hoss slowly. Sometimes the pull was so strong it tore the cow's horns from their sockets. A muley cow had to be roped 'round the neck, and if there was very much strain she was soon out of her misery and there was one less muley on the range.

After one roped a bogged cow, his partner waded out into the cold gumbo and started diggin' the cow's feet free with the shovel. The suction of the soil held the animal's feet as if in a vise, and the more it struggled, the deeper it sank. Only with human help would it ever get free. Even with the strongest hoss it was impossible to pull a cow free on a square

N. EGGENHOFER

pull, if as many as two feet were bogged, without breakin' the brute's neck or leg, unless her legs were loosened.

Unless bog riders were kept constantly on the job in sections containin' bog holes the losses in cattle were heavy. If the animal had been in a bog-hole for several hours, it was seldom good for anything afterward. It was usually too weak to walk or its leaders had been strained. If the weather was cold, it might become paralyzed by chill even in less time, and might never walk again. Often when she was discovered she was already dead, or too far gone to live after she was pulled out. All the rancher could salvage was the hide. Cows usually got bogged worse in early spring when they were already weak from the hard winter. Then the bog riders were kept busy, sometimes havin' to work long hours after dark, not because they liked the work, but because of their loyalty to the brand and their sympathy for the animal, which they knowed wouldn't last through 'nother bone-chillin' night.

Inch by inch the cow was pulled toward dry ground. The man with the shovel was up to his knees in cold gumbo. He had to work fast to dig the cow's legs free, and durin' that time he had to keep his own legs movin' to keep from gettin' bogged 'imself. As the animal was dragged toward dry ground he continued to lift, boost, and shovel to keep the animal free.

When the riders succeeded in draggin' the cow to dry land, she was allowed to lay there till she thawed out and had gained a little strength. If she wasn't too far gone, and showed any signs of life, she was tailed up. Often she was still too weak to more'n stagger a few steps before she fell down again, and sometimes had to be tailed up a dozen times before she could stand on her feet to stay. To the shovel man it was exceptionally disagreeable work, and sometimes it was hard to tell which was the muddiest, him or the rescued cow. A cowhand hated doin' footwork anyway, and when he had to wallow in the mud besides, he'd shore refuse to do it if he didn't consider it a duty.

When the bog rider found a cow caught in the river quicksand, he worked different than when she was in a boghole. It was sometimes best to pull off his pants and boots to keep the sand from fillin' his boots and pockets to weight 'im down. When quicksand got in his boots it held his feet as in a vise and he had to pour water into 'em to get 'em off.

Methods of gettin' an animal out of quicksand varied with the animal and the bog rider. A hoss's neck was easy broke, but it could pull a lot of weight with its tail. A cow could stand a lot of pullin' by the head, but its tail would pull off easy. Because a hoss gets up in front and a cow behind, the last-used legs were liberated first so the animal wouldn't begin to flounder, and break the legs still in the sand. A hoss'd fight to get out, but a cow jes' gave up and settled down in dumb hopelessness. She did her fightin' after she got out.

After strippin' 'imself of his garments, the bog rider approached the victim and began trompin' the sand which held her front legs. As he tromped the sand down, the water rose till he freed one leg at a time. By workin' fast he could soon loosen the hind legs before the front one got bogged too much again. With the front legs freed and the hind ones partly loosened, a rope could be slipped under the body and tied to the horn of the saddle. The cow could then be pulled out. The pullin' had to be in line with the body, and if the pull was even slightly to one side the neck might be cricked or a leg snapped.

"As ungrateful as a cow fresh pulled from a boghole" was a common figger of speech. Weak, cold, worn out by her long imprisonment, she felt no gratitude toward her rescuer. If she had any strength at all, she turned on 'im and tried her best to hook 'im or gore his hoss. Fortunately, she was usually too cold and stiff to more'n stagger a few steps before she fell again. If she appeared to have 'nough strength to do any real damage, he roped her again and busted her, lettin' her lay there till he could get safely away and let her get over her mad spell.

RIDIN' THE MILLS

Nothin' changed life on the range like the comin' of the wire fences. Fenced off from livin' water, somethin' had to be done to bring water to the cattle. Water locators with their water witches began to come in, and they were followed by well drillers. A cow could do without grass for a day or two, but if she didn't get water the cowman might as well hang his saddle on the fence. With the comin' of fences he began to breed up his herds and sell cattle by the pound instead of by the head, so he had to do somethin' to keep her from walkin' off her tallow by goin' so far to water. No matter how much he paid for the bull that sired his calves, if they followed their mothers goin' back and forth for water too far, they'd become dogied and rusty. Therefore windmills began to dot the range. The first ones were crude, wooden things, and the cowhand had little use for either them or wire fences. He didn't like anything that changed his free open-range way of life. He had little faith in windmills takin' the place of livin' water. "No wind, no water," they said, and a cow got jes' as thirsty on still days as she did when the wind was blowin'.

The first windmills were the U. S. Mills, called "Government mills." These had a big wooden wheel, double vanes, and a direct stroke. Because they were crude wooden affairs without grease cups or oil reservoirs, they had to be greased by hand and greased often. This created a special job for the cowhands, and a ranch which had a lot of mills kept one or two men busy ridin' 'em. He was knowed as the "mill rider," or "windmill monkey," since he had to do a lot of climbin' over the mill to grease it. 'Bout the only thing he packed with 'im was a beer bottle full of oil, but this was so messy he soon learned to hide it in the bracin' of each mill to be used when he rode by.

When one of the first windmills in the Texas Panhandle was installed and put into operation, the owner took his crew of riders out to see how it worked before acceptin' it from the contractor. When he saw the little trickle of water flowin' out he was as tickled as a cub bear with a honeycomb, and declared that the windmill would revolutionize the cow business. One skeptical cowhand eyed the small stream, and said, "Hell, Boss, I could get behind a bush and do a better job than that."

It didn't take much runnin' to make one of them old mills start cryin' for oil. The rider could hear it long before he got to it, and he knowed what it needed. Skinnin' up the ladder with his bottle, he was soon

drenchin' the sucker rods and gears till they quit squawkin'. The smaller outfits hired only one man for this job. If there was a breakdown he reported it, and the ranch had to send for outside help because the average hand wasn't a mechanic. The larger outfits with many mills kept a whole crew of repairmen with wagons and tools.

If the mill rider found the mill wheel racin' like mad and no water comin' forth, he knowed the sucker rod had been pulled in two. The bawlin' cattle 'round an empty trough told 'im how important it was to get to headquarters for help, a team, and tackle. 'Bout all he could do alone was grease one. No cowman liked to see cattle suffer from thirst, so he rode fast for help. Even then it took hours to repair a broken-down windmill. While they worked, the thirsty cattle tromped the troughs, bellowed, hooked each other, and made a general nuisance of themselves. He was grateful when he saw the water comin' forth again, but then he had to fight the cattle to see that each had an opportunity to get its share.

Barbed wire and windmills helped the cowman breed up his herds. He went in for heavy beef when cattle began sellin' by the pound. The old longhorn could walk miles for water without tirin', but the finer bred animals couldn't go far without losin' weight. Long walks to water even stunted the growth of the young cattle. So the rancher began buildin' more wells in the larger pastures, and the mill rider was kept busy on the mills. One could tell the depth of the well by the size of the wheel and the lay of the land by the height of the derrick. In a flat country they averaged 'bout twenty-five feet in height, but below a hill or caprock they were sometimes forty feet high. This latter height made the climbin' harder for the miller. With the cowboy's talent for givin' ever'thing a name, each mill soon received one and they could be used to give directions.

When the mill rider got to the top of the mill, he shoved the vane 'round so the wheel was out of the wind, and tied it off with a hobble rope or some wire till the greasin' job was done. It got to be quite a job to climb the tower and fight yeller jackets each time. Some few of 'em have been knocked off and seriously injured, but this didn't happen often if he was sober, and he usually was if on the job. They shed their spurs and chaps before startin' their climb to lessen this handicap. More have been injured by fallin' through rotten timbers of the old wooden mills than in any other way. If he received a serious injury when workin' alone, he might lay there till he was missed and someone came searchin' for 'im. This might be hours later.

In later years, with the comin' of gasoline engines, the mill rider's job became one for a mechanic who understood carburetors, spark plugs, and jack pumps. Though a mill might be equipped with them gasoline engines, they wasn't always used, but saved for windless days. However, the old-time mill rider who was ignorant of its operation was put to work at some other task and some young feller with garage experience was put on the job. This was no longer a greasin' job, but one which called for the savvy of the general cussedness of gasoline engines. Most of the old-time riders were glad to quit when this new-fangled method was introduced. They didn't like the smell of gasoline. As herds improved, so did the mills. The windmill later also brought a touch of luxury to the ranch by puttin' runnin' water in the house and makin' green gardens possible.

Many a thirsty cowhand has rode out of his way to visit some nearby mill to quench his thirst with its pure water. The old-time cowhand quenched his thirst with the first water he came across, no matter what the kind. It might be clear or muddy, cool or warm, or alkalied and gyppy. Water from stagnant pools gave many an old-timer boils and chills and fever, but they was made of rawhide and whalebone, and soon wore them afflictions off.

Here's a story I was told 'bout Bud Puryear, an old cowhand of the Texas Panhandle. The ranch had sent several cowboys south to drive in a small bunch of cattle to the home ranch. They had to drive them cattle through a dry desert section nearly all day before reachin' the ranch, and both cattle and men suffered extremely from thirst. By the time they reached the southern edge of the ranch where there was a surface tank, the cattle were frantic and the men's tongues were swollen. When the cattle smelled the water of the tank they made a run for it, and the men followed.

Bud rode right in among the cattle, lay down on his belly, and stuck his muzzle in the water. The other boys rode to the other side of the tank where the water wasn't muddied.

"Hey, Bud!" one of 'em yelled over to the other side. "Why don't you come over here where the water's clear?"

"Hell," answered Bud, "what difference does it make? I'm goin' to drink it all anyway."

RIDIN' THE BRUSH

The brush rider was different from any other cowboy. He worked different, dressed different, and looked different. He was an expert at runnin' cattle in the brush, somethin' a plains cowboy couldn't do. He had to be a good rider because he had to ride in ever' position to dodge the brush. At one time or 'nother durin' his ride, he was practically all over the hoss, first in one position, then in an entirely different one as he dodged. In order to dodge successfully, he had to keep his eyes open, although thorns and limbs were constantly tearin' at his face. He had to look to dodge and he had to dodge to keep lookin'. He used his arms, hands, shoulders, legs, and feet as shields.

The country he worked in was called the "brasada," or "brush country." The Spanish word is *brazada*, from *brazo*, meanin' arm or branch. This term was particularly applied to parts of Texas in the region densely covered with thickets and underbrush.

The brush rider went by such names as "brush buster," "brush thumper," "brush hand," "brush whacker," and "brush popper," the latter bein' the most pop'lar title. He was also sometimes called a "limb skinner," but his limbs were the ones that got skinned. It was characteristic of 'im to grab his hoss with the spurs and break into a run when he started into the brush. He never lost respect for the brush, but he knowed he'd never ketch a cow by lookin' for a soft entrance. He hit it on the run and tore a hole in it.

When he came out of the brush he had knots on his head so his hat didn't fit like it did when he went in, his face was scratched and skinned, he was full of thorns, and there was 'nough wood hangin' to his saddle horn to barbecue a side of yearlin' ribs. Maybe his hoss was full of thorns, and holdin' one foot up as he stepped outside to blow, with his head low and his flanks heavin'. He had to go back into the brush for practically ever' cow and bring 'em out one at a time. Then they were tied to a tree, or necked to some other cow, drove farther out into a big clearin' where they were held by several riders, or put into a corral.

Compared to the romantic cowboy of fiction, the brush hand was a sorry-lookin' cuss. No big hats or fancy trappin's for 'im. He wasn't much in the sun, and a big hat gave too much surface for the brush to grab. His hat was usually pinched or rolled to a point in front, and some of 'em were kept on with a chin strap. His chaps were never of the hair variety, and flappin' leather bat wings were likely to be snagged. His chaps were much heavier'n ordinary ones, close fittin', and with no buckles or conchas exposed.

He wore a strong close-fittin' jacket without a tail. Leather jackets would be picked to pieces. He might take off his hot jacket in the brandin' pen, but he'd feel as naked without his chaps as he would without his pants. Besides, he never knowed when he'd have to go back into the brush again. If he could afford gloves he wore 'em; otherwise his skin had to pay the penalty.

The brush buster's saddle was a good one, though smooth and without fancy stampin', or raised designs to invite the hold of thorns to get in their work. Ever' saddle was equipped with heavy bull-nosed tapaderos, never the long, fancy eagle bills of other sections. They were used strictly as brush busters as the rider extended his legs in some direction to brush aside the limbs. These, together with his duckin'-covered elbows, fended away most of the whippin' brush. When one had worked in the brush very long, his costume was torn and scarred till he looked like it wasn't good 'nough for the ragman. But little did he care. His feller workers looked as bad, and there wasn't any audience to criticize.

As a roper the brush hand was without a peer. His rope was much shorter than that of the plains cowboy, often a scant twenty-five feet.

Fightin' his way through the brush, there was neither time nor space to swing a loop. He used a small loop and frequently had nothin' but a hind foot to dab his rope on. To avoid entanglements his cast had to be made expertly at jes' the right moment. Often the brush was so thick he didn't even take his rope down, but tailed the animal down till he could slip from the saddle and place his loop on the animal's horns. Such brush was so thick it was said that snakes had to climb up to see out. The plains cowboy, with his long rope and wide swingin' loop, would be worthless in the brush country. It was said that jes' two things were required to make a good brush roper—"a damned fool and a race hoss."

His hoss was usually lightweight, and he'd learned to twist and dodge like a good cuttin' hoss in dodgin' the brush. He required little reinin', for once he got sight of the cow nothin' could stop 'im. Like his rider, he was a brute for punishment, and as game as they come. The number of hosses in the brush hand's string was greater than in other mounts because the work was too hard to keep a hoss at it long at a time. Between rides each hoss was given a rest to allow the thorns to work out and the wounds to heal. Yet no matter how stove up he became, he was always ready to break into the brush at the first opportunity.

The brush roundup was more of a drive than a roundup. Men were scattered throughout the brush, and they drove the cattle before 'em as quietly as possible so that there'd be no undue excitement. The drive'd be headed toward some natural openin' in the brush, or toward some trap or corral. These were indispensable in the brush country. All the cattle in a selected space couldn't be gotten on the first drive, but the accumulated cattle were driven into the trap with each drive and the men returned to rework the same territory till they'd gotten all the cattle in that section.

Most of the drivin' in the brush country was done real early in the mornin', as soon as the first break of dawn was in the east, and the drive was then usually over by ten or eleven o'clock. The brush got hot in the middle of the day, and cattle didn't work good in the heat. Drivin' was often done on moonlight nights, and was called a "moonlight roundup."

If it had rained and the brush was wet, them cattle were especially hard to work. Some outfits kept trained dogs to help with the work, and these cut down the work of both hoss and man.

27

Blizzards and Droughts

THE old-time cowhand had to work in all kinds of weather. In fact, the worse the weather, the more ridin' he had to do. When the sun went down in a murk of boilin' clouds, or when the horizon was hung with gray trailin' skirts of showers and a black cloudbank shot through and through with crinklin' lightnin', he knowed he was in for a wet night.

Such rains often lasted for days, but the work of the roundup couldn't stop. Men moved 'bout in noisy and clumsy yeller slickers, all of which made the hosses spooky. Ever'thing was wet and stiff and sticky. Boots were clogged with mud till the spurs on his heels looked like 'nother hunk of mud. The work was dangerous now, for stirrups were slick, saddles wet, and hosses cold and touchy. Wet, slippery stirrups and muddy boots shore didn't make it safe to fork a spooky hoss.

Slippery footin' made 'im worry and wonder if his hoss'd fall and pin 'im, and he wished right then that his hoss had as many legs as a centipede. Ropes were muddy and stiff, latigos were wet, and so was his bed. This was one of the drab sides of his life, but most of 'em kept their good humor because they knowed that this was a part of their job. He might cuss a little when he went to saddle his mount that'd wallowed in the mud and had to be scraped off before he could put the wet saddle and soggy blanket on 'im while the bronc stomped thin mud in his face.

But the thing that hurt 'im the worst was havin' to wait for chuck when he was hungry, while the cook cussed the wet wood and the damp salt and flour in tryin' to get his meal under way. If he had a fly set up over his fires and workbench, things wasn't so bad, but even then it was hard to bake bread from damp flour.

At night he had to sleep in damp beds on soggy ground and he knowed this'd cause 'im to suffer with rheumatism in later years.

Some mornin' the men in the bunkhouse might wake up to hear the wind howlin' 'round the corners to find its way through chinks and crevices, bringin' with it a thread of snow that quickly built itself into a little mound. With ever' hour the world outside changed into a place of white mystery. The ranch buildin's, blotted out by the thick mantle that clung to 'em like wet fingers, were jes' blotches of black and white. The haystacks and corrals were lost in a veil that swirled 'bout like the skirt of a mad dancer. Yet somewhere out there in that mad, blind world was life—cattle and hosses, and maybe men.

To one who, when ridin' far out on the wide plains, experienced the sudden blizzard out of the north sweepin' in fury across the land, it was an experience he never forgot. The howlin', freezin' wind drivin', swirlin', blindin' sheets of knifelike sleet and powdery snow that stung your face and seemed to smother you as it blotted out the rest of the world left you with a sense of absolute desolation and helplessness.

It affected cattle the same way. When a storm hit a herd they instantly turned tail to it and drifted with the storm. With the stingin' sleet cuttin' into their eyes and faces, it was a waste of time to try and stop 'em. There wasn't any panic like a stampede, but the cattle were determined not to face that punishment. Even men couldn't face such a storm. Shortly they became hungry and numb, thin and gaunt. Glistenin' icicles hung from their mouths, ears, and eyes. On and on they plodded before the storm, lowin' their misery to a seemingly empty world, heads lowered, hairy backs snow-covered and crusty, their eyes but dark holes peerin' out of an ice pack.

With heads down and tails tucked, they stumbled on. With legs and hocks sore, hairless and bleedin' from walkin' in crusted snow, they left a trail of blood and frozen bodies of them that got down and couldn't get up. Here and there was a thin-flanked cow with a shiverin' rough-coated calf trailin' at her heels, maybe wonderin' at what cruel world he'd come into. Also there was an occasional humpbacked yearlin' with little nubs of horns tellin' that they were jes' comin' out of calfhood. Such drifts and "die-ups" made the large cattle owners cuss their great loss, the small determined rancher to make a fresh start in the spring, and the weak ones to throw in the sponge.

Most wagon bosses, when the cattle first began to drift, made some effort to stop 'em, but never succeeded, and in the end would order the boys to make it back to the wagon while they could still find it. He knowed the cattle would stay together, and he'd find the survivors against some drift fence or under a cutbank when the storm was over. Besides, chousin' the hosses too much in tryin' to turn 'em would make the hosses too hot and sweaty to unsaddle 'em.

Hosses usually survived severe storms because they sought shelter and pawed down to grass. The constant action of this pawin' also seemed to keep 'em warmer. For water they ate the snow. If the snow was light and the dry grass long, cattle could exist for a time because they ate a quantity of the snow with the grass. Some soon learned to eat snow for moisture. This was better'n choppin' holes in the ice in a stream for 'em, because such a water hole held 'em to the stream where the grass was soon exhausted, and rather than leave the water they ate the willow branches. This caked their stomachs with dry murrain which couldn't be cast off, and many died a horrible death.

Occasionally in the north a Chinook wind would melt the snow and ice, then turn cold again and seal ever'thing under a frozen mass, even the trees and brush. The cattle then, with their very vitals chilled, would quit tryin' to find forage and stand in helpless despair. As long as cattle held together, they've been knowed to drift for hundreds of miles if there was no drift fence or natural barrier to bar 'em, but if they became separated a lone animal would be apt to give up and lie down to die.

Sometimes the snow drifted into ravines till it was level with the earth, and cattle piled into these and couldn't extricate themselves, thus causin' great loss. Followin' the trail of a drift was the trail of death and financial ruin. Ever' few yards some animal had reached the end of its endurance and laid down to die. They were soon chilled to the marrow of their bones, and didn't seem to care. When comin' to a fence a few might turn aside and search for an openin', but most of 'em jes' tried to push through. As they piled up, sometimes a post was flattened and they continued on with the wind, but if the posts held they trampled each other underfoot till they were piled high 'nough for the last ones to walk over their bodies to the other side.

Nothin' was so destructive to the cattle business as them sudden and severe blizzards. There were usually preliminary warnin's which the wise plainsman knowed and prepared for if he had the warnin' far 'nough in advance. But most of them storms were of surprisin' suddenness, and before one knowed it the air was suddenly a whirlin' mass of cuttin' ice and blindin' white. This was especially so in Texas. One old cowman, in describin' such a blizzard, said, "Them Texas northers jes' pour off the North Pole with nothin' to stop 'em but a bob-wire fence, and it's full of knotholes."

After a hard winter, the survivors of the herd were weak till the spring grass came. Durin' this time the cowhand worked overtime tailin' up them "downers," and it was a back-breakin' job when you had to follow it all day. Because even when a weak cow had been tailed up she often fell again if she was frightened or attempted to run, the cowhands moved cautiously among 'em. The cattle had to be tailed up ever' mornin' till the prairie greened up and they got a little strength. By that time the heel flies got after 'em, and they beat it to the nearest boghole where they had to be dug out and tailed up again.

Though drifts and die-ups of the blizzard years were the Number One tragedies of the range, the drought years were a close second. Water has always been the problem in the cattle country. In the early days the ranchman, in locatin' his ranch, first established his water rights by squattin' on some stream. But even large streams could dry up in the drought years. Meetin' the long drought months that periodically plagued the range called for a special kind of courage. There had to be patience, too, and a willingness to help his neighbors toward a common end.

Hot sun and dry wind, day after day, week after week, baked all the moisture from the earth, leavin' the grassland brown and lifeless till there wasn't 'nough grass in the whole state to winter a prairie dog. It was now a country where the unpityin' sun came up day after day and burned deep lines into men's faces, stampin' the mark of age long before the debt was due; where men got used to seein' shimmerin' objects through the unvaryin' haze of heat; where no man could tell the color of his neighbor's eyes because he never saw more'n they showed through the narrow slits that kept out the scorchin' rays.

The whole earth got as dry as a covered bridge and as gray as the rocks and as bare. Here and there the ground had cracked under the heat, and giant fissures gaped for the feet of the unwary. Cows stumbled hopelessly into canyons to learn that there, too, there was no water. Their dried skins drew tight over the bones, and the panic of desperation glared from their dull eyes. Gorged buzzards strutted ever'where. They'd cluster on a carcass, unwinkin' and insolent. Here and there were orphan calves, bawlin' impotently against echoin' canyon walls, and carrion crows hung 'bout in flocks, their shadows flittin' swiftly on the earth.

Rivers dried up till they became as dry as a tobacco box, and it got so hot it'd slip hair on a bear. Never a cloud in the sky to offer the hopeful prospect of rain, the blisterin' heat witherin' and shrivelin' the grass, yet the cowhand went patiently on with his work, his task now more than doubled. He took pride in it, as always, and there was nothin' that could tempt 'im to neglect it.

Each mornin' he got up from a sultry night to go outside and search the sky hopefully for a cloud, no matter how small. Water holes and rivers dried up to a stagnant, boggy mire where cattle became mired tryin' to suck a drop of moisture for their parched tongues. What little moisture there was at first became a foul and poisonous fluid, a death trap for the weak. Some cows went mad and broke their horns hookin' trees, rocks, and other objects; others went blind and staggered 'bout lowin' and moanin' with such pitiful appeal that it tore the heart of a cowman.

Maybe that brassy sun would keep burnin' the earth till the whole country seemed like it was jes' a thin sheet of sandpaper between it and hell. It became so hot that, as one cowhand said, "If a man died here and went to hell he'd wire back for blankets." With the sun hot 'nough to sunburn a horned frog, it didn't take long till there wasn't 'nough grass to wad a smooth-bore gun. Cattle got so thin they looked like they had only one gut, and you'd think they was a herd of jerky on the hoof. When they could go no farther they laid down and died till the whole country was as empty as a church on Saturday night.

Some ranchers were able to foresee a long drought and were able to ship or trail their cattle to 'nother state or Territory where there was still grass and water, but this was an expensive and exasperatin' job, especially if the drought area was extended and they had to make a dry drive for any distance. At such a time when the whole country was as dry as a lime burner's hat, it could easily develop into one of the tragedies of the range. As one cowhand said, "It was so dry the bushes followed the dogs 'round."

Prairie Fires

O<small>NE</small> of the worst enemies of the rancher was the prairie fire. It was always a source of worry to ranchers and cowboys alike, for the destruction of grass was like the destruction of the cattle 'emselves. Men worked for, fought for, and died for grass ever since they've been ridin' in the dust of cattle. Fires were hardest to control when there'd been an abundant grass crop, especially in the fall when the grass'd been cured on the stem. There were dangers of fires durin' more'n half the year, for both spring and fall offered several months when the grass was dry. The cattle country was usually level, the climate dry, and the wind strong, all this addin' to the hazards of fire.

The inferno of cracklin' grass and sagebrush deprived cattle of winter feed, and burned homes, corrals, and haystacks as well. After a range had been burned in the fall, there'd be no grass till spring, and not much then, for a burned-off range recuperated mighty slow. Sometimes it took several years for it to get back to its normal state. It was a serious matter when a rancher lost his winter feed. Often he had to sell off his cattle at a loss, find other ranges at a high cost, or let his cattle starve.

So it was quite natural that men of the cattle country took ever' precaution to prevent fires, but they started anyhow, either through neglect, by accident, or an act of nature. There were many causes of fires. The cowhand had to be careful with his smokin', and many of 'em got the habit of breakin' their matches in two before throwin' 'em away.

Cooks also got careless when breakin' camp, and failed to soak their ashes with 'nough water, sometimes leavin' a live coal to smolder till caught by the wind and blowed into some dry grass. But the people the cowhand hated like a snake were the campers passin' through the country. They were seldom acquainted with the dangers of fire to the cattle country and were careless in the handlin' of their campfires. Fires have been started by some thoughtless greener tryin' to burn out a pack rat's nest, by the careless flip of a match or cigarette, or by birds peckin' at an unstruck match dropped from some cowhand's pocket.

Sometimes in the early days grass fires were deliberately set by Injuns in their fight against the white man, or some nester might hate a ranchman 'nough to burn 'im out. Fire was often used as a fightin' weapon. At times, also, the lightnin' might set a fire, but usually durin' such a storm there was 'nough rain to put out them fires before they got much start.

Most ranchers, and even the nesters, would plow a fire-guard 'round their homes, corrals, and haystacks as a protection against fire. This usually worked, but it wasn't infallible. Much depended upon the size of the fire and the strength of the wind. In a high wind sparks could easily be blowed across the fire-guard to set a new blaze. The fire-guard was made by plowin' sets of furrows from fifty to a hundred yards apart, with four furrows in each set. Then in the fall when the grass was dry 'nough to burn, he selected a windless day and burned the grass between the sets, trailin' the fire with water-laden wagons. In settin' them fires the cowhand would use a gunny sack soaked in kerosene and fastened to a wire several feet in length. This wire would then be tied to a rope and the rope fastened to his saddle horn. The soaked sack would be lighted and dragged some distance behind the rider, settin' the grass afire as he went. The fire was set on the lee side of the strip of grass so that if there was any wind the fire'd have to run against it.

Other cowhands followed with sacks soaked in water from the barrels carried in the accompanyin' wagon, and beat out any fire that broke over the furrow at any time. While fire-guards were often a protection, they didn't, as we've said before, always make a ranch property immune from fire. Burnin' cowchips were often caught in a high wind and rolled 'long the ground like a tin plate, settin' new fires as they went. Or tumbleweeds and other brush were often shot into the air and sailed like balls of fire for great distances, kindlin' new fires wherever they landed.

Back firin' has long been used to check prairie fires. This is a pur-

posely set fire controlled on the advancin' side and drove toward the oncomin' blaze till the two meet and burn 'emselves out. Ranchers sometimes used this method of protectin' their outfit if they'd neglected plowin' fire-guards and there was a fire burnin' itself toward 'em. Many times this method was successful, but it was always dangerous. The old sayin' "Fight fire with fire" can be applied here, but if it ain't controlled properly you only add to your troubles. It was best to have some such background as an arroyo, a creek, or cow trail from which to start a backfire. While the oncomin' fire was still miles away the backfire could be set, providin' there were plenty of men with wet sacks to watch that the fire didn't jump back with the wind. When 'nough space had been burned to prevent the grass on the leeward side from ignitin', the sack men moved on down the sides to keep the fire from breakin' over at other places. In this way the backfire was forced to burn slowly into the wind till it met the oncomin' fire and they burned 'emselves out.

The best way to fight fires seemed to be the drag. A steer was shot and cut in half the long way; the head was cut off so as not to be in the way of the ropes. One side was skinned from belly to back, leavin' this floppin' skin as the carcass was dragged to help put out the little embers that the carcass didn't extinguish. Ropes were tied to front and hind legs, and with this half-carcass two cowhands pulled it over the edge of the blaze, one ridin' on either side of it. Each animal made two drags, and while two cowhands pulled one in one direction, two others pulled the second half in the opposite direction. Hosses pullin' the drag on the inward side of the blaze had to be changed often, for the ground they walked over was hot and apt to bake their hoofs. As they stepped gingerly over the hot ground they kicked up spurts of soot which soon covered both them and their riders.

It made no difference whose brand was on the steer; he had to be sacrificed for the good of the range. It was often better, if some wire was handy, to use this on the legs of the animal, this, in turn, bein' fastened to the rope by which the rider dragged the carcass. This was because the flames sometimes burned a rope in two. The two men draggin' them half-carcasses by their saddle horns paced their speed by the ability of the men behind 'em to keep up with their beatin' out the remnants of the blaze with their wet gunny sacks, saddle blankets, slickers, or by what other means they had at hand.

Fightin' fires was the work most dreaded by the cowboy. The men behind the drags, for instance, beatin' out the little blazes found that job physically very tirin'. Their lungs were on fire from the smoke and ashes they were forced to breathe, their eyes smarted from the same reason, and the heat from the blaze and burned-over ground was intense. Yet they had to keep at it till relieved, for they dared not stop and let the scattered little blazes get ahead of 'em again. Sometimes men worked near 'nough to the flames to get their faces blistered. The stench of burned grass, weeds, sagebrush, and cow chips filled the air, yet men fought till they were ready to drop from exhaustion.

Cattle bellowed and stampeded, circlin' before the oncomin' blaze as if crazy. Wild animals, such as deer, antelope, coyotes, and mustangs fled before the heat, no longer afraid of man, but fleein' from somethin' they knowed to be a common enemy. Sometimes they fled through the blaze onto the burned-over ground where they were safe for the time, but had to forego food and water. The loss of cattle was usually slight because their instinct told 'em to follow the trails they had made to water, and it often happened that they made their way to some creek, tank, or lake where they took refuge. It was the small calves which usually suffered. Bein' deserted by their mothers when they left to seek water, it was their nature to lay hidden in the grass till their mother returned. They didn't know what this strange new enemy was and had no one to guide 'em to safety.

Rarely were humans caught in them fires, yet when the grass was tall and the wind high, especially when it took a sudden change of course, such a thing could and did happen.

Cowmen and settlers on the prairie were always on the lookout for that thin cloud of smoke on the horizon that spelled danger. When such a cloud was sighted he sounded the alarm, and men of the ranch dropped whatever else they were doin' and hurried to help in the fight. Wagons with water barrels, chuck wagons to feed the fire fighters, gunny sacks were gathered, and all made ready to do battle with the most dreaded enemy. It made no difference where the line of smoke was. Even if the wind was blowin' toward it and away from his own ranch, he felt it his duty to help his feller rancher, and besides, one never knowed when the wind would change and push the fire toward his range. Even if he didn't like a certain neighbor, they were now fightin' a common foe, a dreaded and merciless one.

Them smoke clouds could be very deceivin', and men might ride miles before they came upon it. But they went, for they considered it their duty to help one another, no matter how distant the range. The next fire might be on a man's own range, and he hoped his distant neighbor'd then come to his aid.

At night a fire could be seen from a long way by the reflection in the sky, and it was especially hard to tell how far away it might be. One could tell which way the fire was travelin' from the direction of the wind. If it was blowin' toward his range, it was quite natural that he'd speed up his effort to reach it.

When a fire was seen, ever'body turned fire fighter. Even the town people were concerned. Stores closed, and all activity ceased except the preparation for fightin' the fire. They were not only concerned 'bout the safety of the town, but for the ranchers who were the customers and friends of their merchants. Gunny sacks were gathered, brooms handed out, and ever'body made an effort to get to the fire. They raced recklessly over the prairie and hills, toward where the night was aglow. With the ranchmen went the wagons poundin' over the untrailed prairie. Sometimes the wagon was filled with empty barrels which danced a mad jig behind the high seat where the driver sat with his feet braced and a whip in his hand which he was usin' freely. The riders followin' 'im on hossback were hopeful they'd find plenty of water in some pond or at some windmill nearer the fire.

Closer to the fire the hot wind blowed the pungent smell of smoke into their faces, and scattered flakes of blackened grass and ashes settled upon 'em. The nearer they got, the thicker the cinders, till the air was filled with 'em, like a snowstorm done in India ink, and the breath of the wind was hotter on their faces. As the fire approached in a dancin' yeller line, they could hear that roarin' cracklin' as it ate up ever'thing before it. The smoke rolled toward 'em, liftin' here and there to let a flare of yeller through.

Millions of sparks danced in and out among the smoke wreaths which ever curled upward—first red, then a dainty rose, and finally black. Men could be seen runnin' back and forth, now disappearin' in the downward swirl of smoke, now seen again in the open beyond. Ever' so often men ran to the wagon, climbed a wheel, dipped a frayed gunny sack into one of the barrels, lifted it out, and ran back to the nearest point of the fire with it drippin'. One could hear the wet sacks *thud, thud* on the ground, leavin' behind the black ashes and the little thin streamers of smoke where they'd struck. Yet always a new blaze seemed to spring forward, and springin' upon these, their arms continued to swing downward, no matter how tired and numb they might be. As they beat the ragged line of yeller with the water-soaked sacks, they left behind a trail of waverin' smoke-traced rim of smolderin' black where only a moment before had been a gay, dancin' orange light. Quite often the smolder left behind was fanned into new life, and again the dry grass was devoured greedily by the ever hungry red tongues.

Hour after hour men worked desperately till they were forced to stop for short rests from sheer exhaustion. The heat in the wind scorched their faces while the smoke filled their lungs and eyes with intolerable smartin'. Time seemed to cease to be measured accurately and the whole world seemed to be unreal, filled with sultry heat and smoke through which the red sun shone heavily, followed by a moon just as red. Now the smoke rolled up in uneven volumes as the wind lifted it; now it was sucked back down by a change of draft, blindin' 'em as they fought.

If the wind was strong and the grass tall, the fire had to be fought from the sides. The front fires moved too fast and were too dangerous to be fought from the front. The heat from this position could quickly kill a man. There was little hope for checkin' the advance of such a fire unless it reached some natural obstruction like a creek, river, or a barren hill, or unless the wind suddenly reversed itself. Side fires burned slower and could be controlled by the drags.

After the last spiteful flop of a black rag which had once been a good new sack had stamped out the last tiny red tongue of fire, the exhausted men would drop in their tracks, looking back at the damage that had been done.

As one old cowman surveyed the work they'd done, and the damage of the fire, he saw the whole range black with here and there a cow chip, or a mesquite stump smolderin' in little blue wisps of smoke. It was a world of hot, smoke-sodden wind and dead black shadows, a world filled with the stench of burned vegetation, and with the prospects of no forage for months to come. The only words that came to his mind to express his thoughts were: "It shore looks like hell with the folks moved out."

Ropers and Ropin'

WHILE ever' cowboy had to have some ropin' ability to hold his job, not all of 'em developed into top ropers. Ropin' was the hardest of all cowboy attainments, and few mastered the art. The workin' cowboy's rope was in constant use, savin' others much time and hard work, and often his unerrin', quick throw saved a feller puncher from death or injury by a mad cow. Of course, all stockmen could rope after a fashion, but the man who could ketch a cow by the heels or head from a runnin' hoss ever' throw was, as one cowhand said, "As scarce as bird dung in a cuckoo clock."

A good roper had to have a sense of perfect timin' and the ability to judge distance. Calculatin' the speed of a runnin' steer with that of his hoss, he had to judge the amount of rope to span the distance between. Judgment of time and distance was half the battle in good ropin'. Top ropers seemed to know by intuition the proper time to throw. They were experts who went 'bout the business without any fancy flourishes. In heelin' he seemed to know jes' when the loop reached the animal's feet at the split second they'd be off the ground. Yet no matter how much natural talent he had, it took constant practice to coordinate this judgment of time and distance with the actual throwin' of the loop. Watching a smooth roper at work was a beautiful sight.

The ketch hand was usually an expert roper and was appointed to rope out the saddle hosses for the other hands. Durin' brandin' season it was his job to heel the calves from hossback and drag 'em to the iron men. He went 'bout his job methodically and coolly, and seldom missed as he walked his hoss slowly among the calves. This was the prettiest of all cow work and showed the smooth roper to the best advantage. He usually rode a steady hoss, preferably one with a runnin' walk or slow foxtrot. He eased through the herd, flippin' his loop over the calf's head or heels with apparently little attention to where his rope was goin'. When he throwed, his hoss automatically turned toward the bull-doggers to meet the calf halfway to slip the roper's loop off. The loop for this kind of work was similar to the hooleyann, a short half-throw that didn't tear up a herd. If there was a few long calves or yearlin's in the herd, he'd drag 'em out by the front or hind feet as a concession to the bull-doggers.

Sometimes, if he wanted to have some fun with the flankers, he'd rope a big calf by the neck and enjoy watchin' 'em try and wrastle it down. He listened to their sarcasm with a grin as he turned his hoss back for 'nother ketch. His little joke broke the monotony of the job, created a diversion which all the other hands, except the flankers, enjoyed watchin'. If the flankers, however, refused to flank the calf, to save face the roper might have to get down and wrastle 'im down 'imself. If he succeeded in doin' this without too much trouble, his sarcasm was shore 'nough cuttin'.

The term "dally" comes from the Spanish *dar la vuelta*, meanin' to "take a turn with a rope." To the American cowboy it sounded like "dolly welter" and he soon shortened it to "dally." It meant to take a half-hitch 'round the saddle horn with a rope after a ketch was made, the loose end bein' held in the roper's hand so he could let it slip in case of an emergency, or take it up shorter. The dally man needed a longer rope than the tie man, one who tied his rope to the saddle horn, because he couldn't throw it all out, but had to have some left to take his turns. When the rope was wound clockwise 'round the horn instead of the proper way, counterclockwise, it was called "coffee grindin'." The knot he tied in the end of his rope was called a "rosebud."

The tie-fast man tied the home end of the rope fast to the horn. There've been arguments on the range for generations as to the merits of both methods, tyin' and dallyin'. As a rule cowhands tie east of the Rockies and dally west of 'em. Tie men used a shorter rope than the dally man, and were usually good ropers with confidence in their ability. The Texan tied his rope, and when he roped anything he figgered to hang onto it. He wasn't a quitter. The Californian kept his rope untied, and when he roped anything he'd take a dally 'round the saddle horn, and if the critter got too pesky he could turn 'im loose. The Texan didn't say much, but the Californian knowed what he thought of 'em and they didn't like it. Also, the tie man argued there were too many fingers lost in dallyin'.

Openin' the noose of a rope with a few quick jerks toward the front, as the right hand grasped the rope at the honda, was called "shakin' out," and was one of the first things done in buildin' a loop. Buildin' the loop was the first important step in ropin'. The honda was run up the rope accordin' to the size of the loop you wanted to build. 'Bout a foot of the rope ran parallel with the loop and was held this distance from the honda if you wanted a fast-closin' loop. This doublin' of the loop a little way helped hold the noose open. The loop was always held in the hand so the thumb was nearest the honda, and the nearer the hand, the slower the closin'.

"Whirlin' " was mostly used in ropin' from hossback. Its object was to keep the loop open, or make it bigger as it paid out with the whirl, and to gain momentum for a long cast. An amateur'll nearly whirl his arm off long before he gets close 'nough for a cast, but the expert roper whirled the noose very little, perhaps once or twice over his head. The whirl was never used when ropin' in a corral. If tryin' to rope out hosses, whirlin' excited 'em. Some men whirled the rope over their head, others kept the loop at their side, shoulder height. A certain amount of wrist action was used to keep the loop open and from kinkin'. Like other ropin', the coil was held in the left hand to play out as the cast was made.

A roper on foot who, instead of whirlin' the rope 'round his head before throwin', spread it out behind and to one side of 'im, and with a quick graceful throw, or toss, launched it with unerrin' aim over the head of the animal was called a "rope tosser." This method was used almost entirely in ketchin' calves out of a herd, as it was done so quick and easy the animal was snared before it got a chance to dodge or move. A rope cast with a single overhead twist, and no whirlin', was called the "California twist."

The "Blocker loop" was a large loop, takin' this name from John Blocker, a well-knowed roper and trail driver of Texas, who originated and made this loop famous. It was started like a straight overhead loop, bein' taken 'round the head to the left. When throwed it turned over and went over the animal's shoulders and picked up both front feet. The cast was made when the loop was behind the right shoulder, the right arm bein' whipped straight forward across the circle it'd been describin'. At the same time the hand and wrist gave the loop a twist toward the left. The loop went out in front of the roper, appeared to stop, stand up, then roll to the left, showin' the honda to be on the side of the loop opposite its position when the throw was started.

The Blocker was a versatile loop. It could be throwed from hossback or afoot, and could be used for a head ketch, heelin', or forefootin'. Its rep'tation growed fast because it could stand a wide loop in front of the object to be roped and provided a bigger openin' at the right place and angle. It could be throwed on foot from any angle, front and side, without movin' the feet. It was most commonly used for heelin' cattle, as it could be throwed directly behind the animal where he couldn't see the action. The right hand continued to hold the rope after the loop had been throwed, lettin' it play out till it reached its object, and since this was so it was a better loop for close quarters.

Back in the days of the old longhorn it was necessary to use a big loop to get it over their wide-spread horns. Now'days big loops ain't needed, and are rarely used. A big loop wouldn't close fast 'nough to ketch the modern hornless critter. There're many slang names for big loops, such as "Mother Hubbard," "washerwoman loop," "community loop," and "cotton patch loop." When a roper's loop slipped over the shoulder of a roped animal and tightened 'round its belly, as the result of usin' too big a loop, it was said to be "belly roped." This was always funny to ever' one except the roper, and he was apt to get a lot of kiddin' 'bout his ropin' ability. The "small loop man" throwed a little loop often called a "dog loop," and they were usually experts at ketchin' calves.

The "hooleyann" was a fast loop used strictly for a head ketch, bein' especially used to rope hosses in a corral. It was throwed with a rather small loop and had an additional virtue of landin' with the honda slidin' down the rope, takin' up the slack as it went. Carryin' the loop in his hand, when the chance presented itself, the roper swung one quick whirl 'round in front of 'im toward the right, up over his head, and released the rope at the target. As it went over, it was turned in a way to cause it to flatten out before it reached the head of the animal to be roped. It landed straight down and had a fair-sized openin'.

The "hooleyann" could be throwed from hossback or while afoot. The loop was started from the left side, and when the thrower mounted the top of the loop was held at 'bout the left shoulder. When afoot it

could be dragged on the ground on the left side, with the roper's knuckles up. One quick whirl in front toward the right and up over the head sent the loop on its way. It was a good loop to use on an animal that had passed the roper, especially to his right. It could be throwed in any direction the roper was able to turn toward and could be placed in a greater variety of positions than any other method of ropin'. Don't confuse the hooleyann with hoolihanin'. This latter was the act of leapin' forward onto the horns of a steer in bulldoggin' to knock 'im off his feet instead of twistin' 'im down.

Mangana is a Spanish word, meanin' "lasso," "sleeve," "net," or "trap." It's also the name of a throw for forefootin', although, by throwin' the loop higher, it could be used for head ketches. The throw was made by pointin' the hand downward, draggin' the loop forward, and swingin' it out so it practically stood on edge. It stood a big loop in front of the animal, so all he had to do was step into it. It was a loop which needed perfect timin', as it'd cause an animal to stop rather than hit it if stood too far ahead of 'im. It was one of the best throws for forefootin' hosses, and was seldom used on cattle. The animal must be passin' in front of the roper and be reasonably close to make a ketch.

The *mangana de pie* is a fancy throw, and was seldom used in actual work. Pie is Spanish for "foot," hence this throw was made with the foot. The cast was made by puttin' a well opened loop on the ground with the toe beneath the honda, and as the animal to be roped went by, the loop was pitched straight forward with the foot. Like the *mangana*, this cast had to have careful timin'. There have been one-armed cowboys who used this cast successfully, but the modern cowboy scarcely knowed what the term meant, as it's almost forgotten. If it was used now it would be looked upon as a fancy trick ropin' stunt. This was 'nother loop used mostly on hosses.

The "figger eight" was a loop throwed so as to ketch the forelegs of an animal in the lower part of the eight while his head was caught in the upper part. This was done by throwin' the straight overhead loop at an animal passin' to the left, so that the honda'd hit 'im jes' behind the left ear, the loop goin' in front and droppin' over his head. When the loop hit the animal at the honda, it stopped suddenly and caused the loop to fold across. It was then the animal got his forefeet into the lower part of the loop. Many of the throws of a good roper appear to be stunt tricks, but they served a useful purpose. On any ranch a good roper stood head and shoulders above any other cowhand, riders included.

The "roll out" was 'nother loop used for ropin' from the ground. It was a loop made by jerkin' the noose forward over the hand and wrist, and releasin' it so that it'd roll out on edge, leanin' somewhat to the right. It was similar to the *mangana*, but came out faster when throwed into position. It could be used to forefoot hosses, but was better as a heel loop for cattle because it rolled a rather small loop under the belly of an animal in position to ketch both hind feet. It was usually only effective when throwed at animals passin' in front of the roper toward his right. The trick roper at a rodeo used this loop in ketchin' several riders abreast by enlargin' the loop.

The "overhead toss" was a favorite method of ketchin' hosses in a corral. The only difference between it and the hooleyann was that the hooleyann turned over as the whirl was started, and the overhead toss turned over as it left the hand. The loop was fairly small, and while held at shoulder height, the bottom part of it was kept swingin' back and forth. When the throw was made, the loop was swung backward 'round the head and released toward the target. The loop was turned over as it was swung upward before it was let go, so that at the final moment the back of the hand was facin' the left, thumb down. In this way, when the loop came down, the honda was on the right instead of the left.

The "overhead loop" was a whirlin' loop because not 'nough steam could be gotten up for a cast without whirlin'. The throw was made by startin' the whirl across the front of the roper to the left, with two or three whirls 'round the head for momentum, then castin' at the target by whirlin' the loop out in front as it came across the right shoulder. Since it was a whirlin' loop it was never used in a corral. This loop could be used for forefootin' hosses as well as other animals, and could be used as a ketch. This was a fast loop, and as it was throwed to land vertical to the ground the throw'd be missed unless the slack was jerked out quick.

The "underhand pitch" was strictly a heel loop for use on cattle. It could be used on foot in a corral, but it was a fav'rite ketch for mounted men workin' on roundup. It was 'bout the only loop for which it was permissible to whirl while workin' among cattle, and it was kept in motion at the right side in a vertical plane, swingin' up. When the target passed in front, the roper brought the rope 'round with a snap to give it carryin' power, and turned the loop over the back side of the hand as it swung upward. This pitched the loop, standin' up, under the animal's belly so he'd jump into it.

The Spanish word *pial* means "foot," and this name was given a throw called the "peal," and commonly used in stretchin' out a cow or steer— never a hoss—that had been roped by the head and neck. It was tossed underhanded jes' back of the front legs under the belly of the runnin' animal, the loop openin' so that the hind legs step into it. When expertly cast, the loop turned so as to form a figger eight, and one hind foot was caught in one half of the figger and the other in the other half. When caught thus, the animal couldn't kick loose if there was any pressure on the rope at all. This loop was used in the head-and-heel stunt of rodeos in puttin' a steer down against time.

Though various loops could be used, ketchin' an animal by the forefeet was called "forefootin'," or "pickin' up his toes." Usually the roper approached the critter from the left side, and a medium sized noose was throwed over the animal's right shoulder and a little ahead, in position to receive one or both feet as they reach ground. The noose was given an inward twist as it was throwed, which caused the upper side of the noose to flip backward against the animal's knees, ready for the ketch. A hoss to be throwed was always forefooted and never heeled. In makin' the cast the hand was swung up and forward in a swift overhand arc, never higher'n the shoulder, and the noose came down edgeways with the honda at the bottom.

Heelin' wasn't as easy as forefootin', but it could be done by throwin' the loop under the belly jes' ahead of the hind feet and lettin' the animal step into the loop. Instead of throwin' the loop over so it landed edgewise as in forefootin', it wasn't turned so far, but the honda came down on the left. Calves were heeled so they could be dragged to the brandin' fire without a struggle. Some good ropers throwed a big loop in front of the runnin' calf, let 'im run through the noose till it reached his hind legs, then tightened the noose as it slipped down to the feet. If the loop was whipped in under the animal too fast, it was apt to close and ketch accidentally if at all. This cast was used principally from hossback. Most ropers afoot used a small loop throwed under the calf's belly.

The "roll" was a corkscrew, wavelike motion of a rope started at the home end and which, travelin' 'long to the honda, could land on the object roped with a jar. It'd sometimes take the fight out of an animal which started to get on the prod when roped. But its most practical common use was to release the roper's noose when he heeled grown cattle and wanted to recover his rope without dismountin'. This saved time as well as doin' away with the danger of bein' afoot among the cattle. It was especially useful when ropin' alone, and only a few rolls were necessary to loosen the honda 'nough to free the roped animal.

Aside from ropin' hosses for breakin' or for saddlin', most ropin' on the ranch was done on calves. Ropin' grown cattle was done mostly for doctorin', clippin' to read haired-over brands, or to teach some contrary steer a lesson. Calf ropin' at a rodeo was done by ketchin' the calf by the neck, then wrastlin' it down for a hogtie. So the rodeo fan seldom saw calf ropin' as it was done on the range—by the heels. This was a harder ketch, but saved trouble of throwin' 'em by hand. They dragged to the brandin' crew better and it was easier on the flankers and the calf too. Heel ketches were mostly made in a corral or on roundup. If the calf was in the open and started runnin' he was hard to heel and sometimes had to be neck roped.

Ranchers didn't like to have their grown cattle roped because it was apt to cripple 'em or make 'em lose flesh, so it was seldom done on the ranch. 'Bout the only ropin' of grown stuff was for doctorin' screw worms, or for milkin' out a cow that'd lost her calf. Two ropers usually worked on grown stuff. One roped by the horns and held the animal while the second roper heeled the brute for stretchin' out. The front roper tried to avoid a neck ketch because it choked the animal, causin' it to struggle more. The horn ketch gave more leverage for throwin', but in these days horns are gettin' scarce, so a lot of ropin' has to be on the neck.

When a roper wanted to throw a steer single-handed, he rode as close to the animal as possible before castin' his loop. When it settled 'round the horns and had been given a jerk to hold it there, the slack of the rope was dropped jes' under the steer's right hipbone, and 'round its buttocks. The rider then reined his hoss to the left and braced 'imself for the shock that was shore to follow. When the slack was taken up the steer was reversed in midair and slammed to the ground, landin' with his head to the rear of the hoss, which, though the rider was halfway to the steer, was keepin' the slack out of the rope and makin' an effort to drag the steer toward the roper.

The steer'd usually lay still long 'nough for the cowboy to doctor or do whatever he caught 'im for. Then came the ticklish job of gettin' his rope off and back on his hoss before the steer could get up, for he'd get up on the prod. If he had horns, the cowboy twisted his head as far over as possible and pushed one horn into the ground. In this position, the steer'd have to struggle a few seconds to get his head straightened out and onto his feet, by which time the man was back on his hoss, runnin' the kinks out of his rope, and coilin' it back onto his horn string. If the steer didn't have horns and was unusually cantankerous, he might fill his eyes with sand to blind 'im for a few seconds.

If it was an old bull, or ranahan steer, that he was ropin'—and them animals were always mean—he might pick up his forefeet. This was done by runnin' almost neck and neck with the animal and throwin' the loop over its right shoulder, givin' it a roll or twist as it left his hand, so that the loop'd land directly in front of the steer's forefeet. When the loop was throwed, the rider turned at a left angle and rode hard against his rope. The resultin' fall was even harder'n the bustin' referred to. If the ketch was clear and on both forefeet, the animal might fall without a broken neck, but the odds were against 'im. If it happened to be a one-legged ketch, it usually resulted in a broken leg or shoulder. This form of ropin', while requirin' more skill than a head or horn ketch, has always been looked upon with disfavor by cattle owners because of its high mortality. It was seldom used except on a mean bull or outlaw steer, which, because of the cattle he led astray by breakin' herd, or refusin' to be penned, was better off dead.

A cowhand who throwed a steer too hard was likely to get a call-down from the boss. A heavy steer that turned a somersault at the end of a rope, when he was brought up short, hit the ground with terrific force. Often horns and even necks were broken. If the ground was hard the steer was bruised so bad that he was worthless as meat. This steer bustin' was called "pullin' the trip," or "fair groundin'." 'Nother steer ropin' method was what was called "goin' over the withers." The roper leaned over the animal's back and dropped a loop 'round the forelegs. Then spurrin' his hoss square away, he tripped the victim, turnin' it on its back. Throwin' a steer by trippin' was also called a "California."

"Hogtyin'" was tyin' an animal down after it was throwed by tyin' its two hind legs and one front one together with a short piece of rope called a "piggin' string." The ties were made with half-hitches. On one end was a loop which the cowhand slipped on the foreleg of the down animal. Standin' behind the animal with one knee on it to help hold it down, he stuck his foot behind the hocks and boosted the hind legs forward, at the same time drawin' the rope under and round both hind feet. This put the two hind feet on top, pointin' forward, and the forefoot below, pointin' back. With two or three turns and two half-hitches the animal was thoroughly tied. Hosses were never hog-tied.

Much of the cowboy's ropin' was done on foot, especially in corral work. Ropin' out saddle hosses gave 'im no trouble after the ketch was made because the wise cow hoss knowed the meanin' of a rope. But if he roped some yearlin' calf he had to know how to dig in, to brace 'imself for the shock when the slack was taken up. The high bootheels helped 'im anchor 'imself as he leaned backward and wrapped the rope 'round his thighs to keep the rope taut. Of course, if he made a heel ketch he didn't have to do all this, as the calf was helpless. All he had to do was keep the rope taut 'nough to keep the calf from kickin' free. By heelin', most of his hard work was eliminated.

In ropin' from hossback the hoss deserved at least 50 per cent of the credit. No matter how good a roper, much of his success depended upon a well trained rope hoss. Ropin' on hossback was more dangerous than ropin' on foot. On foot you could always turn loose, but when a roped steer and a hoss got tangled in a mixup you didn't have much chance to leave the party. Heavy ropin' was always done from hossback. Grown cattle would attack a man on foot, and were dangerous. The roper saw that the cinch was tight, and never let the steer get a side pull, but either kept the hoss turned toward, or away, from the roped animal.

Platin' the Ponies

Some of the larger ranches had a reg'lar blacksmith shop and hired a professional blacksmith to repair the wagons and shoe the hosses. But on the average ranch when a rider was hired he took on the responsibility of shoein' his own string. Shoein' hosses was a long way from bein' the easiest work in the world, nor was it the safest, but it was a part of his job. As one old cowhand said regardin' the shoein' of hosses: "This shore is hard work and has wrecked a lot of promisin' cowboy careers. All hosses hate to be shod and won't cooperate with the cowboys in these well meanin' efforts. The young hosses is bad; the older ones is worse; and the idea that cowboys is bowlegged from much ridin's all wrong. Cowboys is bowlegged from holdin' up nine hundred pounds of kickin' hoss while at the same time raspin' his feet down and puttin' shoes on 'im. Shoein' hosses and tryin' to break some of 'em to ride accounts for all cowboys' most painful and embarrassin' moments."

Mighty few cowhands liked this duty, and some of 'em disliked it so much they'd dicker with some other puncher to plate their ponies in exchange for somethin' that puncher liked even less, such as takin' the frost out of some hoss on a cold mornin'. On most ranches where there was no blacksmith to fit each individual, shoes were bought ready made and were put on cold. "Good 'noughs" was the slang name for them shoes, and they were bought by the keg in various sizes ready to put on the hoss's feet cold.

Of course, a neater and better fit was obtained with anvil and bellows where a shoe could be heat shaped to the animal's foot, but in the haste of the roundup and other cow work, there wasn't always time. So them malleable shoe plates had to be used, and with some raspin' and hammerin' these could be made to fit fairly well.

Some claim that a hoss should be shod ever' two months, but a good deal depends on the kind of country you're workin' in. In the flat country a shoein' before the roundup will usually last through that work, and the shoes could be pulled off when the hosses were turned out to run the range till the next roundup. But in a rough and rocky country hossshoein' equipment was a reg'lar part of the wagon.

A cowhoss could only work if his feet were in good condition, so the cowhand was careful to watch his mount's feet. They tacked a shoe on ever' time one was lost, came loose, or worn. Even though he had ten or twelve head in his string, and maybe never rode each one more'n once a week, he rode 'em in rotation and didn't want to find one with a throwed shoe the day he had to ride 'im.

A heap of folks think a saddle hoss should be shod all the time. This is a mistake, for when the hoss was turned loose after the cow work was over he'd be healthier and more contented if the shoes were pulled and he could run barefooted. It'd be like keepin' shoes on a healthy kid in the summertime.

A careful cowhand watched his hoss's feet closely and found that he had to reset their shoes frequently because in a little while the hoof growed out and 'round the shoes, and if not reset they caused the shoe to bear on the tender sole instead of the hard wall of the hoof. This'd soon cripple the hoss and make 'im unfit for work.

In pickin' a shoe to fit each foot of the hoss, the cowhand'd measure the width of the hoof at its widest point and the length from toe to heel. Then he chose a shoe nearest them measurements. Because the shoe was usually fitted before the foot was worked on, it'd be ready to put on after the foot was trimmed; it wouldn't be necessary to let the foot down once it was picked up or tied up.

Ever' shoe had to be altered some, either widened or narrowed so that it'd exactly fit the outside edge of the hoof. The heel of the hoof must rest on the iron, so if the shoe was too wide or too narrow at the heel it had to be adjusted to fit, and this called for some hammerin'.

Now that he was ready to prepare the hoof for shoein', the cowhand put his tools in his boot top, or near at hand on the ground, and placed the nails in his mouth. These were sometimes slightly bent at the point beforehand so they'd be shore to come out on the side of the hoof. Often the bronc had to have his foot tied up. It shouldn't be tied high, but to jes' clear the ground. It was mostly to make the hoss think he was helpless anyway. Even a gentle hoss sometimes objected to bein' shod, especially after some careless cowboy'd drove a nail into the tender part of his hoof.

A good way to shoe a hoss was to push 'im against a corral fence and lean against 'im with your shoulder. Your leanin' against 'im made 'im put his weight on the opposite foot and it was easy to lift the one you wanted to work on. In liftin' a hind foot it was a good idea to carry the leg a step to the rear before placin' it between your knees. Say you're platin' a rear foot, you run your hand slowly down his rear leg to the hock, then pick up the foot, take your step back, and place his foot between your knees as you face his tail. Most cowhands talked to the hoss while all this was goin' on to give 'im confidence and also to distract his attention.

It was also important to clean the hoss's feet to free 'em of dirt, gravel, and other accumulation. All the depressions 'round the frog, especially them near the heel, should be thoroughly cleaned. The cleanin' should be done from heel toward the toe. The frog, sole, and outer wall should all be pared and trimmed to remove rough edges and loose parts, but the frog should be left as full as possible, and the wall should be left a little higher than the sole.

Now you would cut and rasp the hoof to get it level and smooth. It was well to try the shoe between rasps to see that it sets plumb flat and snug. It was vitally important that the rasped wall be absolutely level for the surface of the shoe. All them preparations were of great importance, and the shoe should be fitted to the foot, not the foot to the shoe. The raspin' of the outer wall of the hoof to fit an undersized shoe was a great mistake that'd eventually ruin the hoss's hoofs.

In nailin' the shoe on the hoof the nail was held between the thumb and the index finger, lettin' the other fingers be free to hold the shoe in place. The nail was held between the fingers as long as possible to guide it. The first nail was put in the second nail hole from the back on one side, the straight side of the nail toward the outside. Then seein' again that the shoe fit, a nail was drove on the other side to hold the shoe in its proper place. Because nails drove in too close to the heel were apt to penetrate the tender part of the heel, this had to be watched. As each nail was drove, its sharp end was twisted off so there was no chance of it injurin' the shoer if the hoss got his foot loose.

At no time were the nails drove far up into the wall of the foot to make 'em hold. To keep from doin' this, small nails were used because they could be made to come out well down on the hoof, thus destroyin' the least amount of the hoof when the hoss was reshod. In this position, too, the nail clinch was nearer at right angles to the wall of the hoof than if it had been drove higher with a large nail. Old nail holes, if higher up, weakened the hoof, but, on the other hand, if the nails were placed too low the holes would tear out easy.

As soon as a nail was drove in, its point was bent toward the shoe or twisted off with the claw of the shoein' hammer. With the clinchin' block, or "alligator," held on the outside wall underneath the nail, the head of the nail should be hammered down into the crease of the shoe.

After the points had been clipped off or clinched down, a good shoer would file a small groove in the hoof wall with the edge of the rasp jes' below where the nail protruded. This made the nails clinch better, because when a clinchin' block was held against the head of the nail and the hammer used on the point of the nail more surface was given for a better clinch.

In a mountainous country hosses were often shod only on the rear feet. This was because they had to slide a lot, and with their unshod front feet becomin' tender they soon learned to slide on the hind feet, which was the right way for a hoss to stop. Also, he could be trained to turn faster if he stopped on his hind feet, and thus be a more useful hoss.

There're several kinds of shoes used in cow work, each with its own name. The shoe had a calked heel, while the slipper was smooth without calks. A bar shoe was one with a metal piece welded across the heel, and a boot was one with both heel and toe calked. It might be said, too, that a hoss with white hoofs needed shoein' ofter'n one with black hoofs, because a white hoof's softer and wears quicker.

When old shoes were taken off, the ends of the clinched nails should be cut with a clinch cutter. Usin' the pinchers under the heel of the shoe, they should be moved forward and pressed straight down to get the nails loose. When the shoe was off, all the dirt and foreign matter should be removed from the frog and sole of the hoss's foot. Then, workin' from the rear of the hoof, all the undergrowth of the sole and hoof should be cut off with a hook knife or cutters.

Philip A. Rollins once wrote: "The shoeing of the average range horse was disturbing to human tranquillity. The shoeing of some horses was a miracle or a devilment according as one viewed it." Then he proceeded to tell of the boss of the ranch sending two cowhands down to the corral to shoe a "pinto cayuse," and after hearing much noise in that vicinity he sauntered down to where he "found an angry pony glaring at two perspiring men and asked: 'Shod him?' He was answered by Bill: 'Guess so. Tacked iron onto everything that flew past. It sure is a heaven-sent mercy that broncs ain't centipedes.' "

Yet, no matter how wild the bronc, the shoein' of 'em was one of the early-day cowhand's jobs. But sometimes platin' them broncs was like huntin' for a whisper in a big wind, or like tryin' to scratch your ear with your elbow.

The Roundup

ONE of the wholesale operations in handlin' range cattle in the old days of free grass and fenceless pastures was the roundup. It was a harvestin' of cattle, a great gatherin' up and a sortin' out; and a brandin' of beasts young and old, that had no marks of ownership burned into their hides. While the roundup was a proposition quite different from that of puttin' and drivin' a large herd on the trail, the two were great companion pieces of the range-cattle industry in the old days.

Unlike most customs of the cattle country, the roundup was neither Spanish-American nor Western-American in origin. It originated in the mountain country of Kentucky, Tennessee, the Carolinas, and the Virginias. The people of them states let their cattle run loose and annually held roundups to gather 'em, but they performed the function in a haphazard sort of way. The Western cowman perfected the system and brought it to the attention of the public as an important phase of the cattle industry.

The primitive Western forerunner of the roundup was a gettin' together of a few neighborin' stockmen to look over each other's herds for strays. Them small neighborhood affairs didn't include a thoroughly organized, systematic search of a large extent of territory, nor an equally systematic identification of the ownership of all the cattle gathered, that were the purpose of the great roundups of the open range in later years.

Them neighborly gatherin's were called "cow hunts," "cow drives," or were spoken of as "runnin' cattle."

The roundup of the open range developed as the cattle business increased and extended. Like ever'thing else in a movin' world, it improved in scope as demanded. It was one of the necessities that arose with the general occupation of the country by men with enlargin' herds. As ranchers and herds became more numerous, ranges began to overlap their borders, offerin' opportunities for neighborin' herds to intermingle. Therefore, the stockmen had to adopt cooperative plans, and under 'em work each other's ranges to gather up in one operation and sort out the cattle on 'em. Roundups varied in detail in different sections, but, in the main, they were essentially the same throughout the cattle country.

There were two roundups a year—one in the spring, the other in the fall. The spring, or calf, roundup was for the brandin' of the calf crop. This work began when the grass came in the spring. Time was measured in a cow camp, not by calendar dates, but by the "comin' grass" when the range began to green up.

The fall, or beef, roundup was for the purpose of gatherin' all cattle for shipment to market, and for the brandin' of the late calves and them overlooked in the spring work. It was conducted 'long much the same lines as the earlier one except it was usually done with more deliberation, for the animals then were heavier in flesh. Them roundups were the most important functions in cattleland, the harvestin' of the range, and the term "work" was applied to all this roundin' up, gatherin', and brandin'.

This industry growed and spread over the West till it became the perfect system as we know it today. When fences came, the custom passed, but in the open-range days the roundup sometimes covered thousands of miles. Stockmen found it necessary for their mutual protection to take some cooperative action; therefore the roundup system was adopted and perfected. Each ranchman of the district bein' worked furnished men and bore his share of the general expense, this share proportioned accordin' to the number of cattle owned. Each ranch furnished 'nough hosses for its riders, but only the larger outfits sent chuck wagons. Each district was worked successively by ranges till each was cleaned up in reg'lar rotation. At the end of the drive ever' owner knowed by the carefully kept tally the increase of his herd and the number of older cattle he owned that had been gathered in this rakin' of the range.

The open-range roundup system lasted only a comparatively few years, but durin' its existence it was the event ever' cowman looked forward to with interest and eagerness. Not only was it his harvest time, but it served as a reunion with old friends and a means of cultivatin' new acquaintances.

After stock associations were organized, they passed laws regulatin' roundups, designatin' both the time and the place at which these should be held. Originally organized for protection against rustlers, they soon passed laws to prevent any individual from workin' ahead of the reg'lar roundup for his personal gain. Them set dates gave ever' man an equal chance, as well as avoidin' workin' the range more'n once. Men who worked the range before the official roundup date were called "sooners." By workin' ahead of the reg'lar roundup them men could pick up many mavericks and strays to which they weren't entitled. When a few smaller ranchers got together and sent out a roundup wagon in defiance of the association roundup, it was called "runnin' a shotgun wagon." Ranchers suspected of rustlin', or bein' in sympathy with rustlers, were blackballed from association roundups.

The plan of campaign that was to cover a broad extent of wild country was carefully worked out with a view of producin' the most satisfactory results within the allotted time. The size of the big circle to be worked was determined partly by the number of men present, partly by the nature of the country.

The cowman never had more need of the cowboy than on the roundup, where the work required a somewhat specialized skill, as well as considerable personal darin'. The preliminary days while waitin' for the clan to gather might be spent in romp and frolic because they knowed that there'd be no play after the work started. Yet each man knowed the work he was to do and made all his preparations for it. His personal outfit was overhauled and put in repair. His rope was limbered up, his straps softened, and his wearin' gear put in order. If he had a semi-bronc in his string, he took the opportunity of givin' it a few lessons in higher education.

The roundup was strictly a business proposition, and the few days that preceded active work were, in the main, devoted to organization and other preparations. Still, the gatherin' was largely in the nature of a reunion, as it brought together a large number of cowmen from over a wide stretch of country, most of whom had some acquaintance with or knowledge of one another.

The real test of the cowboy on roundup wasn't the work done in camp, such as ropin' and brandin', but his ability to bring in cattle from the roughest or most densely covered country. This called for familiarity with the country that was rode over. It demanded a quick eye and good judgment, as well as mere ability to ride.

The wagon boss, whose duty it was to tell 'em off, rode in the lead on a steady cow hoss, as was his privilege. When he reached the point he considered proper, and the boys in the rear had caught up, he'd pull up with his men gathered 'bout 'im; then he'd send 'em out singly or in pairs to specified points where they'd turn back, drivin' before 'em cattle from them sections. This was called "tellin' off the riders," or "scatterin' the riders."

When the men stopped to receive them orders, or "powders," they dismounted to reset their saddles and recinch for the hard ride to come. The men were usually sent in pairs. A man unfamiliar with the country'd be paired with one who knowed that particular range; one ridin' an unreliable hoss'd be accompanied by one ridin' a more trustworthy one.

There was a sort of technique in scatterin' men so that the country'd be covered with no gaps between riders where cattle might be missed or dodge back. It required a knowledge of the range to be worked on the part of the boss and the utmost dependability on the part of the men and hosses he sent out to do the job. The distance between riders depended a heap on the kind of country and the number of cattle.

Men workin' the outer circle were given an earlier start. Though they used the toughest hosses they needed more time, since they rode the outside limits of the territory to be worked. Them men who drove in the cattle from the farthest edges were called "lead drive men." The shorter, or "inside circle," was usually rode by men whose hosses hadn't yet been hardened to cow work. On the out trip each man tried to save his hoss in order to have 'im in good shape for the actual hazin' of the cattle from the brush and canyons. Sometimes in the rough country where cattle found hidin' places, they'd "smoke 'em out" by firin' six-guns to scare 'em out.

As this group of cowboys rode over the range, it spread out, dividin' into smaller parties, and later these scattered till the men were separated by distances that varied accordin' to the topography of the country. Each man had to hunt out all the cattle on the ground over which he rode, and, if it was much broken, carefully search for scattered individuals or small groups.

Soon clouds of dust were seen in ever' direction, and dust clouds on the range meant stock bunched and movin'. As the circle became smaller the bunches became larger and the dust thicker. As the roundup advanced, the strain on the men growed greater, their hours longer, and their work more tryin'. Few were on duty less than twelve to fifteen hours. They were hardy and tough and could stand as much punishment as any set of men on earth. This work was attended by many dangers and there were bound to be fatalities.

This gather of cattle was drove toward a designated holdin' spot where they were worked. Back and forth through the dust they swung and charged, swoopin' wide to round in a gallopin' steer, flingin' their sweatin' hosses at the congested herd. Calves lumberin' awkwardly in a half-hearted gallop after their mothers, their tongues hangin' from the side of their mouths and dribblin' with a lathery foam. Here and there some mother cow with a heavin' of ribs and flanks busted into a long-drawn bawl that rose for an instant to a high pitch and then ended in a throaty rumble. All this bawlin' and bellerin', the cracklin' of horns and poundin' of hoofs, the dusty whirl of worried cattle was a part of the roundup. Added to all this frenzied babel that went boomin' skyward were the shrill yells and yips of the cowboys, all of which made a mighty savage music.

As soon as the convergin' circle riders had urged their drive onto the holdin' spot, they surrounded the cattle and held 'em in close herd. After 'nough time to allow the men to change hosses, this concentrated mass of cattle were invaded by cowboys on cuttin' hosses. This cuttin' out called for bold and skillful ridin' and involved some personal danger. It was hard, wearin' work, keepin' man and hoss constantly on the alert. As a rule only three or four men did the cuttin', because too many riders cuttin' at once got the cattle stirred up, and mothers and calves got separated from each other. Speed in this game didn't save time. It was best to work at a slow steady gait.

A "cut" was a group of cattle separated from the main herd for any definite purpose, as for shippin' or for brandin', and this was usually started with a "decoy herd," or "anchor cattle," a few cows used in startin' a cut of cattle. A "cut of cows with calves" was the segregatin' of all cows with unbranded calves into a separate cut. If any cattle were cut out for shipment to market this was called a "beef cut." Usually one man cut a single animal, but occasionally cuttin' an animal was done by two men, and this was called "cuttin' double-barreled."

The men keepin' the cut under control were said to be "holdin' the cut," and this called for some ridin' and vigilance, as the cut cows try to return to the main herd, especially till the cut growed to some size. This cuttin' out from the main herd to smaller cuts for any purpose was called "workin' the herd," but the term "work" or "general work" applied to all handlin' of cattle on roundup.

Often after the first day, when work was pressin', there was what was knowed as the "night drive" or "moonlightin' 'em." Small squads of men, consistin' of one or more from each outfit, were sent ahead ten or fifteen miles from the mess wagon to camp on their own hook. Very early in the mornin' they began drivin' cattle from the country designated for that day. Because they worked without chuck wagons and packed their food in small cotton bags, this was sometimes called a "greasy sack ride." Workin' in a country too rough for wagons was also called "moonshinin'."

The final cattle drove in from circle on roundup were called the "combin's." All coulees, canyons, foothills, and flats had to be combed thoroughly for the hidin' cattle. Close combin' of the range was necessary because if a calf wasn't branded before it quit followin' its mother it became a maverick and was likely to acquire an owner other than the owner of the mother. Sometimes riders were sent back to "prowl" a range; this was to go back over a territory after a roundup in search of cattle that might have been missed. If a man was sent out to prowl alone and stayed for some time, he took an individual camp outfit, and was then said to be "rawhidin'." When the wagon boss had gathered all the cattle in a given region, he was said to have "covered his dog."

Some ranches hired a cowboy to visit ranches, sometimes as far away as fifty or more miles, and pick up stock branded with his employer's brand found anywhere, takin' it with 'im to the next ranch or range. He took his gather to the home ranch as often as he could, changed hosses, and went again. A man on this duty was called a "renegade rider."

When cowmen over a wide range of territory pooled their resources and men, it was often spoken of as a "pool roundup." This could be a gigantic affair. The roundup camp of such a gatherin' was also a "pool camp." In the early eighties the Wyoming Stock Growers' Association took in such a vast territory that it sent out notices of dates for the start of the roundup by hand bills. From this the cowboy dubbed 'em "hand-bill roundups."

Movin' a roundup camp was quite a spectacle. The wagon boss gave instructions which no one but a cowhand familiar with the country could understand. The nighthawk drove up the remuda early. Saddle hosses were caught and saddled, and the rest of the hosses left to graze nearby. The rope corral was coiled and put into the wagon, beds rolled and piled into it, and ever' hand found somethin' to do or he wasn't a cowhand. Some harnessed the cook's teams while others helped 'im pack and stow his pots and kettles.

When ever'thing was ready, the cook crawled on his wagon seat and was handed the lines by some thoughtful puncher who, before he realized the lines were out of his hands, saw the cook herdin' his raw broncs across the rough, roadless country. With the mess wagon rattlin' and swayin' behind that runnin' team, he wondered how the outfit held to-gether. By the time the cowboys reached the new camp at noon, the cook had camp set up and a hot meal waitin' for 'em.

Some of the larger outfits hired a pilot whose duty it was to guide the roundup wagons over the plains and brakes to the next campin' place. He had to be well acquainted with the country and use good judgment con-cernin' the location of the next camp with regard to water and suitable surroundin's for workin' the cattle.

In the fall if an outfit gathered ever' animal fit for market and drove 'em to the loadin' pens, they were said to be "shippin' close." This was often done because of grass conditions, overgrazin', or market prices. Sometimes in the fall months in the mountain ranges cattle would be rounded up from the higher country and drove into the valley or lower country to winter, and this was called "shovin' down." The men doin' this work were called the "shove-down crew." Some ranches kept a floatin' outfit, five or six men and a cook, to ride the range in the winter months to brand the late calves and the ones that had escaped the roundup.

The cowhands often spoke of the roundup season as "sleepin' out" or "beddin' out," for at this time he did his sleepin' in the open. The open roundup system lasted only a comparatively short while, but even in later years when a roundup was held where the final bunchin' of cattle wasn't within a corral, but in the open, it was still called an open roundup.

It's fittin' to refer to the roundup as a thing of the past, although in some parts of the Western country it lingers in emaciated form—little more'n a ghost of what it used to be. The term's still in common use, but generally extended in its application, and may be applied to almost any sort of gatherin' together of cattle. If a herd of cattle's to be drove to a railroad station for shipment, roundin' up them animals is one of the preliminaries. But the real thing was a different procedure. It was the gigantic pageant of the cattle country. The great open plains formed its true field of action, but as fences came in to nullify its usefulness it passed out, leavin' only a memory of days never to be seen again.

Brands and Ear-Marks

THE language of brands is a special one requirin' particular knowledge, both symbolic and useful, and this knowledge marked the genuwine cowman more'n anything else. It couldn't be bought with anything except experience. A volume could be wrote 'bout the origin of brands, their use and methods of application, but it's our purpose to try and stick with the language of the cowboy as each phase of the work's dealt with.

The origin of the brand dates back to antiquity, and there's never been anything to take its place as a permanent mark of ownership. As the cowman says, "A brand's something that won't come off in the wash."

There's many kinds of brands, as well as innumerable forms, and each has a name of its own. They're the cattleman's mark of identification, his trade-mark. Brandin' soon became a systematized business, and brands had to be registered with the proper official of his county, or state, a written instrument claimin' the executive right to burn, upon a particular part of an animal, a particular design, and certain specified cuts in the ears, or other skin. If no one had a claim upon this design, it was formally allowed, and entered into the official brand book.

If a man wished to sell an animal, the buyer could place his own brand upon it. Yet how could this be done without his neighbor becomin' suspicious that he'd stolen the animal outright? This was accomplished by what was knowed as a "vent brand," from the Spanish *venta*, meanin' sale. The original owner placed his brand upon 'nother part of the animal, which meant that he'd deeded the animal to a new owner, whose brand it also bore. It had the effect of cancelin' the ownership brand, thus servin' as the acknowledgment of a sale. It was usually placed on the same side of the animal as the original brand. The term "fire out" was sometimes used instead of "vent," but it meant the same process of barrin' out a brand. "Counterbrandin' " had the same effect.

When a brand was superseded, by purchase or by discovery that the wrong brand had been placed on an animal, or that the brand had been put in the wrong place, the custom was for the brander to burn a bar through the original brand, put his own brand above or below it, and also on that part of the animal where it properly belonged, if the correct mark was differently situated. Later in the cattle industry, counter-brandin' was done by repeatin' the undesired brand and placin' the new one upon the animal where it belonged; and the use of the bar through the discarded brand was discontinued.

With the openin' of the cattle trails there came into use 'nother brand called the "road brand." This was a special brand of any design for trail herds as a sign of ownership en route. This brand helped the herders keep from minglin' their herds with outside cattle and spiritin' off their home range them animals of disinterested ownership.

This type brand originated in Texas durin' the trail days when a law was passed that all cattle drove beyond the northern limits of the state were to be branded by the drover with "a large and plain mark, composed of any mark or device he may choose, which mark shall be branded on the left side of the stock behind the shoulder." With the passin' of trail drivin', this brand was no longer used.

There was 'nother brand, used only in Texas, called the "county brand." It consisted of a separate prescribed letter or group of letters for each Texas county, and, if employed, went always, and unlike other brands, upon the animal's neck. This brand was intended to make stealin' more difficult, as the rustler would now have to see that his doctored brand was recorded in the county of the county brand or alter that brand too. Trail cattle which had changed ownership often upon their home range, and then went up the trail to government agencies, might, at the end of their journey, have their hides thoroughly etched, or, in the language of the cowboy, be "burnt till they looked like a brand book."

Brands were composed of letters, numbers, symbols, monograms, and numerous combinations of each. The readin' of brands is an art. To the tenderfoot, brands are so many picture puzzles, and he's almost shore to misread 'em, and be dazed by their queer jumble of lines, letters, and curves. The cowboy, on the other hand, took pride in his ability to call 'em correctly. He recorded the brand of ever' animal within his vision, and could see brands from a distance that'd be impossible for an unpracticed eye.

Brands have made necessary the coinin' of a language all their own, and this language, like other languages, follow certain rules. The characters of a brand read from top to bottom, from outside to inside and from left to right. The ability to read them brands was referred to as "callin' the brands."

A "stamp brand," such as used today, is made with a set brandin' iron which burns the complete brand with one impression.

It was harder to drive one or two head of cattle than a large herd, and a good cowman avoided drivin' his stock as much as possible, hence his recourse to brandin' on the open range. In the early days all brandin' was done in the open, but later it was looked upon with suspicion unless done in the presence of a roundup crew. Cattle branded in the open were said to be "range branded."

"Corral brandin'" was the brandin' of stock in a corral. This might not be so picturesque as brandin' in the open, but it was easier on the men, the cattle, and the hosses. Havin' no herd to hold, ever' man could take part in the brandin'. The actual work was done in the same manner as brandin' in the open, but before reachin' the pens the steers and dry cows were worked out. When the pens were reached, the mother cows were cut outside, where they bawled till the calves were turned out to relieve their anxiety and receive their sympathy.

Modern ranches now use "chute brandin'." The animal's run into a narrow chute, a bar's placed in front of the animal and a second dropped behind 'im so he can't move. He's then branded through the side railin's.

The reg'lar "calf brandin'" occurred in the spring, and this was called "ironin' the calf crop," because it was the brandin' of the season's calves. There were usually at least two "ketch hands" to do the ropin'. There was no prettier work than to watch a smooth roper as he moved into the herd, shakin' out his loop and selectin' the calf to be dragged to the fire. With a short half-swing of his rope to keep from excitin' the herd, he made his cast. His hoss turned mechanically and headed for the fire. The roper made a mental note of the earmark and brand of the mother when he roped the calf, and as he approached the "flankers" he called out to the "iron men": "Calf on the string," and the brand of the mother. Usually the cow'd foller her calf to the edge of the herd, or a little beyond, as her calf was dragged, a protestin' bundle of stiffened muscles pullin' against the rope. If the boys who were holdin' the herd didn't turn her back, she'd sometimes foller her calf all the way and create havoc with man and hoss.

The "ketch hand" wasn't particular how he'd ketch the small spring calves because they were easy handled. But when he'd ketch a long-aged, or last fall's calf, as a favor to the flankers he'd rope it by the hind feet. If he had it in for some flanker, or, as we've said before, wanted to see some fun, he'd sometimes bring a big calf roped by the neck, then sit on his hoss and laugh as he watched the flankers try to wrastle this calf down.

When the calf arrived at the end of the rope, one flanker'd step in and ketch the rope with his left hand, halfway between the hoss and the calf, lettin' the rope slide through his hand till the calf was near the fire. Then the one doin' the flankin' would ketch the calf's ear on the opposite side of 'im, and slap his hand into the flank on that side. By jerkin' upward and with a pressure of the knees against the calf's side when it took the next jump, the flanker sent the calf's feet outward, and it came down on its side. The side they throwed 'im on depended on which side the brand was to be placed. The rope was freed from his neck or heels early so the ketch hand could go back for 'nother calf.

After the flankers got the calf stretched on the ground, one sat on the ground behind the animal, with one foot shovin' the lower hind leg forward as far as possible, his boot instep wedged in jes' above the hock. The upper hind leg he held with both hands drawn far back into his lap. The second flanker, back of the calf, rested one knee on its neck, the other on its shoulder, while he held the upper foreleg doubled at the knee, in both hands. He yelled "calf on the ground," and the animal was now ready for brandin', ear-markin', and other operations. All the calf could do was wriggle a little and bawl a-plenty. Each set of flankers had their roper, and a good roper could keep 'em busy. Flankin' calves was no vacation.

The "brander," or "iron man," was the one whose immediate duty it was to place the brand on the animal. As soon as the calf was stretched out, he yelled "Hot iron!" with the name of the brand wanted. The "iron tender," the man who heated and attended to the brandin' irons, came on the trot from the fire with the brandin' iron wanted as it glowed a cherry red. The brander hit the rod against his forearm to jar away the coals and pressed it to the calf's hide. This was called "slappin' a brand on," or "runnin' a brand." It required but a few seconds to mark the ears with a sharp knife and stamp the hot iron on the flank, but them few seconds were an ordeal of terror to the calf. Usually it bore the knife without a sound, but the sizzlin' iron caused a doleful wail of agony and fear. When released, the calf struggled to its clumsy legs and trotted off to seek its mother and sympathy.

The success of the brands depended upon the brander's wisdom of his business. He had to have expert knowledge to apply a brandin' iron properly. If the brand was not burned deep 'nough it wouldn't peel, and if the iron was too hot it'd burn too deep, cook the flesh, blot the brand and leave a wound that'd become infected. If too cold it'd leave no brand, only a sore. Yet it had to be hot 'nough to burn the hair and quickly sear the surface of the hide 'nough to form a scab which peeled off in time, but allowed no hair to grow over it. The iron had to be free from scale and rust to make a sharp brand. Very little pressure was necessary to put on a good brand if the iron was at the right heat. Here are a few don'ts the cowman usually kept in mind:

Don't let the iron get too hot; that starts a hair fire, and usually results in a poor brand; don't use a forge or coal fire; wood's the best fuel for brandin' fires; don't use acids or similar humane agents; they leave a scar, not a brand, often causin' a bad sore, and the result's unreadable; don't use a small hoss iron on cattle; you never get a readable brand with a small iron; don't use a thin or burned-up iron; it'll cut too deep or make a thin scar which covers over with hair; don't try to brand a wet or even a damp animal; the brand'll scald, leave a blotch, bad sore, or no brand at all; don't get in a hurry; the cow'll wear the brand all her life, and you want it to bring her home; don't get tenderhearted. The iron must burn deep 'nough to remove hair and outer layer of skin; when the iron's lifted the brand should be the color of saddle leather.

It's a good idea to avoid brands with sharp corners or them with narrow spaces between the marks if you want a clean burn. Even with a stamp iron it's hard to put such a brand on an animal that wasn't layin' there like a sleepin' babe all the time. The narrow gaps will be burned across and the whole brand would peel, thus leaving a brand that might be subject to dispute, if not suspicion.

In puttin' on a brand it was best to rock the iron a little as it was pressed down, and in this way some air was let under and it burned more uniform. Deep brandin', especially in the Southwest where the animal's skin was thinner, was apt to cause "wartin'." It didn't necessarily hurt the brand except make it look ungainly because it caused a scaly growth that sometimes stood up and often caused the animal's tail to get caught on it, when it needed that tail to switch flies with.

The hot iron itself was called such names as "iron," short for brandin' iron, "hot stuff," "scorcher," or "cookstove." After a calf was branded it was usually booted toward its anxious mother, and brandin' was spoken of as "burnin' and bootin' 'em," or "burnin' and trimmin' up calves," and they did get some trimmin' before the work was done.

The "iron tender," or "fireman," was the man who tended the fires and kept the brandin' irons hot. He had to look to his supply of fuel in advance and see that he had plenty for the work to be done. In the early days, when workin' in a timberless country, he had to depend on cow chips, and it was hard to keep such fires goin'. His was a hot job, the heat and smoke searin' his eyes, but he dared not let his irons get cold till the work was done. Addin' fresh fuel, fannin' a sickly blaze with his hat while he tried to keep the smoke from his tired eyes, and runnin' to the brander with the irons wanted kept 'im on the jump. Not before the sun shone redly through the smoke was he free to kick the half-burned sticks apart and pour water on 'em.

Like the rest of the brandin' crew, he had to know brands and the irons they called for. When the brander called for a certain brand the tender had to know which to grab. When the brand had been slapped on the calf, he took the iron back to the fire and buried it in the coals to get hot for the next victim of that brand.

The men who cut the ear-marks, dewlaps, wattles, and other marks of identification on the animal's anatomy were knowed as the "butchers," or "knifemen," or "cutters." They squatted on their heels, built cigarettes, and sharpened their knives on a little whetstone while the irons were gettin' hot. They used a cowman's ordinary knife which they re-sharpened ever' time the work slackened a bit. Theirs was a bloody job, for calves had a way of slingin' their heads after they've been ear-marked. Not only did they mark the calves, but made future steers of the young male animals. They had to know the various ear-marks of the brands called, sometimes each ear havin' more'n one different mark on it. Workin' in the dust, the acrid smoke of scorchin' hair, the blood of cuttin' operations, and amid the confusion of bawlin' sufferers and bellowin' mothers, they were a sight when the work was finished.

The "doctors," or "medicine men," put the finishin' touches to the whole operation. They jumped 'bout nimble as a flea with their daubs and pot of tar, or other disinfectin' dope to smear the wounds of the operation. The "needle man" quickly and expertly used his hypodermic needle to give vaccine and shots for blackleg and other diseases. Them "medicine men" were often smeared with their own concoctions, and smelled like a medicine chest.

Nothin' 'bout the work of brandin' was clean or easy except maybe the "tally man's" job. He was usually appointed by the roundup captain. He was an older man, one recently injured, or one not in good physical condition to do heavier work. Above all he was chosen for his honesty, for this position offered many opportunities to falsify the records. Upon his count depended the owner's estimate of the season's profits. If he had some clerical ability, it helped. Though his job was the easiest one of the entire work, he'd rather be takin' an active part in the more strenuous work if he was a real cowman.

Ever' time a calf slithered to the fire he listened for the flanker's chant of the brand of the animal's mother and its sex. He echoed this call as he set it down in his tally book. As the number of unbranded calves growed smaller, the record in his book growed longer, and as time passed it became more grimy and smudged. At ever' lax moment he took the opportunity to sharpen a stub pencil which was wearin' down steadily. Durin' them periods of lull the brander was callin' for more calves by yellin', "More straw!" but this was music to the tally man's ears because it gave 'im a moment to stretch.

Workin' in a corral full of burned cattle was no job for a weaklin', and it had its perilous moments. Anxious mama cows and husky bull calves made brandin' interestin'. When some old cow heard the anguished bawl of her calf and came on the prod, the cowhands had to be alert to keep from gettin' gored. When the cry "Hook 'em cow!" or "Lookout cowboy!" went up, it was no disgrace to run.

There was a lot of funny things happen 'round a brandin' fire. Cowhands were always puttin' up jokes on each other, and as there was usually hands from a half-dozen outfits workin' 'round the fire, a feller could never tell what was comin' next. When some ornery calf kicked a ketch hand in the middle, they laughed so hard they nearly fell off their hosses, even if this hand was stretched out cold as a meat hook with some busted ribs.

And so the work proceeded with a skill that made ever' move count till the last calf had scampered to its anxious ma. The air was full of smoke, dust, and animal odors; the men were dirty, bloody, with eyes smartin' from dust and smoke.

A brand burned deep 'nough to be permanent was said to be a "fast brand." One not burned deep 'nough would hair over, and when this happened, in order to read the brand it had to be clipped, and this was called "clippin' a brand." "Tally brandin' " was takin' an inventory of cattle.

Gettin' back to the readin' of brands, I hope I can give you a few hints 'long this line. A "boxed brand" is one whose design bears framin' lines; an "open brand" is a letter or figger not boxed, although the letter *A* havin' no cross-section's also called an "Open *A*." A "bench brand" is one restin' on a horizontal bracket with its feet downward as a bench, and a "drag brand" is one with a bottom projection that angles downward to some degree. A "flyin' brand" is one whose letter or figger has wings, and a "forked brand" is one with a **V**-shaped prong attached to any part of the letter.

Any letter or figger "too tired to stand up," and lyin' on its side, is called a "lazy brand." One leanin' in an oblique position's a "tumblin' brand"; one with lower designs like feet or legs is a "walkin' brand"; and one with curves at its end or either side's a "runnin' brand." A "rafter brand" is one havin' semi-cone-shaped lines above it similar to the roof of a house; a "rockin' brand" is one restin' upon and connected with a quarter-circle, while a "swingin' brand" is one suspended from a quarter-circle. However, when the quarter-circle's unjoined from the letter or figger, it's read a "quarter-circle."

A letter or figger havin' one or more enlarged termini's called a "bradded brand"; a "barbed brand" is made with a short projection from some part of it. A straight line's a "bar" if it rests in a horizontal position. If it runs through a part of a letter, it becomes a "cross"; if it's perpendicular it's apt to be a "one," sometimes an "I," but if it leans at an angle it's called a "slash." A brand usin' this symbol leanin', one one way and the other another, is called a "cut and slash." The straight horizontal line, if long, like John Chisum's brand, which extended from shoulder to tail is, knowed as the "fence rail."

The letter "O" if perfectly round, is called an "O" or "circle," but if it's flattened to the least degree it becomes a "mashed O," a "squashed O," or a "goose egg." If only a part of the curved circle's used, it's a "three-quarter circle," "half-circle," or "quarter-circle," dependin' upon the amount used. A circle within a circle's called a "double-circle."

Roman numerals are also used in brands. Such a brand as "IV" is not called "IV," but the "Roman four," yet when the numeral "X" is used, it's called after the letter rather than the numeral, as "LX" is "LX" brand rather than "Roman sixty." A "connected brand" is one which combines two or more letters or figgers so that they run together similar to the monogram seen on the Eastern housewife's pillow slips. The "bosal brand" is a stripe burned 'round an animal's nose; a brand placed on an animal directly in the rear or on the buttocks is called a "butt brand," and to burn a bar or bars across the back of an animal and extendin' to both sides is a "saddle brand." The "tailbone rafter" is two lines burned on the rump of an animal and meetin' at the top of the tailbone.

Ever' conceivable symbol was used in brands: triangles, bells, pots, kettles, tools, spurs, bits, hearts, and countless others. These were usually easy to read, but there were many that even a cowboy would be at a loss to call correctly, had he not lived in the immediate vicinity and heard its name numerous times. An odd-lookin' brand, brought into a district from the outside, havin' no letters, numerals, or familiar figgers by which it might be called, was dubbed by the cowboy the enigmatical name of "fluidy mustard." The "whangdoodle" is a brand with a group of interlockin' wings with no flyin' central figger. A brand too complicated to be described with a brief name was called a "fool brand."

Mexican brands were more complicated and perplexin' than the

American brands, and the American cowboy, in speakin' of them intricate Mexican brands, didn't attempt to translate 'em, but slangily referred to all of 'em briefly, but descriptively, as "the map of Mexico," "a skillet of snakes."

Ranches commonly took their names from the brand burned on their cattle, and owners also lost the identity of their Christian names and were called by their brand. Very often, too, a cowhand workin' on a ranch was called by its brand, as "Fiddleback Red," to distinguish 'im from the other redheads of the range, and signifyin' that the one mentioned worked for the "Fiddleback brand."

Cowboys at a brandin' delighted in givin' some brand a new name to see if they could stump the firetender. It developed into quite a game with some of 'em. When the ketch hand dragged up a calf and called out its mother's brand, the flankers, or brander, called out somethin' entirely different, yet one that'd fit this particular brand. S. Omar Barker gave some good examples of this when he told 'bout a ketch hand callin' out "T Bench" and the flanker yellin', "Tally one tea party," or maybe 'nother would sing out, "T at a meetin'." Wasn't the T settin' on a bench? Or if the brand was a "Quarter-Circle Jug," he'd call "Gimme a jug in the shade," or if the brand was an "LN" with the N on top of the horizontal part of the L, he'd maybe call it "Sparkin' LN." Wasn't N settin' on L's lap?

Some brands received a permanent, though unintended, name because no one knowed their correct interpretation. The odd brand in Texas which no one seemed to know what to call's now the "Quien sabe." Also, a brand in Wyoming which is really the "Revolvin' H" is now better knowed as the "damfino" because when asked its name some cowhand answered, "Damn if I know."

Ear-marks are an added means of identification. There were times when it was hard to read a brand, especially in winter when the animal's hair was long, and ear-marks proved to be quite convenient and could be seen from a distance. Like brands, each mark has a name that forms a part of the cowboy's language.

The "overbit" is a **V**-shaped mark made by doublin' the ear in and cuttin' a small piece, perhaps an inch, out of the upper part of the ear, an inch in length, and maybe one-third that in depth. The same cut made in the lower side of the ear's an "underbit." When two such triangular cuts are made they're a "double overbit" and "double underbit."

The "seven-overbit" is made by cuttin' the ear straight down near the tip for 'bout an inch on the top side, then from near the upper base of the ear, makin' a cut which slopes to meet the straight downward first cut. The "seven-underbit" is made the same way by makin' the cut on the lower side.

A "crop" is made by cuttin' 'bout one half of the ear off smoothly, straight from the upper side. Though this can be said to be a "cropped ear," what the cowboy calls a "crop-ear" is in speakin' of an animal with its ears shortened by freezin' or sunburn. The "upper half-crop" or "over half-crop" is made by splittin' the ear from the tip, midway 'bout halfway back toward the head, and cuttin' off the upper half. The "lower" or "under half-crop" is made the same way on the underside of the ear.

The "steeple fork" is made by cuttin' two splits into the ear from the end, back one-third and halfway toward the head, and cuttin' out the middle piece, the splits bein' 'bout an inch apart. The "split" is made simply by splittin' the ear from the tip midway 'bout halfway back toward the head. The "oversplit" is made by makin' the split from the upper edge of the ear to 'bout the middle; the "undersplit" bein' the same on the lower side.

The "swallow-fork" is made by hollowin' the ear lengthwise, beginnin' halfway back, and cuttin' at an angle of forty-five degrees toward the end. The result's a forked notch in the ear. The "swallowtail" is made by trimmin' the tip of the ear into the form of a bird's flarin' tail.

The "overslope" is made by cuttin' the ear 'bout two thirds of the way back from the tip straight to the center of the ear at the upper side; the "underslope" is the same cut on the lower side. The "sharp" is made by cuttin' an under- and over-slope on the same ear, givin' it a sharp or pointed appearance, and sometimes called a "point." The "grub" is a cruel ear-mark made by cuttin' the entire ear off smoothly with the head. One of the sayin's of the range is "When you see a man grubbin' and sharpin' the ears of his cows, you can bet he's a thief." A man who "grubbed" or "sharped" was looked upon with suspicion, as them marks were resorted to by rustlers to destroy the original ear-mark.

The "overhack" is made by simply cuttin' down an inch on the upper side of the ear, and the "underhack" is the same cut on the lower side. The "over-round" is made by cuttin' a half-circle from the top of the ear, while the "under-round" is cuttin' the half-circle from the bottom. The "hole ear-mark" is made by simply punchin' a hole in the ear; the "sawtooth" is made by cuttin' the end of the ear in and out in the shape of the teeth of a saw, while the "saw-set" is made by croppin' the ear, then cuttin' out the center in the shape of a rectangle, and it's sometimes called the "crop and mortice." The "jingle-bob" is an ear-mark made with a deep slit that leaves the lower half of the ear floppin' down, one of the most hideous marks ever devised. This mark was made famous by John Chisum, a pioneer rancher of Lincoln County, New Mexico.

Cattle without ear-marks are called "full ears," or "slick ears," and one that has been ear-marked is a "stick ear." Ear-marks can be used in innumerable combinations.

There's other marks of ownership made with a knife other than them of the ears. The "dewlap" is made on the underside of the neck or brisket by pinchin' up a quantity of skin and cuttin' it all, but not entire off. When healed it leaves a hangin' flap of skin. Some were slashed up and called "dewlaps up," others slashed down and called "dewlaps down." The "jug handle" is made by cuttin' a long slash on the skin of the brisket and not cuttin' out at either end, which, when healed, looks like the handle of a jug.

The "wattle" is made on the neck or jaw of an animal by pinchin' up a quantity of skin, and cuttin' it all, but not entirely off. When healed it left a hangin' flap of skin. The "varruga" is also a wattle made by cuttin' a strip of hide down 'bout two inches and lettin' it hang. "Buds" are made by cuttin' down a strip of skin on the nose.

As a mark of identification the brand's perfect. It's put on in a moment, yet it remains as long as the animal lives, and no matter how far a cow or hoss might stray from its home range, identification by the owner, through the brand, is positive. The ability to read brands and ear-marks correctly and at a glance ranks almost as high as dexterity with a rope, and higher on a cow ranch than the ability to ride buckin' hosses.

Burnin' and Bootin' 'Em

EASTERN people heard a lot 'bout the cowboy and the life he lived, but they had their own ideas 'bout the brandin' of cattle. Knowin' how painful a hot iron would be if it seared their own tender skin, they made much to-do 'bout the cruelty of brandin' cattle. At one time the Humane Society of the East raised quite an objection to the cowman's method of identifyin' his cattle.

A few years back I read a story in the *Cattleman Magazine* which said in part: "The most unanswerable argument for not brandin', that I ever heard, was given by a lady from the East. Instead of being prompted by a desire to lessen or eliminate the pain to the branded animal or thinking of it as an economical sin, she viewed it with an artistic eye and reasoned with an aesthetically charged mind and stated: 'That brand is undecorative. It is crudely executed. It is not properly proportioned nor geometrically correct.'

"While the boss was taking the count from this verbal knockout, a sharp-witted, fun-loving cowboy came to his assistance and with convincing seriousness said: 'Lady, these cows don't care. Everyone of 'em was country-raised and the calves ain't goin' to college.' "

The best story I ever heard on the cruelties of brandin' was told by the boss of the Swingin' L. On this particular day he'd rode out from headquarters to see how the roundup was goin'. He was too old for strenuous work, but with the crew out on the range, the loneliness of the ranch had palled on 'im, so he'd come out to hear the cows bawl and smell hair burn.

After supper the silence of the crew was but respect for his age and superior position. They were givin' 'im the floor if he cared to spin a yarn, and he usually did. If he didn't, he'd let 'em know in due time.

"You know, boys," he began after knockin' the fire from his pipe on his boot heel, "brandin' them big yearlin's today takes my mind back to Texas, 'way back in the early eighties, when the cattle bus'ness was boomin'. With the trail drives to Kansas and the big price beef was bringin', the folks in the East thought all the money was in the cow bus'-ness. Settlers come pourin' into Texas till the whole range was cluttered up with 'em.

"Cap'talists who don't know a heifer from a horned frog come foggin' in, grass-bellied with cash, and farmers who don't own nothin' but a span of skinny mules, a faded wife, 'nough offspring to start a public school, and a hound for ever' kid, come runnin' a close second to take up a section and git rich quick.

"The old cow gits to be such a pop'lar subject back East that some fool shorthorns begin writin' pieces 'bout the cruelties of brandin', comparin' the cowman with the savage Injun. Them wart hogs'd never been closer to a cow than a city milk wagon, but the people believed all this tommy-rot and right away they start plannin' to teach us cowmen how to run our bus'ness.

"In them days I'm workin' for the Pothook spread. We've jes' started the calf brandin' and are camped on the lower range where there's a pole corral to hold the calves. 'Long 'bout sundown one evenin' old Pop Jackson come drivin' up in a buckboard from his livery stable in town. Settin' 'longside 'im is a stranger a-wearin' one of them hard-boiled hats and a lot of other dude trimmin's.

" 'Hey, Jed,' shouts Pop to the boss. 'Yere's a feller from Bostin whut wants to savvy the brandin' bus'ness. I brung 'im yere 'cause I knowed you'd learn 'im if anybody would.'

" 'Yes, Mister Jed,' says the tenderfoot, holdin' out his slim white paw, 'I've been sent by my Boston paper to secure some firsthand information upon the cruel Western custom of brandin' cattle. The Eastern humane societies are strongly agitatin' the abolishment of this savage custom, and are contemplatin' makin' a national law at Washington to that effect. Through this urgin', my paper has sent me West so I can reveal to the readin' public that actual process and cruel method you cow persons employ.'

"We stands there listenin' to all that high-falutin talk plumb flabbergasted. The boss fin'lly recovers 'nough to snort his disgust, but he's full of Western hospitality and holds back his feelin's.

" 'Well, hop out, son,' he says, 'set and eat a bean with us. We're jes' fixin' to throw a little fodder to our tapeworms. We'll teach you whut we kin 'bout the brandin' bus'ness.'

"A hummin'bird's appetite is robust compared with Boston's that night. He don't like beans 'less'n they're Boston baked, and he can't drink coffee without it's diluted with cream. 'Bout all he eats is a little of the fillin' from the dried apple pie, leavin' the crust untouched. Right there he makes an enemy of the cook.

"The next mornin' Boston's all spraddled out in a cowboy outfit he's bought back East, and he looks like a mail-order catalogue on foot. His boots are too tight and he stumbles over a pair of long-shanked spurs ever' step. His chaps flap somethin' ridic'lous when he walks, makin' 'im look 'bout as out of place as a pig in a pawnshop. His eyes look like he ain't slept none all night, and his appetite ain't improved none either.

"When the remuda comes in I offer to saddle a hoss for 'im, but he's kinda suspicious and 'lows he'll walk over as the pen's only 'bout a hundred yards.

"We're hard at work when he gits there, and he perches hisself on the top rail to git a good view of the op'ry. He pushed that pencil for all he's worth. Sometimes he crawls down for a closer view and stands 'round in the way, but when he gits a whiff of fried hair on his empty stomach it makes 'im kinda seasick.

"He musta thought he was in bedlam: calves bawlin', cows bellerin', men yellin', and smoke and dust ever'where. The boys try to see how rough they kin handle the calves. Some of 'em, when a calf bawled, would give its throat a tremolo effect that made its voice sound plumb pitiful.

"Sometimes when they thought Boston's lookin', one of 'em shouts loud 'nough to be heard at the home ranch, 'Dang your on'ry soul! Kick me, will you? Jes' for that I'll cut your leg off,' and as they turned the critter loose this cowhand puts one of the calf's forefeet over its neck and lets it hop off on three legs. With all that smoke and dust it shore looks like that calf's lost a leg in the shuffle.

"Boston writes so much he soon runs out of paper and goes back to camp for more. He leaves what he's wrote in the wagon, and as he comes back with his fresh supply Bud Lucas calls 'im over to the fire.

" 'Boston,' says Bud, 'if I was one of them writin' fellers and wanted to show them folks back East that I shore knowed whereof I spoke, I'd take a whirl at helpin' at this brandin' myself, 'stead of settin' on a fence and watchin' the other feller. That's the only way to git true knowledge, and I'll guarantee your writin'll be more convincin'.'

"Boston admits it sounds reasonable, and agrees to try it, but he ain't a-bilin' over with the idea. Right away the ropers start bringin' up calves by the neck 'stead of draggin' 'em up by the hind feet like they should, and Bud puts 'im to flankin' them necked calves. He shows 'im how to reach over the calf's back, grab a handful of loose flank skin, and how to heave up, kick the critter's feet out from under it, and let it down with a flop. Of course, this ain't much of a job for a cowhand 'less'n it's a big calf, but Boston don't know much 'bout it and he's soon wore down to a nubbin'.

" 'Bout an hour 'fore noon he looked so weak and pale I feels sorry for 'im and tell 'im if he'll heel 'em a while I'll do the flankin'. I show 'im, after the calf's down, how to ketch one hind leg while he pushes his boot heel against the hock of the other leg and shoves forward. That's easier and he likes it better, but with the smoke blowin' in his face he's shore glad when we knock off for chuck.

"We fogs it to camp, and I know as soon as I see Cookie that he's got somethin' on his mind besides his hat. His curiosity's got the best of 'im and he's dug up Boston's notes and read 'em. Most of it's with big words that'd make a hoss buck, so Cookie don't savvy it completely, but he gits the drift 'nough to tell us that our cruelty to pore animals would bring tears to anybody that's got a heart one degree softer'n a boulder.

" 'We'll show 'im jes' how cruel brandin' kin be,' growls Bud, and I know somethin's on his mind that'll be as refreshin' to Boston as bein' burned at stake.

"When we're halfway through eatin', Boston comes snailin' in, lookin' like a motherless calf. The boys'd got all the choice helpin's of beef and pie, but he goes to the wagon and helps his plate with the leavin's, and he shore put away a square meal for once.

"Ridin' back to the corral, I noticed some of the boys up in front with their heads together, but right then I'm pretty busy tryin' to iron the humps out of a green bronc I've saddled, so I don't know what they're hatchin' up. Pretty soon Boston comes walkin' over like he feels better, and he pitches right into the work again.

" 'Long in the middle of the afternoon when the sun's the hottest and the dust thickest and Boston's gittin' so weary he's weak, Bud musta give the signal for the dirty work to start. Brazos comes 'long pullin' a great big husky calf up by the neck, the biggest one in the pen. With 'im settin' back stiff-legged, it's 'bout all Brazos's pony kin do to drag 'im. Bud has lots to say 'bout a puncher that don't know better'n to bring up a calf that big by the neck.

" 'Well,' answers Brazos like he's plenty touchy, 'I missed my throw at his toes and he jes' nacher'ly pokes his head through my loop. Maybe you'd better git someone else to do your ropin'.'

" 'Well, I guess we'll have to flank 'im,' says Bud, payin' no attention to Brazos. 'Now, Boston, yere's your chance. If you want to tell the folks back home that you've done somethin', pitch in and flank that rascal. The boys'll help you.'

"I don't know whether Boston's game or jes' plain dumb, but he starts right in tryin' to flank that yearlin'. The boys all grab a-holt, too, but don't seem to do nothin' more helpful than grunt and git in the way. Boston wrastles that calf till he's plumb tuckered out, and jes' 'fore he gives up the boys manage to git the critter down.

"Brazos leaves the rope on the calf's neck, somethin' he's never done before. Bud tells Boston to heel 'im while the rest of us is a-settin' on his carcass—the calf's a-course. Brazos goes 'round to help Boston, and I see 'im tangle the rope 'round Boston's feet, all the time bein' genial as a bartender to a sheriff. As soon as he's done that, seems he's got bus'ness somewhere else.

"When the hot iron's slapped on that calf, he lets out a bawl and manages to jerk loose from ever'body but Boston, who's a-hangin' on to one hoof like an Injun to a whisky jug. That calf gits up on three legs, and when he kicks Boston in the mouth he breaks all holts as well as four of Boston's front teeth.

"The yearlin' breaks for the gate, the rope's tangled up in Boston's feet, and he goes skimmin' through the dust like one of them water skipper birds. The boys're runnin' 'longside the calf, tryin' to stop 'im and yellin' like Comanches, and in some way they head 'im right toward the fire. When the critter sees that fire in front with no chance to dodge it, he gives a big leap and lands on the other side, but Boston's jerked through the air and lands plumb in the middle of it, a-squirmin' in them hot irons and yellin' till the calf takes up the slack and pulls 'im out.

"We fin'lly manages to down the calf and untangle Boston. He's the dangdest-lookin' sight you ever seen. Bloody, dirty, shy 'nough skin to half-sole an elephant, and his clothes still a-smokin'. All he kin do is moan and cuss, and he can't even cuss good with all them teeth missin'.

"Bud puts 'im on a gentle hoss and tells 'im he better take the rest of the day off. He don't need no urgin', and the boys kin hardly hold in till he's out of hearin'.

"When we finish brandin' and make it to the wagon again, old Cookie's holdin' his sides a-laughin'. He points to a flock of torn paper scattered over the prairie, all that's left of that masterpiece on cruelty. I reckon it needed revisin'.

" 'He's a-packin',' says Cookie between laughs, 'the brand of the old Pothook 'tween his shoulders that he'll always have to remember us by. He's a-cussin' all cowboys, cow brutes, and the hull cow country. Says tell you he'll leave your hoss at Jackson's barn in town, and for the hull outfit to go to hell.'

"Cookie gets 'nother laughin' fit.

" 'When he's tearin' up all that highfalutin writin',' he continues when he kin talk again, 'he says out loud to hisself, "Bunk, jes' plain bunk." He's shore changed his mind as to who bears the sufferin' of brandin'.' "

The old man filled his pipe again.

"Well, that ain't quite the end of the story," he resumed. "When Boston gits back home he resigns from the paper, and as soon as he kin git his bridle teeth fixed, he comes back down in that country. He buys out the old Pothook, and changes the brand to one he kin smear all over the critter's hide till you kin read it in the moonlight. He says he's gonna show them critters how to suffer from a hot iron."

On the Trail

No OLD-TIME feature of the cattle business was more picturesque or more important than the movements of herds goin' up the trail to market. Them drives saved the Texas cattlemen from bankruptcy; they furnished the North and East with needed beef and the Northwest with breedin' cattle. The first trail men learned by trial and error the science of drivin' cattle. They learned that cattle weren't drove, but trailed, or grazed northward so that they'd gain flesh as they went. They learned the science of waterin' a herd, of swimmin' rivers, beddin' down cattle, and handlin' stampedes.

As long as the trail days lasted, it was the ambition of ever' ranch boy in Texas to go up the trail to Kansas. It was to 'im what a college education is to a high-school boy. It gave 'im an opportunity to break the monotony of range life and offered a chance to "see the world."

The act of movin' cattle up the trail was called "trail drivin'," but the only time they were actually drove was to get 'em away from familiar territory when they first left the ranch, to tire 'em down in an effort to avoid stampedes, or to reach feed and water in sections where these were scarce. At other times they were merely trailed or kept headed in the direction the drover wanted 'em to go as they grazed. In this manner they'd travel ten or twelve miles a day. The cattle usually traveled in single file, or in twos and threes, formin' a long, sinuous line, which, if seen from above, would've looked like a huge serpent in slow motion. Nothing could be more absurd to the old-time cowman than to see TV and moving pictures of herds driven at a gallop and closely bunched without any chance to graze.

The men who made the drive were knowed as "trail hands" or "trail drivers" and the crew consisted of the "trail boss," his assistant, the "secundo," or "straw boss," the cook, the wrangler, and 'nough men to control the herd, usually one puncher to ever' two hundred and fifty or three hundred head of cattle. A "lookout" was a man who rode ahead, usually the trail boss, to seek grass and water for the herd.

Only the best men of the range were hired to make the drive up the trail unless men were mighty scarce. The hours were long, the work hard and dangerous. The pay was usually a little better'n that on the range, and the trail offered the boys a chance to "see the elephant and hear the owl hoot" at the end of the trail. The trail was no place for a man with jumpy nerves or one without courage. He had to be a man dependable in any crisis.

Near the head of the marchin' trail herd were two men, one on each side, called "point riders," "point men," or "lead men." These were the most experienced men, and them with good judgment in meetin' obstacles, swimmin' rivers, and such. This was the honored post of the drive, and also the most dangerous and responsible. They were the first to swim rivers or meet the attack of Injuns. They worked in pairs and acted as pilots for the herd. No one rode immediately in front of the herd, but off to one side near the head. When they wanted to change the course of the cattle they rode abreast of the foremost cattle, one on each side of the column. Then they quietly veered in the desired direction, and the lead cattle swerved away from the one approachin' 'em toward the one goin' away from 'em. A point man might turn occasionally to twist in his saddle and look back over the slow-movin' river of horns and bodies, half-hidden in the dust cloud the cattle kicked up. Leadin' the herd plodded the "lead steers," their heads swingin' from side to side like the pendulum of a clock in steady rhythm.

Occasionally native cattle would be in the path of the driven herd, and the point men would ride ahead to drive 'em out of the way. Only one point man would leave the herd at a time, as it was necessary for at least one man to stay on point to keep the cattle movin'. When a point man left his place for anything, the swing rider on his side advanced to take his place till he returned.

Stationed 'bout a third of the way back of the point riders were the "swing riders," one on each side of the ploddin' line of cattle. Their function was to keep the cattle from wanderin' to the side away from the rest and keep away any native cattle tryin' to join the driven herd. This, however, didn't keep 'em from lettin' an occasional stray join the drive to replace one that had been lost en route. Each man was loyal to the boss and wanted to see 'im arrive with as many cattle as he started with. The section of the line of cattle he rode was called the "swing."

The "flank riders" were stationed 'bout a third of the way back of the swing riders, and they performed a similar duty. Like the swing riders, they had to ride up and down the herd to keep the cattle in line and zigzag out onto the prairie to keep away foreign cattle. Drivin' stragglers back into the herd from which they'd wandered was called "cuttin' in." Often them cattle were stubborn 'bout the matter, and both the swing and flank riders had to do a heap more ridin' than the point and drag men, and their hosses tired sooner. In spite of the hard ridin' he did durin' the day, he had to take his turn at night herdin' when the cattle were bedded down.

At the rear of the trail herd rode the "drag," or "tail rider." His was the most disagreeable job of all because he had to ride in the dust kicked up by the entire herd, and contend with the weak, obstinate, and lazy, the weary and footsore critters till his patience was sorely tried. While the other riders might be singin' in the pure air ahead, there wasn't no music in the soul of the drag rider, and he used his vocal powers to cuss beneath the neckerchief he kept over his nose and mouth to keep from bein' suffocated. This part of the column was called the "drag," or "tail," and it represented both a hospital and a home for the incompetents. The cattle occupyin' this position were called "drags," and the word was often applied to lazy humans.

The drag rider had to weave back and forth, roundin' the corners and never crowdin' an animal or his hoss up into the herd, which would have caused the cattle to tromp on one another's heels, thus bruisin' 'em. The least experienced men were placed on drag because they could be taught in a couple of hours.

The drag rider spent a good part of his time with rope or whip, tryin' to beat a little life into his charges to keep 'em from quittin' on 'im. This was spoken of as "poundin' 'em on the back," and his occupation was commonly referred to as "eatin' drag dust," "bringin' up the drag," or "swallowin' dust."

In startin' out there was a heap of confusion, and cattle gave some trouble till they became used to travelin' with a herd. They were pressed to a fast drive for the first day or two in order to get 'em away from familiar range, and to make 'em so tired they'd lie down at night. After them first few days the herd'd organize itself, with the stronger cattle in the lead and the weaker ones in the drag. They were said to be "herd broke." And even though the cattle were wild and had been gathered from different ranges, if properly handled they'd soon become a well behaved unit.

Some trail bosses wouldn't throw their cattle off the bedground till the dew was off the grass, as dew moisture softened the hoofs of the cattle and caused 'em to wear easily. But this wasn't usually necessary if the cattle were slowly drifted and spaced far 'nough apart to keep 'em from trompin' on one another's heels. The last watch would usually throw 'em off at daylight and let 'em drift 'bout a mile and a half before throwin' 'em back on the trail and drivin' till 'bout 11 o'clock. Then they'd be throwed off the trail again and grazed toward their next bedground. They tried to make the shortest drive in the forenoon because of the heat.

The average herd was from 2,500 to 3,000 head, and a herd of this size would be strung out for 'bout three-quarters of a mile. The leaders were always held back to the pace of the sore-footed ones of the drag.

After the cattle left the bedground in the mornin' and were strung out in a thin line, the trail boss and 'nother man stationed on the opposite side of the herd began countin' cattle. Their forefingers rose and fell as they pointed directly at each animal that passed. As each hundred head was counted, each man dropped a pebble into a handy pocket, or any other counter his individual selection dictated. When the herd had passed, each man counted his counters and announced his tally to the other. Chances are that their first count checked. If not, and there was a wide margin of difference, they rode to the head of the movin' column and started over again. If many were missin', a puncher or two would drop back, if possible, and join a followin' herd to search for the missin' cattle. This was the "trail count," and necessary at times to check up on the cattle.

The expression "keepin' up the corners" meant keepin' the stronger cattle movin' in such a way as not to impede the progress of the others, seein' that the rear of the column was no wider'n the swing, or the cattle'd be overheated, and seein' that the herd didn't become spaced so that the marchin' column became too long.

Followin' the cattle was the chuck wagon drove by the cook, though often in the afternoon he took the lead so he could make camp and have supper ready by the time the herd was bedded down. Behind 'im came the remuda drove by the wrangler. Occasionally in the early days some drovers carried a two-wheeled cart to pack cow chips when goin' through a country where wood was scarce. The vehicle occupyin' this rather menial social position was knowed as the "chip wagon." Also, sometimes a more humane drover would carry a "calf wagon," or "blattin' cart," to save the calves born en route. But most drovers scorned its use and, rather than delay the drive, killed the calves or gave 'em to settlers if any happened to live nearby. The driver performin' this humiliatin' task was called "Little Mary," or "Nursey." What this driver answered back was salty but unprintable.

The bedground was the place where the cattle were held at night. The trail boss tried to get his wagon to the place he was to camp for the night somewhere 'round five o'clock in the afternoon. The bedground was chosen with a heap of care. A good trail boss was particular to avoid a site near timber, washouts, or ravines. One never knowed when cattle might stampede, and them natural obstacles were dangerous. High and dry ground was chosen if possible because cattle lie better on high ground where insects were more easily blowed away, and again where the ground was usually more level than lower ground and not apt to encounter streams in case of stampedes.

It was the duty of the day herders to have the cattle on the bedground and bedded down before dusk. This beddin' down was the formin' of the herd for their night's rest—a scientific job requirin' that the herd not be crowded too close, nor yet allowed to scatter over too much territory. With a trail herd, as the sun began to sink in the west, the men in charge would carefully and gradually work the cattle into a more compact space and urge 'em toward some open, level ground selected for the bedground. If the herd had been well grazed and watered durin' the day, they'd stop, and gradually a few would lie down to their contented cud chewin'. With patience the cowboy would stay with 'em till relieved by the men on first guard. He was said to "father the herd." The expression "ridin' 'em down" signified this gradual urgin' of the point and drag cattle closer together, preparin' to put 'em on the bedground. Where such a herd had been well handled and grass was plentiful, the animals, if not disturbed by some unusual noise, would lie thus for three or four hours without movin'. Then as with one accord they'd all get onto their feet, mill 'bout for a few minutes, and then lie down again, this time on their other side.

The herd should be bedded loose 'nough to give each animal room to rise and turn over without disturbin' the animal next to it. But they shouldn't be bedded so loose that it'd scatter the herd so that it'd take too much time to ride 'round it, and thus give some steer time to slip out and be gone.

The wagon boss set his direction by the North Star. At night, after locatin' this star, the chuck-wagon tongue was pointed in the direction to be traveled the next day. This was called "followin' the tongue." Usually a lantern was hung inside the wagon sheet of the wagon, or on its tongue for a beacon to guide the riders back to camp on dark nights, but a cowhand with a good night hoss could always find his way without a light.

The next mornin' when the herd was started out again, the leaders were pointed in the direction the drover wanted it to go, and this was called "headin' 'em up." The start was called "stringin' 'em out." The herd now grazed its way toward its destination, leavin' the wagon the last to break camp. The trail boss loped far ahead to search out water and a noon campin' location. Soon the wagon, followed by the remuda, swung wide 'round the slow-movin' herd and gained its position in the lead.

Havin' selected a suitable campsite, the trail boss rode back within sight and wig-wagged directions with his hat, and the cook whipped his teams into a gallop. Arrivin' at the chosen location, camp was made and the monotonous routine of cookin' gone through again. While the men ate, the herd was allowed to scatter somewhat to graze and rest. In the evenin' this same process was gone through again.

Night herdin' was the watchin' of the cattle at night after they'd been bedded down. Each man in camp, except the cook and the wrangler, had to serve his turn. Usually there were two men to each guard for the average herd. Upon reachin' the bedground, they rode in opposite directions as they circled the herd. This answered the double purpose of keepin' the men separated and havin' a man lookin' each way so that no animal could slip away unnoticed in the dark. Two punchers ridin' side by side and talkin' were apt to neglect their job.

They usually rode from forty to fifty feet away from the herd so as not to disturb 'em, and sang as they rode. This not only reassured the cattle, but diverted their attention from other things. If things went smooth, they kept this up till they were relieved by the next guard. On many nights a puncher had no stars to comfort 'im and couldn't even strike a match. If the cattle were nervous, as they often were on stormy nights, he had to be extremely cautious, and would have to ride a mile to spit. On pleasant nights the work wasn't so hard, but even then the cowboy had to stay in the saddle all the time, and the hours seemed long and lonesome. Somewhere an animal might cough, and a black shape move out from the shadows. A rider would swing toward it, and the shape then melted again into the splotch of shade which was the sleepin' herd. To his nostrils came the peculiar animal odor of the herd, across the way the slow monotonous chant of a song, and if there was no song for an instant his pardner could be located by the dim glow in the dark of a cigarette.

When workin' with the roundup or with a trail herd, the cowhand didn't get much sleep, and what he did get was interrupted by his havin' to take his turn at night guard. But after he was on the job a while, he rarely needed to be awakened. Sleepin' with his ear to the ground, he could hear the rider comin' off herd when he was still a long distance away, and by the time he reached camp the new guard was ready to take his place.

There were several periods of guard durin' the night, and "cocktail."

This was the last watch before daylight, and the one despised by all herders because it was at a time when men most loved to sleep. Before the watch was over, it was mornin', the cattle were beginnin' to stir, and the other hands were eatin' their breakfast and gettin' hot coffee. The period between sundown and eight o'clock was called the "killpecker guard," in some sections, and "bobtail guard" in others. The "graveyard shift" or "graveyard stretch" came from midnight to 2:00 A.M., and all others had various slang names. New men comin' on duty were referred to as "relief men," and them jes' finishin' their period were then "off herd."

The expression "standin' guard" was seldom used. Night herdin' was knowed as "singin' to 'em" because at this time the cowhand did a lot of singin' to help quiet the cattle.

In ever' herd there was a steer who, by his aggressiveness and stamina, took his place at the head of the herd as a self-appointed leader and retained this leadership to the end of the trail. He became knowed as the "lead steer," and was usually honored with a name. To the drover he proved 'imself to be invaluable, and some of 'em rendered such valuable service that they were retained and drove back home to be used on the next trip. The cowboys became as attached to 'im as they would a feller rider.

It was natural for the stronger animals to work toward the front and the weaker ones to fall back to the rear. Whatever position an animal took at the beginnin' he'd usually hold it to the end of the drive. The muleys in a herd soon found each other and stayed close together. They tried to avoid the horned stuff even at night when bedded down.

Waterin' the herd meant more'n jes' turnin' the cattle loose uncontrolled to fight for a place 'long the riverbank. Waterin' a trail herd was a science. A good trail boss knowed to slow up his herd before hittin' the river, then cut 'em into small bunches and let each drink, or he'd throw 'em up and down stream as they came to water, lettin' all cattle get a clear drink. When a herd hit the stream all at once, the leaders were crowded out before gettin' 'nough water and the drags got a muddy drink. If the wind was in the right direction, cattle could smell water for miles, and the trail drivers sometimes had a hard time controllin' a herd of thirsty cattle to keep down panic. After a long, dry drive this sometimes gave plenty of trouble. If a herd was bein' watered on a creek with a fairly long stretch of water, the boss would throw 'em 'long the water by pointin' 'em upstream and downstream as they came in. Cattle properly watered like to take a first fill, go out on the bank to "blow" for a few minutes, and then come back for more water. They'd repeat this process several times if 'nough time was given 'em.

As a rule cattle were watered only once a day, in the evenin'. Charlie Goodnight once said that the "science of the trail is in grazin' and waterin' the cattle, but the waterin' is the most important of the two."

"Squeezin' 'em down" was the narrowin' of the width of a trail herd for the crossin' of a river, or for any other purpose. If the river was swimmin' water, too deep to cross without swimmin', puttin' the leaders of the herd into the water for a crossin' was called "startin' the swim." Crossin' rivers was no easy task, but many of 'em crossed the old cattle trails, some of 'em well knowed for their treachery. Gettin' cattle to take water often called for a heap of patience, a knowledge of cow psychology, and a lot of experience.

Once cattle balked at crossin' a river it was hard to get 'em into the water. If the hands could get a lead steer in, the rest would usually follow. If the cattle were dry or thirsty they'd take the water easier, but even then they seemed to need a leader. The pilot rode out in front, swimmin' his hoss not too far ahead, and the other riders swam their hosses on the downstream side of the herd to keep it from driftin'. Hosses swelled up in swimmin', so it was wise to loosen the cinches. Reins don't mean a thing to a hoss in water and tied reins were dangerous. The best way to guide an animal was to splash water in his face the opposite direction you wanted 'im to go. Pullin' on the reins was apt to cause the hoss to go over backward and drown both 'imself and his rider.

High water, quicksand, and treacherous banks offered plenty of hazards. Muscular cramps, suck holes, undercurrents, swift water, and a number of things could take the life of even the best swimmer. If the sun shone in the eyes of the cattle, they had a hard time seein' the opposite bank, and wouldn't take to water. A good trail boss knowed this, and didn't put cattle into the water under this circumstance.

Sometimes startin' a swim was accomplished by keepin' the cattle away from the water a day or so and then gradually workin' 'em down to an easy takin'-off place. Frequently, jes' as the cattle reached the water's edge, the hoss herd would be eased into the river ahead of the lead cattle and started for the opposite bank. Usually the drovers had no trouble in gettin' the cattle to follow the hosses.

In swimmin' the herd, if the river was at medium stage and calm, there was usually no trouble in gettin' the leaders to take the water; but if the river was high and turbulent, "big swimmin' " it was called, much vigorous urgin' was required. Once the cattle reached swimmin' depth they usually went ahead to the other side unless some floatin' log or unexpected event caused 'em to start millin' in midstream. This millin' in a stream was called a "merry-go-round in high water," and was a most dangerous thing. Although it was highly desirable to get a stampedin' herd to mill on land, when they did so in water the results were anything but desirable. When they got to swimmin' 'round in an ever tightenin' circle in water, they became hopelessly massed, and the loss from drownin's was enormous unless the herders were lucky in breakin' this mass up in the early stages. To stop 'em was a difficult and dangerous job, as the rider couldn't enter the center of the mass to break it up, and pushin' from the outside caused it to become tighter. The cowboy sometimes had to desert his hoss and crawl over the backs of the cattle to get 'em turned. If successful he'd slip back to be ferried over by hangin' to the tail of some animal.

When the trail boss had advance information 'bout some river bein' at flood stage, he held up the herd at a safe distance and rode down to give the river his personal inspection. If he returned and gave his report of the river as bein' "over the willows," he meant that it was at flood stage and there'd be several hundred yards of swimmin' water. Crossin' a river with a herd of wild longhorns under any circumstances was no job for a weaklin'. It took courage, and no higher compliment could be paid a man than to say of 'im, "He'd do to ride the river with."

Often a herd started, say from South Texas, in the spring while the northern ranges were still covered with snow, yet the early washy grass of their startin' point was already green. As they traveled north the grass, with the passin' of time in their slow progress, became green as they went. This was called "travelin' with the grass."

Sometimes they encountered weeks of rain, which made it mighty disagreeable to both cattle and men. It was bad 'nough to stay in camp for a week in such weather, but to have to break and make camp ever' day was still worse. Ever' night beds had to be made down in wet grass and soaked beddin' spread to absorb still more moisture. Hands and faces were muddy, and it was useless to clean or dry 'em; soaked clothes, if he forgot to bring his slicker, the splashin' mud from the herd—all them things made for his great discomfort.

One of the things that caused losses in the trail days, as well as lots of trouble for the drover, such as quarantines—some of 'em "Winchester quarantines"—ill feelin' with the settlers 'long the trail, and lots of other calamities, was the Texas fever. This was a splenic fever caused by ticks and spread by the immune, but tick-infested cattle of the southern country to the cattle of the more northern latitudes. This disease was also knowed as "Southern" and "Spanish" fever. It brought 'bout the plowin' of furrows to designate the side limits of the trail to keep drovers within certain bounds. Kansas recognized this as constitutin' a fence, and passed trespass laws to prosecute anyone crossin' them furrows, which became called a "furrow fence."

The cattle trails served an excellent purpose in the development of the country, for they brought the North and the South of the Mississippi Valley into close business relations followin' the Civil War. That was of great economic, educational and political advantage to both, bringing the two sections to a better understandin'.

Stampedes

A STAMPEDE was the runnin' wild of cattle or hosses from fright, or, as sometimes, pure cussedness. The word's from the Spanish *estampeda*, meanin' crash, loud noise, or a general scamper of cattle. It's used both as a noun and a verb, and in later years also became used to express the rush of humans to new localities. The old-time Texan called 'em "stompedes," and his description of one was, "It's jes' one jump to their feet and 'nother jump to hell."

Perhaps the most dreaded of all things in his life, the cowboy hated a stampede at night. There was always a heap of danger of death or of bein' crippled; of course, the wagon boss and the owner dreaded it because of the loss of cattle, both in the killed and maimed and loss of flesh. There were some stampedes in daylight, but the majority of 'em happened at night when the boogers were unseen. And the stormier the weather, the more apt was there to be a stampede.

"Boys, the cattle's runnin'!" is a short sentence, but it portrayed a situation without any other explanation and brought the punchers back from dreamland and to grabbin' clothes. Ordinarily when a cow rose from the ground she got into a "prayin'" attitude on her knees and rose on her hind feet, but when she was scared she jumped straight into the air and landed on all four feet quicker'n a stutterin' man could holler "shucks."

Nothin' could happen so quick as a stampede. It was hard to realize how sudden so many cattle could rise up on their feet and be gone. As the cowman said, "They jes' buy a through ticket to hell and gone and try to ketch the first train," and it was like startin' from the back door of hell on a hot day and comin' out on the run. As soon as a cowhand could mount his hoss, he heaved a prayer in the general direction of Heaven and *rode*. On stormy nights they usually left their hosses saddled, ready for any emergency.

A stampede was dangerous both to the runnin' cattle and to the men herdin' 'em. Holdin' a herd on a dark and stormy night was a hazardous job. Ridin' buckin' hosses, swimmin' rivers in flood, nearly ever'thing the cowboy did was plenty dangerous. But ridin' at breakneck speed through the night in a frantic effort to check a stampede was the most dangerous of all his work. If the country was broken and filled with prairie-dog holes, his life depended on the shore-footedness of his racin' hoss. A spill meant certain death, and many were the graves on the prairie that marked where some cowhand had given his life to perform his duty. A hoss could go over a bluff or river bank, slip in the mud, or step into a badger hole, and both hoss and rider be throwed into the path of the on-comin' cattle. However, cattle would split and go 'round a fallen object if they saw it in time, but often this happened too near in front for 'em to see, or the pressure from behind, or on the sides, was too great for 'em to give way. Even if nothin' happened other than the cripplin' of his hoss, he was still in a bad way.

A stampede spoiled cattle and made 'em nervous and hard to hold for many days. Herds that stampeded often early in the drive didn't recover from the experience for a time, and were spoiled to the extent that they'd stampede on the slightest provocation. Often many of 'em were killed or crippled, and others were so scattered they'd never be recovered.

When cattle stampeded they often ran for miles till they were forced to stop from exhaustion. This was damagin' both to their weight and condition, and a good cowman did his best to keep down stampedes. A good wagon boss wouldn't bed his cattle on rough ground, near gullies or trees, but tried to pick a level place much like the cattle would natu-rally pick for 'emselves if allowed to. He kept the camp quiet, allowed no firin' of guns or unusual noises, and he watered the cattle thoroughly and saw to it that they had a bellyful of grass before they were bedded down. If cattle had plenty of grass and water jes' before they were put on the bedground, they'd be more contented and would lie down and rest.

But when cattle were hungry and thirsty, they became restless and would keep gettin' up and disturbin' them that were down—all of which got 'em well primed for a run at the slightest excuse. Keepin' 'em contented on the bedground and givin' 'em plenty of room in which to lie down was the secret of preventin' stampedes—always, of course, barrin' unfortunate accidents or storms.

Some trail men wanted a few cows with calves mixed in with any herd of steers. In any run a calf'd become separated from its mother, and she'd soon stop and bawl for it, and that bawl'd tend to bring the steers to their senses and a halt. On the other hand, mixed cattle wouldn't travel uniformly, and in a bad run the young and the weak were liable to be mutilated.

A good wagon boss bedded his cattle down loosely and not too close together, for if too close one steer switchin' his tail might hit 'nother in the eye with it. This steer'd be apt to jump up with a bawl and start the whole herd off on a run. When cattle stampeded over their own bedground, you'd hear a few steers bawl suddenly, throatily—they were the ones that were a fraction of a second too late in gettin' to their feet, and they were payin' the penalty under the lungin' bodies of them that stumbled over 'em. The fact that the majority of stampedes occurred on stormy nights made 'em harder to bring under control and more dangerous to the riders.

Anything could cause a stampede. No matter how gentle a herd, it was forever on the lookout for somethin' to booger at. Maybe lightnin' and thunder caused more stampedes than anything else. Cattle became frantic from the terrifyin' noise of thunder, and wanted to get away. Sights, sounds, odors, all have caused stampedes. A tumbleweed, a jackrabbit, a hoss shakin' his saddle when unmounted, the flare of a match—thousands of causes have been listed by the cattlemen, some of 'em so simple that they sounded ridiculous to the greener.

Stampedes happened most often in the early stage of the drive. This was because they were travelin' a country strange to 'em and were naturally nervous and suspicious. The change from the familiar home range to strange surroundin's and from the custom of sleepin' in free solitude to bein' bedded down with hundreds of other cattle and all guarded by that hated enemy, man, naturally made 'em nervous. On their home range cattle were familiar with ever' bush, gully, hill, and stone, and so when they were drove into a territory where nothin' was familiar they were

naturally apprehensive. Also, in trail days the country through which the trails passed was full of thieves and Injuns who often stampeded a herd in the hope of retrievin' some of the scattered cattle.

Quite often a stampedin' herd would split in two or more sections. This made controllin' 'em difficult because of the lack of men. However, since they often ran parallel to each other, the riders could sometimes

N. EGGENHOFER

merge 'em back into the original herd. At other times they scattered all over the prairie, and daylight found the scattered groups bein' held by some wet, weary, and hungry cowhand who'd stayed with 'em all night. This scatterin' caused much delay and loss of labor in gettin' 'em together again. Some were lost altogether, and all of 'em would lose some valuable weight. Often early in the run the herd would be split by some natural object, and sometimes each division would be split again and again till the cattle would be scattered all over the country.

As a rule cattle grazed against the wind, and if in a stampede they started out by runnin' with the wind or at cross current, they'd soon circle to run against it. A stampedin' herd rarely ran in a straight line. They split and turned to avoid some object, yet always swung back into the wind.

Often in a herd there'd be some particular animal that'd start the herd on stampedes till they'd be spoiled. This individual was called a "stampeder," and he spent his time lookin' for an opportunity to find somethin' to scare at. After his evil ways were discovered he was gotten rid of at the first opportunity.

Ordinarily the cook had nothin' to do with cattle, but durin' a stampede it was "all hands and the cook," and this phrase signified an emergency when ever' man was called to duty. With the clashin' of horns a herd would be up and away like flushed quail. There was no warnin', no preparation for flight, no hesitation as to direction or leadership. Whatever the cause, it made the drags wake up and forget all 'bout sore feet.

Cattle weren't alone in their fear of thunder and lightnin', for if there was anything the trail driver feared it was lightnin'. Fightin' a stampede was hot work, and they believed that heat and steel both attracted electricity. Durin' an electrical storm many cowhands would cast away their six-guns, spurs, knives, or anything else made of metal for fear they'd draw the lightnin'. Some of 'em preferred to shed their slickers and get wet to cool their bodies and thus be less liable to attract lightnin'.

The phosphorous light so commonly seen playin' on the horns and ears of cattle and hosses durin' such a storm was called "fox-fire" by the cowman. Such balls of fire dancin' on the hoss's ears, from the horns of cattle, and even sometimes runnin' 'round the brim of the cowboy's hat was a weird, uncanny sight. Even at times when the cowboy spit, it seemed he was spittin' a stream of livin' fire. In the blackness of night, between flashes of lightnin', such a scene seemed ghostly.

The most profane man among 'em would give 'nother a wide berth if the latter was doin' any cussin' 'bout the weather, or takin' the Lord's name in vain. Them men might not have much religion in their own name, but they feared the wrath of God's punishment by the elements if they were near anyone mockin' Him.

Many a report has been given about a trail outfit jes' after the herd had been bedded down for the night, with the first guard ridin' 'round 'em with never a thought of disaster, when all of a sudden it got warm and sticky, and there was a thick, muffled feelin' in the air. It wasn't long till the air moved kinda heavy and seemed to be saturated with sulphurous smoke. Then thunder began to mutter beyond the horizon. There suddenly seemed to be a tense expectancy in the air, a hush as if the world held its breath before a calamity, and the cattle began to grow more restless.

Steadily it growed darker, and two dense clouds were convergin' in heavy ragged columns. The air became oppressive to the lungs. Suddenly a flash of lightnin' licked silently toward the cloud banks. The men waited for the thunder, countin' off the seconds till it should strike. Then it burst with a muffled sound and a long rumble. By now the cattle that'd been lyin' down got to their feet to let out an uneasy bawl or two.

Then the sky growed blacker; the slow-gatherin' clouds appeared to be suddenly agitated; they piled and rolled and mushroomed. The storm was upon 'em with thunder growlin' threats and lightnin' playin' behind the sullen jumble of black clouds. A fork of white lightnin' flashed, and, like a boomin' avalanche, thunder followed. A blue-white knotted rope of lightnin' burned down out of the clouds, and instantly a thunderclap cracked, seemin' to shake the foundations of the earth. Then it rolled as if bangin' from cloud to cloud, and boomed 'long the peaks, and at last rumbled away into silence till the next one.

The roar of approachin' wind, the increasin' claps of thunder, the more and more vivid flashes of lightnin', the electric glow on the horns of the cattle, all made the cowboy yearn for a dry bed at home. The cattle on such a night, as the roar of thunder filled the air with the noise of battle, would nervously wander this way and that in their fright. Then, when all was panic in the pitchy black, made more terrifyin' by the sizzlin', spittin', snappin' flashes of lightnin', they suddenly were gone.

There was some confusion, some crowdin', here and there a jumble of bodies where a steer had stumbled; but the men on guard saw nothin' of it, and even while they wheeled their hosses for pursuit, the herd was gone, thunderin' away in the darkness. It was then that the boss was thankful he'd ordered ever' man to saddle a night hoss. Always the thunder boomed overhead, and by lightnin' flashes riders glimpsed the boilin' sea of cattle fleein', they knowed not where or why, only blind fear crowdin' at their heels. The noise of their hoofs was engulfin'. It sounded like hell migratin' on cartwheels. Their bellowin' was an even higher roar than the thunder of their hoofs, and through all this noise could be heard the clackin' of horns and the collidin' of bodies. The rush of horns looked like a movin' thicket of skeleton brush. But the thing the rider was most conscious of was the shakin' of the earth.

Durin' a stampede the riders made ever' effort to gain a position alongside the lead cattle and try to head 'em into a millin' circle. Once at the head he tried with voice, quirt, or gun to get the lead cattle to swing in the opposite direction. The cattle behind would usually follow the leaders in front, and by continuously swingin' 'em into a smaller circle they'd soon be into a mill. Each rider kept up some sort of noise, and if he could hear his pardner above the other noises he knowed he was safe. If he didn't hear 'im he might be down. Turnin' the leaders more and more till the column formed itself into a U, they rode till the two ends merged together. As this compact mass raced in a circle, they were said to be "millin'," and they kept this up till they stopped from exhaustion, and the stampede was over. After windin' 'emselves into a narrowin' mass which became tighter'n tighter till finally it was so tight they couldn't move, there was nothin' for 'em to do but stop.

Racin' neck and neck with the leaders, the cowboy urged his hoss in so close to the plungin' mass that the hot breath was on his leg and the smell of panic in his nostrils. He used his slicker as a flail, bringin' it down with wide, overhead strokes into the faces of the foremost steers. He yelled, screamed, and cussed them wild brutes till he felt a yieldin' of their close-packed bodies. In the darkness some sixth sense of the cowpuncher's art told 'im he was turnin' the leaders.

Finally when they were stopped there was water standin' ever'where and it was hard, or impossible, to bed 'em again. Then the cowboys, wet to the skin, cold and miserable, stood guard for the remainder of the night. Maybe one or two broke into song, but it took a brave man to sing under such conditions.

The big job awaited 'em at dawn. First they counted the cattle, and if any were gone they followed their tracks on fresh hosses. Maybe they weren't far off—maybe they were twenty miles—but get them back they had to do even if they were halfway back to the home range.

All this was part of the cowhand's work, but a stampede was an experience that tried his soul and left 'im with tormented dreams. Maybe when it was over the clouds overhead broke and trailed off in ragged streams, still torn by a wind the earth didn't feel, and the moon showed now and then swimmin' the black cloud patches left from the storm. But he had to stay with the cattle till daylight, perhaps miles from the wagon and the camp of the night before, cold, wet, no sleep for the night, and a long way from breakfast. It was an experience he wouldn't soon forget, but he had the satisfaction of havin' done a hard task well.

36

Ridin' the Roughstring

THE roughstring riders were the fellers who followed the hazardous trade of hoss breakin' as a steady business. They had to be good, even better'n the man who jes' broke hosses, and a good one was hard to find. The best cowhands could ride the snuffy ones, but wouldn't. This was the buster's job, and he got a few extry dollars a month more'n the average hand. The ordinary cowhand didn't claim to be a bronc rider. In fact he'd usually quit if asked to ride a bronc because there was always a job somewhere else where he could ride the gentle ones.

The buster's job was spoken of as "bustin'," "gentlin'," "snappin' broncs," or "twistin' out." No man hired to break hosses ever abused 'em. He took great pride in his work, and it was an honor to be pointed out as the rider of the roughstring for a big outfit. He did his best to make good hosses and not spoil 'em. No outfit wanted spoiled hosses.

Some twisters preferred slippin' a blind on a bad hoss while they saddled, and took it off when they mounted. Some bridles were equipped with *tapaojos* which could be slipped down, or they used a neckerchief, a sack, or anything else that was handy. If the hoss was real mean and tried to bite, kick, and paw he was apt to have one hind foot tied up. This was done with a Scotch or crow hobble, and when tied thus he couldn't strike or kick without fallin' down.

A top twister wouldn't give a dime for a bronc that didn't buck and show some spirit when first rode. Yet, if he was a good one, he had to have patience and take plenty of time, especially if he was breakin' young hosses. It was the twister who was bustin' 'em at so much per head that hurried 'em 'long by rough methods. This was one reason why ranchers who wanted good cow hosses put their busters on the reg'lar payroll.

Ever' cowhand took a heap of pride in bein' able to top his own string of hosses, but he wasn't so proud that he wanted to ride them that was unbroken. It was a kind of disgrace to tie your stirrups or pull leather when ridin' a buckin' hoss, and very few cowhands tied their stirrups, but a heap of 'em grabbed the apple rather than be bucked off. And it was a good thing they made them saddle horns strong, or they'd a-been pulled out by the roots.

As a rule the tall, wiry-framed cowhand could stand the ridin' game better. A man followin' this game had to be reckless, darin', and know how to laugh when things seemed bad. When he got old 'nough to quit enjoyin' the game and started bein' careful and serious, he'd better tell the boss to give 'im reg'lar cowboy wages and a gentler hoss to ride. Then when he heard that terrifyin' bawl of a mad bronc, he could enjoy it 'cause the other feller was ridin' 'im.

Ever' cow outfit of any size had its roughstring. It was made up of broncs, young hosses, and old outlaws or spoiled hosses that the average cowhand couldn't or wouldn't ride.

There's an old sayin', "The rider of the roughstring maybe ain't strong on brains, but he ain't short on guts." It took courage to ride the mean ones. He knowed he wasn't attendin' no knittin' bee. An occasional ride might be play for some reckless spirit, but it was work for a veteran. Bronc busters were mostly young men, and they were too old for the game at thirty, all crippled and busted up inside. Then they had to have some younger man do their breakin' and were satisfied to ride the gentle ones. He never had any trouble gettin' a job because a buster don't last long. If he didn't get killed or crippled, he soon got so stove-up he couldn't take the punishment.

Breakin' hosses on a ranch was a heap different from ridin' one out of a chute for ten seconds with a pick-up man right there to get 'im as soon as the whistle blowed. At the ranch he tried to keep the hoss from buckin', but at the rodeo he wanted 'im to buck his best so he could show his ridin' ability. If he was a rough bucker of course that ten seconds seemed like a long time. Ridin' buckin' hosses at the ranch wasn't for show unless the buster wanted to put on a little show of his own. Mostly it was strictly business, and the rider was tryin' to build his rep'tation as a gentler of the wild ones.

Each bronc twister had his own way of breakin' a hoss, but all good busters tried to break so that the hoss's spirit remained unbroken, for a spiritless hoss was worthless. The buster strove to break quickly, as it meant time and money to the boss. He usually turned the hoss over to the cowboy after "three saddles." No matter what his manner of breakin', he was more interested in stayin' on the hoss than in his performance. His very callin' demanded that he stay on, as a matter of pride and because hosses become outlaws when they consistently throw their riders. But when a rider boasted that he'd never been throwed, it was a shore sign he hadn't forked any bad ones, or hadn't been ridin' long, or he was jes' a blamed liar.

A hoss was usually at the breakin' age when he was between three and one-half and four years old. It was a heap harder to break a hoss after his fifth year because he had to be handled a lot more to make 'im realize he'd been set on. Havin' run the range all his life, he was usually strong, wild, and hard to ride. In the old days when hosses were plentiful and cheap, most busters would jes' "rough break" 'em. This meant to rope, choke down, blindfold, and saddle a green bronc, then mount, strip off the blindfold, dig in with the spurs, slam the hoss with a quirt, and proceed to fight it out.

Later when good hosses were more in demand, the buster took more time with his gentlin'. He might spend a good part of that time teachin' the bronc the terrors of the rope. The roped hoss might drag 'im 'round the corral a few times, but eventually the buster would get the rope looped 'round the firm snubbin' post in the center of the corral. After the hoss had run on the rope—that is, dashed to the end of it and got throwed a few times—he'd soon learn it was useless to fight the string. Maybe he'd spend some time tryin' to quiet the hoss with soothin' breakin' patter, jes' sayin' anythin' to let the hoss hear the human voice.

On some ranches a hazer was employed to help the buster. His duty, especially when the hoss was broke outside a corral, was to keep the animal turned so that his buckin' wouldn't take 'im too far away. He also helped with the sackin' and earin' down. "Sackin' out" was done by fannin' a saddle blanket, or a grain sack, 'round the hoss, eventually droppin' it on the bronc's back many times to get 'im used to it. It was usually started by lettin' 'im smell the object, then rubbin' it 'long his jaws, neck, and shoulders, sides and back to convince 'im there wasn't any harm in it. After that he flipped it easy-like 'bout the back and hindquarters, gettin' a little rougher as he went. Most broncs blow up at the first sackin', but they soon become convinced it won't hurt 'em.

Frequently the buster would put the saddle on and let the hoss "buck the saddle" while he was held by a rope to convince 'im that the rig was on his back to stay. Some busters used a "blinder," a sack or cloth to cover the bronc's eyes while saddlin'. This was called "blindin'," and it caused the hoss to stand still while bein' saddled. Others let the hazer "ear down" the bronc, distractin' the hoss's attention so the rider could mount. Sometimes the men doin' the earin' would ketch the tip of the ear that was above his hand with his teeth. This caused the hoss to stand very quiet to avoid the pain. When obliged to ride without the help of a hazer, the rider sometimes diverted the hoss's attention by stickin' his thumb in the brute's left eye.

Many hosses, when bein' cinched up, would take in a lot of wind so that the saddle became loose when the ride started, but the rider was wise to this trick, and as he was pullin' the cinch tight he'd kick the brute in the belly. The surprise of this move caused the hoss to expel the air in his lungs and let the rider pull the latigo straps up 'nother notch or two. If the hoss was on his feet and bein' eared, the buster forked 'im as easy as he could, but when the bronc had to be throwed to be saddled the rider eased 'imself into the saddle while the hoss was still down. He then told his helpers to "turn loose," "throw off," "ease up," "let 'er go," or "give 'im air," and the fight was on.

If the breakin' was bein' done in a corral, you'd likely find the top rail full of spectators givin' useless advice and encouragement. This top rail was knowed as the "op'ry house," and the watchers were knowed by such names as "chute roosters," "rail birds," or "top railers."

Ever' rider tried his best to keep a hoss from gettin' his head between his forelegs. This was the first step in buckin', and when a hoss's head was held high he couldn't do much serious buckin'. When a hoss started to buck there were a lot of slang expressions the cowhand used for a description of this act. The hoss "arches his back," "boils over," "breaks in two," "blows up," "comes apart," "comes undone," "folds up," "kettles," "hops for mama," "kicks the lid off," "shoots its back," "unwinds," "wrinkles his spine," or was said to be "slattin' his sails."

The buster's job required strength and skill, and he had to possess a "sixth sense" of knowin' which way the hoss would jump next. If he was

throwed he'd be certain to crawl back on the animal immediately, providin' he hadn't been crippled. It gave the hoss bad ideas to let 'im think
he'd won the fight. Maybe after a hard ride you felt that all you needed
to make you a cripple was a handful of lead pencils, but falls had no
terrors for the seasoned rider. But the thought of bein' "hung up," that
is, havin' his foot caught in a stirrup or findin' 'imself under a man-
killer's hoofs, worried 'im plenty. More'n one rider's been kicked into a
funeral procession. And there was always that fear of a "throwback"
when the hoss suddenly throwed 'imself backward, the trick of a killer.

A buster wasn't ashamed of bein' grassed if the job was done by a good
bucker. It took a man with whiskers to curry the kinks out of some of
them broncs when they warped their backbones and hallelujahed all over
the lot, or stuck their bills in the ground and tried to kick the teeth out
of the man in the moon. Sometimes it was like tryin' to ride a cyclone
with the bridle off, and many a good rider has met his shadow on the
ground. Maybe after some rider had gone up to fork a cloud, when he
came down he didn't break nothin', but chances are all the hinges and
bolts was loosened. It was funny to see some rider go sailin' off, his hind
legs kickin' 'round in the air like a migratin' bullfrog in full flight.

In tellin' of his defeat one cowhand said: "I had trouble gettin' my
wood on 'im, and when I did git my tree laced up it didn't do me much
good 'cause I didn't git settled 'fore I goes sailin' off, flying' low and
usin' my face for a roughlock till I lost 'nough hide to make a pair of
leggin's."

Most ever' buster has experienced rides that took the curl out of his
hair. Many was the time, maybe, when he'd been throwed so high he had
St. Peter's initials whittled on his boots, and he admitted he had to keep
dodgin' his head to keep from bumpin' the stars.

A rider had to know how to get off them broncs without 'em stickin'
a hoof in his vest pocket or stampedin', but most of 'em got off the hard
way when some bronc was pitchin' to beat a straight flush.

One of the first things a bronc rider learned was how to fall when he
was throwed. He learned how to kick free of the stirrups, to go limp and
hit the ground rollin'. He always knowed he was goin' a jump or two
before he actually went, though he didn't always have time to pick a soft
spot to land in. He was liable to land in a cactus patch, and would have to
be picked for a week to keep 'im from lookin' like a porcupine, or he
might land in some hard place where he was spread out flat as a wet leaf
and be headed for a week in the bedwagon.

There're a heap of slang terms for bein' throwed from a hoss, such as he "bit the dust," "chewed gravel," "dirtied his shirt," "kissed the ground," was "piled," "spilled," "flung away," "grassed," was "pickin' daisies," "takin' up a homestead," "tasted gravel," "takin' up a squatters' right," got "unloaded," "dumped," "busted," or "turned the pack." If he was throwed head first, he "landed on his sombrero," or "landed forked end up." If he was throwed with arms and legs outstretched, he was doin' the "spread-eagle." If he was throwed high into the air he was "chasin' a cloud," "cloud huntin'," or "went up to fork a cloud."

As a rule the larger ranches had a first-class buster on the payroll the year round, though maybe part of the time he had to perform other duties. But there were men who made their livin' goin' from ranch to ranch breakin' out hosses. Them fellers were employed by the smaller ranches which were unable to maintain a first-class rider throughout the year. They traveled through the country from ranch to ranch, breakin' hosses as they went at so much per head. Them men were called "contract busters." When the hosses on one ranch were broke, they moved to 'nother and thus found work long after the hoss-breakin' season was over. Often they were young fellers tryin' to make 'nough money to start a spread of their own, and they'd ride anything that wore hair.

The roughstring rider's got many slang titles too, such as "bronc breaker," "bronc buster," "bronc stomper," "bronc snapper," "bronc scratcher," "jinete," and "bronc fighter." However, this last title better fits the man who fights the hosses and had never learned to control his own temper, and he, therefore, usually spoiled the hoss instead of conquering it. At all times the buster let the hoss know who's boss. Gentle words and caresses won't break a jug-headed bronc, unless the process is spread over a period of many months. Yet the buster don't fight the hoss more'n necessary unless he wants to make the animal an outlaw.

No two hosses bucked exactly alike. Each had a different temperament. The majority bucked from fear, but some bucked because they were touched with a spur, or for the pure fun of it, while there were many that bucked from pure viciousness. Them were the ones that usually became outlaws.

Each mode of buckin' had a descriptive title, as had ever'thing else in the West. "Buckin' on a dime," was said when the hoss did his buckin' in one spot. "Buckin' straight away" consisted of long straight jumps ahead without any twists, whirlin', or rearin', an easy hoss for some to ride, yet poison for others. Straight-away buckers were usually big and strong and rough in their actions. Their chief stock in trade was to jump extremely high, then, as they started down, to kick high with their hindquarters. At the same time the cantle of the saddle hit the seat of the rider's pants, and the rider hit the dirt. A hoss of this type usually hurt his rider when buckin' 'im off, because he generally throwed 'im high and hard.

A "high-roller," or "high-poler," as he was sometimes called, was a hoss which leaped high into the air when buckin'. While not quite so fast as others, he was extremely rough and went after his rider with cool and deliberate aim that seldom failed to disqualify 'im. Also, in rodeo work, this type hoss pleased the customers for he put on a great show, and his actions were easy to follow. "Pitchin' fence cornered," or "fence wormin'," was said when a hoss bucked in a zigzag direction, and he was said to be "layin' a rail fence." When a hoss reared wildly and vaulted upward, pawin' with his front feet, he was knowed as a "cloud hunter."

An extremely exasperatin' variety of buckin' hoss was the "weaver." His feet never struck the ground in a straight line. He had a peculiar weavin' motion which was plumb disconcertin' to a man who didn't have a mighty firm seat in the saddle. A "pioneer bucker" was an animal that bucked in circles and figger eights. He was called a pioneer because he was always seekin' new territory. A "sunfisher" was a hoss that twisted his body into a crescent, or, in other words, when he seemed to try to touch the ground with first one shoulder and then the other, lettin' the sunlight hit his belly. Such pitchin' was called "sunfishin'."

"Swappin' end" was where a bronc quickly reversed his position, makin' a complete half-circle in the air, sometimes called "windmillin'." Such buckin' could soon make a rider dizzy. One cowhand said such a hoss gave 'im a better merry-go-round ride than he'd paid a nickel for at a carnival. "Walkin' beamin'," or "pump handle" buckin', was the seesaw effect of a buckin' hoss, wherein he landed alternately on his front and hind feet. He was an easy hoss to ride, and as one cowboy said, "A baby couldn't fall off 'im." A man who drawed such a hoss at a ridin' contest felt 'imself cheated, and the sarcastic remarks from the side lines didn't improve his temper none.

A "pile-driver" was a hoss that humped his back like he had a water-

melon under the saddle, and came down with all four legs as stiff as ramrods, and high he went and hard he hit. The result was a grindin' shock that'd drive any ordinary man's spine through his hat, but the experienced rider settin' in the saddle gave no sign. A "spinner" was a hoss which bucked in a tight circle, spinnin' either to right or left. This type hoss generally did his buckin' in a small space, but his actions were so violent as he whirled and bucked with a backward motion as he hit the ground, that the average rider mighty quick became dizzy, lost his sense of balance, and was soon eatin' gravel. This type bucker seldom hurt his rider when throwin' 'im, because he didn't throw 'im high. He merely whirled and turned from under 'im, lettin' 'im down comparatively easy.

A "fall-back," or "rear-back" was when a hoss hurled 'imself backward intentionally, and he was said to "pinwheel." A hoss that did this was very rare. It was the trick of a killer. A "show bucker" was a hoss that bucked hard, straight away, and with nose between front feet, though he was not hard to ride. In rodeos he looked good from the grandstand, but he was never used in the semifinals.

A hoss which jumped 'bout with arched back and stiffened knees at a pretense of buckin' was said to "crow hop," "cat back," "pussy back," "frog walk," or "goat." The playful buckin' indulged in by both hoss and rider in the spirit of fun was called a "whing-ding." A hoss makin' little short, stiff-legged jumps was also said to be "sheep jumpin'." A hoss was said to "buck jump" when he leaped as he bucked.

A "blind bucker" was a hoss that lost his head when rode and would buck into anything. He was also called a "suicide hoss" because he seemed to go insane from fear and was more dangerous to 'imself than to his rider, as he was apt to kill 'imself by buckin' over some obstacle. An "honest bucker" was a hoss which started pitchin' as soon as he was mounted, and tried ever' device to unseat his rider. Some hosses would make no effort to pitch till they got their rider off guard, then, before he was aware of the hoss's evil intentions, he found 'imself on the ground. Them latter hosses were not classed as honest buckers.

The "circle buck" was the buckin' of a hoss in a long, rapid, and evenly timed leaps in a circle of thirty or forty feet, the hoss leanin' inward toward the center of the circle. The "close-to-the-ground bucker" was a type hoss very quick in his actions, and though buckin' very hard, he never got very high off the ground. He kicked sideways with his hindquarters and seemed to be tryin' to explode and disintegrate. He shook his head from side to side, and with ever quick-changin' movements he hurled his body through the air, doin' ever'thing possible to confuse his rider. With his fast and violent actions it seemed no task for 'im to befuddle the rider and cause 'im to lose his sense of timin' and direction. Very frequently he lost track of his mount entirely, and found 'imself gatherin' a handful of somethin' he didn't want.

There was 'nother type of hoss called a "runaway bucker." He started out on the run instead of buckin', then 'bout the time his rider decided he'd let 'im run till he run down his mainspring, he'd break in two and start buckin'. Generally his first leap'd be high and mighty, and if the rider was caught nappin' he didn't have much chance to stay on. When a hoss was runnin' his best, then leaped four or five feet into the air and came down stiff-legged, he lit mighty heavy. The fast forward motion stopped so abruptly that the hoss appeared to shove 'imself backward as he hit the ground. This trick has caused many a rider to meet his Waterloo.

"Jackknifin' " was a clippin' together of the front and rear legs, sometimes as a part of a "straight buck." When a hoss bucked backward he was said to be "crawfishin'," and the sudden shift in the gait of a buckin' hoss was called a "double-shuffle." Any hoss that bucked was called a "bucker," but a buckin' hoss of ability was called a "gut twister," a "hard to set," a "can't-be-rode hoss," and "livin' lightnin'." Of the man makin' a good ride it was said, "He sets that bronc as easy as a hossfly on a mule's ear," that he was "stickin' like a tick makin' a gotch ear," "stickin' like a postage stamp," or it was "jes' like buckin' off a porous plaster," and you "couldn't have chopped 'im loose from that hoss with an ax." 'Bout the man who had little or no ridin' ability it was said that he "couldn't ride a covered wagon," "couldn't ride a cotton mule," "couldn't ride a pack hoss," "couldn't ride nothin' wilder'n a wheel chair," or "he musta learned his ridin' on a hobby hoss."

The first few saddles could be mighty important to the hoss's future usefulness. The buster's job was to give the hoss his start as a cow hoss. After the first few tries to take the rough edges off, he turned 'im over to the other riders as gentled, or broken, but it'd be a long time before the rider who inherited 'im could ride 'im on duty without first takin' the kinks out of his backbone, which the cowboy speaks of as "toppin' off," "uncorkin'," "unroosterin'," "settin' the hair," "workin' over," "kickin' the frost out," "smoothin' out the humps," "curryin' out the kinks," "lettin' the hammer down," "ironin' 'im out," or "ironin' out the humps." Even a gentle hoss'd pitch on cold mornin's to warm 'imself up. If there was anything that'd cause hosses to pitch it was grass fat. After a winter of idleness the cowboy had to do some tall ridin' before he succeeded in smoothin' the humps out of them hosses.

What cowboys in other sections called "buckin'," the Texan called "pitchin'," and a term used in South Texas, though seldom heard in other sections, was "cayusein'." "Thumbin' " was jabbin' a hoss with the thumb to provoke further buckin'. When a rider successfully rode a buckin' hoss he was said to be "settin' the buck," or was "ridin' it out." Usin' the quirt was called "wipin' 'im out," "throwin' the buckskin," or he was said to be "pourin' the bud into 'im." A man who rode 'longside with a blacksnake whip to assist in breakin' work hosses to a wagon was called a "whipper-in."

A bronc rider might be long and thin, and then again he might be short, but no matter how he was built, one thing was certain, he was made of whalebone and rawhide. He didn't ride the rough ones jes' for a close-up view of the stars, but many a time some gut-twister had 'im soarin' so high it was damned scary to a man without wings.

Ridin' a buckin' hoss, if not an art, was shore a contest requirin' skill, courage, and strength, especially if it happened to be a hoss that was spoiled or had acquired the habit from general cussedness. I doubt if there was any one thing in connection with ranch work or a rodeo performance that was more excitin' than a good rider on a good buckin' hoss.

At Play

37

Ridin' the Shows

RIDIN' the shows is what the cowboy calls competin' for prize money at rodeos, usually done by the professional rider. The word rodeo's from the Spanish *rodear* (ro-day-ar), meanin' to encompass, the act of encirclin', and used in the sections under Spanish influence to mean the roundin' up of cattle. The word has recently become used in two different senses as well as with two different pronunciations. Nowdays it refers strictly to cowboy contests and is mostly pronounced *ro*-de-o, while for the roundup it was pronounced ro-*day*-o, but in this sense it's rapidly becomin' obsolete.

I guess the idea of the rodeo started back in the early days when on roundups the cowhand got to banterin' and augurin' as to who was the best rider or the fastest roper of the group, or maybe who could ride a certain bronc knowed to be a good bucker. There'd soon be some bets made, and at the end of the roundup a ropin' and ridin' contest would have to settle the issue.

Maybe when a bunch of good riders on one ranch heard that there was one of them "can't be rode" hosses at a neighborin' ranch they'd ride over some Sunday on a kind of busman's holiday. This hoss and some like 'im would be rounded up and hazed to the home corral. After some braggin' and bettin' the contest'd be on. This could've been the very beginnin' of today's rodeo.

Such local contests soon moved to town, and there're several towns that claim to be the first to stage such ridin' contests. At Pecos, Texas, in 1883, on the Fourth of July, some cowhands staged such a contest to celebrate the Fourth and at the same time settle some arguments 'bout certain riders bein' able to stay on certain hosses of that section, and how fast certain ropers could ketch certain steers. There was no admission charged, no prizes, no grandstand, no chutes nor fences. Only a judge and a pen to hold the steers to be roped.

Without buckin' chutes the broncs were snubbed out in the middle of the arena to the snubber's hoss. This was done by pullin' the bucker's halter rope so that his head was practically in the snubber's lap. The hoss was blindfolded while this battle between the snubber and the hoss was goin' on.

Sometimes the bronc had to be eared down. This was done by a man or two holdin' the bronc's ears and tryin' to keep 'im in one spot while the saddle was bein' put on. This was a dangerous job because the bronc still had two loose forefeet and wasn't afraid to use 'em. Sometimes the bronc'd have to be throwed and saddled while he was down, and the rider'd ease into the saddle before the hoss was let up.

Them little ridin' and ropin' contests caught on and became frequent in different sections of the country. In 1888, at Prescott, Arizona, again on the Fourth of July, the first rodeo where prizes were given and admission charged was held. Since that time rodeos have become a big business, but it took a long time to get it where it is today.

The cattle country has always been interested in the ridin' of buckin' hosses and the work of ropin'. Even when loafin' in town a group of cowhands liked to pit their skill against the ability of some well knowed bucker, and this desire of contest between man and animal is no doubt what started the idea of the rodeo as it is today.

They looked upon it as a sport, and with so few means of entertainment they used it as both recreation and entertainment. Such contests weren't only held on the ranch between members of the same outfit, but also between rival outfits. The work the men did developed skills along his line, and so a buster naturally could ride better'n the ordinary hand, jes' as the top roper could rope better'n the bronc buster. Each man strove to be superior in his specialty. So this work of the range appears to be the beginnin' of that lusty American sport with its full share of broken bones and stiff competition.

His work bein' what it was, it was only natural that his sport should grow out of it. All outdoor men have that spirit of competition, and the cowboy's strength, darin', and skill provided the spark that set this competition workin'. From the days of its simple beginnin' the rodeo's gone through some great struggles and changes. It wasn't called rodeo in the beginnin', but "ridin' and ropin' contests." Soon after the beginnin' each contest had its rules, but the lack of uniform rules caused many misunderstandin's and conflicts. There was no organization, no co-operation, and consequently no order, but ever'thing was confusion and conflictin' dates.

Nowadays the competition is keen and highly specialized, so the contestant has to spend considerable time practicin' for improvement, jes' like a good ball player has to keep in practice. His is different from most other sports in that he assumes all the expense and pays for the privilege of enterin' each event at the same time. He not only has to provide his own equipment, but pay his own expenses and travel fare, and expenses for rodeo folks are particularly high because most towns raise their rates durin' them events. If he's a professional he travels many thousands of miles durin' the year. With no wages, nor guarantee for his performance, all he can ask in return for his entry fee's a fair chance with the stock he drawed. If he's good and the stock's good he might be lucky 'nough to win prize money plus the entry fees of his feller contestants. He's got to be good to the highest degree to survive this rugged sport because only the top four men in each go-round and finals of each event are paid any cash awards. So it's that skill he constantly practices for that takes 'im to the pay window after the judges tally up. He has to attain that professional skill or find 'imself at a great disadvantage in competition, especially in contests of considerable size. He had to have some luck too, especially in drawin' a good buckin' hoss. This hoss had to have 'nough wickedness in 'im to let the rider put up a good ride. Some mighty good riders miss prize money because the hoss they drawed wasn't mean 'nough. Nobody got credit for ridin' a rockin'-chair hoss.

The least little slip could put a man out of the money and send 'im back home broke. He'd have a lot of company, though, in the cryin' room, which is the headquarters office where alibis are offered and disappointments aired. Some of 'em are lucky if they have 'nough for get-away money. Prizes and silver cups is what makes 'em follow rodeos 'round. They'd put up a lot of money in railroad fare and entrance fees and didn't want to see it washed down the drain. But it was always a gamble whether they went home broke, loaded down with prize money, or on a stretcher.

The modern rodeo employs a heap of people. Like the circus, it has its advance agent, publicity man, ticket sellers and takers, ushers, and all the rest. Then there's the stock contractor who furnishes the stock, and with 'im are his stock tenders. The rodeo has its starters, time-keepers, judges, pick-up men, flag men, and, of course, secretaries, bookkeepers, and such. Also such participants as don't compete for prizes but are paid straight salaries, such as trick riders, trick ropers, clowns, and such.

There're five standard events in rodeo: saddle bronc ridin', bareback ridin', bull ridin', calf ropin', and steer wrestlin'. In the early days there wasn't any calf ropin' or trick ridin', fancy ropin', or clowns. Winnin' points were allowed for steer ropin' and team ropin', and there were championships awarded for them two events. Also, wild-cow milkin' was a timed event. In this event a wild cow's turned loose in the arena and two cowboys dash after her. One ropes the critter and the other one mugs her. After this the roper runs on foot, packin' a pop bottle, and tries to obtain 'bout an inch of milk in it. After securin' the milk he runs to the judges to show it.

Aside from the reg'lar events a good rodeo had many colorful acts that kept things movin' at a fast pace and entertained the customers. Some of 'em were wild hoss races, trick ridin', trick ropin', chuck-wagon races, cuttin'-hoss contests, mounted square dances, mounted drill teams, barrel races, mad scrambles, which was usually the finale when fifteen or more Brahma bulls, steers, and mules, with cowboys on their backs, rushed into the arena from the chutes and bucked in all directions. Sometimes there were many more acts, dependin' upon the producer's money and imagination.

There's a heap of difference in ridin' a bronc in a rodeo and one on the range. On the range the buster tried to teach the hoss to be a good cowhoss, and there wasn't no eight- or ten-second ride like in rodeo ridin'. You'd think this'd make rodeo ridin' easier, but, on the other hand, them rodeo broncs ain't young, well meanin' colts boogered up with fear. They're older hosses that's been spoilt by mean riders, or jes' bad by nature. If a rider lets a hoss get the best of 'im on the range without takin' it out of 'im, he's apt to have a spoilt hoss on his hands. A good twister'll learn the hoss to work and be of some use to the outfit, but the rodeo rider wants the hoss to buck hard so he can show off his ridin' ability, but he's always glad to get the hell off when that whistle blows.

In the early days of rodeo there was no time limit on bronc ridin' like there is now. The judges jes' let the contestant ride and the hoss buck till they felt like the ride had gone long 'nough to show the rider's ability and endurance. The ride was over when they fired a gun into the air if the rider hadn't already been spread out on the arena like a rug. Today, if the hoss is a good bucker, that ten-second limit we now have seems like a mighty long time, and ever' gut-joltin' move seems like the last you can stand.

When a rider drawed his bronc's number out of the hat, he was hopin' he didn't draw some sulker or chute-crazy animal. A sulker was especially aggravatin' because he wouldn't leave the chute till he was good and ready. He'd squat back on his haunches, bunchin' 'imself, after the gate was opened. No amount of coaxin'd make 'im come out till he was ready. Then he'd suddenly leave with a mighty and un-expected leap which caused most riders to break their balance across the cantle board, and he was mighty seldom able to get his seat back and usually wound up by goin' up for a little air. A chute-crazy bronc was 'bout as bad, for he reared, backed, fought, and kicked till he wore 'imself down.

The rodeo's now well organized and has some strict rules. In the beginnin' a bronc rider could use any kind of saddle he wanted to, but in the 1920's the Association adopted what they called the "As-sociation" or "contest" saddle, and its use is now compulsory. Built on a modified Ellenburg tree, medium in height, with a fourteen-inch swell and a five-inch cantle, it has nothin' 'bout it which allows the rider to anchor 'imself. The original association saddle was made with small round skirts, three-quarter rigged, with a flank rig set farther back than on a reg'lar rigged saddle. This flank riggin' makes the bronc buck, and though most hosses used in buckin' contests buck without it, this riggin' makes 'em turn the works loose.

The buckin' rein's the most important piece of equipment used in bronc ridin'. It's usually a single rope attached to the hackamore. By grippin' this, the rider has an aid in keepin' his balance, but in contests he's not allowed to change hands. This single rein's of braided grass or cotton rope, and mustn't be more'n one inch in diameter. No tape or knots are allowed on it, and it mustn't be wrapped 'round the hand, but held in plain grasp while the other hand remains free. It must be held by the hand on the same side as it is on the halter, and with daylight showin' between the hand and the hoss's neck as he leaves the chute. By this rein the rider gets his balance, timin', and feelin' of the hoss.

So the present-day rules for a bronc-ridin' contest, as devised by the Rodeo Association of America, are: that the ridin's to be done with a plain halter, one rein and a saddle, the latter to be supplied by the management of the rodeo. A man could use his own saddle if it was of the accepted Association make and recognized gear. The rider must leave the chute with both feet in the stirrups and both spurs against the hoss's shoulders. He must scratch ahead for the first five jumps, then behind. He has to stay on the hoss and ride clean for ten seconds and at the whistle get on behind his pick-up man. This pick-up man's a hossman who stands ready to take up the hoss bein' rode by the contestant when the ride's over.

A rider's disqualified if he's bucked off, changes hands on the rein, wraps the rein 'round the hand, pulls leather, blows a stirrup, touches the animal or saddle or rein with his free hand, rides with locked spurs, failin' to spur throughout the ride to the satisfaction of the judges, not bein' ready to ride when called, touches the hoss with his hat, or looks cross-eyed at the judges. Fannin' a hoss with the hat used to allow the rider to ride better by its balance and was spectacular, but modern rodeos forbid quirtin', fannin', or even touchin' the animal with the hand.

Usin' the spurs in the act of ridin' came in for many of the cowboy's technical and slang terms. "Scratchin'" is the act of keepin' the feet movin' in a kickin' motion while ridin' buckin' hosses. "Rakin'" is generally applied when the rider gives his legs a free sweep, rollin' the rowels of his spurs 'long the hoss's sides from shoulder to rump, and is one of the highest accomplishments coveted by the bronc rider. This is one of the rules of rodeo, but on the range the rule was that behind the cinch belonged to the rider, but in front of it belonged to the company, and the company didn't want their hosses spurred on the shoulders.

"Bicyclin'" is the act of scratchin' with first one foot and then the other in the manner of ridin' a bicycle. "Coastin' on the spurs" is ridin' with the spurs locked in the cinch, or under the hoss's shoulder blades, and is not tolerated in contests. "Screwin' down" is the act of sinkin' the spurs into the cinch and failin' to move the feet in a kickin' motion as provided by rodeo rules. It's also called "ridin' on the spurs." "Locked spurs" are them whose rowels have been fastened with a string or hosshair so they won't move. When them spurs are held firmly in the cinch it's next to impossible to unseat the rider, and their use is also barred at rodeos. When not locked, spurs don't help the rider in stayin' on; on the contrary, they act in the manner of ball bearin's to throw 'im. The cowboy's said to "curry 'im out" when he rakes with his spurs; "reefin'," "combin'," and "shove in the steel" are terms also used. "Throwin' the steel" is usin' the spurs freely, and the spur marks on a hoss's hide are called "panther tracks," or "hundred-and-elevens." A "buck hook" is a blunt-nosed, up-curved piece added to the frame of the spur and used to lock in the cinch or in the side of a plungin' hoss, and of course is barred at rodeos. "Spur buttonin'" is slidin' the button of the spur 'long the sides of a buckin' hoss when scratchin' instead of turnin' the rowels against the flesh. This is practiced by some rodeo riders.

Contestants can also be disqualified for bein' under the influence of likker in the arena, by bein' rowdy or quarrelsome on the rodeo grounds, by the mistreatment of stock, by refusin' to contest on an animal drawed for 'im, by not bein' ready to compete when called upon, and by cheatin' or attemptin' to cheat.

Bareback ridin's similar to the saddle-bronc event except that the hoss is encircled with a surcingle, and this and the flank strap's the only pieces of equipment allowed. No reins or stirrups are allowed, and the rider has nothin' to hold to except a handhold on the surcingle, and this can't be over ten inches wide at the hand hold and with not over a six-inch D ring. The rider's permitted to use only one hand durin' the ride, and can't change hands. He must keep his other hand and arm free of the hoss and the riggin'.

He's judged by the manner in which he rides, how he spurs his mount, and how rough the hoss is. He can be disqualified much the same as the saddle-bronc rider. It's one of the spectacular events of the rodeo, and a heap of times the rider ended up by soarin' up to see what the moon was made of.

Even if the cowhand did do a lot of calf ropin' in his work on the ranch, it wasn't introduced into rodeos as a timed event till later. But after its introduction it became pop'lar and is now one of the five standard events. The roper starts from behind a barrier and has to give the calf a start before he breaks it. Since it's a timed event, there are three timekeepers, a field judge, and a deadline referee.

After the calf's roped, the rope's tied fast to the saddle, the rider dismounts, and has to throw the calf by hand. If the calf's not on his feet after bein' roped, it must be made to stand and then be throwed by hand and tied. The tie's made like the puncher ties calves on the range, a three-legged cross tie, and it must hold till inspected by the tie judge. After his inspection, he gives his approval to release the calf, but if the calf works free 'imself before inspection the roper's marked "no time." Them sad words have wrecked many a contestant's hopes for a chance at the final money.

To qualify, the roper's loop must be released from the hand; the rope must be on the calf when the rider reaches it; if he breaks the barrier he's penalized ten seconds. He's allowed no assistance, and if the judges think he busted the calf intentionally, he's disqualified. If his hoss drags the calf, the field judge can stop the hoss and impose a penalty. The roper's allowed two ropes, but if he fails on both of 'em he's given "no time."

The bull-ridin' event is one of the most sensational of the rodeo. There's always that chill of expectin' to see a man throwed, tromped, gored, or tossed on the horns of a mad bull. In the beginnin' ordinary bulls from the range were used, and each bull was equipped with what's called a bull riggin'. Also, in the early days of rodeo the rider was allowed to hang on with both hands, settin' 'imself well back, with his feet well forward, and spurrin' the shoulders and neck only. This riggin' consisted of a heavy leather strap, three inches wide and 'bout two feet long, with two hand holds 'bout three inches apart. At each end of this surcingle were attached heavy rings to which the latigos and cinch were fastened as on a saddle. Now two hands are barred and the surcingle has also been discontinued.

Now only a rope is used, and each bull rider owns his own. It's braided flat from the same material as a buckin' rein's made from. It's 'bout twelve feet long, and both ends are tapered flat. In the center where it fits under the middle of the bull's belly there's an extry loop woven which holds a brass cowbell. The rope has to be smooth, free of bristles, and kept well resined. The purpose of the bell's to give the rope weight 'nough to allow it to drop when turned loose.

When the animal's placed in the chute his front quarters receive this loose rope that's fastened in such a manner that it'll fall off at the completion of the ride. There're no knots or hitches allowed, and if the bell ain't attached no ride's allowed. The animal's also equipped with a flank strap which makes 'im buck, though this ain't needed.

The rider has to stay on eight seconds from the time the bull leaves the chute, and though this don't sound like it's long, it's a mighty long time when on the back of a whirlin' bull. The ridin' has to be done with one hand on the rope, with the other kept in the air at all times, and the bull must be spurred to the satisfaction of the judges. The rider can be disqualified by cheatin' in any way, bein' bucked off, for not bein' ready when called to ride, for touchin' the bull with his hat or free hand, for usin' sharp spurs, or for usin' spurs with locked rowels, and the bull mustn't be spurred in the chute. If the rider's knocked off at the chute or the bull falls while in the chute, he may get a re-ride if the judges think he deserves it.

In the early 1920's at the Fort Worth, Texas, Live Stock Rodeo, a Brahma bull was first used, and this proved to be such a thrillin' and dangerous exhibition, all of which pleased the crowd so, that it was made a permanent part of all rodeos. Them crossbreed bulls have all the bad qualities of their ancestors and none of the good. None of 'em can be trusted. Them heavy animals are loose-skinned, have a hump on their shoulders, sharp hoofs, and are as active as a cat. When you're in the same arena with one of them meanies, he looks like a bad dream on the hoof. They're the toughest of all animals to ride, and as soon as they come out of the chute they start a spinnin' jump and keep up this tight spin till the rider's throwed.

With the use of them dangerous animals came the rodeo clown. He was a necessary protection for the bull riders. The bull had only two things in mind, to get rid of the rider on his back, and to hook, trample, and kill any other man or animal within sight. A clown's supposed to be funny, but his main task is the protection of the rider. That's what they're hired for, and their funny antics are jes' incidental. They may not be funny to some folks, but they've got guts. When a rider's down the clown takes great risks to bait the bull and get 'im away from the down rider. With his baggy britches and barrel-jumpin' antics, he's entertainin', and if he can create a laugh he likes it, but if he's succeeded in savin' some rider from bein' gored he's satisfied whether he made you laugh or not. In his years of follperhapsowin' rodeos he soon learns the individual characteristics of the bulls and how best to handle 'em, but he's not immune from bein' crippled.

Bulldoggin', as it's now knowed, is to throw one's right arm over a steer's neck, the right hand grippin' the loose, bottom skin at the base of the right horn, or the brute's nose, while the left hand seizes the tip of the animal's left horn. The dogger then rises clear of the ground, and, by lungin' his body downward against his own left elbow, so twists the neck of the animal that the latter loses his balance, and falls. The first bulldogger was a Choctaw-Negro, Bill Pickett, who in 1903 was given credit for inventin' this stunt. He astonished other cowboys by droppin' off a runnin' hoss onto the neck of a steer and throwin' the animal by hand.

The term bulldoggin' came from the fact that after leapin' from his hoss and grabbin' the steer by the horns, Pickett twisted the animal's neck till its nose was turned upward. He then bit the animal's lip, turned loose his hand holds, and leaned backward. He no longer needed hands because the tenderness of the lip caused the steer to fall to ease the pain. By the use of teeth in this manner, the stunt took the name of bulldoggin' after the manner of bulldogs throwin' cattle when set upon a steer. When the steer lowered his head to fight off the dog, the bulldog would sink his teeth into the steer's lip. Other cowboys began tryin' it, but not likin' the lip bitin' they learned to twist 'em down by hand. It wasn't till several years later that 'nough of 'em were present at any one rodeo to make a contest, but it was sometimes put on the program purely as an exhibition. More and more took it up till it became one of the timed events in all good rodeos. The name bulldoggin' was soon dropped as a rodeo term, and its common name now is steer wrestlin'.

Steer wrestlin's governed by arena conditions, as are also the start and deadline rules. There're usually three timers, a field judge, a deadline referee, and any other officials the management sees fit to appoint. The dogger has to furnish his own hoss and hazer. The steer belongs to the dogger after it leaves the chute and has a head start of crossin' the ten-foot line. With the hazer on one side and the dogger on the other, they try to keep the steer in a straight line till the dogger's ready to leap on the animal's neck. After that the hazer leaves to ketch the dogger's hoss.

After ketchin' the steer, the wrestler has to bring 'im to a stop by throwin' his body forward and usin' his heels as a brake. Though he kicks up a heap of dust, he gets the steer stopped, and it's now a battle to twist 'im down. If he knocks the steer down when he flies on 'im from the hoss, and without twistin' 'im down with a wrestlin' hold, it's called hoolihanin', and ain't allowed. In such a case he has to let the steer up on all four feet and then twist 'im down, and this loses a lot of valuable time. The steer's not considered throwed till all four feet are out and straight ahead.

A good deal depends on the size of the arena whether the doggin's done from behind a barrier or is "lap and tap." In a small arena the dogger can jump on the steer's neck as soon as the chute's cleared, and this is called "lap and tap." But usually the doggin's done from a barrier, and this is a rope stretched across in front of the dogger and his hoss somewhere in front of the chute. It can be anywhere selected from ten feet to forty, and is released by a spring fastened in a latch under tension with a piece of twine. After the steer comes out of the chute and his nose crosses the line—a white tape fastened to the ground—the flagger drops his flag and releases the barrier. The dogger's given a ten-second penalty if he breaks the barrier.

His hazer don't worry 'bout a barrier, and is out in front from the start. His job's to keep the steer in a straight line while the dogger ketches up. He can't give the dogger any help in gettin' the steer down, and if he jumps his hoss at the steer he'll be disqualified. Cattle used in other events like steer ropin' or cuttin' can't be used in wrestlin', and neither cattle with broken horns nor crippled stock can be used.

Some states, owing to Humane Society laws, won't allow steer wrestlin', so an event called "steer decoratin'" is substituted. It's less spectacular but also less dangerous. The stunt's performed by the dogger leapin' from his hoss to the head of the steer, and while the animal's goin' at full speed he places 'round the nose a rubber band, or puts a band decorated with ribbons 'round a horn. The steer must be on all four feet when decorated, and the dogger's disqualified if the rubber band breaks or the ribbon's shortened.

While bronc ridin' and ropin's part of the cowhand's work on the range, bull ridin' and steer wrestlin' had nothin' to do with range work, and because of this cowhands had to practice up on them stunts when the boss wasn't 'round.

The rodeo's now a big business and has been taken out of the hands of the workin' cowboy. Most men followin' it now are professionals specializin' in only one or two stunts, and constantly practicin' to become better. There's still a few little annual rodeos like the one at Stamford, Texas, put on by the Cowboy's Reunion ever' Fourth of July, that's strictly for the workin' cowhand, where professionals are barred. It don't get much national notice, but it's one of the best I ever saw, and it gives the ordinary rider a chance to compete for the fun of it. After all, that spirit was the cause of them contests in the first place.

Cowboy Pranks

LACKIN' such amusements as movies, radio, phonographs, and television, the cowboy had to create his own. There were few women in his life and therefore little refinement in his behavior. His was a humor with hair on its chest like the life he lived.

He was usually unmarried and free from domestic worries, and his chief aim in life was livin'; he cared little 'bout accumulatin' wealth and property. Usually he wanted to be nothin' but a cowhand. The life suited 'im, and he was plumb content with the $30 or $40 a month a cowhand drawed down. He loved this life of freedom. If he wanted to see 'nother section of the country, he could quit and ride toward it. He had all the fun with none of the responsibility, and could get up in the mornin' with nothin' on his mind but his hat. If he had a good hoss and saddle and a bedroll, he had no further financial worries. His kind rarely considered the problem of life seriously.

As a class he was always runnin' over with wit and good humor, and always ready for some fun. In spite of the movies and Western stories, he wasn't forever huntin' a fight. He was usually at peace with all men from choice. True, their love of fun often led to trouble, but that was because sometimes their victim wasn't man 'nough to "take it." The Westerner has always been quick to size up visitors and fill 'em with misinformation. Though he was uneducated, he was rich in the understandin' of human nature, and quick to deflate conceit in others.

His vigorous good health filled 'im with prank and play, and much of his humor found release in the rough hossplay of tricks and pranks.

All cattleland loved a joke—when it was on the other feller, and a good joke or prank was the cowboy's staff of life. Livin' in the open, in a high and dry climate, filled 'im with so much vinegar he was like a kid on a holiday. Not bein' hobbled with conventions, he was mighty apt to give his sense of humor free play, which meant that his pranks were likely to be plenty rough and robust, like the life he lived. By nature he was a reckless, don't-give-a-damn fool that'd forgot there was such a thing as consequences.

Lookin' for the unexpected was what kept 'im primed up. Many a smart cowman hired some feller jes' for laughin' stock, some greener who wanted to be a cowboy. Such a feller maybe didn't get much out of life 'imself, but he shore kept the punchers happy and matchin' wits to see what prank they could pull on 'im next. The kid hoss wrangler got it in the neck, too. It was a part of his education and was what made 'im a real hand later.

Ever' tenderfoot was fresh meat for the cowhand, and stringin' a greener was the fav'rite sport of the cow country. Fake Injun raids usually brought out what was in the tenderfoot. This was a good joke if ever'-thing went well, but if, as once happened, they forgot to take the lead from the cartridges in the gun they handed 'im, it wasn't no nursery game.

Distances in the West were deceivin'. Sometimes a mountain that looked close, but wasn't, was pointed out to a pilgrim, and he'd be asked to ride over to a ranch at its foot to borrow a screw-worm screw-driver, a corral key, or sent on some other silly errand. If there did happen to be a ranch there, they'd send 'im on to the next, and if this greener didn't soon ketch onto the game he'd be in for a lot of saddle sores.

Shootin' at a tenderfoot's feet to make 'im dance was mostly done in a story books, and didn't happen often on the range. The cowboy in real life wasn't so good with a gun that he'd chance cripplin' a human bein' for the fun of it.

Puttin' a pilgrim on a gentle-lookin' hoss that bucked was legitimate, and playin' tricks on 'im with snakes and lizards was often indulged in. Fake quarrels, with a greener in the line of fire, was a heap of fun for the boys too.

Cowhands got a lot of fun playin' tricks on each other too. Durin' the first days of a general roundup, while waitin' for the outfits to gather, there was always a session of kangaroo court where cowhands were tried on a heap of ridiculous charges and always found guilty. Various penalties were imposed and executed. Maybe it was a case for a chappin', or bein' throwed into a nearby creek to wash his sins away; sometimes the sentence called for the ridin' of a wild young steer to be picked out of the first bunch of cattle rounded up; or, if the defendant happened to be a brag who claimed he could ride anything that wore hair, he'd maybe be sentenced to ride some notorious outlaw hoss.

All this rough play was given and taken in good nature. It was a part of the life. It was mighty seldom a feller wanted to make a leppy of 'imself by losin' his temper. He jes' waited till he had a chance to get even. Things got pretty rough for the feller who couldn't take it.

When sleepin' out on roundup, some prankster might drag a set of trace chains rattlin' close to some sleeper's bed and holler "Whoa" in a loud voice. This made the sleepers close by come out of their bedrolls quicker'n hell could scorch a feather. When they thought the chuck wagon team was runnin' over their bedground, they got pretty nimble-blooded.

Puttin' a burr under some rider's saddle blanket after he'd saddled to see a little buckin' and find out how the rider could stick on was routine on frosty mornin's. Or somebody might suddenly yell and throw his hat under a rider's mount jes' as he forked 'im to see if he couldn't be entertained with an unscheduled ridin' contest to break the monotony. A late sleeper's bed with 'im still in it might be pulled into a creek or rough ground by some practical joker.

They got a heap of fun puttin' salt and horned toads in each other's bedrolls or lizards and cactus in each other's boots, or two might gang up on a sleeper, and while one pulled a rope slowly over 'im the other would shake a rattlesnake's rattles.

When the fall work was over at the ranch and the cowhand was paid off, some of 'em made their way to town to loaf till the spring work started. With time hangin' on his hands, and bein' used to an active life, it didn't take 'im long to study up some devilment. Nobody could beat an idle cowhand in thinkin' up devilment. All them practical jokes were played to get the victim to "treat." If this victim was a good sport, he'd invite the crowd to the nearest saloon for the drinks. If he couldn't take it, and got nasty 'bout it, he was soon throwed into the cutbacks. From then on, life got to be mighty unpleasant for 'im as long as he stayed in that community, and he got to be 'bout as welcome as a polecat at a picnic.

The loafin' months in the winter came to be knowed as "snipe huntin' season" and "badger season." A group of cowhands, with maybe some natives—for the town folks enjoyed jobbin' some newcomer too—would gather and act excited 'bout the comin' snipe hunt they were plannin'. They'd make it sound so enticin' to the tenderfoot that he'd ask what the chances were for 'im to go 'long. Of course, he was welcome. They'd leave town 'bout dark, and as they rode 'long would explain to the greener how easy the snipe was to ketch and what a delicious dish he made. They rode across prairie, over bluffs, through gulches, jumped creeks, and on for 'bout six hours, not always in a straight course, but often circlin' not to get too far away from town, but the greener didn't know it.

Of course, the visitor didn't know a blamed thing 'bout snipe huntin', so he followed the instructions and advice of the experienced cowboys. Finally they'd find a suitable place to set the trap, and if it was swampy and a country full of mosquitos, all the better. When they got to such a place one or two cowboys would dismount and have the greener light too. They'd light a lantern, give 'im a gunny sack, and show 'im how to squat down and hold the mouth open. They explained how the light would attract the snipe to go into the sack if he was always careful to keep the mouth open wide. After some careful coachin' they said they'd better go and help the others drive in the snipe, as they'd have to cover a wide range of country, and they said they'd better take his hoss off a ways to keep it from scarin' the snipe away, and with this they'd ride off to join the others as they all went back to town. While they were laughin' on their way home, the greener was sweatin' and fightin' mosquitos, hopin' he'd soon ketch plenty of snipe to show the boys he was a good snipe hunter.

But when dawn came and still no snipe drivers, he began to realize he'd been jobbed. If he wasn't too far from town he'd be left to walk in, but sometimes a cowhand with an extry saddle hoss would jes' happen to see 'im stumblin' 'long, and give 'im a lift.

"Pullin' the badger" got to be a standard joke, and one worked many, many times in the cattle country. It got to be so well knowed that, in order to pull it successfully, it had to be pulled on an Easterner who knowed absolutely nothin' 'bout the West. They usually tried to pick some party who looked prosperous 'nough to buy drinks for the crowd. After they selected their victim they'd gather 'round 'im casual-like and begin talkin' excitedly 'bout the comin' badger fight. They'd talk 'bout the fightin' qualities of the dog selected and of his past record, and the size of the badger they had under cover at the time.

Their zeal and eagerness couldn't help but rub off some on the stranger, and he'd soon become mighty interested. They'd place big bets, some on the dog, some on the badger. Then they'd begin' arguin' as to who'd referee the fight, some would suggest one, some 'nother, but they'd always decide it should be someone who didn't have a bet on the fight. Maybe several would volunteer, but when asked they'd admit they had bets on the fight too. Declarin' they'd have to have some disinterested party, they'd begin lookin' 'round and suddenly discover the greener. They'd maybe ask 'im if he'd bet on the fight. And would he serve as a disinterested referee? Naturally he'd feel highly honored.

By now it was time for the crowd to make its way to where the badger was kept, usually at the livery stable or maybe back of some pop'lar saloon. By now the whole town had closed shop and come to witness the great fight. On the way some cowhand would give the new referee some advice as how to pull the badger. If he'd pull hard he'd be helpin' the dog, if slow, he'd give the badger the best of it. Naturally he was always in sympathy with the dog.

When they got to the place of the fight, there was the dog. Chances are he didn't look like a fighter and was nothin' but a lazy flea trap. Nearby was the tub the badger was supposed to be under, and there was a rope runnin' out some distance from beneath the tub. Some cowhand explained to the referee what his duties were, and he took his place to pull on the rope, a mighty proud and serious official. Since he was in sympathy with the dog, when he was ordered to "pull" he gave the rope a hard yank jes' as one cowhand tipped up the tub from the rear.

To his great amazement there was no badger on the end of the rope at all, but he found 'imself with a mighty red face as he gazed down on one of them vessels usually found under the bed at night. If he didn't jerk it too hard, he was apt to see it still half full of stale beer, with maybe a link sausage and a little wad of tissue paper in it. That explodin' yell from the crowd brought 'im back to life and made 'im realize he'd been jobbed. If he took it with a grin they all headed for the saloon, makin' more noise than a bluejay camp meetin'. They knowed he was goin' to be a good sport, and treat.

With no outlet for his humor it's doubtful if the cowboy could have survived, not the violence of his work, but the monotony of his loafin' season.

Bendin' an Elbow

A LOT of them romantic town-gaited writers would have us believe a cowboy never had nothin' to do but wear his boot soles out on a brass rail while he's gettin' callouses on his elbows from leanin' on a bar. Fact is, he did less drinkin' than the city man who had his drinks handy ever' day.

The cowhand did his drinkin' periodically—when he went to town, which wasn't often. But when he did ride in to hear the owl hoot I'll admit he kept them swingin' doors busy. Because whisky and cow work didn't mix, a strict rule of the cattle country was "no whisky with the wagon." Consequently when he got to town he was thirsty as a mudhen on a tin roof, and had developed a bad case of bottle fever.

When a bunch of 'em went to town they didn't lose no time in puttin' on the rollers, and it was a familiar sight to see a dozen wiry ponies slide to a sudden slitherin' halt at a hitch rack and as many sun-baked punchers hit the ground. With spurs a-jinglin', boots clackin', and loud-mouthed kiddin', each one tried to squeeze through the swingin' doors ahead of the other. Then they kept the bartender busy as a beaver makin' a new dam.

Drinkin' wasn't particularly the besettin' sin of the cowman, but after long hard months of lonesome work hogtyin' his drinkin', it was kinda natural that when he hit town after the roundup he cut his wolf loose and freighted his crop with likker. When a trail outfit pulled in near some cowtown of his destination, or on the way, the wagon boss usually let some of the men go into town, leavin' only a skeleton crew to hold the herd.

After weeks on the trail, fed up with the dangerous, monotonous work and their own company, the boys were pretty apt to be on edge and in search of what excitement and good times the town afforded. The boss usually only advanced 'em 'nough money to last till nighttime in the hope that they'd be back by then. But some of 'em were lucky in gamblin' for a time, and as the night wore on and the likker began to take hold they more'n likely decided to resent the authority of some marshal. Or maybe they got to fussin' with each other, when some hand got sore because 'nother was more successful with the lady of the evenin'. The old-time marshal didn't make a target of 'imself when there was trouble afoot. More'n likely he shot from shelter because he had no cravin' to be fingerin' music out of a harp. Whenever cowboys, likker, soldiers, and buffalo hunters were throwed together there was usually a fracas of some kind.

The world's attention has been attracted to the cowboy's drinkin' because when he got drunk he wanted ever'body to know it, and they usually did if they were in the same county. Most of his trouble was the mixture of spirits—high spirits with strong spirits. Bein' a young, healthy, and reckless cuss, he proceeded to get noiser'n a Mexican revolution till he was a thorn in the town marshal's shortribs. The law never knowed whether he was goin' to fight or frolic, sing or shoot. A heap depended on the brand of booze he drank. The saloon and poker joints got plumb fat and prosperous when a bunch of cowhands hit town.

Here and there you might see some rancher, his hand cupped 'round his glass, silently shovin' it 'round in studied circles on the damp bar as he listened to the troubles of his neighbor. Maybe at the other end of the bar some of the punchers were gettin' boisterous, givin' the ever smilin' barkeep some cause for worry. Over all was a tobacco cloud that settled in stratified layers, changin' and swirlin' with each movement of men.

There's a lot of exaggerated stories told 'bout how a cowhand likes his likker. There's one told 'bout two cowhands who'd saved their money for a few years and went to a little cattle shippin' town and bought the only saloon. They closed the place up for what the natives thought was a redecoratin' job. After a week passed and they still didn't open, the thirsty began to gather in front and holler at 'em to open up the place. One of them cowboy owners got tired of the noise out front and went to the door.

"When you goin' to open this place up?" asked one of them dry waddies.

"Open hell," answers the new saloon owner. "We bought this joint for our own drinkin'."

Some of that frontier scamper juice would draw a blood blister on a rawhide boot. It made you wonder how they kept such stuff corked. Three drinks would grow horns on a muley cow. After nosin' your way to the bottom of a half dozen glasses, you'd begin to get a free snake with ever' drink. No man could gargle that brand of hootch without annexin' a few of them queer animals that ain't natural history.

There used to be a story told of two cowboys who'd been on a bender for days. One of 'em looked up the doctor and asked 'im to come take a look at his pardner. When the doctor got there he didn't find anything wrong with 'im except too much joy juice, and he told his friend so.

"The hell there ain't nothin' wrong with 'im," yells this friend. "The room's full of pink elephants and green tigers, and he can't see 'em. I say he's gone blind as a posthole!" When a feller begins to see them things in broad daylight it's time to taper off.

I once heard a story of two cowboys takin' their first train ride. They took a quart of hootch 'long with em, and after they'd been on the train a while one of 'em opened the bottle and took a big drink. Jes' as he passed the bottle to his friend they went through a tunnel. He tried to grab the bottle back and shouted: "Don't drink that stuff, Shorty! It's made me blind as a snubbin' post."

You'd wonder if that snake charmer in the white apron had been spittin' tobacco juice in the barrel to make it pleasant to the taste when you drank some of that stuff he served. If a man had a fightin' disposition this'd bring it out, and he'd soon be givin' the town hell with the hide off, doin' his best to uphold the cowhand's rep'tation for bein' wild and woolly. Hell went on a holiday when his kind hit town.

When a cowhand rode to town to spill a pot of paint and hear the owl hoot, he usually made a night of it—stayin' out with the dry cattle, he called it. He was first of all a good-'nough hossman not to leave his mount fightin' flies at a hitch rack while he was fightin' booze at a bar. He went to the livery stable to find a place to lean his hoss, and see that he got grain, hay, and water. Then he bowlegged it over to his fav'-rite bar to belly up and inoculate 'imself against snake bite. Old **Cap** Mulhall used to say, "It don't take backbone to belly up to a bar."

At the bar the first thing he did was plant his boot heel on the brass rail like he intended it to take root. While that brass rail was a handy place to hook a boot heel, it also turned out later to be a good thing to keep a man on his feet. He asked that aproned man on the sober side to sort out some bottles, then he proceeded to lap up likker like a fired cowhand. This puncher didn't have no educated thirst that called for bottles with pretty labels and silver foiled bonnets on 'em. He mighty seldom wasted his time on wine and fancy mixtures, and he didn't have much appetite for beer because in the old days he could seldom get it cold. Very few frontier saloons carried stocks of fancy likker. Whisky was his drink and he took it straight—till it took 'im. Some called for a chaser, but mostly he didn't want to put the fire out. The only thing most cowhands used to chase a drink was a pleasant memory.

When a bardog with his deceivin' smile asked you to "name your pizen," it was jes' a matter of form, and 'bout all he got for an answer was a nod of the head because all he had in stock was rye and bourbon. They didn't have any truck with drinks that called for olives or red cherries or fizz water, and they shore didn't waste no ice puttin' it in drinks to weaken the whisky.

In his younger days Charlie Russell and Kid Price opened up a saloon. One day a stranger walked in and asked for a cocktail. Charlie didn't know a cocktail from a peacock, but he tried to build one. He put ever'-thing on the back bar into it, even to a piece of lemon peel he had.

"I guess he wasn't a hard drinker," says Charlie, "because he only took one swaller and left the house and was never seen again. Maybe he went to Milk River to put out the fire and bogged down in the quicksand."

Now usin' his rope arm to h'ist a glass, the newly arrived cowhand proceeded to take the first layer off his tonsils and let his weakness for booze run wild. The first few burnin' sensations of this conversation fluid brought out the tongue oil, and he started augurin' with the bar-tender. Most likely this individual was an old stove-up ex-cowhand, and maybe he was the best bardog that ever waved a bar rag, but his heart was still out on the range, so they started talkin' cow. A few more drinks and this cowhand was the best cowman in the county and the barkeep was gettin' a little tired of listenin' and started yawnin' on the glasses to give 'em a polish.

A few more and he was the best cowman in the Territory and the barkeep got busy with his bar rag. It wasn't long till he was 'bout the best in the whole West and began to lie 'bout the herd he owned, even if he was jes' a common $30 a month hand. It was then the barkeep got disgusted, reached for the bottle, and hammered the cork home with the heel of his hand, which told this cowhand plainer'n words that his credit had run out.

After some useless augurin', he zigzagged off to the next saloon lookin' like somebody'd stole his rudder. Feelin' his way 'long the buildin's like his legs was a burden, he wondered why they didn't stay put and why they'd never thought to build them board walks wider. To watch 'im you'd a-thought walkin' was a lost art.

At the next saloon his tongue was a lot thicker and his lies a lot bigger. He was gettin' to the point where he believed 'em 'imself. It was gettin' pretty late and he was talkin' mostly to 'imself by now, the barkeep bein' down at the other end of the bar out of earshot and cussin' under his breath. A little peeved at the neglect he's receivin', this cowhand might decide to do a little target practice to command the attention he deserved. When he reached for his iron he clawed an empty holster, not knowin' his friend behind the first bar had lifted it to keep 'im out of trouble.

His swing, as he started to reach, also started 'im to reelin' 'round like a pup tryin' to find a soft spot to lie down in. He wound up by beddin' down all right, but it wasn't in no soft spot.

Though most cowhands drank when they hit town, some of 'em were reg'lar walkin' whisky vats, and could hold more likker than a gopher hole. But there were others like watched Puritans, who stayed sober as a muley cow. Others jes' took on 'nough joy juice to get a talkin' load. Their tongues could run a long time if kept well oiled. If their tongues got too thick to talk they resorted to the sign language, but they stayed as peaceful as a church. Drinkin' was a means of relaxin' from a season of hard, dusty work, and it gave 'em a chance to blow off steam. Most of 'em drank in the spirit of fun and for a friendly get-together with the others of his breed.

There were others with bronc dispositions, and when they got a full-growed case of booze blind they wanted to smoke up the town. They kept filin' away that nosepaint till they either got floored or frenzied. His kind were the ones that gave the other cowboys a bad rep'tation. If he couldn't wait till he got outside to start trouble, the bartender was usually a fighter, and had a bung starter, blackjack, or six-gun handy. More'n one bad hombre has had his hair combed where it was thinnest with a six-gun barrel, raisin' a knot that'd sweat a rat to run 'round. When a cowhand started takin' on a load, you'd think he was dry as a sponge the way he was soakin' up that cow-town neck oil. Pretty soon he was knockin' 'round like a blind dog in a meat shop, and couldn't hit the ground with his hat in three throws. He was gettin' to where he couldn't walk any more, but jes' went feelin' 'round. At this stage he began to see things that wasn't there, but he didn't know when to quit. He most likely ordered the barkeep and that twin brother of his to set out 'nother drink.

A corkscrew never pulled no one out of a hole, but there are men who go into a barroom to build up their courage when they're "lookin' for someone." He mighty often has to prove this courage. There were others who try to drown their sorrow in likker, but they only irrigate it. Givin' some folks likker's like tryin' to play a harp with a hammer.

When a man made a night of it, the next mornin' he was apt to feel like the frazzled end of a misspent life, and had one of them headaches built for a hoss. His head felt so big he could've eat hay with the hosses and he wouldn't bet he could crowd it into a corral. He usually had a brindle taste in his mouth like he'd had supper with a coyote and felt like goin' out and buryin' his teeth on the prairie. Besides, he was so shaky he couldn't pour a drink of whisky into a barrel with the head knocked out. This dark brown taste in his disposition and his oversized head made 'im wish he'd gone broke sooner.

When the drought was over, this celebratin' cowboy usually rode out of town with nothin' but a head and some debts. As one once said, "The head's mighty heavy, but the pocket's plenty light." If he did have any money left, maybe he slipped a bottle into his saddle pocket to take the hair off the dog on the trail home. He usually tried to empty the bottle before he got to the ranch. When one cowboy was asked by a new hand ridin' to the ranch with 'im how far it was to headquarters, the boy with the bottle held it up to the light and answered, " 'Bout a half-quart down the trail."

I remember a saddle-pocket bottle, though, that cured one cowboy of drinkin'. When he and his pardner started for the ranch from town, his friend put a wrapped quart bottle in this cowhand's saddle pocket because his own saddle wasn't equipped with pockets. A few miles out of town the one packin' the bottle had a burnin' thirst that couldn't resist temptation. He sneaked the bottle out, peeled the paper down the neck, and took a cow swaller of the stuff.

It wasn't long till he was so sick he heaved up ever'thing but his socks. When he got through he couldn't have been emptier inside if they'd used a vacuum cleaner on 'im. When his pard took a look at the bottle and saw what he'd done, he grinned like a possum eatin' yeller jackets.

"You damned fool," he busts out, "what you mean drinkin' up my Neat's foot oil?"

This sick cowboy was helpless as a frozen snake. He needed sympathy like a fresh-branded calf, but he didn't get none. By the time he got back to the ranch he was weak as a dragged cat, and was never knowed to look up the neck of 'nother bottle. His bottle-fever days were over.

The cowman has a lot of slang names for the booze he drinks, and calls it' such things as "lightnin' flash," "base burner," "brave-maker," "bug juice," "coffin varnish," "dynamite," "gut warmer," "neck oil," "red disturbance," "redeye," "scamper juice," "joy juice," "snake pizen," "tarantula juice," "tonsil varnish," "tornado juice," "wild mare's milk," and many others. A particularly low grade of rot-gut he called "sheep-herder's delight," and near the Utah line a strong whisky was called "Brigham Young cocktail." He claimed that one drink and "you're a confirmed polygamist." The cowman sometimes used the Injun's name for whisky, "firewater." This was derived from the custom of traders demonstratin' the alcoholic content by throwin' a little of the whisky on the fire to let it burn. Unless this was done, the Injun didn't trade, fearin' he'd been cheated.

Many of the early frontier towns were towns of saloons, dance halls, and gamblin' places where hard-eyed men came to revel in wine, women, and song; they were towns where morals were flung to the winds, like a deck of unlucky cards.

There were some tough saloons on the early frontier, and they soon got the name of "Bucket of Blood." The original "Bucket of Blood" was Shorty Young's dive in Havre, Montana, and since its rep'tation spread the term became used in describin' other dives. Most of them places were so low a rattlesnake'd be ashamed to meet his mother there, but no saloon's quite like a ladies' finishin' school.

The "Whoop-Up" was 'nother famous place. The original "Fort Whoop-Up" was a dive on the Canadian border north of Shelby, Montana. The boundary line ran down the middle of the buildin', and that coincidence came in handy, for the chief business at Whoop-Up was sellin' whisky to Injuns. Later there growed a whole crop of "Whoop-Ups," a fact which worried the law-abidin' Canucks more'n it did the Americans. The word "whoop-up" finally growed to embody a thought rather than a place. "What tribe does he belong to?" someone would ask. "He's a whoop-up," would be the answer and this was always funny. Many a cowboy went into such a place to "lay the dust," but he'd wind up by bein' laid in the dust. It wasn't no place for 'im to try and put on the rollers, that is, have a high old time.

There were many places in the old Northwest, too, called "hog ranches." Them were places of loose women, but they sold whisky too. Most of 'em were as cold-blooded as a rattler with a chill.

Seems like when a rootin'-tootin' cowboy got drunk he wanted to tear up somethin'. If he shot up a mirror or busted a few lights he was always good for the damage, and the saloonkeeper kept some extry in stock. But some bartenders hated brawls and were men of action. If he saw that some cowhand had it in mind to shoot up the place, he slapped the gapin' barrels of a sawed-off shotgun across the bar, and this playful cowhand could imagine many disagreeable things it could do.

The pioneer saloon was an important establishment. It filled a needed place in the social life of the community. It was the place where many business deals were transacted and many pardnerships formed. It was 'bout the only place a cowhand could meet his friends and loaf without havin' to spend money, and still be welcome. It was a place where a man might look at a paper or inquire 'bout jobs, because it was here the unemployed sought work and the employer hunted men to fill his needs. In cold weather there was a potbellied stove red with heat, and this, with the fire the cowboys packed in their bellies after a trip or two to the bar, helped thaw 'em out. The saloonkeeper of them days was usually a solid citizen who gave of his business advice and was generous with his charity.

Ever' saloon had one of them cow-town bums who did his hibernatin' there. He acted as janitor, changed the sawdust, kept the tobacco-box spittoons cleaned out, and swamped out the place. 'Bout all the pay he got was a few drinks when somebody bought for the house, and the loose change he found in the sawdust 'round the poker tables or near the bar. He wasn't familiar with water, neither by taste nor feel.

Maybe some travelin' tramp artist had passed through and painted the picture of a naked woman on the back-bar mirror for a drink or two, but mostly the art decorations were pictures cut out of the *Police Gazette*, or advertisin' some distillery.

Outside in the front were usually a few empty beer kegs that the broke loafers set on till someone came by and invited 'em in for a drink. Ever' cowhand packed a knife because he needed it in his work. When he got to town and hung 'round in front of a saloon, the first thing he did was pull it out and start whittlin' on the awnin' posts, cuttin' his initials or the brand of his outfit. Some of them old posts had been whittled on so much they were jes' hangin' together.

In them days a good woman wouldn't walk on the same side of the street a saloon was on. The barkeepers in them days, too, were more particular in lettin' a minor sneak into the place. They didn't want to have no part in startin' some kid on the road to ruin.

Back in them days, too, drinkin' was a social custom and not looked on as much of a sin except by some pious church members. There's a story of a cowboy who was scolded for his drinkin' by one of the good Christian sisters.

"What will the Lord think when you arrive in Heaven with whisky on your breath?" she asks 'im.

"Lady," he answers, "when I get up to the Lord I'm a-goin' to leave my breath down here."

Chips That Pass in the Night

THE average cowhand had a strong passion for gamblin'; it was a kind of second nature with 'im. He was mighty apt to gamble recklessly too. After he bought a few clothes and a good ridin' rig, he didn't have much further use for money. He was seldom ambitious to save any of the stuff. Gamblin' was one of his most widely advertised sins. Accordin' to the modern magazines, the movies and TV, he spent most of his days at this pastime.

Most cowhands were young men, footloose, reckless, and without responsibilities. And while card playin' furnished excitement and a fascinatin' pastime, it wasn't an obsession with 'em. A heap of the time they played to kill time, or to practice for a day they hoped to get to town and buck the professionals. They might even practice some second dealin', hopin' to get even with the slick town dealers.

Very few ranchers allowed gamblin' on the ranch, as it created enemies and took the players away from their duties. But they were not always there to see what was goin' on, nor did they visit the bunkhouse very often. There might be some gamblin' goin' on, too, 'round a camp-fire where a saddle blanket would be used. Charlie Russell once said, "You can tell a saddle-blanket gambler's luck by the rig he's ridin'." Them games were usually small, and a small-time gambler became knowed as a "saddle-blanket gambler."

The cowhand's work on the range was hard and dangerous, and the pay small. He couldn't help hoping that he could beat the game in town and win more in a few hours than he could earn by workin' in several months. He remembered how easy it seemed to be for the gamblers in town. After the cattle were delivered to the shippin' point, there was a letdown for the cowhands and they felt free to do as they pleased for a day or so.

After the long hours of hard work and responsibility while on the trail, when he hit town it didn't take 'im long to get his money into circulation. The gamblers knowed the lure of the games for the cowboy, and they had the cards stacked for 'im. All of a sudden he was as pop'lar as a snake in a prohibition town.

Against the professional gambler the cowhand had 'bout as much chance of winnin' as a grasshopper that hops into an anthill. Them dealers always seemed to know both sides of the cards. After the cowhands had got their pay checks you'd see a bunch of happy-go-lucky daredevils slidin' from their saddles in front of some saloon. The bartender greeted 'em with professional cordiality, a phase of it bein' to set a bottle and glasses on the bar in front of 'em. He was jes' as anxious as the other town people to get the cowboy's money.

After a few drinks, the tickin' of the roulette wheel seemed mighty invitin'; the rattle of the marble on the slowin' wheel, the drone of the croupier's voice, the clickin' of celluloid chips between the long fingers of the dealers at the poker tables, the sight of others stacked before 'im in beguilin' cylinders of red, white, and blue—all them things held the cowhands with fascination.

Poker was the most pop'lar game with 'im because he felt like he knowed somethin' 'bout it. Usually the game started kinda small, but it jes' naturally seemed to gather a heap of moss as it went 'long. Sometimes he tried all night to get somethin' higher'n a two-spot, but it was no trick at all for the dealer to keep showin' 'im hands that looked as big as a log house.

For 'im somehow there never was 'nough spots on the cards, but luck shore kept a-settin' on that dealer's shirttail. It seemed like the best he could hold was maybe some very young clubs, while that dealer could always seem to outhold a warehouse. If he did happen to draw a hand of two pair or three of a kind, the dealer'd show 'im a hand of five, all wearin' the same complexion.

When he started out maybe he'd be grass bellied with spot cash and thought he had 'nough to be called "mister," but the trouble was he was jes' called—too many times. After a session of poker he could usually count his coin without takin' it from his pocket, and he didn't ride home singin' with his tail up. He wished now he had all the change them bartenders forgot to give 'im back. One cowhand said he started out with plenty of money and six bits over, but when he quit he'd a-settled for the six bits.

When the dealer and some other house man started seesawin' 'im, his luck would shore 'nough ravel out and he'd soon be cleaned down to his spurs.

Some of the ranch owners had a weakness for draw poker, too, but rarely were they equal to the professional. Maybe he'd start with a roll as big as a wagon hub, but it wasn't long till his luck was runnin' kinda muddy. As Charlie Russell once said, "When he come he had a roll that'd choke a cow—one of them rolls that needs a rubber band. When he left he didn't need the rubber band and his roll wouldn't choke a chickadee."

Men settin' 'round a poker table were usually as silent as so many owls and as mirthless as high priests at some sacred rite. They let the chips and cards do all their talkin' and made signs when they chose to pass. The rancher tried to watch the dealer through the haze of tobacco smoke, but if this individual was dealin' from the bottom he was too practiced to get caught at it. He had to be mighty careful, 'cause he didn't want to be lyin' there beside the table with sawdust in his beard, starin' at the ceilin' but seein' nothin'. If there was any sign of trouble, each player was ready to ease his chair back and slide under the table.

Sometimes a whole herd of cows or a band of hosses would be lost on the turn of a card, or he'd lost money like he had a hole in his pocket as big as a pant's leg, but when he left the table he kept a poker face and you'd never know he didn't have a tail feather left.

When the cowhand, after he was cleaned, looked over at that dealer wallowin' in velvet with 'nough money in front of 'im to burn a wet mule, he couldn't believe it was all luck that put it there. He knowed he'd somehow been cheated, but he couldn't prove nothin'. But that didn't keep 'im from wantin' to fill up on brimstone and tarantula juice and pack his belt full of shells to blast a lot of them tinhorn gamblers all the way into Boot Hill. This was one of the things that gave the cowboy a bad rep'tation when they reached the end of the trail in such towns as Abilene, Dodge, Caldwell, and Wichita.

The cowboy's easy money attracted thugs from ever'where. The gamblers, pimps, and painted women were hoverin' 'bout like so many vultures on ever' hand. The cowboy resented this concerted effort to rob 'im of his hard-earned money, and when he realized that he was again broke he had that empty feelin' that comes when one knowed he'd been robbed. Bein' unable to prove anything whetted his desire to burn some powder in revenge. So he rode up and down the street unravelin' some cartridges, hopin' some of 'em might come close 'nough to some gambler to raise a blister. He'd liked to have filled 'em so full of lead they couldn't walk uphill, but he didn't want to commit murder. After his gun was as empty as a banker's heart, he'd maybe lost some of his steam and beat it for the camp before some town marshal ambushed 'im from behind a water barrel. On his way back home he was a broke but wiser man, but not so wise that he wouldn't do the same thing on his next trip up the trail.

Like the old sayin', "Play 'em high and sleep in the street," but still a faint heart never filled a flush and a cowhand keeps a-hopin' and buckin' the games.

41

Range Calico

THE early West was a man's country. Until it became more settled, range calico was as scarce as sunflowers on a Christmas tree. This scarcity of women made her kind of awesome to the cowboy and he looked upon her as bein' somethin' holy and plumb precious.

No other breed of men on earth respected women more'n the range man. He was apt to be pretty touchy in protectin' her character. He felt that a man was pretty low that'd bring a woman into contact with dirt, or allow her to touch it of her own accord. He placed her on a high fence because he wanted to look up to her. He wanted her feminine with frills and fluffs all over. He had no use for them he-women who wore pants and tried to dress like a man.

A few years ago I was standin' on the sidewalk in Amarillo, talkin' to an old JA cowhand. While we were talkin' a very stout lady, beef plumb to the hocks, passed by. She was dressed in a man's shirt and wore thin tight silk slacks. This cowhand lost all interest in our conversation till she'd turned the next corner. He seemed plumb fascinated with the rear view he saw. Finally he looked at me, shook his head, and said, "By God, it looked like two boar shoats fightin' under a wagon sheet."

In later years more married men came out to the range, bringin' their families. If there was a pretty daughter the whole range would soon be sufferin' with Cupid's cramp, and some favored puncher'd be callin' on her as reg'lar as a goose goes barefooted. The fewness of women didn't lessen a cowhand's wish to go a-courtin'. He called this courtin' "gallin'," "ridin' herd on a woman," "settin' the bag," "callin'," "cuttin' a rusty," or was said to have the "calico fever."

A pretty woman could choose from the whole range. Of course, them gals could cause a heap of jealousy, and men, once good friends, would soon be gettin' 'long like two bobcats in a gunny sack. A fickle woman's like a careless man with a gun. They're both apt to hurt somebody.

That naked little runt with the bow and arrow we call Cupid could shore booger up a peeler. Once he was shot with that weapon he started campin' on the trail of some filly till he'd slapped his brand on her and tied her to the snortin' post, or she had 'im walkin' the fence. When the game was love a cowhand with the calico fever took the bridle off. When he dropped his loop on the gal of his choice, he throwed her into the home pasture and nailed up the gate.

There not bein' 'nough women to go 'round in the early days, some punchers didn't have no more show in their courtin' than a one-legged man at a kickin' contest. You couldn't say he didn't try, but losin' in that game didn't improve his temper none. Till he got over his lovesickness he was so disagreeable a shepherd dog couldn't get 'long with 'im.

I'd hate to tell how far some of them old waddies would ride jes' to look at a gal. There was Brazos Joe, who used to ride twenty miles to town ever' chance he got to spend his wages for pies and such throat-ticklin' truck, eatin' like a hoss balin' bunchgrass till he developed a chronic bellyache, all because there was a biscuit shooter workin' there that was easy on the eyes. After he met this gal, he swore there was a mistake in the census report, and there wasn't but one gal in the U.S.

A Mill Iron puncher used to ride plumb off his range to drop by old man Johnson's little spread where there was a daughter who was pretty as a red heifer in a flower bed. Of course, he always had that common excuse of the range—huntin' hosses—framed up. One day he dropped by casual-like and found the old man at home a-settin' on the front porch.

"I'm out lookin' for strays," says this puncher, kind of surprised at findin' the old man at home. "Have you seen a little blaze-faced sorrel mare with our brand 'round here?"

"Go right on into the parlor. You'll find her a-settin' on the sofa, but she ain't wearin' your brand—yet," said the old man, grinnin', and jerkin' his head toward the front door. This hoss hunter didn't fool 'im none. He'd been young once 'imself.

When some of them lovesick cowhands was settin' the bag on a gal, her old man'd have to pour water on the porch steps to keep 'em from settin' there all night. More'n one courtin' cowboy nearly starved his Sunday hoss to death keepin' it tied to the old man's hitchin' rack, and post hay don't make a hoss no fatter.

Maybe some cowhand liked to show off to the gal he was a-courtin'. When he rode up, if she was out on the porch to meet 'im, he gigged his hoss in a tender spot so he'd buck a little. If she was visitin' from the East, a few crow hops or a little goatin' 'round might impress her, but he had to do some real ridin' to fool a ranch-raised gal. Sometimes that hoss swapped ends quicker'n a flea could hop out of danger, and this rider was pickin' 'imself up with two handsful of somethin' he didn't want. Maybe there was nothin' busted except his ego, but all his bolts and hinges might be loosened.

A Turkey Track puncher mounted his hoss to ride out to look after some fences. As he swung a leg over his hoss, an Eastern visitor came out on the back porch to see 'im off. Thinkin' he'd make a hit by showin' her some real ridin', he shoved the galves into this old hoss he was ridin'. He was makin' a straight-up ride too, but he'd forgot 'bout that clothesline stretched across the yard. When this caught 'im under the chin it stripped 'im from the saddle. While he was hangin' there like a man doin' a strangulation jig, she went into the house all doubled up, and it wasn't from pain. She saw 'im off all right. When he caught his hoss and crawled on again he didn't say nothin', but it wasn't safe to ask questions. He was mad 'nough to kick a hog barefooted. After that he avoided this gal like he would a swamp.

When the nesters began driftin' into the cattle country, some of 'em would bring a daughter pretty as a painted wagon. It didn't take a cowhand long to find out where she lived. He'd find some excuse to ride over her way and somehow ever' time he'd ride by he'd develop a burnin' thirst and stop to ask for water. No matter how gyppy it was, he'd drink it like it was nectar. When he looked into her eyes over the rim of that tin cup and found 'em soft and leathery as blackstrap lick poured onto a tin plate, he'd take to her like honeysuckle to a front porch.

She soon had 'im cinched to the last hole and they was gettin' 'long

like two pups in a basket. When he went 'round advertisin' that she was
so sweet bee trees was gall beside her, or talkin' 'bout her bein' as pure
as the Chirstmas snow, it wouldn't be long till she was puttin' the hobbles
on 'im.

Her old man was usually kind of religious and didn't like cowboys.
They drank and gambled, were wild and quick to fight, and spent their
money as free and easy as suicide. But the daughter found 'em more
attractive than the sodbustin' boys. She liked their jinglin' spurs, their
gaudy dress, their broad grin and free-heartedness. When a nester boy
came a-courtin' he thought he was a sport when he brought her a ten-
cent bag of gumdrops. The cowhand brought her the biggest box of
candy he could find in town, and apologized because he couldn't find a
bigger one. He was generous with her little brothers and sisters too,
and soon won 'em for allies. Anyway, a ridin' man has always been
more romantic than a man on foot.

In ridin' over the range, if he came across a little house with a garden
in the back, or a flower bed out in front, it was a shore sign there was a

woman livin' there. A few plants in tomato cans settin' in a curtained window would make 'im stop and do a little wishful thinkin'.

While thumbin' through some thick wish book, he'd lingered many a time with a heap of wonder at the women's more personal wearin' apparel pictured there. If he passed a place and saw them same garments hangin' on a clothesline, he didn't need a gizzardful of gravel to find an excuse to stop. Of course, he was hopin' them clothes belonged to some single gal livin' there.

As the West became more settled, wisdom-bringers were imported to teach the range yearlin's their three R's. Some of 'em was from the East, educated to a feather edge, and as full of information as a mail-order catalogue. Bein' soft and pretty as a young calf's ears, they never lacked a good saddle hoss and a willin' escort to ride home with 'em. Some admirin' puncher jes' happened by with an extry hoss or buckboard as school was turnin' out.

It's been said that a good-lookin' schoolteacher was better in the cow country than a sky pilot. Ever' cowboy wanted to marry her, and she could make 'im walk a straighter path than any preacher could. One season was 'bout all a lady teacher got to teach, as some cowboy always got his loop on her before school was out. On one range it was so bad that if they hadn't brought in an ugly old maid to teach the kids wouldn't have got much schoolin'.

Some old range waddy even might decide his own education had been neglected and try to enroll as a private pupil. But she knowed what he was after and that teachin' 'im would be as risky as braidin' a mule's tail. She'd as soon learn a bull calf to drink out of a bucket as to try and teach that old dog new tricks. She had other ways of educatin' 'im. It wasn't book learnin' he was after.

Sometimes she'd left her heart back East and was as aloof as a mountain sheep. A cowhand didn't have no more show with her kind than a stump-tailed bull in fly time. But it occasionally happened she fell for one of them bowlegged range riders. If she did he wasn't long in mortagagin' his here and hereafter for the papers necessary to file a permanent claim on her affections, and huntin' a sky pilot to weld 'im to the neck yoke. After that she'd have 'im so bridlewise he'd stand hitched with the reins hangin' down. Bein' that she was from the East, she'd soon have 'im so civilized he'd tote an umbrella and wear galluses.

But all them wisdom-bringers wasn't as soft and fluffy as a goose-hair pillow. Some of 'em was of the old-maid variety and looked like they'd been weaned on a pickle. Her kind wouldn't attract as much attention as an empty bottle. A man'd shore look at his hole card before droppin' by with a saddle hoss for her kind. If he was loco 'nough to do so, she'd probably greet 'im with a look sour 'nough to pucker a pig's mouth. She always seemed soured on life and couldn't get the acid from her system. If one wise school board hadn't hired one of them ugly old maids when they did, ever' cowhand on that range would've had a schoolteacher wife. The pretty ones was gettin' married off so fast the kids hardly learned what the last one looked like.

Many an old alkali got plumb dissatisfied with the boar's nest he'd been livin' in when some filly cut his trail. Most unmarried men are as homeless as a poker chip. Some of 'em would like to settle down and stay in one place till they rust, but nearly all cowmen are skittish of widders, both grass and sod. It's the voice of experience against the amateur. Some of them widders might have a short rope, but they shore throwed a wide loop. Once she'd got a man in her trap you couldn't turn her no more'n you could a runaway hog. It was like watchin' a bag of fleas to see which way she'd jump next. You take some old buck-nun who'd never been hogtied with matrimonial ropes, and he didn't savvy she-stuff. When some widder plucked the emblem of bondage from the third finger of the hand she'd once give away and fastened that hand onto 'im, he was as helpless as a cow in quicksand.

I remember watchin' one widder spinnin' her web like a spider after a fly. She had so much tallow she only needed four more pounds to get into a sideshow, and she had 'nough offspring to start a public school. Personally, I'd jes' as soon have married an orphan asylum. Bein' in the lead when tongues was give out, she could talk the hide off a cow, and she soon had her man convinced he needed her worse'n a fish needs water. From then on his leg was tied up and she was wearin' the bell.

The grass widder, too, is a dangerous critter. Bein' of the grass variety didn't mean she was lettin' any of it grow under her feet. When she adjusted her sights for a poor male she didn't seem to have no trouble gettin' a rake to gather her hay crop.

The Heart and Hand woman was 'nother who sometimes came West to shake her rope at some lonely batch. She got this name from that old magazine put out by a matrimonial agency. Some love-hungry cowboy'd get a copy through the mail and read it with a heap of interest—that is, them that could read. His simple soul believed all them descriptions. Hell, wasn't it printed? He didn't believe you could print anything that wasn't the truth. At one time the cowman depended on them matrimonial bureaus for a wife like he did the mail-order houses for his winter underriggin'.

Sometimes he started a letter courtship with one of them catalogue widders who wanted her weeds plowed under. Maybe it started out of curiosity, to pass the time and learn the news from the outside, or jes' for a joke, but he often found out too late that he'd put a spoke in his wheel, and some gal was on her way out, ready to surrender like a willow to the wind. He'd find 'imself drivin' a buckboard fifty miles to the railroad station to meet a lady love he'd really never intended seein' 'im in his home corral. He knowed such a wife was a gamble, but the suspense was what fascinated 'im. There was always that thrill of expectancy, like openin' a box of Crackerjack to see what prize was inside. Them prizes usually turned out to be somethin' you wouldn't want if you'd seen it first, like a little wooden whistle or some such gadget, and the chances were when this catalogue woman stepped off the train the photograph she'd sent didn't show up all the blemishes, and she'd forgot to tell 'im 'bout all the kids she owned. Maybe she had a face built for a hackamore and wasn't nothin' for a drinkin' man to look at, but, as a rule, he wasn't no parlor ornament either.

Anway he was of a breed whose word was as bindin' as a hangman's knot on a hoss thief's neck, and let 'imself be hooked up in double harness. Occasionally, by the time she had 'im harness broke, he found out she was a cook that could put real flavor in his grub. Once she slipped the nosebag on 'im he was like a grain-fed hoss, and was never again satisfied with the hay shoveled out by some old roundup coosie. More'n one such marriage has turned out good, both for a man's digestion and his contentment.

Maybe Eve pluckin' that first apple started this whole thing, but from that day to this, when a woman starts draggin' her loop there's always a man willin' to step into it. Woman has always influenced man, either for good or bad, and most of us know that a smile from a good woman's worth a heap more'n a dozen handed out by a bartender.

Shakin' a Hoof

You seldom see a cowhand that ain't crazy 'bout dancin'. When a love-hungry puncher rode to town for a high-heeled time he usually wound up in a honky-tonk to storm the puncheons with the calico queens and painted cats. Here he found the gal that'd got his bankroll the last time he was in town waitin' with her paint and glad smile to trim 'im again. In daylight some of them gals looked kinda frayed 'round the edges, but at night in the light of smoky lamp chimneys and behind a paint job that'd make an Injun on the warpath jealous they looked pretty good to an excited cowboy.

There was no such thing as beauty parlors in them days, and the gals of a busy dance hall had little time for more'n a daub of paint smeared into a poor imitation of the bloom of youth. Their hair was frizzled by curlin' irons heated in the chimney of an oil lamp. Their dress sparkled with cheap gauds, and they reeked with a cheap perfume that was supposed to dull a man's senses. Most likely as the couple danced they left a swirlin' eddy of tobacco smoke behind, and the stompin' of high-heeled boots caused the big tin hangin' lamps to flicker constantly from the concussion. Maybe such a dance didn't raise a cowboy's moral standard and kept 'im broke while in town, but it made 'im forget his troubles and helped keep 'im contented.

When he left town he was broke but ridin' home singin' with his tail up, and likely sportin' some gal's fancy garter on his arm. With this he tried to fool his friends into believin' he was a lady killer. He never stopped to figger how much that emblem cost 'im.

But the really big social event in any cowhand's life was the dance that was held somewhere on the range after the fall roundup. Nobody got a special invitation. Some puncher jes' happened by and dropped the word. If you heard of it you considered yourself invited, and needed no special urgin'.

The range dance was a heap different from the honky-tonks. Here he met the gentle heifers and not the drags of the she-herd. This called for his best wagon manners, and gettin' ready for it made for a lot of fixin'. Gopherin' through his war bag for the low-necked clothes he saved for special occasions, he dug out a fancy shirt that was wrinkled as a burnt boot and hung it out on a limb to let the wind smooth the wrinkles.

Some puncher who was handy with the shears was asked to trim 'nother's mane so he'd look like a white man instead of an Injun. There was a lot of painful face scrapin' before a busted mirror that suddenly got to be plumb pop'lar, but with a stiff beard and a dull razor it took more'n a lookin' glass to keep from dewlappin' yourself till you looked like the U.S. flag.

Throwed into the refinin' influence of a good woman, a puncher'd do things he couldn't be hogtied to do any other time. He'd wash, iron, and even do a little mendin' to dude up for some nester gal he knowed would be there. All this slickin' up was tough on the soap supply and stock water, but when he was through soakin' his hide he was clean as a baby's leg.

Now all spraddled out in his full war paint, with boots fresh greased and spurs let out to the town hole so they'd sing pretty, he hit the trail for a ride of maybe twenty miles.

The more settled feller rode his Sunday hoss, but some more reckless one saddled a half-broke bronc in his string which he figgered needed some more miles put on 'im. He had an interestin' time ironin' the humps out of this bronc's back, sometimes wonderin' if he hadn't wasted a lot of time and comfort in the barber work he'd jes' finished because this devil he's a-ridin' could've bucked them whiskers off.

The rancher who was puttin' on this hoe-dig has been busier'n a one-armed man saddlin' a green bronc. Him and his boys've been broilin' beef over a barbecue pit; his women folks've been bakin' pies and cakes for days, and fryin' bearsign by the tubsfull. With a lot of hungry mouths to feed, if there wasn't a wagonload of grub it wouldn't last as long as two bits in a poker game. The city woman might feed her guests salad sandwiches that a cowhand could eat till he starved plumb to death, but a ranch woman knowed she wasn't feedin' hummin'-birds. All them cakes and pies she was makin' for fluff-duffs were jes' to remind the boys they wasn't eatin' at the wagon.

The first guests arrived early to help with the final fixin's. Some set the long table for the big feed, while others moved the furniture out of the front rooms for the dance. If the weather was pretty this was piled out in a front yard that included plenty of territory. Boxes were put 'long the walls with boards laid across 'em to make benches for the ladies. The floor was scrubbed clean and some corn meal sprinkled on to make it smoother. The home stock was fed early and turned into the starve-out to make room in the corral for the guests' hosses.

After all this was done and coffee was a-bilin' in a pot big as a dippin' vat, the other folks started waggin' tongues 'bout the range gossip. Most of the talk was 'bout the last dance, the weather, the calf crop, the price of beef, the grass, and such things that affected their daily lives. Waitin' for the rest of the guests to arrive, they laughed and joked 'bout this and that till they all ran out of smart answers.

The younger punchers soon started a poker game in the bunkhouse, and somebody was always thoughtful 'nough to bring a jug. There was some whose bankroll could be swallowed by a chickadee without much strain, and they jes' sweat the game. Tirin' of this they bowlegged it over to the corral where a few were talkin' hoss and checkin' up on the brands to see who'd arrived.

Guests kept pourin' in till you wondered if there was goin' to be 'nough grub to go 'round. They came on hossback, in wagons, buck-boards, and buggies. The nester gals were spruced up in their Sunday best with calico and gingham dresses that nearly dragged the ground. Gals in them days didn't show much of their fetlocks. Some of 'em had faces red with excitement and travel, but they wouldn't think of powderin' their noses in public. Some few fillies from town came out, dressed in more style, with silks and satins that swished like high wind in tall grass. The sight of them gals shore boogered up the range heifers with a load of envy.

The boys dressed accordin' to their own taste and wardrobe, but none of 'em would take any blue ribbons at a bull show. There was a few nester boys, too, tryin' to imitate the cowboy, but they didn't have no luck at it. Their hand-me-down sodbustin' boots gave 'em away and you could tell by their walk that they'd followed a mule's tail down a furrow more'n they'd forked a hoss. Now and then some puncher showed up public as a zebra, wearin' a b'iled shirt and smellin' of bear grease and lavender soap, lookin' as miserable as a razorback hog stroppin' 'imself on a fencepost. You could always tell the married men. Their womenfolks made 'em put on a choke rope, button their vests, pull their britches legs out of their boots, and stick their shirt-tails in.

Durin' the first table there was a lot of laughin' and joshin' shouted above the rattle of dishes. Them waitin' for second table were talkin' outside in quieter tones, hopin' it didn't take the first ones long to fill out their equators. Maybe above all this noise some nester gal was heard gigglin' like a lost filly colt at some joke a cowboy'd told.

Finally you heard the sound of scrapin' chairs and knowed it was time for the second herd to be hazed to the feed trough. Supper over, the boys strolled outside with a bag of Bull Durham in one hand while they gophered through their vests for papers with the other. Outside they rolled a pill and took a few puffs while the table was bein' cleared.

The old range fiddler had a wide rep'tation, both good and bad. In ordinary times he was knowed as a lazy, worthless cuss, spendin' most of his time calfin' 'round a saloon, and when it came to drinkin' he didn't belong to the garden variety. But durin' a dance he was the man of the hour. The dancers considered it an honor to be noticed by 'im. Even the gals, ordinarily shy, flirted with 'im to get 'im to play some tune they liked best.

If he was late there was a heap of worry, but if he was on hand and sober, by the time supper was over he was on his box unwrappin' his fiddle. Bein' mighty fond of that instrument, he handled it with a heap of care. He packed a rattlesnake's rattles inside to keep away dampness, but its belly was white with the snow of resin dust that was never wiped off.

Usually he didn't know one note from 'nother, but could play all night without playin' the same tune twice if it was in the key of G. He spent a heap of time gettin' ready, twistin', listenin', thumpin', and sawin'. He was the center of attraction, and liked it. It looked like he was makin' slow headway, but finally he got things fixed and drawed the bow across the strings a few times to get warmed up.

By the time the fiddler was warmed up the caller took his place. He was an individual who felt as important as a pup with a new collar. When he stepped into the room, talk kind of stopped and ever'body backed against the wall to make room for the dancin'. With leather lungs and a loud mouth he could beller like a bull in a canebrake. But he had a sense of rhythm and 'nough personality to get the crowd into the spirit of the dance.

As a rule he was a dude for dress, goin' in for fancy doodads like silver conchas, beaded vests, rattlesnake skins, and bright shirts. He called from memory, and if he forgot the words he was good at puttin' in some patter of his own. He was more forward than the average and had to be a leader to do a good job. Now, with his head reared back like a coffeepot lid, he yelled, "Podners to your puncheons," and the dance was on.

> "Choose your podners, form a ring,
> Figger eight and double L swing."

The fiddler forgot his laziness and became a mighty animated human. He beat time with his head, feet, and ever' part of his body at the same time. He was now doin' the work he loved, and with the soul of an artist he was shore makin' that fiddle talk a language that put ginger in your feet. Music like that roused a crowd to action, and even the ones not dancin' helped beat time as the caller shouted:

> "Ducks in the river, goin' to the ford,
> Coffee in a little rag, sugar in a gourd."

At most range dances there was a lot more men than ladies. In order to complete a set some of the boys volunteered to be "heifer branded" by havin' a white handkerchief tied 'round their arms. This meant they were to take the part of a female and dance lady fashion. Their reward was bein' allowed to set with the ladies between dances, at which time they felt 'bout as out of place as a cow on a front porch. Sometimes some playful puncher ignored this white emblem of woman-hood and got plenty rough, but them self-appointed females could take it and pay back with interest if "her" pardner got too frolicsome.

Most of the boys were kind of timid at first. They'd run in a straight steer herd so long they were shy as a green bronc to a new water trough. But the whinin' of the fiddle, the scrapin' and stompin' of high-heeled boots, and the shouts of the caller soon made ever'body forget he was skittish. Added to this noise there was always some high-pitched cowboy yell that quickened the blood and made the fiddler bear down with more vigor.

No woman who wanted to dance was ever a wallflower. Even if she was ugly as a tar bucket, she was always in the thick of things. Sometimes there were one or two who refused to dance in spite of the shortage of females. They were what the range called "puncture ladies." Their churchgoin' feet were too religious to let 'em dance, but they could shore set on the sidelines and puncture other folk's rep'tations. Their breed was always in the lead when tongues were handed out, and you couldn't check 'em with a three-quarter rope and a snubbin' post.

When the men got tired they could sneak out to the bunkhouse and snatch a little rest, but this luxury was denied the women. However, they didn't put so much labor into their dancin' because the men swung 'em with such vigor they needed little effort on their part. Still this wasn't always the case, Maybe across the room you'd see some bow-legged runt tryin' to swing a woman who had so much tallow she was big 'nough to hunt bears with a switch. She was doin' all the hard work. He jes' moved 'round like he had hobbles on, hangin' on like an Injun to a whisky jug.

Some punchers danced like a bear 'round a beehive that was afraid of gettin' stung. Others didn't seem to know how to handle calico, and got as rough as they do handlin' cattle in a brandin' pen. I'll bet the women would jes' as soon dance with a grizzly, but most peelers go more or less loco when a female's 'round.

Dancin' in them days wasn't jes' wigglin' 'round and shakin' your rump. It was a rompin', stompin' affair. The feet of the dancers pounded the floor so hard that no matter how clean the floor'd been scrubbed, they brought out the dirt from under the boards that'd been there since the shack was built.

Somethin' 'bout a cowboy dance jes' gets you. That fiddle music even stirred the blood of the old bone-seasoned alkalies, and though they didn't travel like a colt no more, they were soon limbered up and shakin' as nimble a hoof as the youngest. There was always some religious feller, too, who couldn't stand such temptations, and he didn't need a second invite to dance 'imself right out of the church.

At ever' dance there was always a few who rode from a distance, and they was usually late. Hearin' the caller's voice half a mile down the trail, they came hell-bent and yellin' plumb up to the door. Not stoppin' to put up their hosses till they'd danced a set, they stampeded into the house. Them drags busted into the next room huntin' a place to hang their hats, but findin' the beds piled full of weaners, they throwed their war bonnets over in the corner and broke to where the grass was greener. Wearin' his ridin' gear, chaps, spurs, and all, he was often mighty glad of this chance to show some filly the fancy trappin's he was proud of.

Society in the cattle country was mighty democratic. Ever' man was a man if he was a square shooter, and no questions were asked. Maybe over yonder the town gambler was dancin' with the pretty wisdom-bringer; next to them was a feller whose folks on his mother's side wore moccasins swingin' the host's wife. Further down the line was a ranch foreman shakin' a hoof with the Mexican cook of a neighborin' spread, while not far away was a feller who was suspicioned of lettin' his calves suck the wrong cows with the belle of the range in his arms. Scattered among the crowd there was always some punchers cussin' the blisters on their feet and the new boots that caused 'em, but they wasn't missin' a dance, even if their feet were on fire.

The coffeepot was always on the stove in the kitchen, and a guest was expected to help 'imself when he felt the need of a stimulant, but mostly it was the women who hit the coffeepot. Between dances some peeler winked and motioned with his head. Pretty soon others began driftin' out like a bunch of saddle hosses followin' a bell mare. Outside, they looked at the moon through the neck of a bottle. Some wasn't able to chamber their likker without gettin' rollicky, but as long as they didn't get their tails over the dashboard they wasn't forefooted. If they were short on good manners and wasn't house broke, there was always somebody willin' to teach 'em and let 'em cool off in the harness shed.

Some thoughtful puncher revived the fiddler and caller with a bottle. After smackin' their lips and wipin' the sweat off their faces, the dance was on again with the caller yellin' louder'n ever:

"Come on, boys, and show some ditty,
Shake your feet and ketch your kitty."

Sometimes a puncher who'd rode forty or fifty miles had to leave early. He announced his farewell dance, danced it, and went out to put leather on his hoss. When he rode away he raised his voice in a cowboy yell that made your hair raise on end, a mighty fittin' farewell of a rider startin' on a long, lonesome ride.

A cowboy dance usually lasted all night. When it broke up at daybreak, the ladies retired to freshen up their spit curls, chalk their noses, and sort out the weaners that was beginnin' to stir off the bedground. The old bowlegs on the dance floor passed the last bottle 'round, savin' a big drink for the fiddler to get 'im to play a last tune. Then they throwed a stag dance that ended up kinda rough like a wrastlin' match. Like a hoss with plenty of bottom, them old saddle slickers jes' wouldn't tire down. But finally, havin' no more wet goods to bribe the fiddler with, they called it a success and limped to the kitchen for a farewell cup of coffee, their feet feelin' like they'd wintered on a hard pasture.

Outside, there was a lot of shoutin' and merrymakin' as the men hooked up their teams and saddled their broncs. Here and there some rancher had his hands full tryin' to hook up a skittish team that wasn't used to all that noise, or some rider was havin' trouble tryin' to set a bronc that'd been rim-fired by some rough joker. Most ever'body stopped to watch till things got straightened out again. The first one done with the job shouted a hearty goodbye and hit the trail.

Each man tried to pass ever'thing on the road to show off his rig, and ever'one left the gates open, expectin' the last to shut 'em. But the men who owned the fences kept fence riders on the job to close 'em, glad that this particular shindig had passed into range history.

Afterword

Now I HOPE all this has given you a better picture of the old-time cow-hand, of his life, his work and his play. I don't want you to get the impression he's like them TV cowboys who spend all their time in town. He had to sweat a little to stay on the payroll. He had to ride somethin' besides a brass rail, and he had to accomplish somethin' besides fillin' a flush or a full-house. Life was somethin' besides blood, bullets and bar-rooms. Town was a mighty poor place for a man with his small finances, and where there were no cows to punch his credit soon run out. After the gamblers got through with him all he had left was somethin' to talk about.

Shore, he wanted to have his fun before that old feller with the hay hook come 'long, but he had to do a heap of work between times. You'd never find him to be one of them eyeballers that's always feedin' off his own range. Usually he had more friends than there's fiddlers in hell be-cause he had a heart in his brisket as big as a saddle blanket.

Maybe the name he went by wasn't always tallied in the family Bible. He might have dropped it in some river as he came West. Sometimes he was as salty as Utah and on occasions could be as techy as a teased snake, but he had his own code of honor. When he pawed up a little sand he was usually justified. From seein' too many TV westerns some folks got the idea that he was the kind to take a long squint at the sun and a quick squat in the shade. They got the idea that he was so lazy he had to lean ag'in a buildin' to spit, but he wasn't the kind that had nothin' to do all day except set 'round on his one-spot. When he was a-settin' on the south side of his pants he was in the saddle doin' the work he was hired to do.

I'm not tryin' to make a hero of the old-time cowhand, but I want to show you that he had some virtues too. Maybe I've waited too late, for they say it's only after a man's dead that folks dig up a heap of virtues to pin on him. As an old-timer myself, I've found his virtues were plenty numerous. Neither did I want to let you think, like some folks do, that he was a double-dyed villain with an everlastin' thirst and a finger with the trigger itch. He had his faults, but in my opinion his virtues outweighed these, and I know for shore that we'll never see his like again on the American scene.